" But when in the course of Divine Providence, these American States became independent with respect to civil government, their ecclesiastical independence was necessarily included; and the different religious denominations of Christians in these States were left at full and equal liberty to model and organize their respective Churches, and forms of worship, and discipline, in such manner as they might judge most convenient for their future prosperity; consistently with the constitution and laws of their country."
(Preface to The Book of Common Prayer, page vi)

Presented to Fl. Wallace Owen, III as the third award for faithful service as an acolyte.

Presented by Donald M. Nickson, Assistant Minister, Saint Chrysostom's Church, Chicago, Illinois

May 1954

A History of the
American Episcopal Church

A HISTORY OF THE
AMERICAN EPISCOPAL
CHURCH

BY THE REVEREND

WILLIAM WILSON MANROSS, Ph.D.

MOREHOUSE-GORHAM CO.

NEW YORK

1950

PREFACE

THE AIM of this history is to show the American Episcopal Church as a living institution, and to supply a connected narrative of its development, both internally and in its relations with the society in which it is situated. Such an object necessarily involves some lessening of the emphasis placed upon dramatic incidents and striking personalities, but I hope that the inherent interest of the Church's story, which I have endeavored to bring out as fully as possible, will more than compensate for this loss, if it is a loss.

As to sources, I have relied rather extensively upon secondary authorities in preparing chapters one, two, and eight, and for a few details elsewhere. Otherwise, the history has been based entirely upon a study of original sources, though in this class I include a large number of contemporary biographies which are not "primary" sources in the technical sense, but which generally represent the nearest approach that can now be made to their subjects. The excuse for using secondary sources in the chapters mentioned is that they deal with subjects which have been exhaustively treated by previous historians, and it seemed advisable to devote the time available for research to an investigation of the extensive portions of the history where a fresh approach appeared to be necessary. Parts of chapter nine are based on a sketch of Bishop White which I prepared for the Bishop White Prayer Book Society while already engaged in the present work, but that sketch was the result of a careful study of all the available sources.

The secondary sources to which I am most indebted are W. S. Perry's *The History of the American Episcopal Church*, Volume I, for the first part of chapter one and for most of the material in chapter two which was not taken from William Bradford's *History of Plymouth Plantation* or John Winthrop's *Journal*; F. L. Hawks's *Contributions to the Ecclesiastical History of the United States*, Volume I, for the portion of chapter one dealing with

Virginia; and A. L. Cross's *Anglican Episcopate and the American Colonies* for chapter eight. All other secondary works consulted, together with a portion of the original sources, are listed in the bibliography.

Acknowledgments are due to Professor Frank Gavin of The General Theological Seminary, without whose advice and encouragement the work would never have been undertaken; to Dr. Louis C. Washburn of Christ Church, Philadelphia, the librarians of General Seminary, the New York Historical Society, and the Wisconsin State Historical Society for their courteous cooperation, especially in permitting the use of valuable manuscripts; to Professor H. C. Robbins of The General Theological Seminary, who has kindly read over the later chapters of the book and offered many helpful suggestions; to Miss Mary Beattie Brady of the Religious Motion Picture Foundation, Mr. F. L. Olmsted of the General Convention Committee of the Diocese of New Jersey, "The Spirit of Missions," and Mr. Alexander B. Andrews of Raleigh, N. C., for friendly assistance in obtaining illustrations; and to my friend, Miss Catharine Wisner, for invaluable assistance in reading proofs.

WILLIAM W. MANROSS
October, 1935.

* * *

I am indebted to a number of critics and correspondents for suggestions and corrections incorporated in this edition. Special acknowledgment is due to the Rev. Dr. Walter H. Stowe, president of the Church Historical Society, for friendly help and encouragement.

W.W.M.
June, 1949.

CONTENTS

ix

A History of the
American Episcopal Church

CHAPTER I

Beginnings—The Church in Virginia

It is a circumstance whose importance to our cultural history
can scarcely be exaggerated that the voyage of Columbus Introductory
preceded the publication of Luther's Ninety-five Theses by but a
quarter of a century, and that the period of exploration and early
settlement in America corresponded with the struggle of Protestants and Catholics for the control of Europe. The New World
thus inherited, at its very birth, the ripe religious controversies
of the old, and the conquest of a wilderness was conditioned by
some of the most abstruse issues of theology. To discover and
explore a new region served not only to enhance one's personal
glory and the greatness of one's country, but to extend the influence of one's particular form of Christianity as well, and even
piracy, if directed against the enemies of one's faith, seemed to
possess a religious sanction. It was therefore inevitable that, as
Spanish explorers brought with them the Roman Catholicism of
Spain, and Dutch explorers the Calvinism of the Netherlands,
so English explorers should carry with them the Church of England, and English colonists, except when they had migrated from
motives of dissent, should be colonists of the Church as well as
the State, making the beginning of the Episcopal Church in this
country contemporaneous with the beginning of English settlement.

The claim of England to a foothold in North America rested
primarily on the voyage made by John Cabot in 1497, under the Early
patronage of Henry VII, which resulted in the discovery of the Explorations
northern continent, but the great internal changes which took
place under the succeeding monarchs interrupted the activities
of English explorers, and it was not until the strong arm of
Elizabeth had brought a certain degree of stability at home that
they were resumed. In 1578 a fleet under the command of Martin

1

Frobisher crossed the ocean to seek for the Northwest Passage and gold along the icy shores of Hudson's Bay. With them went a clergyman of the Church of England, "one Master Wolfall," who, according to Hakluyt, the great chronicler of English explorations, had left a good living and a virtuous wife in England to go as chaplain of the fleet, solely out of his love for the souls of the infidel natives. What he did for them is not recorded, but at least he celebrated the Holy Communion for the officers and gentlemen of the fleet, on land, and this was the first service of the Church ever read upon North American soil.

Voyages to America, for either exploration or plunder, became more frequent as the years went on, and in all of them the Church was represented in one way or another. During his circumnavigation of the globe in 1679, Sir Francis Drake landed on the Pacific coast, within the present boundaries of the United States, where prayers, possibly including some from the Prayer Book, were read by his chaplain, a Church clergyman though of the Puritan party. In 1583 Sir Humphrey Gilbert made the first attempt to settle an English colony in America. One of his motives was declared to be the planting of Christian inhabitants in the new land and the conversion of the natives, and his patent, originally granted in 1578, contained a clause, which was to become more or less standard in colonial charters, to the effect that the laws of the colony should agree as far as possible with those of England, and that they should not be "against the true Christian faith or religion now professed in the Church of England." Gilbert landed in St. John's Harbor, Newfoundland, August 4, 1583, and after solemnly taking possession of the forest as its feudal lord, proceeded (with admirable economy) to issue three laws for the government of the colony, one of which provided that the public exercise of religion should be according to the use of the Church of England. The colony, however, was short-lived. The loss of one of his ships on an exploring voyage forced Sir Humphrey to return to England, and ere he had reached that country the frigate which bore him went to the bottom, carrying him with it.

Gilbert's colonial projects were at once taken up by his half-brother, Sir Walter Raleigh, a favorite of Queen Elizabeth, from whom he obtained a fresh patent in substantially the same terms as that of 1578. In the spring of 1584 Raleigh sent two English naviga-

Gilbert and Raleigh

tors, Philip Amadas and Arthur Barlowe, to reconnoiter a site for a colony. They spent two months on the coast of North Carolina, returning with two captured natives and a glowing but not very accurate description of the country. Their reports excited great interest in England, and Elizabeth graciously permitted the new region to be called Virginia, in honor of the state of life on which she appears to have prided herself.

In 1585 Raleigh dispatched a fleet of seven vessels under the command of Sir Richard Grenville with colonists for his new dominion, under the governorship of Ralph Lane. With them was Thomas Hariot, a distinguished scientist, who was interested in studying the natural history of the country and in the conversion of the natives; and an artist, John White, who was to supply pictures of the various objects of interest that might be encountered. Under Hariot's direction, prayers were regularly read, and some impression, of a religious nature, was made upon the Indians, chiefly because the weapons and other mechanical contrivances of the settlers seemed to them to be the results of special divine favor. But the colonists did not remain long at Roanoke, the island on which they had settled, and the next summer saw them returning to England with the fleet of Sir Francis Drake, who had chanced to come along at a time when they were sorely discouraged by the failure of supplies to arrive from England. When the supply ships did arrive, a few weeks later, they found the colony deserted, and were obliged to return home, leaving behind fifteen men, who were never heard from again.

Raleigh, however, was undaunted, and the favorable reports of Lane and Hariot on the soil and climate of "Virginia" gave him some grounds for encouragement. The year 1587, therefore, saw the departure of one more ill-fated expedition for America. Its governor was to be John White, the artist of the earlier expedition, and it was furnished with a municipal charter for "The City of Raleigh in Virginia," an early example of that irrepressible optimism which was so often to inspire the settlement of our country. It was also enriched by a donation of one hundred pounds from its founder, to be invested for the planting of Christianity in America.

The expedition had been directed to the shores of Chesapeake Bay, but settled instead at Roanoke, where it found the dwelling-houses built by Lane, and the bones of such of the fifteen as had not fled to an unknown fate. On August 13, 1587, the colony witnessed the baptism of Manteo, one of the Indians captured by Amadas and Barlowe, who was honored with the resounding title of Lord of Roanoke and Dasmonguepeuk. A week later occurred the birth of Virginia Dare, a granddaughter of the governor, and the first English child born in the New World, who, in due time, was also christened. From these incidents it has been inferred that a priest of the Church was present, either as chaplain of the colony, or of the fleet which brought it over, but of this there is no definite proof.

The colony, however, though it had an auspicious beginning, was destined to have a mysterious end. Governor White presently returned to England, for reasons which are not entirely clear, leaving behind him, with the rest of the colonists, his daughter and her child. When he reached the homeland, the Spanish Armada was approaching, and the ensuing conflict, followed by the financial embarrassments of Raleigh, which obliged him to transfer his patent to a company, delayed the relief of the colony for over a year. When White again reached Roanoke he found that the colonists had departed, leaving behind them, as had been arranged, an indication of their destination by cutting the word CROATOAN in the bark of a tree. This inscription was unaccompanied by any indication of distress, so it is presumed that they had merely sought a more satisfactory location, but before the ships could look for them a series of accidents forced their retirement to the West Indies, and the colonists were never located. They may have been killed or starved, or they may have mingled with the Indians, but certain it is that no white person ever saw them again.

The next attempts at colonization were made in the region that was soon to be known as New England, and under the patronage of promoters other than Raleigh. In 1602 Bartholomew Gosnold, with a small company, spent some weeks on the island of Cuttyhunk in Buzzard's Bay, off the Massachusetts coast. A settlement was apparently projected, but when a cargo of native commodities had been collected, the expedition returned to England, where the proprietors became involved in a suit with Raleigh, who sought to confiscate their cargo on the strength of his patent, because

Fate of the Colony

Projected Colonies in New England

the voyage had been made without his consent. In 1603 another brief settlement was made, this time by Martin Pring, in the harbors of Plymouth and Duxbury. With Pring was one Robert Salterne, a candidate for Holy Orders, who may have read the services of the Church upon the site of the future home of the Pilgrims.

In 1605 George Waymouth visited the shores of New England and, after a brief sojourn, returned with some captive Indians. These were seized by the governor of Plymouth, where Waymouth landed, and stimulated in that officer, Sir Ferdinando Gorges by name, a lifelong interest in American colonization, which was to cost him a great deal of trouble and expense, and bring him little profit. They also, together with the reports of the returned settlers, served to revive the general interest in America so that a new company was organized for the purpose of colonization, with which Gorges and Sir John Popham, the Lord Chief Justice of England, presently became associated. The first two ships sent out by these adventurers were captured by the Spaniards, but a third ship, dispatched by Popham, succeeded in reaching the coast of Maine, and, as the season was summer, brought back such glowing accounts of the country that it was determined to send out colonists without delay, and the following spring (1607), two ships under the command of Raleigh Gilbert, a son of Sir Humphrey, and George Popham, a brother of the Chief Justice, sailed for Maine. They landed on the island of Monhegan, and on the ensuing Sunday their chaplain, Richard Seymour, read the services of the Prayer Book, and preached. A week from the following Wednesday, a site for the settlement was finally chosen, another sermon was preached, the President's commission was read, George Popham was chosen for the office, and the laws prepared by the proprietors were promulgated. Among them was one providing for the practice of religion according to the use of the Church of England, and another calling upon the colonists to make exertions for the conversion of the Indians. The colonists remained at their settlement through the winter, under the leadership of Popham, and, after his death, of Gilbert, but with the coming of the supply ship in the spring they returned to England, where family affairs required Gilbert's presence, though it is possible that a few of the colonists had

Sir Ferdinando Gorges

Colony at Monhegan

withdrawn to the mouth of the Sheepscot River, where they may have remained. The Chief Justice had died in England about the same time as his brother in America, but Gorges was to continue his efforts for colonization, with indifferent success, until the territory was swallowed up by Massachusetts.

These instances of the early appearance of the Church of England upon American shores, which were assembled through the erudition of Bishop William Stevens Perry, the most distinguished of our Church historians, are items of antiquarian or sentimental interest only, for they led to no results of historical importance. It cannot even be said that the failure of the early experiments at colonization taught later settlers what blunders they should avoid, for nearly all of the mistakes of the previous adventurers, as well as some fresh ones, were made in the planting of the Jamestown colony in 1607, and the fact that this settlement succeeded where others had failed was due to accident rather than to any superiority of design. Nevertheless, it did succeed, and with it begins the continuous history of the Episcopal Church in this country.

The Settlement at Jamestown, 1607

There was, indeed, one respect in which the Virginia colony was more favored than those which had been attempted before, and that was that it enjoyed the more active support and protection of the monarch. James I, who would have been a great statesman had he been able to live up to his best moments, saw more clearly than his predecessors the value of American colonization. To encourage settlement, therefore, he chartered two great companies, one of London and one of Plymouth, who were to settle, respectively, the southern and northern portions of the territory claimed by England, with a large neutral area of two hundred miles along the coast, in between, which might be claimed by the first company establishing a colony in it. Of these two corporations, the London Company appears to have been the most active, and to it belongs the honor of planting the first successful English colony in America.

Pedagogy requires classification, and teachers are constantly obliged to simplify their subjects by the creation of categories which are only roughly accurate and which, if taken too literally, tend to impress the minds of the pupils with a sharpness of division which does not in fact exist. Of such a sort is the distinction, commonly drawn in the teaching of American history, between the colonies which were founded for religious motives and those which were established for other purposes. Insofar as the most conspicuous motives of the first settlers and promoters are concerned, this distinction is probably valid, but if it is understood to imply that considerations of self-interest were altogether unknown to the founders of religious refuges, or that those who established other colonies were entirely oblivious to the concerns of religion, it is certainly fallacious. The London Company, for instance, was undoubtedly founded in the hope, though it was to prove a vain one, of making a profit, but, nevertheless, missionary activity in the New World was one of the objects expressed in its charter, and the earliest instructions which it supplied to its colonists called for the practice of Christianity in conformity with the standards of the Church of England.

One of the original petitioners for the charter of the London Company was Robert Hunt, a clergyman of the Established Robert Hunt Church, and when the first group of colonists departed for their new home in the spring of 1607, he sailed with them to devote his life to building up the Church in the infant settlement, where he remained until his death, the date of which is unknown. On the fourteenth of May, the day after landing, he celebrated the first Eucharist upon the soil of Virginia. Thereafter, services were held daily, at first under an old sail suspended from four trees, and later in a crude wooden church which the colonists erected as one of their first buildings. The colony at Jamestown was hampered by over-elaborate instructions, a division of leadership, an unsatisfactory location, the expenditure of the colonists' time in a search for gold when they should have been planting crops, the incapacity of most of the settlers for husbandry, and the discouragement to industry involved in requiring all to work for the Company, bringing their produce to a common store. Hunt is said to have done what he could to keep peace among the leaders, but his efforts were unsuccessful, and when a relief ship arrived at the end of the first winter, it found most of the officers either dead or in jail. A majority of the inhabitants had also succumbed to the hardships of their situation. The condition of the colony was precarious for several years, and the settlers were at least once on the verge of returning to England, when the arrival of a new governor and fresh supplies induced them to remain.

They struggled on, and in time evolved a properly functioning community. In 1608 the first recorded marriage in the colony was celebrated, probably by Hunt. In 1610, Lord Delaware came over as governor and brought with him a chaplain, who was apparently the second clergyman in the colony. In the same year, the charter of the Company was revised, in the hope of strengthening it, and one of the clauses of the new charter required that all persons migrating to the colony should take the oath of supremacy, whereby the King was acknowledged as the head of the Church.

"Dale's Laws"   In 1611 the Company, in an effort to improve the discipline of the colony, many of whose inhabitants were not very amenable to control, issued a set of laws which had the effect of practically placing the colonists under martial law. These laws were promulgated by the then governor, Thomas Dale, and under the name of "Dale's Laws" they have become a byword for severity, scarcely less famous than the partly legendary "Blue Laws" of Connecticut, but Dale acted only as the representative of his superiors, and was not himself responsible for the provisions of the code.

The ecclesiastical laws in this collection, had they ever been enforced, would have set up a Little Inquisition in Virginia, and made the clergy one of the most powerful classes in the community. All military officers were to see that "Almighty God be duly and daily served," to call upon the people to hear sermons, and to frequent daily Morning and Evening Prayer themselves. Offenders were to be punished according to martial law. No one was to speak impiously against the Trinity or any person of it, "or against the known articles of the Christian faith," on pain of death, and death was also prescribed for blasphemy of the Divine Name, or for saying or doing anything which might "tend to the derision or despite of God's Holy Word." Severe penalties were provided for unlawful oaths, and anyone failing in respect for the clergy was to be whipped three times or to apologize publicly on three separate Sabbaths. Every person was required to attend service twice daily, on penalty, for the first offense, of the loss of one day's rations, for the second, of a flogging, and for the third, of six months in the galleys, though it is doubtful if such an institution existed in Virginia. For Sabbath-breaking the penalties were even more severe. All preachers and ministers were to preach every Sunday morning and catechize in the evening, and to say prayers twice daily. They were also to choose four of the most religious and best-disposed persons in their parishes to inform them of the sins of the people and to keep up the church buildings (that is, to act as a rudimentary vestry), and were to keep a record of all christenings, marriages, and deaths, "upon the burthen of a neglectful conscience, and upon pain of losing their entertainment." Finally, every colonist was to repair to the minister immediately upon his arrival and inform him as to the condition of his religious faith. Should the minister decide that the colonist was in need of instruction, he must submit to it, or be whipped, upon complaint of the clergyman to the governor.

Actually, these laws were never enforced strictly if they were enforced at all. If the severity of the penalties (which were harsh even when judged by contemporary standards) had not forced them into desuetude, their disregard of the actual conditions of colonial life would have done so, for they presupposed an effective Church Establishment in a community where there were probably not more than two clergymen, ministering to a handful of scattered and ignorant settlers. For many of the colonists, attendance at daily services would probably have been not so much a hardship as an impossibility, and had the ministers undertaken to give private religious instruction to all who were in need of it, they would have had but little time left for preparing their sermons and keeping their records.

A brighter incident of the year was the founding, by Governor Dale, of Henrico Parish, the second in the colony. Its first minister was the Reverend Alexander Whitaker, who, because of his long and devoted service in the colony, earned the title of "Apostle to Virginia." He was the son of Dr. William Whitaker, Master of St. John's, Cambridge, and is said to have been well to do, having gone to Virginia from religious motives only. It was he who baptized and married the romantic Pocahontas, the reputed savior of Captain John Smith, and the actual wife of John Rolfe, the father of the Virginia tobacco industry.

Dale's laws did not remain even nominally in force for a very

Henrico Parish

long time, for Governor Argall revised them in 1618, substituting milder penalties, though persons who failed to attend church on Sundays and holidays were still to be severely punished.

In 1619 the Company was again reorganized and a more liberal party obtained control. The new charter provided for a local legislature with an elective lower house, the first representative assembly in America. This body, when it met, in the same year, adopted a number of laws concerning the Church, including some relating to its internal discipline. Ministers were required to read service, in conformity with the use of the Church of England, twice on Sundays, in addition to catechizing the young, and all persons were compelled to attend these services. The clergy were also directed to file lists of baptisms, marriages and burials with the provincial secretary, to admonish drunkards, to report persons guilty of scandalous offenses to the governor, to excommunicate those who were unrepentantly incontinent, and to meet quarterly, as a sort of ecclesiastical court, to consider such cases. Fines were imposed for profanity, the money received to go to the Church. It is doubtful that these disciplinary provisions were ever strictly enforced.

The governor, at this time, divided the colony into four "corporations," setting apart glebe lands, for the benefit of the Church, in each. Steps were also taken to increase the number of ministers, of whom there were then only five. The Company undertook to settle six tenants on every glebe, and the Bishop of London agreed to try to find priests who would come over, an action which may have been one source of the jurisdiction which that prelate eventually came to exercise over the Church in the American colonies.

More important than these measures was the project for a college and preparatory school at Henrico, to educate both Indians and settlers. This was already in contemplation in 1619, and was referred to in some of the acts of the first assembly. It assumed for a time a promising aspect, with donations from the Company, the Bishop of London, and others, but an Indian war, which began in 1622, and nearly resulted in the destruction of the colony, forced its temporary abandonment. It was never entirely given up, but not until it obtained the energetic support of Commissary James Blair at the close of the century did it find practical realization. In the meantime, the honor of founding the first institution of

The First Assembly, 1619

College Projected

higher learning within our borders was to go to the Puritans of the north. The Church historian can, however, find one bright spot in the dark history of the first Indian war, for it is recorded that a portion of the colony was saved from slaughter by the loyalty of a Christianized Indian named Chanco.

In 1624, when Francis Wyatt was governor, the legislature made some further provision for the Church. Places of worship and burial grounds were to be provided wherever the people were accustomed to assemble for religious services. The Church was to adhere as far as possible to the canons of the Church of England, and fines in tobacco were provided for unexcused absence from Sunday worship. March twenty-second, the day of the Indian massacre, was to be kept as a holy day, and the regular holy days of the Church were to be observed except when two of them came together in summer. Then one only might be kept, so that work in the fields would not be too long interrupted. A minister who was absent from his cure for more than two months in a year was to forfeit half his salary and, in the case of an absence exceeding four months, would lose his entire yearly stipend and the cure. Anyone who disparaged a minister, so as to alienate the affections of his people and thereby decrease his usefulness, was to pay five hundred pounds of tobacco and ask forgiveness publicly in the congregation, unless he could produce satisfactory evidence to substantiate his charges. In order that the minister's salary might be secure, no one was to dispose of any of his tobacco until the claims of the minister had been satisfied, on pain of a double assessment. It was decreed that one person be appointed on each plantation to collect the minister's portion out of the best tobacco and corn.

This is the first known reference to clerical salaries in Virginia law, but it does not represent the first institution of legal stipends, for it clearly presupposes their existence. Ministers were publicly supported, by some means, from the start, so it may be said that the Church was always established in colonial Virginia in some degree, but it never, anywhere in America, obtained a complete establishment, such as existed in England, since it was never, prior to the Revolution, provided with bishops, or with an adequate system of ecclesiastical courts. This defect was to prove a serious handicap in the maintenance of discipline.

Ecclesiastical Laws of 1624

It is interesting to compare these laws with the code which bears the name of Governor Dale. Both have the same object, and deal with substantially the same matters, but the laws of 1624, being passed by a legislature made up of practical colonists, and not by a group of theorists across the sea, are expressed in terms which have some relation to the actual situation in the colony. The duties they require are possible of performance under normal conditions, and moreover, the penalties they exact are sufficiently moderate to give them a reasonable prospect of being enforceable.

Virginia a
Royal Colony

About this time, the Company, which had been torn by dissension for some time, and a number of whose leaders, being inclined toward the Puritan party, had but slight favor with the court, was brought to an end by royal edict. Thus the colony passed under the immediate control of the King. This change, of which most of the settlers approved, had but little effect upon the internal affairs of the colony, whether ecclesiastical or civil. Under Sir John Hervey, in 1629, severe penalties were provided for failure to observe the canons of the Church, but it is not likely that these were very generally enforced, for the great body of canon law could have had only slight application to the still somewhat primitive conditions of the colony.

A more important act of the same year was one which provided that no minister should be allowed to officiate unless he could show the governor a certificate of his ordination by some bishop in England and would promise to conform to the standards of the English Church. Any other minister was to be silenced by the governor, and if he proved obdurate, expelled from the colony. This law, of course, merely carried out the principle of the earlier acts requiring conformity to the Church of England in the public services of the colony, but it furnished a convenient means of enforcing that principle by excluding ministers not likely to conform. It may be worth noting that the act makes no specific reference to the authority of the Bishop of London, the certificate of any English bishop being considered sufficient.

Reception of
Ministers

When the newly arrived clergyman had satisfied the governor of his episcopal ordination, and had given the promise of conformity, the governor was requested to "induct the said minister into any parish that shall make presentation of him." This provision, which formed the basis of ministerial tenure in Virginia throughout the colonial period, was to be the source of a great deal of discussion and conflict. Taking its terms as they were understood in English canon law, it had the effect of making the parish (which soon came to mean, if it did not already mean, the vestry) the "patron" of the livings, and placing the governor in position of "Ordinary," or general ecclesiastical authority for the colony, dividing the power of appointment between them. It was not long, however, before the vestries discovered that, while a minister who was once presented and inducted as rector of the parish became largely free from their control, they could keep him pretty well subject to their will by allowing the parish to remain technically vacant, and hiring him upon a temporary basis, usually for a year at a time. Such a practice was contrary to English law, which caused the right of appointment to devolve on the Ordinary, if presentation were not made in six months, but the vestries, for some reason, contended that they were not subject to the same rules as other patrons. They were never able to make good their claim legally, but in practice they were generally able to have their own way.

Southern Churchmen in colonial times were generally characterized about equally by zeal for the Establishment, in the imperfect form they had given it, and by opposition to any further strengthening of ecclesiastical discipline. At this early period the former quality was more conspicuous in the Virginians than the latter, and they were generally strong supporters of the High Church policies of Laud, and the claims of the Stuart monarchs, who, indeed, showed themselves well-disposed toward the colony. Early in the conflict which led to the English Civil War, laws were passed against both Puritans and Roman Catholics, though there cannot have been many members of either group in the colony.

The first evidence of the presence of dissent in Virginia comes, as a matter of fact, not from a Virginian but from a Massachusetts source. The Journal of Governor Winthrop records that one Mr. Bennet, a gentleman of Virginia, arrived in Boston in 1642 "with letters of many well-disposed people of the upper new farms (possibly upper Norfolk) in Virginia to the elders in Boston, bewailing their sad condition for want of the means of salvation, and earnestly entreating a supply of faithful ministers." Who these

Dissenters in Virginia

"well-disposed people" were, it is not easy to say. They may have been new settlers from England, with Puritan sympathies; they may have been old settlers who had grown discontented with the existing Establishment, or they may have been a first instalment of that southward migration from the New England colonies which was to fill up a considerable portion of the southern frontier. Their plea, at any rate, so moved the Boston elders that, with the approval of the General Court, they sent two ministers, Knowlys and Thompson, to their assistance. These two gentlemen were, of course, prevented from preaching publicly by the Act of 1629, but they may have had some hearing in private houses.

Whether through their efforts or others', a small Puritan congregation was assembled in Virginia, for in 1648 the colony was again heard from in Massachusetts, with the arrival of one Mr. Harrison, pastor of the Church at Nanseman. He reported that their number had grown to one hundred and eighteen, and that many more were looking favorably upon them, so that Governor Sir William Berkeley had been moved to persecute them—that is, to enforce the Act of 1629—and had banished Harrison and his elder, Mr. Durand. Harrison desired the advice of the leaders at Boston as to whether the Church ought to remove, in view of this opposition, and if so, where. He was advised that as they were growing and, as, according to his report, many of the Council (the upper house in the colonial legislature) were on the point of being converted, "they should not be hasty to remove, as long as they could stay on any tolerable terms," but that if they did move, a good location might be the Bahamas, where liberty of conscience was promised. The readiness of this group to move elsewhere suggests that, in spite of the alleged interest of the Council members, of which there is no other evidence, the Puritans were not among those who had great possessions in the colony.

The Puritan Revolution

The time was now at hand, however, when the tables were temporarily to be reversed and the Puritans were to have their day of power in England and even, by force, to gain at least nominal control of the government of Virginia, the most loyal of the colonies. In 1647, when the Puritan party had already gained the ascendancy in England, the Virginia Assembly passed an act providing that any minister who refused to use the Book of Common Prayer in his public services was not entitled to the support provided by law. When news of the execution of Charles I reached Virginia, Charles II was immediately proclaimed as his successor. The colony was not able, however, to hold out single-handed against the power of the Commonwealth, and when a force was sent over for its subjection, it was felt that an honorable surrender was better than a useless struggle. The terms of capitulation which were then arranged provided that the Book of Common Prayer might continue in use for one year, if prayers for the King were not said publicly, and that the settled ministers, if they were not guilty of active opposition to the new government, might retain their cures and receive their dues for the same length of time. Actually, the services of the Church were probably carried on without great change throughout the period of Puritan rule, though some Separatist congregations may have been formed at this time, and there is some evidence that the Church had declined before the coming of the Restoration. In 1653 an act was passed excluding clergymen from the House of Burgesses, as the popular house of the Assembly was called, on the ground that their presence there might "produce bad consequences." In 1656, as it was reported that many places were destitute of ministers, measures were taken to encourage their immigration and settlement. In 1657 an act was passed for settling the religious affairs of the province, which provided "that to the people of the respective parishes should be referred all matters touching the church wardens and vestry, agreements with their ministers, and, in general, such things as concerned the parish or parishioners."

The vagueness and generality of this act may be accounted for by the need which was probably still felt of avoiding any direct   Vestries opposition to the Puritan power, although its rule was rapidly drawing to a close. The institution of the vestry, here alluded to, was to become a characteristic feature of Episcopal Church government in this country. The date of its introduction into Virginia is uncertain, but it was undoubtedly early. The first statutory reference to it that has been found is in a law of 1643, but this is a reenactment of earlier legislation, now lost. In a legal document of 1718, vestries, elected by the people, are said to have existed in the province from the earliest times. The institution, in fact, had its origin in the English canon law of the period. In ordinary

English use, the term vestry is applied to a meeting of the whole parish, which any resident is eligible to attend, but by the seventeenth century it had become customary in some parishes to transfer the function of the larger assembly to a smaller board, known as a "select vestry," which was usually elected by the parish meeting but in a few cases was self-perpetuating. It was in this form that the vestry was transplanted to the New World, partly because it was most common in the parts of England from which the early settlers came, and partly because it was better suited than the more usual form to the need of large but thinly-settled parishes, where the frequent assembling of all the residents would have been highly impractical. In colonies where there was a large dissenting population, which was sometimes in the majority, it had a further advantage in that it was possible to require the vestrymen to take the oaths of allegiance and supremacy, and thus to exclude dissenters from serving as such.

With the return of Charles II in 1660, the Church was again in the ascendant in England and some efforts were made to promote its interests in the colonies also. That stout old Royalist, Governor Berkeley, returned to Virginia, bringing with him fresh instructions, in which the concerns of the Church had a prominent part, for the very first article told him to "be careful Almighty God may be duly and daily served, *according to the form of Religion established in the Church of England."*

The Restoration

In 1662 an act was passed renewing and amplifying the law of 1629. It repeated the earlier regulations as to episcopal ordination, presentation, and induction, but provided further that a majority of each parish should choose twelve of the most able men to be a vestry, which body, once elected, was to be self-perpetuating, and, with the minister, was to have the power of electing wardens. Every vestryman was to take the oaths of allegiance and supremacy, and to subscribe to the doctrine and discipline of the Church of England.

At the time of the Restoration there were fifty parishes legally established in Virginia, though many of them existed on paper only. To supply these parishes there were only about ten ministers, and the securing of the number needed was one of the problems with which the colonial authorities had to deal. To encourage the migration of clergymen, a bounty of twenty pounds was offered to anyone who would transport a "sufficient minister" —that is, a minister in good standing of the Church of England— to the colony. At a later period this amount was paid by royal bounty to any clergyman coming to the colonies, and may have increased the number who were willing to undertake the journey, but at that time the measure had little effect, and the colony was to suffer from a serious shortage of ministers throughout the century.

The ecclesiastical clauses in the instructions of Lord Culpeper, who came over as governor in 1679, though similar in their general purport to those given to Governor Berkeley in 1660, and to other governors before and after, are interesting as containing a clause to the effect that no minister should henceforth be preferred to any benefice unless he could produce a certificate of his conformity from the Bishop of London. This was the first specific recognition, in the instructions to the governor of a continental colony, of the traditional jurisdiction of London over the plantations. The instructions also direct that the ministers shall be admitted to their vestries in the direction of Church affairs—a right that the vestries were sometimes disposed to deny.

As we have not that wealth of information on the daily life of the Church in the seventeenth century which is furnished in the eighteenth by the reports of the missionaries to the Society for the Propagation of the Gospel, and of the Commissaries and other ministers to the Bishop of London, it is impossible to describe that life as thoroughly now as we can later. There are many circumstances, however, which warrant us in inferring that the organization of the Church in most parts of Virginia was still somewhat rudimentary. The shortage of ministers has already been mentioned, and many of the parishes were probably too thinly populated to pay a minister, according to the requirements of the law, even if one could have been secured. There is evidence also that a considerable number of parishes as yet had no church buildings. There was no central ecclesiastical authority in the colony, except such as might be exercised by the governor, and so individual ministers and parishes were practically independent. A law to which reference is made at a later date provided that if a parish had no minister, the vestry should choose a godly layman to read the services of the Church on Sundays and holi-

Church Life in the Seventeenth Century

days, and, whether or not this law was already in existence, it is
very likely that the practice was.

In the older parishes a certain amount of stability had probably
been achieved, and some of the characteristics which were later
to distinguish southern colonial churchmanship may have begun
to develop. The salaries of ministers were most likely paid with
a fair regularity, though perhaps with some grumbling. Neat
church buildings, of brick or stone, had doubtless been erected,
and there may also have been "chapels-of-ease" in the more
remote parts of parishes, where services were held once or twice
a month for the convenience of those who lived there. In the
regular churches, services would be held every Sunday or holi-
day, and would be as well attended as circumstances permitted,
for whatever the private or public morals of the colonists may
have been, the obligation of regular attendance at public worship
seems to have been felt as strongly in the South as in New England. The Holy Communion, however, unless it was celebrated
more frequently than at a later time, would not be held more
than three or four times a year. The calibre of the clergy was
probably higher than at a later period, for their support was not
yet sufficient to attract those persons without hope of ecclesiastical
preferment at home who came at a later time to the southern
colonies in search of comfortable and secure, if not luxurious, livings, and greatly lowered the standards of the ministry, both as
to ability and morals. The long immunity from ecclesiastical discipline, which was the necessary result of early conditions in the
colony, made the people restless at any suggestion of its re-in-
troduction, and when the first Commissary was appointed by the
Bishop of London in 1689, he found it expedient not to attempt
the exercise of any jurisdiction over the laity.

CHAPTER II

OTHER COLONIES IN THE SEVENTEENTH CENTURY

FROM a colony founded by Churchmen, in which the Church was loved and provided for at the very beginning of settlement and consistently nourished thereafter, we must now turn to a plantation settled by those who regarded the Church as but insufficiently purged of the errors of Rome, and who came to the New World to avoid conforming to the corruptions which they believed to exist in her liturgy and government. Although the earliest efforts at colonization in New England were made under Church auspices, and though some Episcopalian colonies were later established in Maine and New Hampshire, the entire section eventually came under the control of settlers who belonged to one phase or another of the great Puritan movement which grew out of the more thoroughly Protestant section of the Reformation party in England. In American usage it has been customary to distinguish between the Pilgrims or Separatists, who settled at Plymouth, and the Puritans who colonized Massachusetts Bay and the rest of New England, though some of the latter were as thorough-going Separatists as the Pilgrims, but this does not agree with the contemporary practice, which was to designate the whole movement by the name of Puritan, and it obscures the fundamental harmony in religious views which existed between the Separatists and the rest of the Puritans.

There was, it is true, a theoretical distinction between the two sets of colonists, for the Plymouth settlers, who were followers of Browne and Barrow and other radical reformers, held that the corruption of the Established Church went so deep as to make it sinful to hold any communion with it, whereas the more conservative Puritans, of which the Massachusetts settlers were examples, were willing to remain in communion with the Church, while in England, provided they themselves were exempted from

conforming to its corrupt practices. In the homeland this difference was of some practical importance, for the Puritans, under a
lenient bishop, might continue fairly comfortably within the
Church, whereas the Separatists were in all cases compelled to
withdraw from it. In this country, however, the distinction proved
largely nominal and after a few years was almost entirely obliter-
ated, for both groups, when freed from the restraints which prevailed at home, found Congregationalism a congenial form of
Church government, and their common Calvinism produced a
substantial agreement as to theology.

The Pilgrims

It was the Pilgrims, so called, who first made good their settlement in New England. Persecuted in the old country, they had
gone first to Holland and had settled for a time at Leyden, but
economic difficulties and a fear that their children would cease
to be Englishmen induced them to seek another refuge. Accordingly, having made an agreement with the London Company
and obtained the tacit acquiescence, though not the official approval, of the King, a portion of them sailed for America, in a
ship believed to have been called the Mayflower, in 1620. They
landed in a region north of the territory of the London Company,
and so had to come to terms with the Plymouth Company, and,
as some of them had come from that part of England, they gave
their colony the name of Plymouth. Its early history was similar
to that of Virginia, as far as the inevitable hardships and blunders
of a pioneer settlement were concerned, though there was less
dissension among the leaders; but in time the difficulties were
overcome, and the colony prospered.

The pilgrims had come to America, not to found a haven of
religious freedom, but to establish a spiritual commonwealth, or
new Israel, in which the state should act in close coöperation with
a Church restored to what they considered its original purity. The
laws of the colony were to agree as nearly as possible with the
legal codes of the Old Testament, and the magistrates were to
secure the Elect, who alone were supposed to form the Church
membership, from being offended by the noise of the ungodly, or
of heretics.

The system thus established, and the similar one shortly to be
set up in Massachusetts and in other parts of New England
except Rhode Island, which was always regarded by the Puritans

as something of a renegade, were destined to function with comparative success for a century or more, but their little Zion did not remain altogether undisturbed during that time. The first threat to its peace from the side of the Church of England (other disturbers do not concern us) occurred in 1623, though it proved not to be a very serious one. In that year appeared Robert Gorges, son of Sir Ferdinando, who had come over as head of one of his father's abortive colonial enterprises, this one being designed for Massachusetts Bay. The attempt was short-lived, though a few of the settlers may have lingered on to trouble the later Puritans, but Gorges had brought with him one William Morell, a clergyman of the Established Church, who remained behind for almost a year after his principal had returned to England, though he performed no ecclesiastical functions during his sojourn. He had with him a commission to enforce conformity to the Church of England in the colony, but he never produced it, because, as Bradford tersely observes, "it would seem he saw it was in vain." *(margin: Representatives of the Church at Plymouth)*

A more serious problem was presented to the rulers of Plymouth by the case of John Lyford, who came over with a group of colonists in 1624. He had been sent out by the company which represented the colony in England, apparently with the expectation that he would serve as pastor for the congregation, which at that time had no regular minister, their old one having failed to come over. Lyford had been episcopally ordained, but he professed to be in sympathy with Puritan views. He is said by Bradford to have been well received and to have allied himself with the local Church, repudiating his former orders. *(margin: John Lyford)*

In course of time, however, he fell in with John Oldom, the leader of a group known as the "particulars," who felt that the terms upon which they came over had been violated by the rulers of the colony, and were, accordingly, disaffected. Though these grievances were primarily political, Oldom appears to have had some ecclesiastical objections also, or else he developed them after coming into contact with Lyford. At any rate, the two of them sent letters home attacking the colony and shortly afterwards endeavored to set up a separate congregation. Oldom was expelled from the colony, and eventually went to Connecticut, where his murder by the Indians was one of the causes of the Pequot War. Lyford expressed repentance and was granted six *(margin: John Oldom)* months' grace. As he renewed his attacks upon the colony, however, he was presently expelled and after various wanderings, finally ended his days in Virginia. Serious charges were brought against his moral character in the course of the dispute, and he certainly proved himself to be of a vacillating temper. It is not clear how far his dispute with the Plymouth authorities arose from a regard for episcopacy, and how far it was due to other causes, but he seems to have performed ministerial functions for a time, after separating from the regular congregation, on the strength of his episcopal ordination.

The charges which he brought against the ecclesiastical arrangements of the colony were in the nature of a caricature of the Separatist position, and contained at least enough truth to be embarrassing to those who were the subject of them. Though they did their author himself no good, they were one of the causes of the break-up of the Pilgrim Company in England, an event which, while it did no permanent harm, caused some uneasiness to the Pilgrims at the time. An ironical note is imparted to the dispute at its close by the fact that one of the charges brought against the colonists by those who withdrew from the Company was that they had received into their Church a man "that in his confession renounced all universal, national, and diocesan churches." According to Bradford, this man was Lyford himself!

Morton of Merrymount

The most famous representative of the Church in early New England was Thomas Morton of Merrymount, but, as in the case of Lyford, it is impossible to say how far his sufferings were due to his attachment to her, and how far to other causes. The circumstances surrounding his first coming to the New World are uncertain, but we know that about 1624 he was located at a place which he called Merrymount, in the neighborhood of Plymouth, with a colony which can probably best be described as a trading post, and that his presence there was highly unwelcome to the Puritans. He and his associates carried on a profitable fur trade, and scandalized their neighbors by their use of the Prayer Book and the free manner of their living. They were also suspected of selling firearms to the Indians, a charge which, whether true or not— and it is a fairly plausible one—certainly alarmed the other settlers, and appears to have been the immediate occasion for Morton's expulsion. He was arrested in 1628 by the Pilgrim captain, Miles

Standish, at the request of some of the smaller settlements, and, after being brought to Plymouth, was dispatched in the next ship for England.

As Merrymount was outside the jurisdiction of Plymouth, this action was clearly illegal, and it is not surprising that Morton was promptly released upon his arrival in England. He returned to Plymouth a year later under the protection of Isaac Allerton, a Puritan, and was lodged for a time at the latter's house. When the authorities forced Allerton to expel him, he went again to Merrymount. He was not there long before the Pilgrims once more found cause to lay hands on him and send him back to England, where he produced a burlesque on Puritanism which he called *The New English Canaan.* In 1633 he joined with some malcontents from Massachusetts Bay in signing a petition against that colony.

In spite of these attacks upon it, he seems to have felt an attraction toward New England which was but coldly reciprocated, for in 1643, when an old man, he again appeared in Plymouth. He was allowed to spend the winter there unmolested, but, rashly venturing within the jurisdiction of Massachusetts Bay, was promptly arrested for having attacked the colony in England, an action which was obviously as illegal as his previous arrests had been. He was held in jail for about a year, but as he proved to be a charge upon the colony, and common humanity forbade subjecting a man of his age to corporal punishment, he was released, ostensibly that he might have an opportunity to raise the money for his fine, but really to give him an opportunity to get out of the colony. This he did, seeking refuge in one of the settlements in Maine which had not yet been subjugated by Massachusetts, where he died a few years later.

Morton's is one of the most hotly debated characters in American history, but the present writer does not feel called upon to enter the controversy. Though he was a member of the Church of England, it is evident that the dispute between Morton and his enemies involved more questions than the difference between episcopacy and congregationalism. It was, in miniature, the dispute of the age between Puritan and Cavalier, between the stern and sometimes harsh, but always vigorous, morality of the middle class, beginning its long struggle upward, and the freer, more generous, but probably weaker standards of the class in power, and of its hangers-on. In such a conflict right can hardly be expected to be all on one side, and to become entirely a partisan either of Morton or his opponents would seem to show an inadequate understanding of the issues involved.

The Salem Colony
As has already been intimated, the other early settlers in the region that was to become Massachusetts were Puritans of a more conservative stamp than those of Plymouth. The colonists at Salem seem, in this respect, to have stood somewhere between the Pilgrims and the settlers at Boston. They were not Separatists before their coming over, and they repudiated the name even after their arrival, but their proceedings did not agree very well with this repudiation. On July 20, 1629, they set apart a day of fasting for the choice of ministers, and two men who had been clergymen in England were questioned concerning their calling. These men proceeded to deny their former orders by declaring that the calling of a minister was a twofold one: inwardly from the Lord, and outwardly from the congregation. This profession proved satisfactory and the two who made it were chosen pastors of the church at Salem.

There were some in the colony, however, to whom this action proved unacceptable. Chief among these were the brothers Browne, one a lawyer and the other a merchant, who were two of the original patentees and men of consequence in the colony. They withdrew, with some others, from the rest of the congregation, and set up a separate meeting in which the Book of Common Prayer was used. They also went to Endicott, the leader of the colony, and charged the ministers with departing from the Church of England, declaring that these were Separatists, and would probably become Anabaptists, but that, for themselves, they would adhere to the old Church. The reply of the ministers to this declaration is characteristic of one phase of the Puritan point of view. They denied that they were either Separatists or Anabaptists (this latter charge, of course, was purely rhetorical, the word Anabaptist having somewhat the same damning power then that Communist has today), and asserted that they had not separated from the Church of England, but only from its corruptions, and that having been persecuted in the Old World for their nonconformity to the Prayer Book and ceremonies of the Church, they neither could nor would use them here, where they had their freedom, as they considered the imposition of them to be a corruption of God's word. At the first Court of Assistants, which met in 1629, the stand of the ministers was approved, and the Brownes were sent home.

The Boston Puritans moved more cautiously toward Congregationalism, but the tendency of their movement was the same, and in the end they all arrived at the same place. The first Puritan settlers on the site of what was to become the metropolis of New England came over in 1629, but a much larger number arrived the next year, bringing with them John Winthrop, who for many years was to guide the destinies of the colony as governor, and was to become its first historian. Before leaving England, these colonists set forth an address to "the rest of their brethren in and of the Church of England" in which they said, "We desire you . . . to take notice of the principals and body of our company, as those who estimate it our honor to call the *Church of England*, from whence we rise, our dear Mother . . . ever acknowledging that such hope and part as we have obtained in the common salvation, we have received in her bosom, and suckt it from her breasts; we leave it not, therefore, as loathing that milk wherewith we were nourished there, but, blessing God for the parentage and education, as members of the same body, shall always rejoice in her good, and unfeignedly grieve for any sorrow that shall ever betide her, and while we have breath, sincerely desire and endeavor the continuance and abundance of her welfare."

The Settlement at Boston

This document was in the nature of a farewell speech, and should be judged by the standards usually governing such productions. It probably said nothing that was not sincerely meant, but it left unsaid a number of things which might have marred the good-will that ought to prevail at a parting. Out of respect for the occasion, it was not thought necessary to specify that the signers of this address regarded their Mother as retaining about her person far too many of the corruptions of a supposedly less reputable woman with whom she had once been associated, or that, while they were willing to accept her orders as being as good as any other, the majority of them by no means regarded them as necessary to a valid administration of the sacraments, or that they were looking forward hopefully to the time when they would be no longer bound by her liturgy. Even so, however, it is not likely that Winthrop and his associates would have spoken quite so strongly had they foreseen how rapidly they were to progress toward separation once they had arrived in their new home.

On July 27, 1630, the Boston congregation kept a fast for the choosing of ministers, as the group at Salem had done a year earlier, and selected John Wilson to be teacher, Increase Nowell to be elder, and two others to be deacons. These four were set apart for their duties in a service in which the congregation laid its hands upon them. This was done with a general protestation "that it was only as a sign of election and confirmation, not of any intent that Mr. Wilson should renounce his ministry he had received in England," but, nevertheless, the breach with the Mother Church was for all practical purposes complete. It is true, that the Bostonians still regarded themselves as being in communion with their fellow-Puritans in the Church of England, and that one of their original objections to Roger Williams was that he held such communion to be unlawful, but they had chosen for themselves the "Independent" or Congregational form of church government, and they soon proved as unwilling to tolerate any other system as were the avowed Separatists of Plymouth. In 1633, when Williams and another minister objected to the holding of ministerial conferences, on the ground that they might lead to "presbytery or superintendency," Winthrop observed that their fears were groundless, as it was agreed by all "that no church or person can have power over another church," and though Endicott was subjected to some criticism in 1635 for having cut the cross out of the English flag at Salem, another year saw this symbol removed from the flags of all of the militia companies.

The Puritans were not the first to settle in the neighborhood of Boston, for when they arrived they found there a few scattered settlers, possibly survivors of Gorges' abortive colony, to whom they gave the name of "old planters." These men were, for the most part, unsympathetic with Puritanism, and two of them, Thomas Walford and Samuel Maverick, were staunch adherents of the Church of England. Walford seems to have offended the Puritans, probably by too great a freedom in expressing his views, and was fined forty shillings and banished from the colony, going

Election of Ministers

The "Old Planters"

to New Hampshire, where he became one of the first wardens of the Church at Strawberry Bank (later Portsmouth), but Maverick, together with William Blaxton, the remaining "old planter," was admitted "freeman" of the colony—that is, accorded civil rights—in 1631. Maverick is praised, even by Puritan writers, for his generous hospitality and his kindness to the Indians, whom he tended during an epidemic of smallpox, but he was distrusted for his opinions and he was forbidden to hold office, required to reside at Boston, and prohibited from entertaining strangers for more than one night, it apparently being feared that he would use his hospitality as a cloak for proselytism. In 1632 he was granted a tract of land in Maine by Gorges' Council for New England, but, in spite of the restraints upon him, he seems to have preferred living at Boston.

Blaxton, the third of these settlers, had built his cabin on the actual site of Boston, and claimed the whole peninsula on the strength of this occupation, a claim which the Puritans respected to the extent of setting apart fifty acres for his use. He was an ordained clergyman of the Church of England, but he had as little regard for prelates as for Puritans, and told his new neighbors that he had come from England because he did not like the Lord-Bishops, and was equally unwilling to join himself with them and be subject to the "Lord-Brethren." He remained at Boston, however, and kept on fairly good terms with the colonists until 1635, when he sold his property to the province and moved into the region which is now Rhode Island, of which colony he became the first settler. In his later years he is said to have made some efforts to exercise his ministry at Providence, though he had to bribe children with fruit to get them to listen to him. When he died he left a library of two hundred volumes—a large collection for that time and place.

The "old planters" were not the only ones to whom the Puritans seemed to be moving too far from the Church of England, for there were some from among their own number who thought the same thing. The story of the Browne brothers has already been told. Another of the Salem Church who disliked the new order of things was the Reverend Francis Bright, one of four ministers sent over by the Massachusetts Company, who, when he felt that the separation had gone too far at Salem, moved to Charlestown,

Objectors Among the Puritans

and finding similar tendencies there, returned to England. Others
followed his example, and it has been estimated that a total of
nearly a hundred colonists returned home rather than accept Independency. It is also probable that there were always some persons
within the colony who would have preferred the ministrations of
the Church, though they were too much in the minority to make
it expedient for them to speak out under ordinary circumstances.
During the period of the Commonwealth, some of them united
with representatives of Presbyterianism to petition the home government for religious toleration, and were fined by the Massachusetts authorities for their temerity.

Efforts to
Subject the
Puritans to
the Church

At the time of the first settlement of Plymouth, the King had
agreed to "connive" with the designs of the Pilgrims, but had
refused to give them any formal sanction, and the Stuart monarchs had never pledged themselves to respect the ecclesiastical
independence of New England. They felt free, therefore, to try to
reduce the Puritan colonies to conformity whenever a fitting occasion should offer, and various schemes for accomplishing this end
were devised by them from time to time. The ineffective authority
given to William Morell when he came over with Robert Gorges
has already been mentioned. In 1634 a commission was issued to
transfer the government of New England to the Archbishop of
Canterbury, the Bishop of London, and others, with power to
regulate the ecclesiastical and civil affairs of the colonies, inflict
penalties, and send the refractory home to England. This commission was, in due time, transmitted to Boston, but nothing was
done about it. Other attempts of a similar sort were made before
the attention of the King became too absorbed in the approaching
revolution to permit his concerning himself with affairs across
the seas, but none of them got beyond being put on paper, and
the Puritans were left tolerably free to regulate their own concerns until after the rise and fall of the Commonwealth.

With the Restoration of the House of Stuart, a more determined
attempt was made to reduce New England to political and ecclesiastical obedience. As a Puritan colony, Massachusetts was naturally suspected in the eyes of the Restoration government, but it
did its best to remove the suspicion by sending a loyal address to
the King as soon as it learned of his accession to the throne. To
this Charles replied in 1662, expressing gratification at the loyalty

of the colony, and promising to restore its charter. He observed, however, that the foundation of the charter was freedom of conscience, and so he required that the General Court should permit all who wished to do so to make use of the Book of Common Prayer and to perform their devotions after the manner of the Church of England, and that all persons of good character should be admitted to the Sacrament of the Lord's Supper, celebrated according to the usage of the Prayer Book, and their children to baptism. This order was not, however, to be understood as implying that any indulgence should be granted to "those persons commonly called Quakers."

In 1664 Charles dispatched a group of Commissioners for the purpose of reducing the Dutch colony of New Amsterdam, and settling the affairs of New England. Among them was Samuel Maverick, whom we have already met as one of the "old planters" at Boston. The Commissioners, or those of them who went about that business, were successful in subjugating the Dutch, but to tame the spirit of the Puritans proved a more difficult matter. They did succeed in getting a law passed which nominally extended the vote to all good, religious persons, but to obtain a sanction for the use of the Prayer Book was more than they could compass.

Commissioners for New England

Charles did not give up at this single defeat. Time and again, through the agency of Edward Randolph, the collector of customs, and others, he ordered the Massachusetts authorities to permit the services of the Church, and in the end he even included in his demands the toleration of the Quakers, but as long as the province retained its independent government, his commands were unheeded, or received but a nominal obedience. Either the Puritans did not realize their danger, or they felt it not worth while to preserve their political independence if they could not use it to regulate their own religious affairs. At any rate, they refused to yield as long as they were able to resist and the freedom of the colony had to be restricted before the freedom of the Church could be obtained.

This, however, did not take place until near the close of Charles II's reign, and it remained for his brother and successor, the unlucky James II, to carry out the measures that he had begun. Charles, who was always in need of money, had, in his later years

Attack on the Massachusetts Charter

hit upon an interesting expedient for raising it. He had discovered, or it had been discovered for him, that many of the oldest cities in England had charters that were technically defective, and accordingly these cities had been compelled, by *quo warranto* proceedings, to surrender their charters, receiving them back only after making a substantial money payment, and even then usually on terms more favorable to the King than had formerly been the case.

This measure could, it was obvious, be extended with equal facility to the colonies, for it was easy to find technical flaws in their charters, though here the object was not so much the improvement of the royal finances as the unifying of colonial government. Action was accordingly begun against the New England provinces, and in due time their charters were declared forfeit, and preparations were made to unite them with New York under a single governor, who was to be located at Boston, and to rule the other colonies through deputies. This plan was not without its statesmanlike qualities, for though it crushed the independence in which, as it now seems to us, the true strength of the colonies lay, it would have united all of the northern provinces under one head, and have greatly increased their outward strength and the efficiency of their government, in addition to enhancing greatly the royal power, which was, of course, the chief object of its promoters. It might, moreover, have been successfully carried through, in spite of its unpopularity with the colonists, had James not succeeded, before he had ruled for more than three years, in blundering himself off the throne altogether.

Even as it was, the scheme was put into partial effect during James's reign, and in the spring of 1686, Joseph Dudley, a resident of Massachusetts, was commissioned "President" of the colonies of Massachusetts, New Hampshire, Maine and New York. The appointment of a royal governor in Massachusetts—for such Dudley, in effect, was, though the title was first accorded to his successor, Andros—necessarily entailed the introduction of the Established Church, and the ship that bore Dudley's commission also carried Robert Ratcliffe, an ordained clergyman, who was to become the first minister of the "King's Chapel" in Boston.

The Sunday after his arrival Ratcliffe preached in the town house of Boston, and read the services of the Church, arrayed in

The Church Comes to Boston

the surplice which was the uniform of his calling. This was a startling event indeed, and, though it can hardly have been a welcome one, a large crowd of people had the curiosity to come and witness the spectacle. They found Ratcliffe, if we may rely upon the testimony of one of them, "a very excellent preacher, whose matter was good, and the dress in which he put it, extraordinary." The following Tuesday he married two couples. Randolph, whose sometimes intemperate zeal for Church and Crown was to make him one of the worst-hated men in Massachusetts history, desired to have Ratcliffe assist at the inauguration of the President and Council, but Dudley, though he had conformed to the Church, was too politic to permit this, nor was Randolph more successful in an effort which he made to obtain one of the three churches in Boston for Ratcliffe's use. All that would be granted by the Council was the privilege of using the room in the town house where the deputies had been accustomed to sit, and here the services of the Church were regularly held for several months.

On June 15, 1686, the parish was formally organized, Dr. Benjamin Bullivant and Mr. Richard Bankes were elected wardens, a sexton was chosen, and some church furnishings were ordered. At a subsequent meeting, Ratcliffe's salary was fixed at fifty pounds a year, in addition to anything the Council might settle upon him. This latter source of income, however, proved fruitless, for though Randolph was lavish of schemes for supporting the Church by taxation, none of them was approved by the government. Had any one of them been adopted, it might have stirred the already restive colonists to revolt, for evidences were daily given of how cordially the Church was hated. Ministers in their pulpits denounced her services in the strong terms which were characteristic of seventeenth-century religious controversy, and the harmless Ratcliffe was branded a priest of Baal. Merchants and artisans who wished to associate themselves with the Church were, if we may rely upon Randolph's testimony, coerced by their creditors and employers into staying away.

Organization of King's Chapel

Near the end of 1686 Dudley was succeeded by Sir Edmund Andros, who was appointed the first royal governor of Massachusetts. Andros, who had served acceptably as governor of New York and who was to become governor of Virginia after the accession of William III, is an important figure in the history of

Sir Edmund Andros

the American colonies and of the Episcopal Church. The task which he had to perform in New England was one which was bound to make him unpopular, and his character was not such as to soften the ill feeling in any way. His manner was arrogant and cold, and his methods of ruling were arbitrary, but he seems, nevertheless, to have been a conscientious public servant, seeking to promote the interests of his royal master more earnestly than did many of his class. He had no sooner been made governor than he demanded the use of one of the Boston meeting-houses for the services of the Church. This was refused after a conference of ministers had been held to consider it, and for a time Andros contented himself with going to church in the town house. In the spring of 1687 he became more insistent, however. On Good Friday he forced his way into Old South Church, and beginning at Easter, the service of the Church of England was held in that building every Sunday, between the morning and afternoon services of the regular congregation. Such an arrangement is likely to lead to friction even when it is voluntary on both sides, and since, in this case, it had been forced on the proprietors of the meeting-house by arbitrary authority, conflict was inevitable. Sometimes, the long sermon of the Church of England preacher would force the Puritans to wait beyond the appointed time for their second service, and at other times, the governor would be annoyed at having to wait for his service because that of the Puritans had been too long. Nevertheless, the joint use of the old church continued, with nothing worse than bickering as the result, until the small wooden structure of King's Chapel was ready for occupancy.

A "brief" authorizing collections for the building of this chapel was issued early in 1688, and nearly one hundred persons contributed £256.9s, to which Andros added £30 and his deputy in New York, Sir Francis Nicholson, who, whatever his faults in other respects, was a consistent patron of the Church, added £25. Some difficulty was experienced in procuring a site, for Puritan landholders were reluctant to sell to the Church, but at length the parish was able to obtain a corner of the old burying-ground, probably through the authority of the Council, which Andros was able to dominate, and there the foundation was laid on October 16, 1688.

Building the
Chapel

The building was not fully completed before news reached the colony of the landing of the Prince of Orange in England in the spring of 1689. This report, which was first brought to the province by John Winslow, was the signal for a local revolution. Andros, Randolph, and a number of other officers of the royal government, most of them Churchmen, were thrown into prison, while excited mobs, encouraged by their pastors, rioted in the streets. Some property of Churchmen and others was destroyed and the new church was much damaged by stones and other instruments of popular violence, the feeling against the Establishment having been stimulated by a treatise on *The Unlawfulness of the Common Prayer Worship*, for whose publication Increase Mather regarded the present as a propitious moment. For a time it was feared that the building would be destroyed, but it survived the popular excitement, and the foothold of the Church in Massachusetts which it represented was retained.

The first successful settlements in Maine and New Hampshire were made by Churchmen, and the Church was present in them, though its life was soon snuffed out by the spread of Puritan power, and it was not revived until well into the new century. In 1622 Sir Ferdinando Gorges and Captain John Mason received a grant of all land between the Merrimac and Sagadahoc rivers, extending inland to the Great Lakes and the St. Lawrence. To this area they gave the classical name of Laconia, and within it, in 1623, they established a settlement and fishing village at the mouth of the Piscataqua. Other small settlements followed in the same region, and in 1629 they combined for mutual protection. Mason, who at his death in 1638 left a bequest of one thousand acres for the maintenance of a preacher, was a zealous Churchman, and it is believed that the colony was furnished with a clergyman, though the evidence for this is not very strong. In 1640 a parish was organized at the principal settlement, Strawberry Bank (later Portsmouth), with Thomas Walford, who has already been mentioned as one of the "old planters" in Massachusetts Bay, and Henry Sherburne as wardens, and a grant of fifty acres for a glebe was made to it by the governor. A church and parsonage were also built, the necessary furnishings for the former having been previously sent over by Mason. The church was served for a time by the Reverend Richard Gibson who, according to Winthrop, had originally been

The Church in New Hampshire

sent over to minister to some fishermen on Richman's Island. In 1642, however, he went to the Isle of Shoals, where he got into a dispute with a Puritan minister, and was hailed before the Massachusetts General Court, which claimed jurisdiction over the island. They released him only on his expressing great repentance, and declaring his intention to return immediately to England. After his departure, the Church in New Hampshire rapidly succumbed to Puritan inroads.

Church Settlements in Maine

Gorges' interests were not confined to New Hampshire, however, and in 1636 he established the first organized government in Maine at Winter Harbor on the Saco River. This was within the territory included in the grant which he held in common with Mason, but he seems to have acted under a separate royal grant, which, like the provincial charter which he obtained in 1639, provided for the Establishment of the Church of England. To this colony and to the other settlements of Scarboro and Casco (now Portland) which were presently established in the same region, came the Rev. Robert Jordan, a minister of the Church of England, who probably arrived about 1640. His marriage to the daughter of John Winter, a well-to-do settler, made him one of the leading landholders of the region, and he became a leader in the unsuccessful resistance to the aggression of Massachusetts. After the authority of that colony had been established, he was occasionally prosecuted for performing the services of the Church, but he continued in tolerable prosperity until the destruction of his home by Indians in King Philip's War forced him to flee to Great Island, where he died in 1679.

Beginnings in New York

As has already been stated, one of the objects of the Commissioners sent over in 1664 was the conquest of the Dutch colony of New Amsterdam, and this conquest was carried through, without bloodshed, by Colonel Richard Nicolls. One of the terms of capitulation provided that the Dutch should have freedom of conscience in matters of religion, which meant that the Calvinistic Dutch Church should remain the Church of the colony until English settlers began to predominate. The English governor and the English garrison had to have a chaplain, however, and, as the only place of worship in the colony was the Dutch church within the fort, the terms of surrender also provided that the English might have the use of this church after the Dutch had finished their service. This arrangement was carried out much more amicably than the similar one in Massachusetts, for the relations of the Church of England with the continental Protestants were, at this time, upon a much more cordial basis than those with the English dissenters. The governor's chaplain continued to be the only minister of the Church of England in New York, as the colony was now called, until after the "Glorious" Revolution of 1689, and the Dutch church in the fort continued to be its only place of worship. There was also an episcopally ordained minister at Albany, in the person of Nicolaus Van Rensselaer, a son of the patroon, but though he had been ordained by the Bishop of Salisbury, he functioned in the colony as a minister of the Dutch Church, and adhered to its usages. His manner of life, moreover, does not seem to have been such as became a clergyman, and he was deposed by Andros in 1677—one of the few instances of the exercise of this episcopal function by a colonial governor.

The accession of William III was marked by a minor revolution in New York, as it had been in Massachusetts. Here a German, Jacob Leisler, raised a force of irregulars and expelled Andros' deputy, Sir Francis Nicholson, a proceeding for which he was hung by that gentleman's successor. Though Leisler, in his wrath against all the Jacobean officers, accused Alexander Innes, the chaplain, of being a Papist, the Church had no real concern in the conflict, except that the dispute between Leislerians and anti-Leislerians, which was to mark New York politics for some years to come, occasionally exerted an indirect influence upon ecclesiastical affairs.

Maryland resembled Massachusetts and Plymouth in that it was founded as a refuge for a religious group which was hostile to the Established Church, but it differed from them in being founded with a view to the toleration of all Trinitarian Christians. Whether or not its founder, Lord Baltimore, believed in religious freedom as a principle, such an arrangement was a matter of practical necessity in his colony. The charter of the province required that its laws should not be inconsistent with those of England, and to tolerate Roman Catholics in the colony, and appoint them to positions of trust, was as far as it was expedient to go in disregarding this clause. That much relaxation had been anticipated, but to go beyond it, and interfere with the freedom of Protestants in the

The Founding of Maryland

colony, would almost certainly have invited an attack upon the charter, for Baltimore, who remained in England, and was a well-known figure at court, could not hope for the immunity which distance and obscurity lent to the Puritans in their early years. Moreover, the Roman Catholics as a whole were a much weaker party in England than the Puritans, and much more subject to popular distrust. And finally, as it soon became evident that not many Roman Catholics wished to migrate to the New World, it was clear that a majority of the colonists would always be Protestant.

Whatever Lord Baltimore's motives may have been for undertaking this experiment in religious freedom, he and his principal agents were thoroughly conscientious in their efforts to carry it out. Not only were all orthodox Christians tolerated, but an effort was made, even in the earliest instructions, to keep peace by forbidding the use of abusive expressions in connection with things held sacred by either Protestants or Roman Catholics, and there are a number of instances on record in which the colonial authorities heard and redressed complaints of the "Protestant Catholics" of the Church of England against their Roman Catholic neighbors.

In 1649, in an effort to prevent the abrogation of his charter by the Puritan power in England, Baltimore had the colonial Assembly give legislative expression to his ideas in the famous Maryland Toleration Act, but the principles which were embodied in that law were those which had governed the colony from the beginning. The efforts to save the charter were unsuccessful, and during the period of the Commonwealth, Maryland was under Protestant control.

The Church in Maryland

It is probable that many, if not a majority, of the first colonists, who came over in 1634, were Protestants, and at least nominal members of the Church of England, and there was already a settlement of Virginia Churchmen, with a minister, on the Isle of Kent, which was eventually adjudged to be included in the Maryland patent. The Churchmen who came over from England had no minister with them, but they did build a chapel at St. Mary's, the first settlement, and they seem to have read services there with some regularity. The first minister of the Established Church who is known to have been in the colony is the Reverend William

Wilkinson, who was there about 1650, but though he occasionally officiated, he was obliged to engage in trade for his support. In 1675 there were three clergymen in the colony. In the following year one of them, John Yeo, addressed a petition to Archbishop Sheldon in which he lamented the poor condition of the Church in Maryland, and said that though there was such a scanty supply of regular ministers for a population which now numbered twenty thousand souls, scattered through ten or twelve counties, there were many irregular preachers, and the Quakers had seen to the provision of "speakers" for their conventicles, not to mention the numerous Roman Catholic priests in the colony. He prayed, therefore, that some arrangement might be made for the establishment of the Church in Maryland.

This letter was referred to the Privy Council in England, and the then Lord Baltimore was questioned on the subject. He replied that in view of the heterogeneous character of the legislature, which included Roman Catholics, Independents, Quakers, and Churchmen, nothing could be done towards an establishment, but that the clergymen then in the colony (he put their number at four) were all provided with adequate plantations. During the remaining years of Stuart rule there was very little change in the ecclesiastical situation of the colony. The Protestants were already well in the majority, and their preponderance increased every year. Ministers were sent over from time to time, but as others died or were removed, the total number was not increased, and in 1689 there were still only three ministers of the Church in Maryland.

The change of dynasties in England brought a new order of things in the colony also. When they learned of the succession of William, the Protestants revolted against the Proprietor, and petitioned the King, in two successive conventions, to end the proprietary government. The petition was finally granted. The colony passed under the control of a Protestant Assembly and a royal governor, and the experiment in religious freedom was at an end. In time the province was restored to the Calverts, but not until the family of Lord Baltimore had itself become Protestant.

Protestants in the Ascendency

CHAPTER III

WHEN does a century begin? In the mind of the average person it begins with the year a new figure appears in the hundreds column, with a double naught following it. An expert in chronology would probably choose the year following, for only then has the tale of the preceding century been completely filled. For the historian, however, no such simple rule of division is possible. He can recognize in any given century certain predominant characteristics distinguishing it from other centuries, just as he can in any other long period of time, but to fix the point at which those characteristics begin their ascendency is by no means an easy matter, and the date chosen must always be an arbitrary one.

Characteristics of the New Century

The division between the seventeenth and eighteenth centuries can be most conveniently fixed, at least in English and American history, by the "Glorious" Revolution of 1689. To be sure, the change which that Revolution effected was not, outwardly, a very radical one, being merely a shifting of dynasties, but as its embodiments guaranteed the Protestant succession, and secured the supremacy of Parliament, it may be said to have brought one long controversy to a close and set the stage for another. From it also evolved a noticeable shift in social forces, for the uneasy compromise between the aristocracy and the upper middle-class which resulted from it in the political field was to have its counterpart in the social ideals of the century. The slow-burning but torrid fires of Puritanism were to give way to a stolid middle-class respectability which stressed the importance of becoming conduct for its own sake, rather than as a means of escaping damnation. The aristocratic ideal, already decadent during the Restoration, was to express itself chiefly in an insistence upon the importance of subordination and stability in society, and, on its lighter side, in the formulation of rules for pleasing fashionable ladies. These two elements, moreover, were to exist not so much in competition as in a state of incomplete fusion, gradually solidifying, with the addition of new forces introduced by the Methodist Revival and the Romantic Movement, into that curiously powerful synthesis of aristocratic and middle-class traditions which was to mark the England of Victoria.

With all things thus in a state of flux, religion, naturally, could not remain unchanged, and the claims of Christianity were subjected to a searching and not altogether favorable examination. It was, of course, still considered illegal, and, what was worse, bad taste, to repudiate Christianity altogether, but to advance its supernatural claims too boldly or to insist too strongly on its authority over human lives was regarded as an even more serious breach of propriety. Among those who felt themselves to be most enlightened, it was regarded simply as a philosophy of life to which certain supernatural fables had been attached, and which should be purged from these superstitions and required to justify itself, like all other philosophies, on grounds of cold rationality. Most of these "enlightened" philosophers, indeed, sincerely believed that such justification was possible, but their attitude tended to deprive the Faith of much of its vitality. There were, of course, many good and many devout men in the Church and in its ministry in the eighteenth century, but, if they wished to be heard at all, at least by the educated, they were obliged to express themselves in the language of the time; to talk more of goodness than of holiness, and more of the rationality of Christianity than of its divine revelation.

In the colonies the situation prevailing in England was reproduced with such modifications as would naturally result from the cruder conditions of colonial culture. There was little genuine aristocracy in America, but there were plenty of aristocratic pretensions, and these combined with the genuine middle-class background of most of the more prosperous colonists to produce a sort of caricature of English society, with the governor and his circle acting as a miniature court. In religion the restlessness of the age showed itself differently here than it did in England. Though we find occasional references to the importation of Deistic or infidel books, there was probably little avowed rationalism in the country until toward the close of the century, but

Religion in the Colonies

there was in all of the colonies a general breakdown of the "standing order," whether that order was Episcopal, Independent, or Quaker. Dissent appeared everywhere, some sort of religious toleration gradually developed in every province, and the older religious denominations joined with two or three new ones in a struggle for position which, though it was temporarily interrupted by the political excitement of the Revolutionary period, was not to end until the second quarter of the nineteenth century saw their ratios fixed upon a national rather than a sectional basis.

Had this struggle taken place at a time when religious feeling in England was stronger, the Episcopal Church would possibly have fared better than it did, for it would have enjoyed a more earnest support from its English friends. As it was, that support cannot be said to have been much more than lukewarm. The Society for the Propagation of the Gospel in Foreign Parts labored, it is true, long and devotedly for the welfare of the colonial Church, but its active supporters never represented more than a small fraction of the membership of the Church at home. By the majority of English Churchmen—and this included most of the ecclesiastics—the spiritual welfare of the colonies was regarded as somebody else's business. They did nothing to promote the work of the Church in America, and they allowed political considerations to prevent the government, which was supposed to be the Church's protector, from permitting the completion of its ministry by a colonial episcopate.

Policy of the Government

The policy of the government with respect to the ecclesiastical affairs of the plantations, insofar as it can be said to have had one, was to obtain the Establishment of the Church in all colonies which had not been founded by persons avowedly seeking to escape from the Establishment at home, and to procure its toleration in colonies where the dissenting interest prevailed. After the accession of William III, no effort was ever made by the home government to force the Church Establishment upon the dissenting colonies. It is true that an Act of Establishment was passed in Maryland at the beginning of this period, but, though the measure was encouraged by Governors Nicholson and Blakiston, and by Commissary Bray, it had its origin in colonial conditions, for, as we have seen, a Protestant revolution in Maryland followed the fall of the Stuarts in England. The act which was passed by the colonial Assembly to provide for the Church was, in fact, disallowed several times before it was put in a form acceptable to the English government, and at least one of the objections brought against it, in its earlier form, was that it extended insufficient toleration to dissenting groups. Moreover, the interest displaced by the Maryland Establishment was that of the Roman Catholics who were not included in the general toleration which the new régime extended toward Protestant dissenters.

This policy, had it been consistently adhered to, would probably, except for its failure to provide for the episcopate, have been as sound a one as could be adopted under the circumstances, but the interest of the English government in the colonies during most of the eighteenth century was not great enough to make it very persistent in following any policy. The more debatable part of the program was, in fact, the part that was most effectively carried out. In colonies where a majority of the inhabitants were members of the Church, the provincial assemblies showed themselves willing to provide for the Establishment on their own initiative, though not always upon terms which were acceptable to the ecclesiastical authorities in England. Acts of Establishment were also obtained, however, through the efforts of the royal governors in the colonies of New York and North Carolina which, though they had not been founded by any definite dissenting interest, probably had a majority of dissenters at the time that the acts were passed. In New York, where the Establishment was obtained at the beginning of the century, so that the hostility aroused had time to wear off before the American Revolution, the Church was probably strengthened by the measure, at least in New York City and Westchester County, but in North Carolina, where a Church Act acceptable to the home government was not obtained until within a few years of the Revolution, and where some of its features were obnoxious even to Churchmen, the ill will produced by it was seriously harmful. With the coming of the Revolution the Church interest in that colony was utterly crushed, and it did not even begin to revive until well into the nineteenth century.

On the other hand, the efforts of the English authorities to obtain religious freedom for the Church in New England were half-hearted and spasmodic. The home government always felt a certain amount of nervousness with respect to these colonies, for

Not Consistently Carried Out

it was feared that any vigorous attempt to interfere in their religious or political affairs would drive them into open rebellion, and
after the fiasco of Andros they were always handled gingerly.
That the Church ultimately obtained something approaching
religious equality in New England was due more to the growing
spirit of toleration in the colonies, and to the combined exertions
of Churchmen and other opponents of the standing order in that
section, chiefly the Baptists and Quakers, than to any active intervention of the English Ministry or its agents. In Pennsylvania, the
only other dissenting colony after the collapse of the Roman
Catholic power in Maryland, religious toleration had been provided for from the start, and a clause in Penn's original charter
had required that a clergyman of the Church of England, duly
recommended by the Bishop of London, should be admitted to the
colony whenever any of the inhabitants should petition for one.

Disadvantages
of the
Church's
Political
Connection

It may be urged that, even though the support which the Church
received from home was not as great as it might have been, it was
more than was enjoyed by any other denomination, and this is
probably true, though the Presbyterians received some help from
Scotland, and the Independents were supported, in their political
interests at least, by the dissenting lobby in England. It must be
remembered, however, that the Episcopal Church also suffered
various disadvantages from its English connection. The great
point made by the dissenters in their opposition to a colonial
episcopate was that bishops, under English law, were officers of
the State as well as the Church, and no amount of insistence could
convince them that a purely spiritual authority was all that was
desired in America. In some cases also, at least in New England,
persons well disposed toward the Church were dissuaded from
joining it by the argument that its growth would threaten the
civil liberties of the colonies. The Church was bound by laws and
customs adapted to a very different situation from that which it
found in the plantations, and every important decision in respect
to its affairs had to be referred across the seas to an authority but
slightly acquainted with colonial conditions. Because its ministry
was incomplete, and because it was under the nominal jurisdiction
of an English bishop, the nearest approach which it could attain
to local self-government was the holding of voluntary conventions
of the clergy which usually included those of only one colony, and

rarely of more than two or three. When the final conflict arose between the colonies and the mother country, the loyalty to the Crown of most of her clergy and many of her laity in the northern colonies cost the Church great unpopularity; the forced flight of many of these clergymen when open hostilities began caused her services to be interrupted and created a shortage in her ministry, which was not to be remedied for many years; and the sudden cessation of aid from the Society for the Propagation of the Gospel at the end of the war, and the repeal of the various acts of establishment left her impoverished and, in many places, temporarily paralyzed.

In the eighteenth century all of the colonies, except Connecticut and Rhode Island, had governors appointed by the King, or by their proprietors, most of them had appointive councils, and all of them had elective assemblies. As all of the proprietors had become Churchmen before the century was very far advanced, the governor was the natural leader of the Church in his colony, and in all of the colonies he performed certain functions which were then considered ecclesiastical, of which the most important were the granting of licenses to marry and the probating of wills. In the colonies where the Church was established (Virginia, Maryland, South Carolina, New York, and later North Carolina and Georgia), the governor was also regarded as in some,measure the "Ordinary" of the province. He investigated the qualifications of newly-arrived ministers, and inducted them into their parishes, either upon presentation by the vestries, as in Virginia, or upon his own initiative, as in Maryland. He sometimes acted, also, to deprive unworthy clergymen of their benefices, and even in a few cases, to suspend or depose them from their ministry, but his assumption of this power was generally opposed by the ecclesiastical authorities at home, and by the Commissaries in the colonies, as inconsistent with the Constitution of the Church of England. As there were no ecclesiastical courts in the colonies, what little canon law was enforced upon the laity was applied by the civil courts, which were more or less subject to the governor's control.

In politics, the governor, if he were honest, sought to advance the interests of the power which appointed him, whether royal or proprietary. The council if appointive, usually, though not always,

The Governor

supported the governor, and the Assembly, which, like the House of Commons, held the purse strings, generally tried to see how many concessions it could wring from the governor in return for paying his salary and granting necessary subsidies. In the game which was thus played out between them, the Church was too often used as a pawn. If the governor chose to appear as her protector, the clergy and others interested in her welfare were more or less compelled to support him, even though his personal and political character might be such as to do but little honor to their religion, and though their support would bring upon them the hostility of the Assembly party. If, on the other hand, the governor preferred to sacrifice the interests of the Church in order to obtain ends which he considered more important, active opposition might only serve to endanger her welfare still further. During the reigns of Queen Anne and of George III, it was generally understood that services to the Church were a means of obtaining royal favor, and governors sought to appear as her protectors whether or not they themselves felt any personal interest in the cause of religion, but under the first two Georges there was no such understanding, and unless they happened to have a personal attachment to the Church, governors sought to promote her interests only when doing so seemed likely to aid their political schemes. As a rule the Church could do but little to control the gubernatorial caprice, though an occasional protest against unfriendly action might be lodged in England. The powerful influence exercised by Commissary Blair in Virginia sometimes enabled him to make and unmake governors, and a similar though less extensive influence was exercised for a time by Commissary Henderson in Maryland, but even in those colonies the Church reaped little permanent benefit from the political victories of the Commissaries.

Jurisdiction of the Bishop of London

The ecclesiastical authority of the governor was supplemented by the uncertain jurisdiction exercised by the Bishop of London over the colonies. This jurisdiction, like so many English institutions, "just happened." It was not the result of any conscious arrangement or formal provision, and the circumstances of its origin have, in fact, never been clearly ascertained. One precedent for it may be found in the request of the Virginia Company to Bishop King to furnish ministers for their colony in 1620, and it is possible that another precedent was furnished by the jurisdiction over the English trading-posts in the Netherlands which Archbishop Laud obtained for the See of London in 1633, and by his less successful efforts to obtain episcopal supervision of New England. It is not until after the Restoration that we find the jurisdiction in actual operation, but by then it is already being justified on the ground of customary usage. In 1675 the Lords' Committee of Trade and Plantations, at the instance of Bishop Compton, directed that an inquiry should be made into the origin of this jurisdiction. The investigation appears to have been fruitless, but, nevertheless, the committee two years later agreed to a proposal of Compton's that, as he was "Ordinary of Jamaica," no ministers should be received in that colony without his license, and that none having that license should be rejected without cause. In 1679, as we have seen, the instructions issued to Lord Culpeper, governor of Virginia, forbade him to prefer any ministers to benefices in the colony unless they had a certificate from London of their being episcopally ordained, and the governor was also directed to confer with the Bishop upon the religious affairs of the colony before sailing. In 1685 the Committee approved the jurisdiction of London over the "West Indies"—a term that was frequently applied to all of the American colonies—except for the disposal of parishes, licensing of marriages, and probating of wills, which powers were reserved to the governors.

After the Revolution of 1689, Compton adopted the policy of delegating his authority in the colonies to resident clergymen specially commissioned for the purpose, to whom was given the name of "Commissaries." These men, who were usually the holders of the principal benefices in the colonies to which they were commissioned, exercised a variable amount of authority, depending upon their personal character and the circumstances in which they found themselves. In colonies where the Church was not established, their position was largely an honorary one. The most that they could do was to preside over voluntary conventions of the clergy, and act as correspondents of the Bishop. In colonies where there was an Establishment, however, they generally attempted to do something more. They called the conventions over which they presided "visitations," and sometimes took the opportunity which these presented of scolding the clergy for their various

The Commissaries

misdeeds. They also claimed the right to suspend a negligent or immoral minister, after due trial, and though the indefiniteness of their authority and the opposition of the clergy, and sometimes of the governor also, made it difficult for them to make this claim good, they sometimes did so.

Compton's colonial policy was followed by his successor, Bishop Robinson, but Edmund Gibson, who came to the See in 1723, was dissatisfied with the basis of his authority, and applied to the Privy Council to have it made more definite. As a result of this application the opinions of the Attorney and Solicitor-General were taken. They ruled that the ecclesiastical jurisdiction of the colonies remained in the Crown, and that if the Bishop of London were to exercise authority abroad, he must obtain a royal commission. With this ruling Gibson complied, and his authority was thus placed upon a basis of formal legality, a fact which seems somewhat to have strengthened the hands of his Commissaries. His successor, Thomas Sherlock, however, professed to believe that the commission was defective, and to be so tender of the royal prerogative that he was unwilling, even with such authority, to run the risk of infringing it. The real reason for his scrupulosity was probably his desire to obtain a colonial episcopate, of which measure he was one of the most zealous proponents. Knowing his politicians, he realized that they would be glad to avoid the difficulties involved in making any fresh provision for the ecclesiastical supervision of the colonies as long as anything like a tolerable arrangement was in existence. He allowed the Commissaries appointed by Bishop Gibson to continue, but when they died or retired, none was appointed to succeed them, except in one or two colonies. The jurisdiction of Sherlock's successors, therefore, was even more shadowy than it had been before, and consisted chiefly in granting the required certificates of episcopal ordination to ministers going to the colonies.

The two most famous of the Commissaries were James Blair of Virginia and Thomas Bray of Maryland. Bray spent but a short time in Maryland, where his chief work was to encourage the passage of a law establishing the Church, but he made the whole colonial Church his debtor when he became the principal agent in the foundation of the Society for the Propagation of the Gospel in Foreign Parts, and of the Society for the Promotion of Christian

Bishop Gibson and Bishop Sherlock

Commissary Blair

Knowledge. Blair remained in Virginia from his appointment in 1689 until his death in 1743, except for occasional visits to England in the performance of his duty, and became in time one of the most influential, though probably not one of the best-loved, men in the colony. He was a Scotchman who possessed all the stubbornness of his race, and he had also a fair share of the irascibility which was almost universal among public men in the early eighteenth century, but he was also a fearless and indefatigable champion of the Church in everything which he felt its interests concerned. His great service was the founding of the College of William and Mary, of which he was the first president. In his capacity as Commissary, he fought with nearly every governor who came to the colony on behalf of the rights of the clergy and the college, and at the same time he sought to raise morals, and increase the clergy's devotion to duty. It must be admitted, however, that his efforts in this latter direction consisted chiefly in giving frequent scoldings. Blair himself reported toward the close of his career that he had only suspended two clergymen, though there must have been many more who needed suspension, and his neighbor, Commissary Wilkinson, wrote to London, "By inquiry, I understand that the Commissary in Virginia does nothing at all in the executing of his commission."

Human institutions are rarely the creations of any one person, and though the honor of being the principal founder of the Society for the Propagation of the Gospel in Foreign Parts belongs to Bray, the work could not have been accomplished without the coöperation of many others. The founding of religious societies had, in fact, become something of a fashion in England by the beginning of the eighteenth century. As early as 1649 a "Corporation for the Promoting and Propagating the Gospel of Jesus Christ in New England" had been established by the Long Parliament to support the work of John Eliot among the Indians, and this society was revived in 1662 at the instance of Robert Boyle, an Irish philanthropist and scientist who displayed a lifelong interest in the conversion of the American aborigines. A few years later, a number of religious societies were organized to combat the attacks upon orthodox Christianity of Socinians, Deists, and other heretics. When, therefore, Bray and other earnest men turned their attention to the needs of Christianity in America, the formation

Commissary Bray and the S.P.G.

of a voluntary society seemed to them a natural means of promoting its interests, just as the obtaining of a royal decree or bounty would have seemed the proper method to men of an earlier day.

Formation
of the
S.P.C.K.

Bray's interest in the colonies began when Bishop Compton appointed him Commissary to Maryland in 1696. As he was not able to leave for his new post at once (he was rector of the parish of Sheldon in England), he devoted himself for a time to sending out missionaries and presenting them with libraries. In 1697 he laid before Bishop Compton a plan for the formation of a society to spread Christian knowledge both at home and in the colonies. His project was shelved for a time, but it led eventually to the formation of the Society for the Promotion of Christian Knowledge two years later. In 1699, by selling his personal effects and by borrowing, Bray obtained enough money to go to Maryland, where he held a visitation, and gave some advice to his clergy, and whence he returned the following year to obtain royal assent for the colonial Act of Establishment. On his return he published a memorial on the state of religion in North America, in which he repeated some information on religious conditions in the colonies which he had obtained and published in 1698, and added a suggestion that to relieve the serious shortage of clergymen existing in the New World, persons in each diocese should be solicited to contribute fifty pounds as the salary, and twenty pounds for the library, of a minister to be sent to the colonies.

S.P.G.
Organized

The next move was made, not by Bray, but by the lower house of the Convocation of Canterbury, which, on May 13, 1701, appointed a committee to consider methods of promoting Christianity in the foreign plantations. Encouraged, perhaps, by this manifestation of interest on the part of the largest body of clergy in England, Bray, within three weeks after the first meeting of the committee, petitioned the King for the establishment of a society to propagate Christianity in the colonies, and the proposal was duly referred to the Crown lawyers for their opinion. The Society for the Promotion of Christian Knowledge had, as we have seen, already been organized, and it now became the sponsor for its younger sister. At various meetings in May, 1701, it considered Bray's petition, a proposed charter, and other documents; received a promise from Thomas Tenison, the Archbishop of Canterbury, to give twenty guineas towards the cost of obtaining a charter, and undertook to make itself responsible for these expenses. At its meeting of June 23, 1701, the charter granted by William III was read to the Society, and thanks were tendered to Bray and Tenison for their efforts in obtaining it. The charter stated that the purposes of the new organization were to provide for the maintenance of orthodox clergy in the plantations, for the propagation of the Gospel in those parts, and the "receiving, managing and disposing of the charity of His Majesty's subjects for those purposes."

As the membership of the two societies was largely the same, the task of promoting the colonial religion was transferred almost entirely to the Society for the Propagation of the Gospel, which held its first meeting within a short time, under the presidency of Archbishop Tenison, an office which was regularly held by him and his successors. On August 15, 1701, the Society instituted an enquiry into the religious state of the colonies, and on October 17 some progress was made towards raising a fund for carrying out its objects. In the spring of 1702 a committee was appointed to recommend measures for carrying out the designs of the Society, and this soon became a permanent Standing Committee. The Dean of Lincoln, who preached the Society's first Anniversary Sermon, declared that settling the state of religion among its own people in the colonies should be its chief object, and converting the natives its second. This declaration defined the relative importance which the Society always attached to these two ends, for, though it resolved in 1710 that the conversion of the heathen should be its principal aim, the resolution was not adhered to.

The first definite effort of the Society on behalf of the colonies was the appointment of George Keith in 1702 to go out as a traveling missionary and report upon the religious needs of America. This interesting personage had been a leader among the Quakers, but, becoming dissatisfied with some of their teachings, he had withdrawn and founded a sect of his own, which became known as the Keithites. He still found his religious position unsatisfactory, however, and in time he conformed to the Church and entered its ministry. He brought a number of his followers with him, while others returned to orthodox Quakerism, and a few continued the struggle to perpetuate their own sect. Because he had lived for some time in the colonies, he appeared to the Society to be the

George Keith Sent to Colonies

proper person to inaugurate its mission. The choice was in many respects an excellent one, for Keith was an energetic and devoted worker who possessed marked abilities as a controversialist, and had a convert's enthusiasm for the cause of the Church. On the other hand, he had the misfortune to possess a contentious spirit and a special rancor against the Quakers, which gave to his mission, at least in the northern colonies, something of the character of a series of controversies with his former co-religionists, combined with occasional flings at the Independents, and may have been one cause of that bias in favor of work among the dissenters which, contrary to Bray's intention, kept the Society from doing very much to supply the many sections of the country which were destitute of all religious services.

Keith sailed from England on April 28, 1702, in the ship *Centurian*. On the way over, he won the admiration of the ship's chaplain, John Talbot, who was so impressed with the importance of the mission that he became Keith's traveling companion in America and, after the latter's return to England, devoted the rest of his life to the service of the colonies. The two of them landed in Boston, where Keith was invited to preach in King's Chapel, then in charge of Samuel Myles and Christopher Bridge. His first sermon was attacked in a pamphlet by the redoubtable Increase Mather, to whom he printed a reply after he had reached New York. From Boston, he took an excursion northward to Portsmouth, where the ferry was wrecked, and he was rescued by a Quaker with whom he promptly got into an argument. Keith traveled slowly southward, preaching in Episcopal churches, and thrusting himself into Quaker meetings whenever he could for the purpose of engaging willing controversialists in debate.

Wherever Keith found Episcopal settlements, he was well received, and he reported that there was a general desire for ministers of the Church of England throughout the North, and that any delay in supplying them might cause the section to be lost to the Presbyterians. At the time of his coming, the only ministers of the Church in New England were the two at Boston already mentioned, and one who had recently been sent to Newport, Rhode Island. In the colony of New York there were no Church ministers except in New York town. There was none at all in New Jersey, nor in Pennsylvania except at Philadelphia, where Evan Evans and an assistant were serving Christ Church. At Philadelphia, Keith had a public debate with another former Quaker, named William Davis, who had published a book "full of blasphemous notions," and from there he reported that he and his associates had baptized two hundred Quakers in various parts of the colonies, besides receiving some who had already been baptized, and converting a number of other dissenters. When he reached the South he found Virginia and Maryland fairly well supplied with ministers, most of whom were men of good repute, though some sections were destitute, as Princess Anne County in Virginia and Annapolis in Maryland. In North Carolina there were no ministers at all, and apparently Keith did not go as far as South Carolina.

When his tour was completed, Keith returned to England, where he accepted a benefice, but Talbot remained in America. After visiting for a time in New York and Connecticut, he went to New Jersey and settled down at Burlington, where he spent the rest of his life, giving as much time as he could to the service of neighboring churches also. In his old age he was dismissed by the Society on suspicion of being a Jacobite, and of exercising unauthorized jurisdiction over his brethren, but he remained at Burlington where the parish had, by then, become strong enough to pay him a salary. The charge of exercising jurisdiction over his brethren was based on a rumor that he had been consecrated by the "Nonjuring" bishops in England, of which more will be said later. He was one of the first to urge that bishops be sent to the colonies, and was zealous for every measure which he thought might strengthen the Church. It is possible that his dismissal was facilitated by his freedom in criticizing the measures of the Society when he disapproved of them.

Talbot in New Jersey

Keith and Talbot were but the forerunners of a constantly increasing number of missionaries who were supported, in whole or part, by the Society until the separation of the colonies from the mother country. The importance of its work can perhaps best be realized by observing that there were not more than three or four self-supporting parishes in all the colonies where the Church was not established. Nearly all of the ministers in these provinces, therefore, were dependent in some measure upon the assistance of the Society, and the great majority would not have been able

Importance of the S.P.G.

to continue their work at all without its help. Moreover, it supplemented the salaries of most of the ministers in South Carolina and New York. Its stipends were small, averaging fifty pounds, but they were regularly paid (which was not generally true of local contributions); they were paid in sterling, an important fact in view of the rapid depreciation of colonial currency; and they were paid in England, so that they could be drawn upon for purchases there without paying the heavy discount which had to be charged on colonial bills to cover fluctuations in the exchange. As all manufactured articles which could not be made in the home, as well as many common foodstuffs, such as salt and tea, had to be brought across the sea, this last item was an important convenience. The Society also aided in the support of schoolmasters in a number of communities, thus helping to lay the foundations of American education.

Its Special Interest in New England   Bray's original intention had been to supply ministers for places which were destitute of all religious services, or which were exposed to the operation of Roman Catholics and Quakers, whom he considered scarcely Christian; but in time the Society came to make its most extensive efforts in New England, and especially in Connecticut. This shift in interest has sometimes been attributed to political motives, but it would seem that there are other circumstances which offer a better explanation. It is true that there were sound political reasons for promoting the Church in New England, where its spread meant the spread of loyalty to the Crown, but the political motives for supporting it on the frontier should have been equally strong, both because the spirit of independence was often highest there and because the settlers there were always in danger of being exposed to the influence of the French.

The real reason for the bias in favor of New England is, I think, more probably to be found in the way in which the claims of the various sections were presented to the Society. The historian today is in a position to know much more about colonial conditions than was anyone in England in the eighteenth century, and it takes a definite effort of the imagination to place ourselves in the position of the Society's leaders. For whatever understanding they had of the situation in the colonies, they were almost entirely dependent upon the reports of their missionaries and other correspondents in

America, and among these, for one voice that was heard in favor of the claims of other sections, there were generally several to be heard in favor of Connecticut or Massachusetts. After the initial explorations of Keith and Talbot, the Society generally followed the policy of sending missionaries only where they were applied for by organized congregations, and where some assurance was given that a church would be built and some contribution made to the minister's support. As Massachusetts and Connecticut required everyone to support some sort of religion, Churchmen there were more ready to make these pledges, and also more likely to keep them. Moreover, the general religious ferment prevailing in New England after the first quarter of the century produced a steady stream of converts to the Church from among the Independent ministers. As these men were generally of higher quality than any who could be obtained for the colonial service in England, the Society hardly felt justified in rejecting them, but, while they could be used effectively in their own colonies, or those with a similar population, the prevalence of inter-colonial jealousies made their employment in more distant provinces a dubious experiment.

Whatever its causes, this apparent partiality did bring upon the Society a certain amount of criticism, both from within the Church and from the outside, and in time its leaders themselves came to regard the policy as inexpedient, especially as it was found to increase the opposition among the dissenters to the cherished project of a colonial episcopate. In 1758 Archbishop Secker wrote to Dr. Samuel Johnson, president of King's College, New York (not to be confused with the English lexicographer), that in the future he thought missionaries should be sent where there were Presbyterians or Independents, only when a competent number of persons would certify "that they cannot in conscience comply with the mode of worship and church government in use, and that they approve ours, but cannot raise a fund to support it among them." This, however, would not have involved any great change from the existing method, as the persons who applied for missionaries were usually those whose consciences scrupled at the forms of Christianity prevailing in their region. In 1772 the Society resolved not to support any fresh missions in New England, but

Criticism of
the S.P.G.

by then the existence of the colonial Church, as such, was so nearly over that the resolution had no time to take effect.

On the other hand, fairness requires the observation that if the spirit of proselytism existed in the Church at this period, it was by no means confined to it. In a number of cases where Church missionaries were sent to places which had hitherto been without the services of any ministers, Presbyterian or Independent clergymen appeared upon the scene within a very short time, and by the third quarter of the century all of the major dissenting groups were engaged in the work of self-propagation in the colonies where the Church was established.

Difficulty of Obtaining Local Support

Though the Society, as has been said, normally required the congregations to which missionaries were sent to pledge something for their support, it was never very successful in forcing them to adhere to those pledges. Even in New England it was reported that the local officers were generally rather careless about collecting ecclesiastical taxes from Churchmen when they had to be paid over to a Church minister, and in the other colonies complaints that the parishes were not living up to their obligations were almost the rule. Moreover, the Society had but indifferent success in solving the problem, which confronts all missionary organizations, of weaning the parishes that had become strong enough to be self-supporting. Parish budgets never increased in proportion to the growth of the congregations, and any suggestion that the Society intended to leave a parish to its own resources would always be met with detailed explanations from the vestry of why the people could not possibly afford to support their own minister—explanations which the missionary, anxious to retain his one sure source of income, would always second, no matter how much he might complain at other times that the people were not doing all they should. In 1774 the Society proposed to cut in half its bounty to missions of ten years' standing or more, but, like the resolution in connection with New England, this decision came too late to take effect before the Revolution. It would, in any case, probably have proven too drastic a measure to be carried out, but had a more gradual scheme of diminution been adopted at an earlier date, the sudden withdrawal of the Society's support after the independence of the colonies was recognized would have proven less disastrous than it did in many parts of the Church.

For its support the Society relied chiefly upon the contributions of its friends in England, but it received some gifts from the colonies also. Several of the governors and some of the other great men of the plantations were among its members, and it also received a present from the King of some lands in the "New Hampshire Grants," later known as Vermont. These were transferred to the diocese of Vermont in the nineteenth century, but so much litigation was involved in making good the title to them that, in the opinion of the son and biographer of Bishop Hopkins, its first prelate, they did the Church there more harm than good. In 1767 the Society was made the residuary legatee of St. George Talbot of New Jersey, a notoriously dissolute person who, for some reason, chose to pose as a patron of the Church. His will, however, was carelessly drawn and improperly witnessed, and the Society was unable to establish its claim to the legacy, which would have involved a considerable amount, could it have been obtained.

The principal executive officer of the Society for the Propagation of the Gospel was the secretary, and it was through him that the contact of the missionaries with the Society was generally maintained. He transmitted to them its directions and rules, and received in turn the reports upon the state of their parishes which they were required to make at least annually, and any other information or complaints that they might care to communicate, for they were forbidden to correspond with private members of the Society, though the Archbishop of Canterbury usually had some correspondents in the colonies, and the Bishop of London was in receipt of occasional official reports from his Commissaries and others. For the most part, the Society was fortunate in its choice of secretaries, who were generally men of conscientiousness and ability, but we sometimes find complaints from the missionaries that their letters home remained unanswered, or that they failed to receive the printed abstracts of the Society's proceedings which were their chief source of information as to its wishes. These complaints were especially frequent in the closing years of Secretary Bearcroft's long administration, when old age seems to have made him negligent. Shortly after his death, in 1762, the clergy of New Jersey asserted that they had had no abstracts since 1759, and received little information of any sort as to the Society's wishes. With the succession of a younger secretary (Burton), con-

Income of the S.P.G.

The Secretary

ditions improved in this respect, yet even under him we find a
missionary reporting that he did not know of his appointment
to a certain station until another clergyman happened to call his
attention to the announcement of it in the abstracts. Some slips of
this sort, however, were inevitable in view of the distance which
instructions had to be sent, and the uncertainty and slowness of
the means of communication.

Discipline of
the S.P.G.
The maintenance of discipline among the colonial clergy, in the
absence of any episcopal authority, was a serious problem, and it is
to the credit of the Society that it erred on the side of strictness
rather than of leniency in this respect. It could not deprive anyone
of his ministerial office, but it could dismiss an offender from its
service, discontinuing his stipend, and, though too many of the
ministers thus discharged were able to establish themselves in the
southern colonies, the prospect of being left without certain support in a strange country was still sufficiently alarming to make
any who felt themselves disposed to stray stop and think. A missionary against whom charges of immorality were brought by
responsible parties was almost certain to be dismissed. He would,
of course, be given a chance to speak for himself, but no formal
trial was required, and, unless he could produce pretty strong
testimony as to his innocence and general good character, he was
sure to be relieved of his duties. The missionaries sometimes
complained that the Society was too willing to listen to charges
against them, and it is possible that injustice was occasionally
committed, but it was better to run the risk of doing this than
to allow the Church to be disgraced by unworthy ministers, especially in colonies where it was already regarded with suspicion.
Dismissal was also the penalty for any serious breach of the
Society's instructions, especial severity being shown to ministers
who went without permission to stations other than those to
which they had been sent, even the best excuses being frequently
rejected. This measure also worked some hardship, for the home
authorities were not always correctly informed as to the character of the posts to which they sent missionaries, but it was
essential if the Society was to retain enough control over its missionaries to use them in pursuing any general policy, as a minister
sent to a difficult but important station was not always capable of
resisting the lure of greener pastures elsewhere.

In spite of all these precautions, unworthy ministers would sometimes be found in the Society's service, but the number was surprisingly small, especially when we consider the remoteness of the field of labor from its seat, and its lack of any local executive. Its men, in fact, constituted a sort of superior caste among the colonial clergy, both as to morals and ability. This was due partly to the superior discipline maintained by the Society and partly to other causes. The excellence of most of the New England con- verts was one, and the fact that most of the missionaries worked under the scrutiny of hostile neighbors was another. More im- portant still in weeding out undesirables was probably the com- bination of small wages and hard work, which kept men who desired a life of ease and comfort, even on a humble scale, from seeking the Society's service. When such men did enter it, they generally realized their mistake in a short time, and left as soon as they conveniently could. *Character of the Missionaries*

Because of this superiority, their common dependence upon the Society, and the general similarity of their religious views (most of them being High Churchmen), the missionaries, though they had no general organization, formed a self-conscious group which transcended colonial boundaries, and to that extent they lent a certain amount of unity to the Church, whose activities in colonial times generally developed along provincial lines. On the other hand, because of the contempt and suspicion, whether jus- tified or not, with which they regarded the rest of the colonial clergy, they also operated in some degree as a divisive factor. This division, however, did not affect their relations with the ministers of the few independent parishes in the North, or with the heads of the colleges at New York and Philadelphia, who, for practical purposes, should be regarded as belonging to their caste. Many of these men had been formerly missionaries of the Society themselves, and most of them maintained some corre- spondence with the missionaries, and with the Society, which, because of the comparative impartiality that their position gave them, often found their advice to be of considerable value.

The general character of the colonial clergy has been too severely dealt with by writers, both at that time and later, though it was certainly not all that it ought to have been. In considering the question, it is necessary, in the first place, to distinguish between *Morals of the Clergy* the northern and southern colonies. Though the number of unworthy ministers who came to the northern colonies from England was rather high, in proportion to the total, the discipline exercised by the Society prevented such men from remaining long in that region, and the generality of the northern clergy may be said not only to have been free from scandal in their personal lives, but to have maintained a reputation for piety and devotion to their duty which was probably superior to that of the average clergyman in England, and at least not inferior to that of the ministers of other denominations in the colonies.

In the South, however, the situation was less satisfactory. The type of Establishment prevailing in that region was probably the worst possible, from the point of view of securing an able and devoted ministry. The salaries, though small, were generally sufficient to enable a man to live without hardship, and the work to be done was simply the ordinary parish routine, so that there was little in the service to appeal to men imbued with a genuine missionary spirit and, on the other hand, the absence of any important posts to which they might hope for preferment (unless the presidency of the college in Virginia could be considered such), chilled the interest of the able and ambitious. The men who came, therefore, were generally men of limited abilities, of little ambition and no influence, and, sometimes at least, of very little religion. In the southern colonies, though they were technically rated as gentlemen, they were not always accepted as the social equals of the planter aristocracy. Nevertheless their parishes were better than the miserable curacies to which they might aspire in England; their livings, unless they were too blunt in rebuking the sins of the people, would be secure; and because of the absence of any strong ecclesiastical jurisdiction, they could feel reasonably confident that neither their private lives nor their public services would be subjected to too severe a scrutiny.

Under such conditions it would, indeed, have been a matter for surprise if unworthy men had not thrust themselves into the ministry. Nevertheless, the sweeping generalizations sometimes made as to the degradation of the southern clergy would seem to have been based upon the impression created by a few extreme cases, rather than upon any adequate knowledge of the facts. If we count up the instances in which ministers are charged with

In the South

specific acts of immorality, the total, though greater than that existing in a healthy religious organization, would never be found to constitute more than a small minority of the clergy in any colony, and this evidence is supported by the preponderance of testimony from the Commissaries, governors, and others who were in a position to have a fairly intimate knowledge of the prevailing conditions. It is probably true that many ministers who were not guilty of notorious offenses were slothful in their work and worldly in their lives. Yet, even on this point, the evidence is not entirely adverse. The rapid growth of dissent in the southern colonies after the first quarter of the century, and the hostility shown to the Church by many of the lower classes during the Revolution and after, would seem to indicate that the ministers had not done all that they should to win and hold the common people, but, on the other hand, from what evidence we have, it would appear that most of them performed the routine duties of their parishes with tolerable regularity, and it must be remembered that a clergyman who did even this would have to work harder than a similarly conscientious minister in England, for the colonial parishes were more extensive, the people more scattered, and the rate of sickness and mortality higher.

The quality of the clergy varied, moreover, from colony to colony, and from time to time. A number of observers testify that conditions were at their worst in Maryland, and this observation is borne out by the large number of specific crimes which we find charged against clergymen there. The evil was partly due to a hostility that existed between the proprietors and the Bishop of London, during the middle part of the century, which made the proprietary governors indifferent to the quality of men they appointed to the parishes. The fact that the salaries in Maryland were higher than elsewhere may also have served to attract a larger number of worldly men to the colony. South Carolina would possibly come next in the scale of ecclesiastical corruption, though between this colony and Virginia there is not much choice. North Carolina and Georgia had too few ministers to make an entirely fair comparison, but among the few they had were certainly some who were evil.

Variations in Quality of Clergy

The situation in most of the southern colonies was probably at its worst during the period that ran roughly from 1725 to 1760. In

the earlier years of the century the colonial service still had enough
missionary character to attract men of earnest faith, and during
the sixties and seventies a reaction against the evil living of some
of their ministers seems to have led the parishes to exercise a
slightly greater care in the selection of new incumbents. Some of
the young men appointed in the southern colonies at this period,
such as David Griffith in Virginia, Thomas John Claggett in
Maryland, and Robert Smith in South Carolina, were to perform
valuable services as leaders of the Church both in the period of
reorganization and afterwards.

The great scandal lay not so much in the frequency of the
crimes alleged against clergymen, or even in their grossness, for
both of these might have been explained by the general crudity of
colonial life, and were paralleled in the experience of other denominations, but in the fact that so many of the offenders went entirely
unpunished. Jacob Henderson of Maryland, for instance, was by
no means the least active or most timid of the Commissaries, yet it
is within his jurisdiction that we trace the shocking history of
William Tibbs. In 1715, shortly before Henderson became Commissary, Tibbs was presented for various crimes to Governor
Hart, who directed three other clergymen to investigate the case,
but did not consider himself empowered to take definite action
until the will of the Bishop of London had been learned. At
Hart's recommendation, Henderson and Christopher Wilkinson
were appointed Commissaries for the purpose of dealing with this
and similar cases, yet in 1724, when the colonial clergy were required to answer a set of queries sent out by Bishop Gibson,
Tibb's name led all the rest, and he reported that he had been
twenty-four years in his parish. In 1732, Henderson reported that
complaints were still being made against him, and that he "con-
tinues as bad as ever," but that, his own commission being somewhat uncertain, he dared not proceed against him, because he was
rich and powerful. So far as is known, the reprobate continued
undisturbed in his living until his career was ended by a peaceful
death. His case was, perhaps, extreme as to the length of time it
covered, but it was by no means an unusual example of the inabil-
ity of the Commissaries to deal with offenders in an effective
manner.

In the later years of the century there was a great increase in

the number of native colonials volunteering for the service of the Native Clergy
Church, not only among converts from other denominations, but
also, though to a lesser extent, among those who had been brought
up within her fold. This circumstance helped, on the whole, to
raise the standards of the ministry, but it created a new problem
for the English authorities in raising the question of what testimonials should be required of candidates from America. Where
the candidate was known to a local clergyman of good repute, the
problem was not a serious one, but there were many cases when
such references were impossible, and, as it was no light matter to
reject a man who had made a long journey across the Atlantic for
orders, the English bishops occasionally felt obliged to accept the
testimonials of laymen. These, however, were sometimes mislead-
ing. There are many otherwise excellent people in the world who
find it almost impossible to refuse to affix their signature to any
document that is presented to them, and in a number of cases men
who had been notorious evil livers in the colonies found it possible
to appear in England with excellent testimonials and be ordained
before information as to their true character could be rushed
across the ocean. In at least one or two instances such men were
appointed to minister in the very communities where they had
acquired their unsavory reputations.

Circumstances compelled some modification of ecclesiastical customs in the colonies, though on the whole it cannot be said that Changes in
the Church showed itself very adaptable to new conditions. Church Life
When changes occurred they were noted with regret, and abandoned as soon as possible. All services requiring the presence of a
bishop, such as Confirmation and the consecration of churches,
had, of course, to be omitted. Where there was a strong Quaker
or Baptist influence, difficulties sometimes ensued about the baptism of infants, and even where these influences were absent, some
parents objected to public baptism, or to the use of sponsors.
Funerals, also, had often to be held from private houses, generally
upon the plea of distance. Holy Communion was celebrated rather
infrequently in most parishes. Many of the clergy felt that its
celebration upon the great festivals was sufficient, and few celebrated it oftener than once a month. When it was held, moreover,
the influence of the Puritans, who maintained that only those confident of being in a state of grace should communicate, sometimes

deterred the people from receiving. Because of the shortage of ministers, candidates for ordination were occasionally permitted to read service, but this practice was frowned upon by the English authorities.

Except where it was provided for by law, the cost of the church building was met by voluntary contributions, by the sale of pews, or by the use of lotteries. This latter method, however, was not practicable in colonies where the government was hostile to the Church, as it required a special license. The architecture, where it had progressed beyond the rudimentary, box-like stage, was generally an attempt at the imitation of the Greek, as Gothic had not yet regained its popularity. The pews were box-shaped, with high sides, and gates to keep out any but the proprietors and their families. The pulpit, which was generally the most conspicuous feature of the church, might be in front of the Communion Table, or behind it, or at the side of the church, or at the opposite end, in which case the pew boxes had seats on either side, so that the congregation could turn around when the minister went up to preach. Nearly everything that went into the church, except the stone or timber, including glass for the windows and sometimes even nails, had to be imported from England, and as such imports were expensive, many of the churches were but poorly furnished. Sometimes the minister could not even comply with the canon requiring him to wear a surplice while officiating, as this vestment had to be made of a finer cloth than could be woven in the colonies.

Though the opportunities for respectable women to earn a livelihood were probably better in the colonies than in the older countries, and though second marriages were rather frequent, the lot of widows whose husbands left them unprovided for was, nevertheless, a hard one, and societies to care for the widows and orphans of clergymen were organized as soon as the number of ministers in the colonial Church was large enough to make such institutions feasible. A beginning was made in Virginia in 1754, when a plan for the relief of widows and orphans drafted by Commissary Dawson was approved by a voluntary convention of ministers, but the first definite organization seems to have been that completed by the clergy of South Carolina in 1762. The most significant of the associations, however, was that organized in the

Church Buildings

Clergy Relief

colonies of Pennsylvania, New York, and New Jersey under the leadership of William Smith, Provost of the College of Philadelphia, in 1767. This was the only important inter-colonial enterprise undertaken by the American clergy, and it was no mere accident that through its meeting one of the first steps in the reorganization of the Church after the Revolution was taken. The societies were organized upon an insurance basis, the minister making a regular contribution, and his family receiving a proportionate return after his death. The New York-Pennsylvania Society enjoyed the special patronage of the Society for the Propagation of the Gospel, whose missionaries supplied the bulk of its members.

Provincial religion tended to be divided along colonial lines, and it is possible to identify most of the colonies with some predominant type of Christianity. As a consciousness of inter-colonial unity began to develop in secular affairs, however, a similar tendency showed itself in religion. Not only did the prevailing denomination in one colony tend to invade the others, but religious groups began to appear which had no definite association with any particular colony or region. The first of these were the Baptists, who, though they appeared first in Rhode Island, spread rapidly throughout the colonies, as traveling artisans and laborers carried their message everywhere, and the Presbyterians, with their more formal ministry, were not far behind them.

The most conspicuous of the inter-colonial religious movements, however, and one which transcended denominational as well as political lines, was that known as the "Great Awakening," which had its origin in the exciting work of Jonathan Edwards at Northampton, Massachusetts, but which in its wider aspects is associated with the preaching of George Whitefield. This brilliant and earnest, but somewhat undisciplined personality made his first appearance in America in 1738 when, though only in deacon's orders, he came over to succeed John Wesley as rector at Savannah, Georgia, the only parish which either ever held. Unlike Wesley, Whitefield was popular in Georgia, but he remained there only long enough to form the project of establishing an orphanage to which he gave the name "Bethesda," and to which he later sought to join an academy and a theological college. The rest of his life he spent as a traveling preacher in England and America,

*"The Great Awakening"

converting sinners, and raising money for the orphanage, which became his hobby. His preaching set the colonies in ferment, every province being in some measure affected, created a temporary schism among the Presbyterians, and gave a considerable impetus to the Baptist Church, which was more or less sympathetic with his views, but his ideas produced surprisingly little in the way of permanent results, probably because they failed to eventuate in any definite organization.

Its Effect on the Church

The ministers of the Episcopal Church, acting on instructions from home, nearly always opposed Whitefield, generally with success so far as their own immediate flocks were concerned, and were roundly abused by him for doing so. In the end the Church probably gained by his preaching, but if so, in the way of reaction rather than of direct conversion. Though Whitefield remained all his life officially within the ministry of the Church, his converts generally found their spiritual home in other denominations, but the success of most clergymen in checking the spread of enthusiasm within their parishes drew to the Church a good many who were distressed by the extravagances and dissensions which that enthusiasm produced elsewhere.

CHAPTER IV

The Church in the South

IN THE preceding chapter we have considered the general circumstances and agencies which conditioned the life of the Church in the eighteenth century, and in subsequent chapters we will consider one or two of the movements which affected the colonies generally. As, however, the work of the Church was carried on in a somewhat different manner in the several provinces, it will be necessary, for an adequate presentation of our subject, to give some consideration to their separate histories. To begin with, therefore, we will turn our attention once more to Virginia.

We left that colony with the Church well established and fairly, though not sufficiently, well supplied with ministers, and we noted that some of the characteristics of later Virginia Churchmanship had probably begun to show themselves already. The Revolution of 1689 brought less change there than in some of the other provinces. Though Virginia had been loyal to the Stuarts in the Puritan Revolution, she had no fondness for Roman Catholicism, and was perfectly willing to accept the Protestant Succession in the House of Orange. King William appointed Lord Effingham governor in 1689, and, as that noble personage could not be expected to exile himself to the plantations, Sir Francis Nicholson, whose service under James II in New York does not seem to have rendered him at all obnoxious to the new régime, was sent as his deputy. With Nicholson came Commissary James Blair, to whose fame we have already alluded.

The project of founding a college in Virginia, which had been begun in 1620, had never been entirely given up, and now both Blair and Nicholson exerted themselves to bring it to fruition. As it was not thought expedient to call an assembly until the sentiment of the colony in regard to the change in government was better known, Blair began his work by opening a private

Virginia

The College of William and Mary

65

subscription for the college. When the legislature met, in 1691, it approved his measures and appointed him its agent to solicit a charter and contributions from the King. Further encouraged by a monetary gift from Governor Nicholson, he sailed promptly for England, where he found that His Majesty had gone abroad to look after his affairs in Holland. He laid the ground for his application, however, by securing the coöperation of Bishop Compton and Archbishop Tillotson, and of Bishop Stillingfleet of Worcester, who enjoyed great favor with the Queen. Mary, in whose person, as daughter of James II, the succession actually lodged, was legally joint sovereign with her husband, but she was much too docile a wife to act upon her own initiative, and would only promise to intercede with her lord and master upon his return. He proved favorably disposed, but his attention was, for a time, absorbed in preparations for war with France, and Blair had to wait several months before he could obtain the desired grant, though he made some use of the delay by securing private contributions.

In 1693 the legislature voted that the college should be located at the "Middle Plantation," which was presently renamed Williamsburg in honor of its royal patron, while the college itself received the name of both monarchs. A beginning was made in the work of instruction with the appointment of one master and Blair as president, though for some time the "College" of William and Mary probably had more nearly the standing of a grammar school. The college building was not completed until 1705, and then it immediately burned down, but by sacrificing the salaries of the faculty and obtaining further help from England, it was presently rebuilt. As its standards improved, the college assumed an honorable place among the educational institutions of the colonies. In time it contributed a number of young men to the ministry of the Church, though not nearly so many as the Puritan college at New Haven.

Lord Effingham's resignation in 1692 caused Nicholson to be replaced by Sir Edmund Andros, and the relations between governor and Commissary were changed from coöperation to hostility. As we have seen, Andros had made himself unpopular in Massachusetts by his inconsiderate zeal for the cause of the Church, but in Virginia he was accused of taking an insufficient interest in her welfare. The reasons for this change in attitude would seem to be

Sir Edmund
Andros,
Governor

a conviction on Andros' part that the Virginia clergy were better paid than they deserved to be, and a personal enmity that soon developed between himself and Blair, whose natural haughtiness clashed sharply with his own. Their quarrel became open when Andros appointed a supply for Blair's parish during the latter's illness, and thereafter Blair devoted himself heart and soul to the undoing of the governor. He presented memorials against Andros, published a pamphlet on the *Present State of Virginia* in which he attacked his administration, and eventually appeared against him at a hearing before the Archbishop of Canterbury and the Bishop of London, which probably contributed to the governor's downfall.

Blair's charges against Andros related to his attitude toward the College and his treatment of the clergy. As to the College, it was alleged among other things that Andros made its friends his enemies, that he interfered with the surveying of the lands granted to it by the King, and gave away some of them, and that he encouraged his followers to refuse payment of the subscriptions which they had made for the College in Nicholson's time. As to the clergy, Andros was accused of not following the excellent example of his predecessor in encouraging their migration from England; of allowing an interpretation of the Church Act which reduced their salaries; of wasting the colonial revenues so that the quit rents, the surplus of which had been granted by the King to the clergy, were all absorbed in public expenses; of permitting the parishes to neglect the presentation of their ministers, though he had the right, as ordinary, to collate when presentation was neglected; of allowing civil courts to try ecclesiastical cases; and of discouraging the parishes from appealing to the Bishop of London against unworthy ministers. The charges in this group relate mostly to customs which had been established in the colony long before the governor's time, and the rest are concerned with debatable questions of policy, but there probably was just ground for complaint against Andros' treatment of the College. At the hearing referred to, Andros' friends accused Blair of filling up the colonial ministry with Scotchmen, and of squandering the funds of the College by accepting a salary as president before the building was completed. The first of these accusations, even if true, was not a very serious one, however much it might jar upon

His Quarrel with Blair

English prejudices, and the second, which was based upon a technicality in the interpretation of the charter, was dismissed by the Archbishop.

Andros was removed in 1697, and was replaced by Nicholson, who had been serving in the meantime as governor of Maryland. Blair gave himself chief credit for both of these actions, but if he was really responsible for the latter, he soon found cause to repent of it. Nicholson had never been distinguished either for the evenness of his temper or the purity of his morals, and his weakness in both respects had lately been increased by a violent but unreciprocated attachment for the daughter of a local planter. He and the Commissary soon quarreled, though, except for Nicholson's private vices, there seems to have been no very good reason for the dispute, which probably had its real basis in the fact that both men suffered from a greatly increased sense of their own importance. In his public policy the governor proved himself as much a protector of the clergy and of the College as he had been before. He obtained an opinion from the Attorney-General of England to the effect that he had the right to collate to lapsed benefices, and by threatening to do this procured the induction of some ministers. He also made some attempt to maintain discipline among the clergy, and as this touched upon the authority of the Commissary, it probably served to increase Blair's hostility. By sacrificing the tribute money which earlier governors had collected, he induced the Indians of Virginia to send several of their boys to the College of William and Mary, where Robert Boyle had provided a fund for their instruction.

Nicholson ruled Virginia for eight years, but at length the violence of his temper became intolerable, and he was dismissed. Though Blair had become his bitter enemy, the majority of the clergy regarded him as their friend, and at a voluntary convention held shortly before his departure, they furnished him with a testimonial, though they had been forbidden to do so by the Bishop of London. At the same time they issued a personal attack upon Blair and asked him if he thought he ought to exercise jurisdiction over them while charges, which Nicholson's friends had brought against him before the authorities in England, were still pending, professing, with mock respect, that they were willing to abide by his decision in the matter. Blair, after offering some

objections to the irregularity of their proceedings, replied that the
action against him in England did not suspend him from office,
and they declared themselves satisfied with this answer, but when
Blair asked them to withdraw their personal abuse of him they
declined, and a rather silly squabble followed, which was terminated by the final departure of the governor.

Nicholson's successor died a short time after reaching the colony,
and was succeeded in turn by Governor Spottswood, who is best
known in Virginia history for his efforts to promote the settlement of the frontier and the exploitation of colonial resources.
He proved a consistent defender of the Church, and for some
time his relations with the Commissary were amicable, but
eventually a dispute arose between them. Shortly before Spottswood's appointment, the Lords of Trade had obtained an opinion
from their legal advisers that the power to appoint ministers in
the colonies was a royal prerogative which could not be destroyed
by a general act. They therefore instructed the governor, as the
Queen's representative, to appoint rectors for the vacant parishes
without regard to the action of the vestries. This ruling went
further than Blair thought proper, and he consequently found
himself in the unusual rôle of a champion of the rights of the
laity. Spottswood, on the other hand, accused Blair of being the
chief promoter of disorder among the clergy of Virginia, both
because of his opposition on this point, and because he permitted
laymen to read services in vacant parishes, though this was required by a law of the colony. The clergy, moreover, whose rancor against the Commissary was still strong, pretended to have
doubts about the validity of his orders, as, instead of the usual
certificate of ordination, he had only a testimonial of his having
served as presbyter in the diocese of Edinburgh.

This controversy soon petered out without reaching any
definite result. Spottswood, or rather, those who instructed him,
had over-reached themselves by endeavoring to assert the dubious
right of collating to all benefices, when they ought merely to have
insisted on the right of doing so in cases where presentation had
lapsed, as this was allowed to them by all impartial legal opinion,
and would have been sufficient to correct the evil of non-induc-
tion. As it was, though a few ministers were probably forced
into parishes that did not want them, the custom of "receiving"

Governor
Spottswood

Induction
Controversy

ministers only upon a temporary tenure continued unaltered in most places, and remained a subject of complaint from the clergy throughout the colonial period. Just how much harm it actually did them, however, is not clear. Blair, in one of his protests, asserted that the insecurity of their tenure prevented the ministers from making good marriages, but if this was the case, the ladies must have been unduly finicky, for most of the rectors retained their cures for a lifetime. It is possible, however, that the theory of temporary appointment made them less self-confident in their dealings with the vestries. In 1752 the Rev. William Kay obtained a judgment of trespass against his vestry, both in the colony and, on appeal, in England, for seizing his glebe after a majority of the vestry had voted to discharge him from his rectorship, to which he had not been inducted. The implication of this decision would seem to be that clergymen who had merely been "received" were regarded as having the same rights at law as inducted ministers.

Church Life
in Virginia

The queries addressed by Bishop Gibson to all the clergy in 1724 enable us to obtain an interesting glimpse of the life of the colonial Church at the close of the first quarter of the century. In Virginia the value of the livings had by now been fixed at 16,000 pounds of tobacco a year, besides the product of the glebes and special fees for marriages, burials, and other services. According to Blair, the total income thus obtained was worth over one hundred pounds sterling in the "sweet scented" parishes, whose tobacco commanded the highest prices, and about eighty pounds in the others, but some of the clergy make the figures much lower. Only five or six of the clergy had ever been formally inducted, but the great majority of them had been many years in their parishes. Most of them had come to Virginia immediately after their ordination, but a few had held minor cures in England, or in other parts of America. The size of their parishes varied from twenty to forty miles in length, and some were even larger. All of the ministers resided in their parishes, as they were required to do, and about half of them had habitable parsonages on their glebes, but the rest were obliged to build houses at their own expense. The parishes were compelled by law to keep both glebes and parsonages in satisfactory condition, but very few of them complied with this requirement. In many cases the glebes were leased out, instead of being worked by the minister and his servants. Most of the churches were but poorly equipped, though a few parishes had schools and libraries.

Service was generally read and a sermon preached once a Sunday in the parish church, the remoteness of many of the parishioners being the excuse for not having two services. If there was a "chapel of ease" in the parish, service was held there once or twice a month. Holy Communion was celebrated from three to six times a year, the occasions on which it was always celebrated being Christmas, Easter, and Whitsunday. Attendance at the Sunday services was fairly good, but other holidays, whether religious or civil, were neglected. Most of the ministers catechized the youth of the parish with some regularity, either during Lent or in the summer. Most of them also professed themselves willing to catechize the negroes when their masters permitted it, but this was seldom the case. In parishes where there were Indians no special effort was made for their conversion, but they were allowed to come to church if they so desired.

Blair died in 1743 and was succeeded by William Dawson, who had been professor of theology at the College. Under Dawson and his brother, Thomas, who succeeded him in 1752, the relations between the Commissary and the governor became more cordial, though, for that matter, the hostility between these two colonial executives had cooled off in Blair's later years, either because he became more mellow as he grew older, or because later governors found it expedient not to offend him. Thomas Dawson also revived the practice of holding frequent meetings of the clergy, which his brother and Blair had allowed to lapse, possibly from a fear of the disputes which frequently developed at such meetings. He opposed the passage of the Tobacco Act of 1756, under Governor Dinwiddie, and he also opposed the deprivation of an immoral clergyman by the same governor, which, though done with the advice of the Council, was regarded by Dawson as an infringement of the rights of the clergy. Neither of these actions, however, disturbed the cordial personal relations which prevailed between Dinwiddie and the Commissary. William Robinson, who became Commissary in 1761, had had a personal quarrel with Francis Farquier, who was then governor, before his appointment, and the ill will between them persisted

Commissary
Dawson

afterwards, but produced slight effect, for the Commissary had become a person of little account in the colony, being no longer even a member of the Council.

The religious care of the frontier, where regular parishes had not yet been organized, was seriously neglected by the Church in Virginia, and in consequence the region was claimed to a large extent by dissenters, a result which was facilitated by the opposition of the new settlers to everything connected with the older portions of the colony, where the earlier planters had become a ruling aristocracy. In 1716 Governor Spottswood sent the Rev. Charles Griffin to the frontier, chiefly to work among the Indians, and in 1738 the Rev. Anthony Gavin went of his own choice, having been moved by reports of the spiritual destitution of the people, but we find few other ministers reporting from that region.

Gavin found that many of the people among whom he worked were Quakers, and from the reports of other ministers also it would appear that these were the first dissenters to appear in the colony in any force, but the strongest dissenting group in Virginia were the Presbyterians. Their first meeting-house was built before 1725, and by the middle of the century they were growing rapidly in the west, where many of the settlers had come from Scotland and the North of Ireland. The movement was strengthened and organized by the work of Samuel Davies, who was sent by the New York Presbytery to take charge of the work in Virginia in 1747. He labored in the colony until 1759, when he became president of Princeton, built up several churches, and made a number of converts from among those who had previously accepted the Established Church, but whether these had been brought up in the Church or not is not clear. Though he had complied with the Toleration Act, some effort was made by the Church authorities to check his activities. It was at first contended that the Toleration Act did not extend to the plantations, and when this contention was overruled, it was argued that the Act did not justify Davies in making proselytes from among the members of the Church, or in serving more than one parish. In 1752, Davies, who already had seven churches, applied to Governor Dinwiddie to license another, and was refused on the ground that he obviously could not serve as a proper minister for

The
Frontier

The
Presbyterians

those which he already had. This Davies frankly admitted, and
made it a ground for asking that another Presbyterian minister
be licensed to assist him, a request with which the governor, who
was on the whole a just man, felt obliged to comply. Other dissenting groups had probably appeared in Virginia before the
Revolution, but they do not seem to have been as numerous
there as in the other southern colonies.

There were also some groups of European Protestants in the
colony, but most of these conformed to the Church. Their ministers received episcopal ordination and were in part supported
by the Society for the Propagation of the Gospel. The first of
these bodies were the French Huguenots, who came to the colony
in 1699, the governor being specially directed to look after their
welfare. In 1715, 291 of them were reported in Henrico County
alone. In 1724 the heads of thirty-two German families informed
authorities that they were sending one of their young men to
England for ordination.

The bickerings over the salaries of the clergy, which continued
steadily throughout the colonial period, culminated in 1756 in the
row over the famous Tobacco Act of that year. For some time
the low price of tobacco had greatly diminished the monetary
value of the ministers' salaries, but an upward swing of the market having reversed the situation, a law was passed permitting
the payment of tobacco dues in monetary equivalents which were
set at a rate higher than the previous prices, but lower than the
present ones. The terms of the Act applied to all debts which were
owed in tobacco, but it was given a special twist against the
clergy by the Burgess' directions to the colonial agent to defend
any suits brought against the vestries in consequence of the Act,
but not against others, so that private debtors took the hint and
came to terms with their creditors. The law was disallowed in
England, but as its operation had been limited to ten months in
the first place, it had expired before the disallowance could take
effect, and the question arose as to whether or not such disallowance was retroactive. The clergy brought several actions for dam-
ages on the ground of the invalidity of the Act, in one of which
Patrick Henry, who appeared for the defense, laid the foundation
of his fame by resorting to dubious legal tactics. In the end the
question was carried to England, where the clergy lost their suit.

Clerical
Salaries

The decision was based upon a technicality, but it was not thought worth while to reopen the case. Other issues were now coming to the fore, and a struggle was beginning in which the Church was to lose official support altogether.

As we have seen, a local revolution in Maryland in 1689-90 led to the overthrow of the Roman Catholic power and, for a time, of the proprietary government. The first important measure of the colonial Assembly, after this upset had been confirmed at home, was to pass an act, in 1692, for the Establishment of the Church of England. The law, however, was allowed to lapse as soon as it was passed, and was not enforced until the arrival of Sir Francis Nicholson as governor in 1694. He showed his interest in religion by ordering a fast upon assuming office, and by instructing the Assembly as to what should be done for the conversion of Indians and negroes, the treatment of slaves, the table of marriages, public morals and work-houses. With Sir Thomas Lawrence, the Secretary, he offered to give one thousand pounds of tobacco toward the cost of every house which was built for a clergyman, and to bear the cost of surveying every glebe that should be laid out. He also caused the back taxes due under the law of 1692 to be collected, and sent the act home for royal approval. Unfortunately, the law contained a clause providing that the rights of Magna Carta should be extended to Maryland, and as the English authorities did not know what this might lead to, they were unwilling to allow it. They sent the Act back, therefore, with directions that it should be repassed and returned without this clause.

A revised act, sent over in 1696, was disallowed because some of its terms were calculated to work hardship upon the Quakers and other dissenters, and another was rejected in 1700 for similar reasons. It was not until 1702 that an act was at last passed which met the specifications of the English government well enough to be approved. This law, which was to serve as the basis of the Church Establishment in Maryland throughout the colonial period, differed in a number of ways from the provisions set up in Virginia. Instead of prescribing a fixed stipend for all clergymen, it directed that each minister should receive forty pounds of tobacco from every person in his parish, besides a fee of five shillings for every marriage. The appointment of ministers, instead of being

Maryland

The Act of Establishment, 1702

divided between the vestry and the governor, was placed entirely in the hands of the latter official, a measure which proved to be productive of even worse evils than the Virginia arrangement. The reason for it was probably a fear that the vestries, being elective, might occasionally pass under the control of dissenters. These bodies were empowered to raise special levies, not to exceed ten pounds a head, for repairs on church or parsonage and other necessary expenses, but an act of 1704 required them to obtain the approval of the county court before doing this. Another law, passed the same year, required a record to be kept of the parish libraries which had been procured through the efforts of Bray, and also directed that they should be regularly inspected by the vestries.

The Establishment of the Church was only a part of the general reorganization which took place in the religious affairs of Maryland after the "Glorious" Revolution. At the same time that the Establishment acts were being passed, laws were enacted which seriously curtailed the liberties of the Roman Catholics, including a statute which empowered the governor to forbid Jesuits from entering the houses of dying persons. A more creditable proceeding was the attempt that was made to provide the colony with a system of common schools, which were intended to prepare students for the College of William and Mary in Virginia. Efforts in this direction began with the arrival of Nicholson in 1694. He offered to give fifty pounds towards the building of a free school, and to contribute twenty-five pounds a year for its expenses as long as he remained in office. Other private subscriptions were made at the same time, but no general appropriation was voted by the legislature. *Common Schools*

In 1696, however, the Assembly did petition King William to grant his patronage for the school, which they proposed to name in his honor. In 1723 an act was passed calling for the erection of one free school in each county, "in some convenient time after the end of the present session of the Assembly." It is not certain how thoroughly this measure was put into effect. In 1724, when the clergy sent in their answers to Bishop Gibson's questionnaire, only one or two of the projected schools were in operation, but, of course, too much could not be expected in a single year.

After Bray's short sojourn in the colony, no Commissary was

appointed for Maryland until 1716. When John Hart came as governor in 1714 he was informed that the clergy of the province had never once met together since its first settlement. This must have been an error, as Bray had held at least one visitation when he was there, but there had probably been none since. Hart called the ministers together shortly after his arrival and questioned them as to the state of religion in the colony. Their replies indicated that conditions were fair, but could be improved. The services of the Prayer Book were read every Sunday in all parishes, and on all of the other holidays in many. Most of the parishes were sufficiently supplied with church buildings, but their repair was somewhat neglected. Some of the glebes were good, others poor, and a few of the parishes had none. The support of the clergy was, of course, regarded as insufficient by the clergy. Every minister was a member of his parish vestry, all had letters of orders, and all professed respect for the jurisdiction of the Bishop of London. They complained of the lack of schoolmasters, and of the general neglect of the requirement that such functionaries be licensed by the Bishop of London. As the moral condition of the colony was bad, they urged the enforcement of the laws against moral offenses and an increase in the severity of the penalties for some, especially fornication. They also prayed that the legislature "would seek an expedient against the damnable sin of polygamy." The growth of "Popery" troubled them, and they also invited His Excellency's attention to "the abuse the dissenters make of the indulgence given them by law."

In 1716, on the recommendation of Governor Hart, the Bishop of London appointed two clergymen, Christopher Wilkinson and Jacob Henderson, to share the commissarial jurisdiction of Maryland between them, one on the Eastern and the other on the Western Shore. Wilkinson appears to have been a mild but conscientious man, who performed the duties of his office as well as he could and kept himself clear of public affairs, but Henderson soon became convinced that the governor was engaged in plotting against the proprietor, the colony having now been restored to the Calverts, and in this he felt obliged to oppose him. As a result, he was necessarily involved in politics, and was rebuked for his meddling by the Bishop, but in the end his judgment proved correct, and after Hart was recalled, he enjoyed great prestige with the proprietary interest. Eventually, after Wilkinson had resigned, Henderson became Commissary for the colony. A rebuke for being overbearing, which was administered to him by the Bishop early in his incumbency, made him cautious of exercising any formal jurisdiction, but he did proceed against a few offenders, and he held regular conventions of the clergy to consider the affairs of the Church.

The answers which the clergy sent to Bishop Gibson in 1724 show religious conditions in the colony to have been somewhat similar to those prevailing in Virginia. All of the rectors had been inducted, but their parishes were smaller than in Virginia. Most of the native negroes, perhaps because of Roman Catholic and Quaker examples, had been instructed and baptized, but no attempts were made to convert the Indians, as the clergy could not understand their language, and found them averse to Christianity. A few clergymen read service on Wednesdays and Fridays, as well as Sundays and holidays, and, though the normal number of celebrations of the Eucharist during a year ranged from three to six, as in Virginia, there were a few who celebrated it as often as twelve times a year, and Commissary Henderson actually held it twice a month. As in Virginia, the youth of a parish were generally catechized at least once during the year, and, also as in Virginia, there was a shortage of church furnishings. The livings were worth from forty to one hundred pounds sterling, depending on size. Most of the parishes, thanks to Bray's efforts, were in possession of small libraries.

Church Life in Maryland

The year 1724 also saw an attempt made by the assembly to set up a lay commission to discipline the clergy. The scandalous lives led by some of the ministers constituted the grounds for this action, and a general attack on clerical morals was made by those who supported the measure. The laity certainly had some grounds for complaint, but it appears, nevertheless, that their charges were greatly exaggerated. Giles Rainsford, an apparently worthy though somewhat self-laudatory clergyman, wrote to the Secretary of the Society for the Propagation of the Gospel, by which he had once been employed, accusing one of the brethren of visiting when drunk, a dying person and saying of another that he was a "mere nuisance." Commissary Wilkinson, in reporting the proposed act to the Bishop of London, also said, "The faults and follies of some

Attempt to Discipline the Clergy

clergymen are too gross to be excused or extenuated." He declared, however, that he knew but two ministers on his Shore who deserved the severe censure passed upon them by the Assembly. The rest he not only held to be free from scandalous crimes, but he asserted that they displayed incredible diligence in the performance of their duties. Many would ride twenty miles of a morning to read service, and in summer they often preached at one church in the forenoon and at another, some distance off, in the afternoon. A few were obliged to preach every day during one week out of every month in order to bring the Church to their more distant parishioners. All of this, of course, was in addition to the many visits which had to be made to the sick and aged, and for the private baptism of children. Governor Calvert, who vetoed the measure as unnecessary and contrary to canon law, also testified that the majority of the ministers had "behaved themselves very well as good clergymen and good subjects."

The Tobacco Controversy

The rapid extension of the area given over to the growing of tobacco created a falling market in that commodity during most of the colonial period, and in 1729 the Maryland legislature undertook an experiment in "controlled production" for the purpose of raising the price. The amount of tobacco that every overseer or laborer might plant was strictly limited, and the vestries, which, in the Southern colonies, as in England, were agencies of the civil as well as the ecclesiastical government, were to divide their parishes into precincts and appoint persons in each precinct to enforce the law by counting plants. In order to offset the expected rise in price, all persons owing debts, or parochial or other dues, in tobacco, were permitted to pay them either in colonial currency, at the rate of ten shillings per hundred weight, or in three-fourths of the amount of tobacco originally called for. The clergy, whose faith in this economic experiment was rather weak, regarded it as in effect a reduction of their salaries by one-fourth and protested vigorously, even threatening to leave the colony.

As a result of their protests and of other objections, the act was disallowed by the proprietor, but another was substituted which allowed one-fourth of the parochial rates to be paid in grain. The object of this act, which was to encourage a greater diversity of crops, was an excellent one, but it proved nearly as obnoxious to the clergy as the former law, for they found that they could not exchange the grain thus received for anything but rum, an article on which, in spite of their reputations, they were not prepared to spend a quarter of their income. Nevertheless, the law was allowed to stand.

In 1768 another attempt was made to provide for the discipline of the clergy, this time by setting up a board composed of the governor, three clergymen, and three laymen. The measure apparently had the approval of the proprietor and efforts were made to prevent the clergy from assembling to protest against it. They did so, however, and, as a result of their vigorous opposition, the act was given up.

In 1767 a list of Maryland parishes showed that the majority of them ranged in value from one to two hundred pounds sterling a year, and that the most valuable was worth £364. Four years later an act was passed requiring the clergy to accept twelve shillings a hundred weight for their tobacco, though the price at that time often ran as high as twenty-five shillings, and sometimes even to thirty. Nevertheless, a table of livings prepared in 1775 showed their average worth to be about the same as in 1767. A few parishes had even increased in value, the maximum then reaching five hundred pounds. *Value of Livings*

The growth of the Roman Catholic Church in Maryland was a constant source of agitation to the representatives of the Church of England there, and if we believed all of their reports about it, we should expect to see the Roman Catholics again in control of the colony before the end of the century. Actually, however, they attained a majority in only one or two parishes. Their growth was partly due to the importation of indentured servants from Ireland, which practice was so extensive as to cause the Assembly to levy a special duty upon the Irish in 1717, but it is probable that they also made some converts, for it was frequently stated that they were "seducing" the members of the Established Church. The Jesuits, in spite of the restrictions placed upon them, came to the colony in great numbers, and as they were probably abler and better trained than the local clergy, they experienced a certain amount of success. *Dissent in Maryland*

The presence of Protestant dissenters in the colony is also noted from time to time. The Quakers had been there almost from the start, and were, with the Roman Catholics, the chief opponents of the acts of Establishment. Before the end of the century the Baptists, Presbyterians, and "New Lights" (*i. e.*, followers of Whitefield) had also made their appearance. The growth of dissent, both Protestant and Catholic, was made the frequent subject of gubernatorial and commissarial addresses and convention resolutions, but it does not appear that Protestant dissenters were as numerous in Maryland as they were in some other colonies. They were also less severe upon the Establishment there, probably because they regarded it as a bulwark against the worse evils of "Popery."

South Carolina

The colony of South Carolina was chartered in 1663, but it was not settled until 1670. Its original proprietors included a number of theoretical philanthropists, and the desire to propagate Christianity in a barbarous country was one of the motives stated in their application for a charter. John Locke, the political philosopher, furnished them, at their request, with an elaborate scheme of government which was never put into effect. In regard to religion, this code provided that the Church of England should alone receive public support, but that all who worshipped God should be permitted to form congregations privately. Like the Maryland Toleration Act, it also provided penalties for those who abused one another's religion. An attempt at settlement in this region had been made from Virginia in 1660, before the granting of the charter, but it was given up. The first successful settlement was made from England in 1670, and Charleston, which was to become the chief town of the colony, and, indeed, of the South, was laid out two years later.

The first Episcopal Church in South Carolina was built at Charleston in 1681, and the first clergyman to officiate in it was apparently Atkin Williamson, who was there in 1680. According to a later witness, he was never able to produce satisfactory letters of orders, but claimed to have been ordained deacon by the Bishop of Dublin, and priest by the Bishop of Lincoln. His character does not seem to have been of the best, and the people would never accept him as a regular minister, but he remained in the colony for many years, and was granted a small pension by the Assembly in his old age. The first regular minister in the colony was Samuel Marshall who came over in 1696, and was elected rector of Charleston in 1698, when the Assembly voted him a salary of one hundred and fifty pounds.

Though the dissenters in the colony seem to have been nearly as numerous as the Churchmen, the latter generally managed to keep control, and their zeal was possibly strengthened by the presence of opponents. In 1703 they passed an act inflicting loss of civil rights and three years' imprisonment on anyone denying the Trinity, or the inspiration of Scripture. In 1704 they made a law requiring all persons elected to the Assembly to take the oaths of allegiance and supremacy, and conform to the Church of England. This act raised a great furore and was disallowed by the proprietors. In the same year the Assembly divided the colony into parishes and provided for the public support of ministers and the building of churches, but this act was also disallowed, because it set up a lay commission with power to remove ministers on complaint of their vestries. According to the governor and Council, the only reason for including this clause was to secure the removal of Edward Marston, Marshall's successor at Charleston, who had made himself obnoxious to the Church party by his vigorous criticism of their effort to exclude dissenters from the Assembly. At any rate, his dismissal was the only use that the commission made of its power during the short time that it had it.

Ecclesiastical Legislation

In 1706 all previous acts relating to the Church were repealed and a law was substituted which was to serve as a permanent basis for the colonial Establishment. This act also set up a lay commission, but its functions were restricted to raising funds and supervising the building of churches. The salaries of the ministers were to be paid out of the public treasury, but if the general funds proved insufficient, the commission was empowered to make a special levy. The salary of the rector at Charleston was to be one hundred and fifty pounds, as before. The other ministers of the colony were to receive fifty pounds. The Book of Common Prayer was to be used in all churches, and the minister was to be elected by all the freeholders in a parish who conformed to the Church of England. These freeholders were also to elect seven men to serve with the minister as a vestry. Church ministers were given the exclusive right of performing marriages, but this clause was not actually enforced, probably because for some time there were not enough clergymen in the colony to make

The Act of Establishment

it practicable. The most influential supporter of this act, and of the preceding laws in favor of the Established Church, had been the governor, Nathaniel Johnson, and his resulting odium with the dissenters was so great that the proprietors felt it wise to recall him, though, at the same time, they expressed a high regard for his services.

Apparently the only ministers in the colony at the time this act was passed, besides the dubious Williamson, were Marston and Samuel Thomas, a missionary of the Society for the Propagation of the Gospel. Thomas had originally been sent over to minister to the Yamassee Indians, who had been converted to Christianity by the Spaniards but were reverting to heathenism since the shift of their allegiance to the English. Governor Johnson had ordered him to go to Goose Creek Parish instead, though whether this was for the purpose of instructing the slaves there, as Johnson asserted, or to check the dissenters, as his enemies alleged, is not certain. As the fifty-pound salaries were in colonial currency, their sterling value was only about thirty-five pounds, which was not enough to supply a sufficient support, even with the returns from the glebe. Thomas was, accordingly, sent to England to ask the Society to supplement these incomes and to recruit five ministers for the Carolina service. He was successful in obtaining three clergymen, but one of them deserted him at Bermuda, on the way over, and the accession was further lessened by his own death shortly after his return. Two more ministers were sent out by the Society in 1707, however.

One of the two ministers who came back with Thomas was
Francis
Le Jau
Dr. Francis Le Jau, who succeeded him at Goose Creek, and who became one of the most devoted and successful ministers in the colonies. He probably did more for the conversion of the negroes than any clergyman not especially appointed for this work, and he also interested himself in the welfare of the Indians. He testified at a later time that his parishioners were among the most sober and best-behaved people in the colony, and one feels confident that the example and teaching of their pastor was the principal cause of the high regard in which they were held. The other ministers sent out at this time were also worthy men, and probably justified Commissary Johnston's statement that "There is not . . . a better set of clergymen in all America than what is

to be met with in this place." One of them, Robert Maule, who
came over in 1707, held a place in the affections of the people
second only to Le Jau's. The latter wrote of him a little later,
"There is not the least person in this province but that expresses
much respect for that worthy brother."

After the disallowance of the Act of 1704, Marston tried to
get reinstated at Charleston, but was unsuccessful. He was
offered a country parish with a special salary of £150 to compensate him for his loss, but this he declined. In the end he was
compelled to accept a rural parish without a special salary, but
he did not get along any better there than at Charleston, and
was finally obliged to give up the ministry altogether. He tried his
hand for a time at medicine and law, but with poor success. After
he had been disposed of at Charleston, the parish was offered to
Bray, and when he declined, the Rev. Richard Marsden from
Maryland was received as *locum tenens*. He gave satisfaction, and
was unanimously elected rector, but unfortunately, his election
had hardly taken place when Gideon Johnston arrived on the
scene with a recommendation to the parish and an appointment
as Commissary from the Bishop of London, whom the congregation had apparently asked to find them a minister. Marsden
was, with some difficulty, persuaded to resign and the people,
also with some difficulty, were induced to choose Johnston as his
successor, but a good deal of ill feeling ensued as a result of the
incident. Marsden received an appointment to a country parish
and some assistance from the Society, but he presently returned
to England where he had received a legacy from his uncle.

The trouble with Marsden was only one of the difficulties that
confronted Commissary Johnston on his arrival in South Carolina.
To begin with, he was accidentally left on an island some miles
from shore on the way over, and had to stay there for twelve
days, without food or shelter, until some fishermen happened to
find him. Then he found that his salary of £150 currency was
only worth about one hundred pounds sterling, and that this, in
turn, would only purchase about one third as much in the colony
as it would in England. As a climax to his troubles, he was sick
for five months after his arrival, and never entirely regained his
health. South Carolina was later described as the "graveyard of
the clergy," and, because its climate was so radically different

Commissary Johnston

from that of the homeland, it rarely proved a healthy place for newcomers from England. Because of these circumstances, most of Johnston's letters home strike a rather complaining note, but he seems, nevertheless, to have been a conscientious clergyman, and to have had a useful career as rector, though it does not appear that he accomplished much as Commissary.

Clerical
Salaries

Johnston's salary was probably larger than that received by any other minister, even though he received no assistance from the Society for the Propagation of the Gospel. However, few of the stipends of the time were adequate. Le Jau once reported that his family had to live ordinarily upon Indian corn bread and water, with a little milk and a joint of fresh meat once a week. Part of his difficulty arose from the servant problem, however, as he had to keep three negroes (not yet entirely paid for), to do the work which could be performed by one maid in England. When he died, he left his wife and two daughters practically destitute, though their immediate necessities were relieved by a gift from the Society.

Grievances of
the Clergy

The dissenters gained control of the Assembly for a time a few years after the passage of the Establishment Act, and partly as a result of this and partly from the general carelessness of the legislators, a number of laws crept into the colonial code which were unfavorable to the Church. In 1713, when Commissary Johnston paid a visit to England, the clergy entrusted him with some complaints to the Society against features of the colonial law which they considered objectionable. They said that four acts had lately passed the Assembly which contained some clauses likely to lessen episcopal authority, and that the practices of the colony relative to the institution and induction of ministers and other matters were contrary to English canon law. Licenses to perform marriages, they complained, were issued to others than Church clergymen and even to "some mechanic persons" (these were Baptist ministers). Ministers, contrary to the law of 1706, were sometimes excluded from their vestries. Those who returned to England within two years were obliged to refund the bounty given them on their arrival—a measure in which there would seem to be considerable justice—and ministers, their widows, or executors were obliged to leave parsonage houses in repair on removal. In elaborating on these complaints, Johnston stated that the lay commissioners had been given indirectly the power of removing ministers which was denied them directly, for they were authorized to pass on the validity of parish elections, and might start an investigation of a minister's title to his parish at any time.

In 1715 the Yamassees revolted against the English authority and the colony was exposed to the terrors of an Indian war. Some of the remoter parishes were entirely deserted, the men all going to fight against the Indians, and the women and children fleeing to the older settlements. In such cases the missionaries, of course, left also, but where any of their parishioners remained, they stuck to their posts, their houses in some cases actually being used as garrisons by the settlers. Several lost their homes and personal property in the struggle and nearly all were adversely affected to some extent, so the Society for the Propagation of the Gospel authorized the Commissary to advance a half-year's stipend where he thought it necessary.

Indian War

Five years later, the colonists themselves were in revolt—this time against the proprietary government. The proprietary officers were driven out and replaced by a government under Colonel Moore, who professed to rule in the King's name, though without any real authority. The situation caused some embarrassment to the clergy, as each side forbade them to accept the marriage licenses of the other. In the end the royal government took advantage of the revolt to annul the proprietary charter, and sent out the veteran Nicholson to restore order. Nicholson's zeal for the Established Church was unabated, and as soon as he had settled the government on an orderly basis, he obtained an act raising the salaries of the clergy outside of Charleston to one hundred pounds, "proclamation money," which was said to be worth from seventy-five to eighty pounds sterling. The act of 1706 had provided that such an increase should take place in three years, but the provision had not been carried out. Nicholson also appears to have adopted the policy of issuing marriage licenses only to Church ministers, but in this respect he was not followed by his successors.

Revolt Against the Proprietors

There were eight clergymen in the colony to answer Bishop Gibson's queries in 1724, and they described usages similar to those prevailing in the other southern colonies. They officiated once a week and celebrated the Eucharist four times a year. Alexander Garden, who had succeeded Johnston as rector at Charleston, read service on Wednesdays, Fridays and holidays, as well as Sundays, and celebrated Communion once a month, as did one other minister. Most of the clergy catechized the youth of their parishes with some regularity. There was a public school at Charleston conducted by the Rev. Thomas Morritt, Garden's assistant. The salaries of one hundred pounds in proclamation money were now estimated as being worth four hundred pounds in paper currency and fifty pounds sterling.

Commissary
Garden

Commissary Johnston had died in 1716 and been succeeded as Commissary by William Treadwell Bull, who, in turn, was replaced by Alexander Garden, in 1729. Garden was more assiduous in the performance of his commissarial duties than his predecessors, probably because he served under Bishop Gibson, who expected more of his representatives than did earlier bishops. He held eighteen visitations during his incumbency, and suspended four clergymen, of whom the most important was George Whitefield. The charge against this famous personage was that he had failed to use the services of the Prayer Book in the meeting-house where he preached in Charleston. He declared his intention of appealing to England, and was granted time for doing so, but as he failed to press his appeal, Garden suspended him *in absentia,* though the suspension does not appear to have had much effect. After Garden's retirement in 1749, no other Commissary was appointed, and the annual visitations became voluntary conventions.

Deterioration
of the Clergy

In 1756 the colony felt itself sufficiently prosperous to relieve the Society for the Propagation of the Gospel of the burden of helping to support its ministers, and the legislature voted to add thirty pounds sterling to the existing salaries of the clergy in cases where the Society's support was withdrawn. This, at the current rate of exchange, was expected to make the total salary worth one hundred pounds sterling. The Society, consequently, discontinued most of its activity in the colony in a short time. The withdrawal of its supervision combined with the increased support to accelerate a deterioration in the quality of the clergy which had already begun to show itself, and complaints against unworthy ministers became more common. As the parishes adopted the practice of hiring ministers recommended by the merchants with whom they traded in England, rather than by the Bishop of London, it is surprising that the number of offenders was not much higher than it was. They had also, for some time, adopted the Virginia practice of not giving their ministers a formal election, but keeping them on permanent probation. This, however, does not seem to have made it any easier to get rid of the unworthy.

The dissenters in South Carolina were strong enough, even from the earliest times, to offer serious political competition to the Churchmen, but it is difficult to determine which group was in the majority at any time. In 1740 it was estimated that the Episcopalians formed forty-five per cent. of the population, the "Presbyterians, French and other Protestants" forty-two and one-half per cent., the Baptists ten per cent. and the Quakers two and one-half per cent., but these figures were probably little more than a guess. Moreover, the classification is faulty, for the Huguenots, who came over in fairly large numbers at the beginning of the century, had conformed to the Church and obtained ministers supported by the Society for the Propagation of the Gospel. The fact that the Churchmen were generally, though not always, able to control the Assembly would indicate that they probably had a majority of the propertied class, or nearly so, but this is not a very reliable index of the rest of the population. In the several parishes the proportion varied from time to time. In some parishes we find indications that the dissenters were increasing, or were already in the majority, while in others it was reported that their churches were being abandoned for want of support. It is probable that the ratio of the different dissenting groups also fluctuated. From the frequent references which we find to the Baptists or "Anabaptists," as they were generally called in the eighteenth century, it seems likely that their strength was generally greater than that allowed them in 1740. In addition to the Huguenots, there were some Swiss Protestants who came to the colony later in the century, and conformed to the Established Church. There were also a few Roman Catholics, but they were not numerous. *Dissenters in South Carolina*

The frontier was neglected in South Carolina, as in other colonies, both because it did not lend itself to regular parochial organization, and because of the difficulty in obtaining ministers willing to perform the arduous work required there. In 1765 *The Frontier*

Charles Woodmason, a prominent layman and magistrate of
Charleston, who had lived for three years in the back settlements,
volunteered to enter the ministry for the express purpose of serving there. He was accordingly ordained by the Bishop of London,
and employed by the Society for the Propagation of the Gospel as
missionary to the frontier, where he served faithfully until driven
out by the Revolution.

North
Carolina

North Carolina was originally included in the same patent as
its sister colony to the south, but its settlement was much more
haphazard and the proprietors were never very successful in establishing their authority over it. The settlers, most of whom drifted
in from the colonies farther north, were largely indifferent to
religion and it was some time before any provision was made for
it. George Fox, the founder of Quakerism, was the first missionary to visit the colony, and as a result of his efforts and those of
other Friends, the Quakers for a time predominated there. In
1703, a Churchman who had been long in the colony wrote to
the Bishop of London that, to his own personal knowledge, it
had been for nearly twenty-one years "without priest or altar" and
that before that time, according to all reports, conditions had
been even worse. A missionary had been sent out, but had proved
unworthy. In 1701 the Churchmen, by careful management, had
obtained control of the Assembly, and had passed a vestry act
which provided a salary of thirty pounds for each minister, but this
was disallowed because the stipend was considered too small, and
the Quakers, who had regained control of the Assembly, refused
to pass another.

Mission of
John Blair

At the time the above report was written, another missionary,
the Rev. John Blair, was touring the colony. He had been sent
out by the Society for the Propagation of the Gospel as the result
of a special donation from Lord Weymouth. He found conditions
in the colony still primitive, and was obliged to hire a guide, as
it was impossible for a stranger to find his way about. Finding
many children unbaptized, he baptized about a hundred. Wherever
he went, he organized a vestry, appointing a lay reader in each of
the three precincts into which the colony was divided. He found
the colony divided into four religious groups, of whom the Quakers were the most powerful enemies of the Church. There were
many who had no religion but who would have been Quakers had

this alternative not involved too high a standard of morality. The third group he described as "something like Presbyterians," though their ministers had no regular ordination of any sort. Those really zealous for the Church, who formed the fourth group, were "the fewest in numbers, but the better sort of people." Later reports indicate the presence of Baptists, Congregationalists, Presbyterians, Moravians, and Germans belonging to the Reformed Church. Blair gave up his mission after a short time, because his funds gave out and the people would not let him settle down in one place.

Lord Weymouth was so disgusted with this failure that he refused to renew his charity, and it was not until 1708 that the Society was able to send two more missionaries to the colony. These men remained in the province for a few years and were then replaced by John Urmiston and Giles Rainsford. Of these, the former was a dissolute person, though it is possible that his vices did not develop until after the death of his wife, which he attributed to hardships suffered in the colony. Both ministers eventually went to Maryland, where Urmiston died in a drunken fit shortly after Commissary Henderson had suspended him, but where Rainsford continued a useful ministry. The Society supported two or three ministers in the colony until the latter part of the century when, the local support becoming more dependable, the number was increased. *Other Missionaries*

The history of North Carolina was a turbulent one throughout the colonial period, and minor civil wars were of frequent occurrence. One of these, known as the "Cary Rebellion," was partly in opposition to an act of establishment passed in 1704. Another such act was adopted in 1715 and renewed, with amendments, in 1741. It provided fifty pounds currency for the support of a minister in each parish, but failed to fix a satisfactory method of collecting even this inadequate amount, though the vestries did succeed in raising it with fair regularity in some parishes. In 1765, thanks to the efforts of Governor Tryon, a law was at last obtained which provided sufficient support for the clergy. It increased their pay to £133.0.8 currency, and allowed them to bring suit in case of non-payment. It also gave them the right to certain special fees. No definite test of orthodoxy was required, but as the right of presentation was lodged in the governor, this irregularity could be covered by his *Act of Establishment* instructions. The governor might suspend an immoral minister subject to the final decision of the Bishop of London, and the clergyman's salary would be uncollectable during suspension. The minister was required to repair the parish buildings and glebes. Unfortunately, this act was very unpopular in the colony, even among Churchmen, as the vestries disliked having a minister forced upon them by the governor. Various expedients were tried to avoid receiving the clergymen thus presented, and the act did the Church little good during the decade that it was in force before the Revolution.

It is probable that the dissenters were always in a majority in North Carolina, though the proportion of Churchmen in the population seems to have been on the increase. Governor Tryon, when he came over in 1765, thought the supporters of the Church were in the majority, but this is unlikely, though they probably did include most of the wealthier planters. The dissenters seem, for the most part, to have been even more poorly supplied with regular ministers than were the Churchmen. As a result they went off into various wild extravagances under local and not very well-educated leaders, so that many of them cannot be identified with any known denomination. There were many who called themselves Baptists, but these went beyond the usual teachings of that Church. Others called themselves "New Lights," but were not followers of Whitefield. He not only disowned them, but took occasion, on his last visit to the colony, to rebuke them sharply for their excesses.

Georgia, which was first settled in 1732, was the youngest of the thirteen colonies. It was founded by the philanthropic General Oglethorpe as a haven for poor debtors, but it probably proved a refuge, as did most of the colonies, for less innocent characters also. Nearly a fourth of the original trustees of the colony were clergymen, and the enterprise was supported by leaders of the Church. A site was set apart at Savannah for a church and glebe in 1732, and Samuel Quincy, a member of the famous Massachusetts family, was appointed its first minister. He remained in the colony three years, until a dispute with Oglethorpe's agent forced his retirement. His successor was John Wesley, who also got in trouble with the authorities, partly because of an unfortunate love affair and partly because he was considered too ardent

Dissenters in
North
Carolina

Georgia

a High Churchman. His brother Charles had come over with him, but left even sooner. John Wesley was succeeded by Whitefield, whose brief stay in the colony has already been mentioned. His successor also stayed only a short time and was followed by Thomas Bosomworth, whose interest in the Indians was so great that he married one, and spent the rest of his life trying to get money from the colony on the ground that his wife alone had power to keep the Indians at peace. He resigned the parish in 1745 and was succeeded by Bartholomew Zouberbuhler, the son of a Swiss parson in South Carolina, who was a devoted minister until his death in 1766 or 1767. When he died he left a fund to be used for the support of a schoolmaster for the negroes, and for other pious purposes.

Georgia became a royal colony in 1752, and six years later the Assembly divided the colony into parishes and appropriated twenty-five pounds a year for a clergyman in each parish, but the only one outside of Savannah to be regularly supplied was Augusta. Special provision was made for Savannah and, at the time of the Revolution, it was described as a "comfortable preferment," worth three hundred pounds sterling. The ministers at Augusta, and some others that were sent to the colony from time to time, had their stipends supplemented by the Society for the Propagation of the Gospel. *Church Establishment*

During the twenty years that Florida was an English colony, some effort was made to settle the Church there, but it was not attended with much success, and was terminated by the return of the colony to Spain in 1783. *Florida*

CHAPTER V

NEW ENGLAND

Contrast with
the South

CONTRASTS are always inviting, and the history of the
Church in colonial New England is in many respects so exactly
the opposite of our findings in the South, that it will be more
interesting, and possibly more informative, to proceed directly
from one section to the other without pausing to examine the
more moderate differences which existed in the Middle Colonies.
In the South we have seen the Episcopal Church everywhere as
the officially-favored denomination, and the other bodies struggling, with varying degrees of strength, in the opposition. In New
England we will find "Independency," or Congregationalism, as
the established order, and our own denomination struggling
amongst the dissenters. In the South we have been obliged to
tell our story to some extent upon a descending scale. Though we
have seen the Church grow in total numbers and in material prosperity, we have been forced to notice a decline in relative strength
and in inner vitality. In New England the growth of the Church
in the eighteenth century was steady, and in some places rapid.

Massachusetts

We have already traced the beginning of the Church in Massachusetts, and have seen that its entrance into that colony was
made possible only by the exercise of a goodly amount of coercion
on the part of the King and his representatives. Forces were
beginning to work, however, which were to give Churchmen and
other opponents of the standing order a hearing such as they had
never been able to obtain before. Within three years of the accession of William III, the Mathers and their colleagues had their
attention temporarily diverted from the evils of episcopacy by
the pursuit of witches. The witchcraft panic, which seized Salem
and the neighboring villages in 1692 and which cast its shadow to
some extent over the whole province, has often been unfairly
represented as an evidence of the peculiar fanaticism of the

Puritans. Up to the close of the seventeenth century, however, practically everyone believed in witches, and all countries had laws against them. In Roman Catholic countries, where witchcraft was a form of heresy, its practitioners were generally burned. In England and her colonies, contrary to popular belief, they were hanged. Earlier in the century, England had seen a witchcraft persecution much more extensive than that which occurred in Massachusetts, and similar outbreaks had taken place in continental countries from time to time. Witchcraft cases had appeared in the courts of other American colonies also, though no one was actually executed for the crime outside of New England.

The real significance of the Massachusetts episode lies in the light which it throws upon the split that was beginning to develop between conservative and liberal within the Puritan party. The conservative ministers, of whom the Mathers were the outstanding leaders, though not directly responsible for the panic, had stimulated it by their writings upon witchcraft. When the charges began to appear, they advised the judges as to what rules should be used in investigating them, and they commented upon the increased activity therein displayed by the Devil as being a punishment for the increasing godlessness of the people, by which, of course, they meant their increasing restlessness under ministerial control. Many of the laity, however, especially at Boston, were opposed to the proceedings. They circulated pamphlets in the Boston coffee-houses ridiculing the Mathers and their writings, objecting to the inadequacy of the tests they applied to the witches, and even casting doubt upon the present possibility of witchcraft at all. To their efforts, at least in part, was due the localizing of the persecution in Salem, Andover, and a few other places. In these efforts, moreover, we may see the beginning of a liberalization of Puritanism which was destined to work great changes in the Massachusetts scene.

The situation created by this movement, together with the rapidly increasing prosperity of the colony, offered the Church a twofold opportunity to advance: through conversion and through immigration. It is a tendency of all liberal movements to dispose some people favorably toward whatever ideas are most opposed to the system that is breaking down. In New England the most dreaded religious evils—or, at least, the ones most widely dis-

Significance of the Witchcraft Panic

cussed—were "Popery and prelacy." To have gone as far as to accept the former would have implied a greater breakdown of the Puritan tradition than had as yet occurred, but prelacy, when examined at first hand, was discovered not to have so hideous a mien as had been supposed, and some were found willing to embrace it. Others, when the Puritan controversies became sharper, observed the comparative harmony prevailing among Episcopalians, and came to the Church in search of peace. At the same time, as the weakening of the Puritan domination coincided with the growing prosperity of the colony, many were attracted to its shores who had no sympathy with Puritanism, and who readily allied themselves with the Church or other denominations more in harmony with their personal religious needs.

The Church
in 1689

In 1689, however, all this was still in the future, and the position of the Church in Massachusetts seemed precarious indeed. The little chapel in the cemetery had not yet been fully completed when the stones of the Puritan mob were hurled through its windows, and its second minister, the Rev. Samuel Myles, arrived in Boston to find the leading members of his parish in jail. It was soon learned, however, that the most important protector of the Church, the royal governor, was to be restored. The Puritans had hoped that the revolution would mean the restoration of their old charter, but, though William III was, perforce, a constitutional monarch, there was probably no man in Europe who had less tolerance for republicanism, and the old charter had made Massachusetts, in effect, a republic. The new charter which he granted was, it is true, more liberal than that of most of the colonies, for it provided for an elective Council as well as an elective lower house, but the governor was still to receive royal appointment.

Samuel Myles

With the restoration of order the political prisoners were released, and the little church to which so many of them belonged began to show signs of increased prosperity. The damage done by the mob was repaired and the building was completed and "benched." Gradually the necessary furnishings were supplied, most of them being gifts of members of the parish or visitors. Myles, who had returned to England in 1692, possibly to receive priest's orders, and remained four years, came back to Massachusetts in 1696, bringing with him various gifts to the parish from Queen Mary, and began in earnest his long and useful ministry.

King William soon presented the chapel with a library, and a stipend of one hundred pounds a year to pay an assistant. As the latter, however, was to be appointed by the Bishop of London, and was not entirely subject to the direction of the rector, the post necessarily became a source of contention. Christopher Bridge, the first assistant to withstand the perils of an ocean voyage (two died in passage) was, unfortunately, not the type of man who could reduce this conflict to a minimum. Though apparently a respectable character, morally speaking, he was of a contentious disposition. After quarreling with Myles for several years, he went to Rhode Island, and began to stir up trouble there. He was succeeded by Henry Harris, who managed to build up an opposition party among the Churchmen, though a small one, and who also courted the favor of the Puritans. This last policy was an unwise one, for it deprived him of any chance to obtain a succession to the rectorship, which eventually became the chief object of his ambition.

By 1722 the number of Episcopalians had grown too large to be accommodated in King's Chapel, and some of them began   Christ Church
the organization of Christ Church. Harris sought the appointment as rector of the new parish, but those who were in charge of the arrangements turned instead to the Rev. Timothy Cutler, late president of Yale College, who had declared for the Church that same year. He accepted, and was sent to England for orders at the expense of the parish. When Cutler returned he proved to be an able and devoted rector, increasing the number of his congregation from four hundred to seven or eight hundred in five years, though it decreased after the organization of Trinity Church in 1740.

The most conspicuous, if not the most effective, champion of the Church at this period was a layman, John Checkley, who   John Checkley
did not succeed in obtaining ordination until after the period of his greatest activity had passed. Checkley was a native Bostonian who had attended the Boston Latin School, and had spent some time at the University of Oxford, though not as a matriculated student. While in England he became converted to the Church, and also developed a certain amount of sympathy for the "Non-jurors," as those clergymen were called who refused to take the oaths to support King William. He returned to Boston about

1710 and set up as the proprietor of a book store and notion shop. In 1719 he fired the first gun in a pamphlet war that he was to carry on for some time in behalf of the Church by reprinting *A Short and Easy Method with the Deists* by the Nonjuror, Charles Leslie. This pamphlet, which was to serve as the chief antidote to Deism for more than a century, had nothing to do with the controversy between the Church and the Puritans, but as an appendix to it Checkley printed one of the epistles of St. Ignatius, the second century advocate of episcopacy. In the same year he caused to be published some *Choice Dialogues* between a countryman and a parson on the subject of predestination, in which he quoted, with apparent approval, a charge which he ascribed to the Lutherans, that the Calvinists worshipped the Devil. He attributed this pamphlet to a "Reverend and Laborious Pastor in Christ's Flock," but it is generally supposed to have been written by himself.

His Contro-
versies and
Trials

These pamphlets, naturally, caused great excitement, and a law was passed, probably for Checkley's benefit, empowering two or more justices of the peace to administer oaths of allegiance and abjuration to any person whose loyalty was suspected. When Checkley was called upon to take these oaths he declined, either out of stubbornness, or because he felt a latent sympathy with the Jacobites, and was fined and placed under bond for his good behavior. In 1722 he went to England, partly on business and partly, it would seem, to try to obtain ordination. In this, if he did try it, he was defeated by the suspicions attaching to his loyalty. While in England he purchased the right to reprint any of Leslie's works that he thought proper, a formality with which he does not seem to have troubled himself before the publication of his first pamphlet.

On his return to Boston, Checkley published a *Modest Proof of the Order and Government Settled by Christ and his Apostles in the Church,* which was answered by two Puritan ministers. In reply, Checkley again reprinted *A Short and Easy Method with the Deists,* which he now enriched with a *Discourse Concerning Episcopacy,* partly compiled from the writings of Leslie and another pamphleteer, and partly the work of his own hand. It denied the validity of any but episcopal succession, and contained some allusions to the dissenters which were more or less abusive, though they did not go beyond the usual amenities of contemporary religious controversy. The remarks were given no personal application to the local ministers, but the pamphlet was, nevertheless, presented as a libel upon those gentlemen, and Checkley, after a trial and appeal, was fined fifty pounds and costs and again placed under bonds for his good behavior.

Checkley carried on his pamphlet controversy while the trial was in session, but discontinued it shortly after, the publication of his defense before the court serving as his last blast. In 1727 he again applied for ordination, and was again refused, probably because Bishop Gibson thought the measure inexpedient in view of the strong feeling that still prevailed as the result of his trial. He had removed the suspicion of disloyalty, as well as he could, by taking the required oaths before his trial commenced. He lived quietly for the next ten years, and when he renewed his application for Holy Orders in 1738 he was accepted and appointed minister to Providence, Rhode Island, where he ended his days. How many converts were made by his pamphlets it is impossible to say, but at least they made the claims of the Church known to most of the literate population of New England.

While these battles were being fought in Boston, the Church was gradually extending itself throughout the rest of the colony. As early as 1703, within a year of Keith's visit to Boston, some citizens of Swansea petitioned the Archbishop of Canterbury for the appointment of a minister, but as it was not found possible to send them one, they drifted back into Independency. In 1706 the Society for the Propagation of the Gospel let it be known that it was prepared to aid any duly recommended graduate of Harvard who cared to come to England for orders, but for a time no one took advantage of the offer. In the same year it was requested by Myles to give some help to the minister of the French Church at Boston, who was episcopally ordained. The first missionary it employed for work outside of Boston, however, was Thomas Eager who was sent in 1713 to Baintree, where some Episcopalians had organized a congregation and asked for aid. Eager, unfortunately, proved unworthy of the trust reposed in him and left the colony in a few months after having created a serious scandal.

In the meantime, a dispute among the Congregationalists at Newbury had led to the formation of an Episcopal church there.

Expansion of the Church in Massachusetts

Newbury

The local meeting-house being badly in need of repair, a majority of the worshippers decided to move to a new location, but a minority insisted upon rebuilding the old edifice. To prevent a split, the majority thereupon obtained an order from the General Court forbidding the formation of a second church at Newbury. At this juncture John Bridges, Her Majesty's Surveyor-General, and a staunch Churchman, promised the dissenters his support if they would declare for episcopacy. They agreed, and the Society, apparently not clearly informed of the circumstances under which the parish had originated, sent a missionary. According to later missionaries, many of the people were very much surprised at being actually supplied with a minister, and some withdrew, but enough remained to keep the church alive, and in time it became one of the strongest in the colony.

The congregation at Baintree disbanded as a result of Eager's misconduct and was not revived until some years later when Ebenezer Miller was sent there. In 1716 a church was organized at Marblehead, and in 1734 one was started at Salem, but the latter did not obtain a minister until 1739. A parish was organized at Scituate as the result of occasional visits from Miller, and in 1736 it received Addington Davenport, later rector of Trinity, Boston, as its missionary.

Struggle Against the Congregational Establishment

The chief obstacle to the growth of the Church in Massachusetts was the exaction from many Episcopalians of money to go towards the support of the Congregational ministers. The charter granted by William III required Massachusetts to allow freedom of conscience and forbade any laws hostile to the interests of the Church of England, but there was a good deal of disagreement between Churchmen and Independents as to what these clauses implied. In 1714, after the organization of the churches at Baintree and Newbury, Governor Dudley secured the exemption of Churchmen there from the taxes to support the local ministry, and, though there were occasional disputes and arrests, this policy was followed wherever regular parishes had been organized until 1727. In that year two acts were passed, of which one forbade traveling more than five miles on a Sunday. The other provided that when Episcopalians lived within five miles of their church and regularly attended its services, their taxes should be paid to their own minister. Thus an Episcopalian who lived more than five miles from his parish church—and there were many such—would not only have to help support a ministry he disapproved of, but would be prevented from attending the services of his own pastor unless he went to some place in the neighborhood Saturday night and returned Monday morning.

Checkley and others protested vigorously against these measures, but they were permitted to stand by the home authorities. In 1732 the Crown lawyers expressed the opinion that they were not contrary to the Charter of Massachusetts and that, in any case, it was too late to disallow them. About 1734, however, Matthew Ellis of Medford, a member of Christ Church, Boston, who had been imprisoned for not paying the required taxes, sought to test the law by prosecuting the constable who arrested him for false imprisonment. The case was decided against him in all of the provincial courts, but he obtained permission to appeal to the King in Council. In spite of the opinion above, the Massachusetts authorities seem to have feared that the case would go against them, or else they had themselves decided that the act in question was unjust. At any rate, they repealed it in 1735, while Ellis' case was still pending in England, and substituted a law which required the taxes collected from all persons regularly attending the services of any Episcopal Church to be paid over to the minister of that church. The act was at first limited to five years, but in 1740 it was made perpetual.

The venerable Samuel Myles of King's Chapel died in 1727 and was succeeded, contrary to Harris' hopes, by Roger Price from England. Price, who had also been appointed Commissary for New England, was the first clergyman to hold that position in Massachusetts. He remained rector of King's Chapel for twenty years, when he resigned to spend his declining years as missionary at Hopkinton, where he had organized a parish. His successor at Boston was Henry Caner, a former missionary in Connecticut, who continued his rectorate at King's Chapel until driven out by the Revolution. In 1740 Trinity Church was organized with Addington Davenport as its first rector, and the Church thus had three strong parishes in Boston, besides the French Church. Whitefield arrived in Boston the same year and business was temporarily suspended while everybody went to hear him. He preached throughout Massachusetts, creating a sensation

Growth of the Church in Boston

everywhere he went, except in the vicinity of Northampton, where most of the sinners had already been converted by Jonathan Edwards. The general effect of his preaching in New England was to hasten the breakdown of the older Puritanism, and to strengthen the newer denominations. Some of the missionaries were alarmed by the first results of his preaching, but they succeeded in holding their people together, and most of them reported considerable accessions when the reaction set in.

Outside of Boston

The decades of the thirties and forties seem to have seen the most rapid growth of the Church outside of Boston, at least as far as the formation of new parishes was concerned, for we find a definite slowing up in the process after 1750. In 1748 it was reported that there were three churches in Boston, two in Newbury, and one each in Salem, Marblehead, Baintree, Bristol, Scituate, Hopkinton, and Taunton. Several of these, however, were without missionaries. In 1759 a church was organized at Cambridge to combat the various heresies with which Churchmen believed Harvard to be infected, and East Apthorp, a distinguished layman of Boston who had been a member of the Society and a vestryman of King's Chapel, was ordained for the post, which he filled very ably for several years. In the same year some land was left to build a church in Dedham, but as the testator's mother had a life interest in the property, it did not become available for some time, and the church was not built until 1771. In 1770 a missionary was sent to the western settlements of the colony, with headquarters at Great Barrington, whence he also served some communities in New York.

Connecticut

The history of the Church in Connecticut does not begin until 1706, and the first minister to remain any time in the colony did not arrive until 1722, yet at the close of the Revolution the Church there was stronger, in many respects, than in any other state. The explanation of this remarkable growth is probably to be found in the fact that the causes which have already been described as contributing to the breakdown of Puritanism in Massachusetts were reinforced in Connecticut by circumstances peculiar to that colony. Connecticut was born in contention, and its history was largely one of strife. It represented, in fact, the not very cordial union of two separate colonies—Connecticut, centering at Hartford, and New Haven—both of them Puritan, but representing very different phases of the movement. Moreover, dissenting groups, chiefly the Baptists and Quakers, appeared early in the colony in fairly large numbers and began a long and eventually successful struggle for religious toleration. In the strife of denominations which resulted, the Church had a chance to be heard, while, on the other hand, it was also helped by the greater narrowness of Puritan Church membership in Connecticut as compared with her northern neighbor. Connecticut Puritans had never acceded to the famous "Half-way Covenant" by which persons not in full communion with the Congregational churches of Massachusetts were admitted to some of the privileges of Church membership, of which the most important, spiritually, was the right to have their children baptized. Consequently there were many respectable and even devout people in Connecticut who could enjoy no religious privileges except listening to sermons and helping to support the minister, and when the first clergymen of the Church came into the colony they found many adults who were unbaptized. Finally, it would appear that the migration of Church people to Connecticut was greater than that to Massachusetts. Samuel Johnson, who was thoroughly familiar with conditions in the former colony, says that a parish usually had its origin in the association of persons who had been attached to the Church of England before coming to America. These would interest some of their neighbors in the Church and would then proceed to organize a parish, applying to the Society for a minister.

The growth of the Church in the colony was, moreover, entirely spontaneous. Connecticut had managed to keep its charter in the dark days of James II and to have it confirmed by William III. The colony was, therefore, never subjected to a royal governor, and consequently there were no important Crown officers to promote the interests of the Church there. Its history began when a few Churchmen at Stratford asked the rector of Trinity Church, New York, to hold services for them. As the distance was too great to make this suggestion practicable, he referred their petition to the Rev. George Muirson, the Society's missionary at Rye, New York.

Beginnings of the Church at Stratford

Muirson complied with their request and visited the colony several times in 1706 and the year following, holding services both at Stratford and Fairfield. He was accompanied on these visits by his patron, Colonel Caleb Heathcote, who, as lord of the "Manor of Scarsdale," which covered what is now Westchester County, was one of the wealthiest and most influential men in the colonies. Without his powerful protection, Muirson would probably have spent some time in a Connecticut jail, and even as it was, the magistrates did all that they could to hinder his activities. On his second visit to Stratford, when he administered Holy Communion, Justices Joseph Curtice and James Judson read a long paper threatening him with legal prosecution, and the former stationed himself and other persons along the public roads to warn all the people against coming to church. Nevertheless, Muirson succeeded in collecting a respectable congregation, and in the spring of 1707 they felt themselves strong enough to petition the Society for a missionary. All those who were acquainted with the situation agreed that Muirson was obviously the man for the post, but unfortunately he died before the petition reached England, and it was not until 1713 that a minister, Francis Phillips, was actually sent out. He soon became discouraged, however, and obtained a position as supply for Evan Evans, the rector of Christ Church, Philadelphia, while the latter was in England. Before leaving Connecticut, he informed the Society that the only adherents of the Church in Connecticut were people who wanted to get out of paying taxes to support the Independent ministers—a statement which helped delay the sending of another missionary to that colony for several years.

This invasion of their colony by the Church of England naturally distressed the Puritans, and they sent one of their ablest ministers, Timothy Cutler, to Stratford to combat it. The choice was not a very fortunate one, from their point of view, for Cutler, according to later testimony, was already strongly inclinable toward episcopacy, but the fact was not known at the time. In 1722, the Churchmen at Stratford having persisted for several years in the face of difficulties and persecutions, the Society relented and sent George Pigot to be their minister. He had scarcely arrived in the colony when his ministry bore dramatic fruit in a way that must have surprised him as much as it did his friends and his opponents, and for which, in fact, he was but slightly responsible.

In his first report to the Society, which was dated August 20,

1722, he stated that though the principal men were strongly preju- The Yale
diced against the Church, he had great hopes of a "glorious revo- Converts
lution in the ecclesiastics of this country." Some of the chief of
them, including Cutler, who had by now become President of Yale
College, and five others, had approached him and expressed their
determination of declaring for the Church of England as soon as
they were assured of being supported at home. The necessary assurance was given, and in October, 1722, Pigot reported that he
had attended the Yale Commencement on September 4, where
Cutler and six others, "in the face of the whole country . . . declared themselves in this wise: that they could no longer keep out
of the Communion of the Holy Catholic Church, and that some
of them doubted the validity and the rest were persuaded of the
invalidity of presbyterian ordination in opposition to episcopal."
The phrase "presbyterian ordination," it should be observed, included the ministry of the Congregationalists in New England
usage. Those fully persuaded of its invalidity were: Cutler; Brown,
a tutor at Yale; Elliot, pastor at Kenelsworth; Johnson, pastor at
West Haven, and Wetmore, pastor at North Haven. Those doubt-
ing its validity were Hart, of East Guilford, and Whittlesey, of
Wallingford. Besides these seven, who stated their views in writing, Buckley, of Colchester, asserted orally that he believed episcopacy to be *jure divino* and Whiting, of "some remoter town,"
declared for "moderate episcopacy." These conversions, of course,
were not as sudden as they appeared to be. Johnson and Cutler.had
been favorably disposed towards episcopacy for some time, and
Johnson had discussed the subject with the other converts, most
of whom were his own age. There is some possibility that Checkley was partly responsible for the conversion of Cutler, though,
curiously enough, the achievement is ascribed to him only by his
enemies.

Some of the converts later relented but four of them, Timothy
Cutler, Daniel Brown, Samuel Johnson, and James Wetmore, Three of Them
went to England shortly afterwards. Brown contracted smallpox Ordained
there and died, but Cutler, Johnson, and Wetmore were ordained
and returned to America. Cutler became the first rector of Christ
Church, Boston, as we have seen, and Johnson succeeded Pigot at
Stratford, where he served many years, both before he became
President of King's College and after his retirement. Wetmore

became missionary at Rye. As might be expected, their conversion caused a good deal of consternation among the Puritans. The Mathers, at Boston, rallied to the cause and sent circular letters to all places in the colony, urging the people to "trace the pious steps of their forefathers." When this was answered by printing Winthrop's farewell address, referred to in our second chapter, to show that their forefathers had not felt so strongly against the Church as the Mathers did, the latter replied by pretending to distinguish two Churches of England, a high and a low, and to be in communion with the latter.

Growth of the Church in Connecticut

The example of the "Yale Converts," as they are commonly called, was followed by a number of their successors, and the Puritan college continued, not only throughout the colonial period, but well into the nineteenth century, to furnish a steady stream of converts to the Episcopal Church. For a time, however, things quieted down in Connecticut, and Johnson remained for five years the only Episcopal minister in the colony, but this does not mean that Stratford was the only place where efforts were being made on behalf of the Church. Johnson visited as many of the neighboring villages as he could, and in other places laymen exerted themselves to organize parishes. In 1727 Henry Caner, who had been acting as catechist and schoolmaster at Fairfield, went to England for orders and returned in the fall to serve as missionary at that town until he was called to King's Chapel twenty years later. As the colonial governor was elected by the people, New London, where the collector of customs had his headquarters, was the nearest approach to a center for royal authority in Connecticut. A church was organized there in 1730 and Samuel Seabury, father of the future first Bishop of the Church, was sent home for orders that he might become their missionary. He also organized parishes at Hebron, Simsbury, and Middletown. In 1732 the inhabitants of Redding and Newtown petitioned for a minister. John Beach, who had been the Congregational minister at the latter place, was ordained·and sent to them three years later. In 1734 the Puritan minister at North Groton conformed to the Church, bringing some of his parishioners with him. He went to England for ordination and returned the following year as a missionary of the Society. In 1736 Jonathan Arnold was sent to West Haven, and a missionary was sent to Derby and Wallingford in 1741. Missions were likewise organized at Norwalk in 1742, at Stamford in 1747, at New Haven in 1752, at Hartford in 1762, and at a number of other villages during these years, so that at the outbreak of the Revolution the Church of England had twenty ministers in the colony.

The struggle for religious liberty in Connecticut followed lines similar to that in Massachusetts, but the Church obtained recognition at an earlier date. In 1708 ·the legislature had passed a law declaring that the churches subscribing to the "Saybrook Platform," the extreme expression of Congregational Puritanism, should be "established," and their ministers supported by taxes levied upon all the people. A proviso attached to this act, however, specified that persons who differed from the established order might hold services in the manner their consciences directed. This exemption has been called a "liberal measure" according to the standards of the time, but it is difficult to see that it went beyond what was required by the English Toleration Act. Its effect upon the Church was that, while its clergymen could no longer be threatened with prosecution for holding services, as Muirson had been, its laity were still required to contribute to the support of a hostile ministry. In 1726 Governor Talcott declared that the only Church of England minister in the colony (Johnson) was allowed the same protection as the Puritan pastors, and his congregation was not required to support any other minister; but if this was true, the concession was an extra-legal one. In 1727, as the result of the petition of Moses Ward, a Churchman of Fairfield, the General Court passed an act which provided that whenever members of the Church of England lived near enough to a minister of that Church to conveniently attend upon his ministrations, and did so, the religious taxes paid by them should be turned over for his support.

This· law, upon which the later act in Massachusetts was modeled, gave the Episcopal Church approximate religious equality in places where it had a settled minister, but it still exposed Episcopalians in places not supplied with clergymen to prosecution for non-payment of Church taxes, and complaints of such prosecutions were not uncommon. This hardship was not removed, either in Connecticut or Massachusetts, until the final disestablishment of the Congregational Church some years after the Revolution. Attempts to evade the law in various ways, as, for example, by paying

Struggle for
Religious
Liberty

Congregational ministers from the general tax funds, were made
from time to time by the local authorities, but they were not ordinarily supported by the General Court. In 1738, however, that body
did permit the towns to divert to this purpose the proceeds from
the sale of some colonial lands, originally intended for the support
of public schools. Churchmen protested vigorously against this
measure, on the ground that they, like all other subjects of the
colony, had a proprietary interest in the lands, and so it was
repealed two years later. The Episcopalians also petitioned about
the same time for the right to tax themselves for the support of
their own ministers, but this was not given them, though the law
of 1727 had allowed them to levy sufficient taxes to supplement the
regular rates.

Whitefield appeared in Connecticut in 1741, and his preaching
there produced much the same effect as in Massachusetts, acting,
perhaps, as an even greater solvent for the standing order, and producing similar excesses. The response of the Church to the movement was the same as in all the other colonies. The ministers
stedfastly opposed it, and though some Churchmen were at first
attracted by it, few were permanently carried away. In the reaction, as elsewhere, some converts were made for the Church.
Whitefield revisited New England in 1764, but his power had
declined.

Whitefield
in Connecticut

The decades preceding the Revolution saw the arrival in Connecticut of a number of clergymen who were to become leaders of
the Church both in the state and the nation after the recognition
of American independence. Jeremiah Leaming, who was one of
the pamphleteers in the controversy over the colonial episcopate,
and was to be the first choice of the Connecticut clergy for their
bishop after the Revolution, was appointed missionary to Norwalk
in 1755, after having served for eight years at Newport, Rhode
Island, part of the time as schoolmaster and part of the time as
rector. Samuel Peters, who was to try very hard to be the first
Bishop of Vermont, appeared at Hebron in 1761. Abraham Jarvis,
who was to become the second Bishop of Connecticut, was ordained in 1763, and sent to Middletown. All of these men were
natives of the colony.

Rhode Island, as has already been intimated, was regarded as
something of a pariah among the New England colonies. It was

founded by Roger Williams, whose religious views were probably Rhode Island as narrow as those of any man on earth, as at one time he was able to hold communion only with himself, but who, perhaps because of that very narrowness, arrived at the principle of separation of Church and State, as a pioneer advocate of which he has attained a well-deserved immortality. Williams was at one time associated with the Baptists, and they as well as the Quakers became one of the strongest religious groups in the colony. The total strength of these two groups was estimated in 1710 as including seven-tenths of the population, though the Independents controlled the important town of Bristol.

The Church of England did not invade the colony until 1700, when Bishop Compton sent David Bethune to be minister at Newport. He is alleged to have had with him a "kinsman" who, like the Poet of Sierra Flat, turned out to be of the opposite sex, but this report does not come from a very reliable source. Anyway, he departed in 1702, and was succeeded by John Lockier, a devout and conscientious minister, who made a good beginning, but unfortunately died after he had been in the colony only two years. The vestry thereupon applied to Lord Cornbury, the governor of New York, to send them a clergyman, and he dispatched the Rev. James Honeyman, whose labors proved highly acceptable to the majority of the people. He had, however, been innocently involved in some scandals in New York, and for this reason, or, at least, with this as an excuse, a faction in the parish opposed him.

Their opposition might not have been serious, but in 1707 the Society sent Christopher Bridge, who had just finished making Controversy trouble in Boston, to Narragansett, Rhode Island. Bridge had not at Newport been long at his station when he decided that Honeyman's was better, and set to work to supplant him. In this he nearly succeeded, for Secretary Chamberlayne of the Society had never approved of Honeyman's going to Newport, and was partial to Bridge. All of the neighboring clergy, however, and several prominent laymen, including Colonel Heathcote, and Colonel Robert Quarry, Her Majesty's Surveyor-General of the Customs and one of the founders of Christ Church, Philadelphia, rallied to Honeyman's support, and their protests, seconded by the Bishop of London, eventually overcame Chamberlayne's prejudices. Honeyman was allowed to continue a distinguished and useful ministry that was to last for forty years. The wagging tongues were finally silenced by his marriage to a respectable local woman in 1711.

As Bridge could hardly be expected to remain next door to Honeyman after his defeat, he was sent elsewhere, and Narragansett was supplied only by such services as Honeyman could give it until 1716 when William Guy was sent there. He remained only two years, and then departed for South Carolina. The parish might have suffered another long vacancy, had it not happened that James McSparran, an Independent minister at Bristol, became converted to the Church in 1719. His former brethren held a conference on his case and hurled a few libels after him, but these were not taken very seriously in England and he was presently ordained and sent to Narragansett, with permission to preach occasionally at Bristol. Like Honeyman, he lived to have a long and useful ministry, though he handicapped himself by getting involved in an interminable suit over some lands in Narragansett, which had been set apart for the support of a minister without specifying his denomination.

McSparran's work at Bristol soon led to the organization of a parish there, and in 1722 it was provided with a missionary. He remained only a few months, however, before accepting an appointment as chaplain of the King's forces in New York, and the parish remained vacant until 1726, when John Usher, a convert from Harvard College, began a ministry of fifty-two years there. Honeyman had been preaching at Providence for several years, and had recommended sending a missionary, but his suggestion was not complied with until 1724, when the Society appointed George Pigot, late of Stratford, Connecticut, to the post. He got into a dispute with his vestry, because he insisted on living on a farm outside of town, though he apparently had an adequate salary, and resigned in 1728. The next minister sent there got into trouble when a woman claiming to be his wife arrived in Boston just as he was about to be married to a local lady. He left shortly afterwards, and was succeeded by Arthur Browne, who remained until 1736, when he went to Portsmouth, New Hampshire. Checkley was sent to Providence, after his ordination in 1738, on Browne's recommendation. The latter's son, Marmaduke Browne, after serving for a time as an itinerant in New Hampshire, was

Growth of the Church in Rhode Island

appointed missionary at Newport in 1761. A church was founded
at Warwick in 1758.

We have seen in an earlier chapter how Churchmen made the
first settlements in Maine and New Hampshire, and how the New
Church was presently smothered by the spread of the Puritan Hampshire
power into those colonies. The first point at which it began to
show signs of renewed life in the eighteenth century was Portsmouth, New Hampshire, where the surveyor-general and some
other royal officers were stationed. In 1734 a parish was organized there and the people petitioned to have Arthur Browne
transferred to them from Providence. This petition, which Browne
seconded, was granted, and he began work at the new station in
1736. At this time New Hampshire was still under the jurisdiction
of the governor of Massachusetts, and the lieutenant-governor,
who ruled in his name, seems to have been unfriendly, or at least
indifferent, to the Church. In 1741, however, the colonies were
separated, and Benning Wentworth began his long career as governor of New Hampshire. Under him the Church was never
without a powerful and loyal supporter in the colony.

Browne preached, whenever he could find time, in some of the
other communities around Portsmouth, and in 1745 he started
churches at Barrington and Nottingham. Browne's son, after
his ordination, acted as an itinerant missionary, serving these
and other stations, until his appointment to Newport left his father
once more the only Church of England minister in the colony.
Young Browne was not replaced until 1767, but after that date
an itinerant was maintained in the colony until the beginning of
the Revolution. Arthur Browne died in 1773, and by the time his
successor was appointed the war had broken out, and it was impossible to reach Portsmouth.

Maine, in spite of its early foundation, remained a frontier local-
ity throughout the colonial period. The first missionary to do any Maine
work there was Jacob Bailey, who was sent over in 1761, after an
earlier appointee, William McClennachan, had decided that the
post was unworthy of his homiletical abilities and had gone southward in an attempt to electioneer for the position of assistant at
Christ Church, Philadelphia. Bailey continued for some years as an
itinerant in the colony, serving Georgetown, Harpswell, Brunswick, and other villages near the mouth of the Kennebec, as well

as Pownalborough (Pownal), a few miles further west. He was also probably responsible for the organization of the church at Falmouth, a village on Casco Bay not far from Portland, which in 1764 agreed with John Wiswall, a local Congregational minister, that he should go home for orders and become their rector, a post which he continued to hold until the Revolution. In 1768 Wiswall complained that his people were taxed to support the local Independent minister, though this was long after Churchmen had been exempted from these taxes by the Massachusetts law, which should have extended to Maine.

Church Life in New England

The general characteristics of New England Churchmanship differed in a number of ways from those which were to be found in the South. The New England ministers were, for the most part, native colonials and converts to the Church from Puritanism, and, except for the small party which surrounded the assistant at King's Chapel, as an almost inevitable result of his position, they were a fairly harmonious group. As might be expected of converts and missionaries who were obliged to commend the Church to a hostile population, they were generally in sympathy with the party which laid the greatest stress upon her distinctive teachings and institutions. Samuel Johnson, it is true, thought that some modification in the external usages of the Church might be permitted to adapt it to colonial conditions. He regarded it as a mockery to enjoin sponsors in baptism to bring their godchildren to the Bishop for confirmation when such a proceeding was impossible, and he approved of allowing candidates for orders to read service, in view of the shortage of ministers. Certain it is, however, that he did not desire any serious modification in principle, and most of the missionaries indeed would never have gone as far as he did. Communion was generally celebrated once a month in New England, and the regular holidays of the Church were faithfully kept. These latter observances at first gave some offense to the Puritans, who disapproved of any stated feasts or fasts, but at a later time we find it frequently reported that many outsiders attended the services on such days.

We probably should not leave this region finally without taking some note of the pamphlet controversies which attended the growth of the Church there. Of the disputes associated with the name of Checkley we have already said as much as is necessary,

and the debates which arose from the efforts to obtain a colonial
episcopate will be considered in a later chapter, but there were
some occasional scrimmages which cannot be placed in either of
these classes. In 1731 George Pigot, then at Marblehead, published
a pamphlet vindicating the observance of Christmas from the
attacks made upon it by John Barnard, the local Congregational
minister. The next year, Jonathan Dickinson, a Puritan clergyman, published a defense of "Presbyterian Ordination" which
involved him in a controversy with Arthur Browne of Providence
and Samuel Johnson of Stratford. In 1736 the same gentleman
printed a sermon on *The Vanity of Human Institutions in the
Worship of God* in which he condemned the usages of the Church
of England. This was answered by John Beach, the missionary at
Newtown and Redding, Connecticut. In 1745 Samuel Johnson
published *A Letter from Aristocles to Authades*, attacking the
Calvinistic theory of predestination, and was answered by Dickinson and supported by Beach. In 1746 some strictures on the Church
in a sermon by the Rev. Noah Hobart were answered by James
Wetmore, the missionary at Rye. Hobart answered this in a small
volume and was in turn replied to by Johnson and Beach. In 1752
James McSparran of Narragansett, published a sermon which was
designed to check the practice of permitting candidates for Holy
Orders to read service. This was interpreted by the Puritans as an
attack on their orders and was replied to by several of them.

CHAPTER VI

THE MIDDLE COLONIES

Their
Characteristics

IT WAS not merely in a geographic sense that the Middle Colonies were "middle." They represented also a mingling of the social and political characteristics of the two extremes, though it should be observed that the individual colonies did not necessarily resemble most closely the section they were nearest. Thus, in New York, with its partial Establishment, the position of the Church was more nearly like that of the South than in Pennsylvania where it enjoyed no special privileges at all. New York also resembled the South more nearly in the number of its slaves which, while not so great as in the tobacco colonies, was still large enough to be a serious factor in the population. On the other hand, in New York, as in New England, the Church had to contend mainly with Independents and Presbyterians, whereas in Pennsylvania the chief opponents were the Quakers. Moreover, the type of Churchmanship prevailing in Pennsylvania seems to have been less predominantly "high" than in New York.

New York

We have previously traced the first appearance of the Church in New York, insofar as it was represented by the chaplain at the fort, and we have also noted that it was apparently the policy of the English government after 1689 to secure the Establishment of the Church in all colonies which had not been founded in the interest of dissent. In New York this purpose was expressed in the instructions given to Colonel Sloughter, the first governor to be sent out by the new government, in 1690. Sloughter endeavored to carry out these orders and in 1691 succeeded in getting a bill introduced into the Assembly for settling a regular ministry in the Province, but it was rejected "as not answering the intention of the House." Sloughter died shortly after this, and the effort had to be renewed by his successor, Benjamin Fletcher. A bill introduced in 1692 was not acted upon before the end of the session,

112

but in 1693 Fletcher urged the matter so strongly that the Assembly felt obliged to do something about it. It accordingly passed an act which provided that a "sufficient Protestant minister" should be settled in the county of New York within a year, another in Richmond County (Staten Island), two in Westchester, and two more in Queen's County on Long Island. No provision was made for King's County (Brooklyn), Dutchess, Orange, and Albany counties, which were predominantly Dutch, nor for Suffolk County, where the people were nearly all Independents. Fletcher objected to the act because it did not specifically give him the right to induct, but, as he was unable to have it amended, he finally signed it. Act of Establishment

The intention of the legislature in passing this law has long been the subject of debate. The phrase "sufficient Protestant minister" in English legal usage meant a minister of the Established Church, but as the Assembly was then controlled by the Dutch and the dissenters, they may have hoped that the phrase would be interpreted in the colonies as applying to any orthodox Protestant minister. This supposition is strengthened by their unwillingness to give the power of induction to the governor, whose instructions obliged him to appoint only ministers licensed by the Bishop of London, but, on the other hand, the fact that no provision was made for Suffolk County, where dissent was strongest, would suggest that they recognized at least a possibility that the ministers introduced under the act would be those of the Church. Moreover, the Dutch members of the Assembly probably did not care a great deal what variety of English minister was introduced into the colony. Their relations with the Church were at least as cordial as with any other denomination.

The act had further provided that the freeholders in each county should annually elect ten vestrymen and two wardens who were, by taxation, to raise one hundred pounds for the support of the ministry, regardless of whether one or two clergymen were employed, and who should also have the power of hiring the ministers. When the first vestry was elected in New York County it was composed of dissenters, and for a time it refused to take any action at all. Finally, prodded by the governor, it voted to call William Vesey, a Churchman who had been serving as a lay

preacher at Hempstead, but apparently it never took the trouble
to inform him of its action. Instead, it inquired of the Assembly
as to the propriety of calling a dissenting minister and was informed by that body that it had a perfect right to do so. Fletcher
then prorogued the Assembly to prevent its taking any further
steps in the matter.

While the question was still in abeyance, Colonel Heathcote,
Lewis Morris, and other influential members of the Church made
preparations to secure the benefits of the act for her in spite of both
the Assembly and the freeholders. The chapel in the fort which
had previously been used for the services of the Church of England
was in a ruinous condition, and so these Churchmen, with the
governor's aid, secured from the Assembly permission to re-
build it outside of the fort. In the spring of 1697, when their building had been enclosed, though not entirely finished, they applied
to the governor for a charter of incorporation, and also prayed
that, as the operation of the Act of 1693 had been delayed by the
want of a suitable building, and as that want was now about to be
supplied through their own efforts, they might be given control
of the money raised by the County Vestry under that act. With
these requests the governor complied, and, as he had previously
placated the most influential element in the Assembly by granting
a liberal charter to the Dutch Church, no opposition was made
from that quarter. Thus the Church vestry became, in effect, the
controlling ecclesiastical power and the County Vestry was reduced to the status of an agency for raising funds. Moreover, subsequent elections to that body had proven more favorable to the
Church, and in 1696 Churchmen formed a majority of its members.

Having thus passed under Church control, the County Vestry
renewed the call to Vesey in 1696, but this time upon the condition of his going to England for ordination, a condition with
which he readily complied. He was the son of a staunch Churchman of Massachusetts, and had been a communicant of the Church
since he was fifteen. His work as a lay preacher was uncanonical,
but he says that it was undertaken on the advice of his fellow
Churchmen. At the time of his second call to New York he was
acting as a lay assistant in King's Chapel, Boston, and studying
theology under the Rev. Samuel Myles. Vesey must have felt

Organization of Trinity Parish

William Vesey

justified in exercising his ministry without episcopal ordination at a time when it probably seemed impossible to obtain it, and yet have felt it his duty to procure such ordination when a way opened for him to do so.

Whatever his motives may have been, Vesey was ordained by the Bishop of London in August, 1697, and on his return to the colony was duly recommended to Governor Fletcher, and by him appointed as "assistant" to the Bishop, who, by the Charter of 1697, had been made titular rector of Trinity Parish. As the interior of the new building was not yet finished, Vesey officiated for a time in the Dutch Church on Garden Street, and two of the Dutch ministers assisted at his induction on Christmas Day, 1697.

The ministry that thus commenced was to last for forty-nine years and be marked by great fruitfulness. The Establishment Act led to a prolonged conflict in some of the other parts of the colony, as we shall see presently, but the arrangement worked out in New York met with very little opposition once it was set in operation, probably because the Churchmen rapidly became the predominant element in the city's population. Vesey's habitual moderation and the integrity and piety of his character also did much to reconcile to his ministry such of the dissenters as were not irrevocably opposed to everything associated with episcopacy. The wardens and vestry of Trinity were entrusted by the city government with the administration of the poor fund, as the deacons of the Reformed Church had been in Dutch times. The board of aldermen usually, though not always, attended service in the church as part of the inauguration ceremony. Governor Cornbury caused a temporary flare-up of hostility by his persecution of two Presbyterian ministers, Makemie and Hampton, early in the century, but the excitement passed over, though the development of the Presbyterian Church which followed their acquittal created a more definite source of opposition than had hitherto existed. In 1714, when a group of ruffians broke into Trinity and desecrated it, the ministers of the French and Dutch churches vigorously expressed their detestation of the deed.

In 1717, Robert Jenney, subsequently rector of Christ Church, Philadelphia, was sent as a schoolmaster and assistant to Trinity Church, in which position he continued until 1722 when the Society appointed him missionary at Rye. He was succeeded by James

Growth of Trinity Church

Wetmore, one of the "Yale Converts," who had originally been intended for Staten Island, and who in turn succeeded him at Rye four years later. The Society continued to aid Trinity in the support of its assistant ministers, who also acted as catechists and schoolmasters. In 1729, it presented New York City with its first public library. In 1704 whatever irregularity had existed in the parochial charter was removed through its being confirmed by a special act of the Assembly, and in 1705 the tract of land known as the "King's Farm," the use of which had originally been granted to Trinity by Governor Fletcher, was fully transferred to the parish by a royal gift. This land, which now covers a large section of downtown New York, has been the chief source of Trinity's wealth. Though a few lots have been sold, the bulk of it has been kept intact.

Vesey died in 1746 and was succeeded by the Rev. Henry Barclay, who had been a missionary to the Indians west of Albany. Under his rectorate the first chapel of the parish, St. George's, was built in 1752. It is now an independent parish. The second chapel, St. Paul's, which was completed in 1766, has remained a part of the parish, and the original structure, which is still standing, is the oldest church building in New York City. Its interior has been considerably changed, however.

After Barclay's death in 1764 he was succeeded by the Rev. Samuel Auchmuty, who had been his assistant for some time, and the Rev. Charles Inglis, former missionary at Dover, Delaware, was chosen to assist Auchmuty. Inglis was one of the few ministers of the Church, in America or elsewhere, to be blessed with the approval of George Whitefield, and his "Methodist" leanings commended him to a portion of the congregation. The rector felt that Inglis' talents would be more useful elsewhere, but accepted him for the sake of peace. Inglis changed his sentiments, apparently, as time went on, for in his later years he was regarded as a High Churchman. He became rector of the parish in 1775 and so continued throughout the Revolution, but left with the British evacuation, to become, after a short time, the first bishop of Nova Scotia.

Though, as we have seen, the Act of 1693 provided for ministers in Westchester, Staten Island, and in one county of Long Island, none was actually sent to these places until the arrival of Lord

Rectors and Assistants

Lord Cornbury

Cornbury as governor in 1702. That individual, a degenerate and a pervert, who is said to have spent half of his time dressed in women's clothes, was one of the most despicable of the colonial governors, a class that cannot be said, as a whole, to have set a very high standard either of decency or integrity. Because he desired to retain the favor of Queen Anne, or for some other reason, he was, however, a vigorous supporter of the Church, which sometimes, in fact, suffered from the excess of his zeal.

In Westchester his efforts were seconded by the more reputable Heathcote, and it is probably because the latter had already reduced that county to some semblance of ecclesiastical order that Cornbury sent John Bartow, the first of the Society's missionaries, there in 1702. Heathcote, in an account of the origin of the Church in Westchester which he later supplied to the Society, said that, as there had been no minister of any description there for some time, a general disregard of the Sabbath came to prevail. To put a stop to this, he let it be known that unless the people of the various communities appointed "readers" and observed the day as best they could, he would direct the captains of the militia to drill their companies on Sunday. This dreary prospect was sufficient to cause the appointment of some lay readers and in time a few dissenting ministers from New England made their appearance. In the village of Westchester the people liked one of these ministers so well that they requested Heathcote to use his influence to get him inducted. Heathcote replied that this was impossible, and diplomatically suggested that they call the Rev. Daniel Bondet, a French minister then at Boston, who had been episcopally ordained, to supply the French church at New Rochelle and their own, at the same time retaining the other minister and supporting him as well as they could. As the latter raised some objections to this scheme, Heathcote contrived to persuade him that it would be advisable to leave the county. The wily Colonel then proceeded, with the aid of Vesey and Bondet, to build up the Church in his dominion by winning over as many as he could of the chief men in every community.

Westchester village at first offered some rather vigorous opposition to Heathcote's plans, but by the time of Bartow's arrival it had been sufficiently tamed so that it accepted his ministry without serious protest. The neighboring village of Eastchester was dis-

Col. Heathcote and the Church in Westchester

posed, at first, to raise some difficulties, but Lord Cornbury soon put an end to that, and Bartow found himself fairly in possession of the field. Of this missionary Lewis Morris wrote in 1707 that he was "a very good man, and of exemplary life, but . . . very inactive." Morris's judgments, however, were seldom impartial, and it is possible that at this time he was annoyed at Colonel Heathcote or happened to have some other reason for being dissatisfied with the state of affairs in Westchester. As a result of his charges Bartow was suspended from the Society's service, but was presently reinstated on the recommendation of others, and continued at his post so long as to be the oldest missionary in the Society's employ after the dismissal of Talbot in 1725.

The Church at Rye

It will be remembered that the Church Act provided for the settlement of two ministers in Westchester County. The second minister to be sent there was Thomas Pritchard who, in 1704, was stationed at Rye whence he also served Bedford and Mamaroneck. He committed suicide, or was murdered, and was replaced by George Muirson, whose pioneer work in Connecticut has already attracted our attention. His labors in New York appear to have been equally useful, but he died three years after his arrival, and the parish was then vacant until 1710, when Christopher Bridge was appointed to it. This gentleman we also met when we were in New England, where we found him something of a troublemaker. Two rebukes to his ambition had, however, been sufficient, and during the nine years that elapsed before his death he served quietly and conscientiously at his post in Rye. Bondet, who remained at New Rochelle after Bartow had taken over the work at Westchester, made a third minister in the county during the early years of the century. He was supported by the voluntary contributions of the French colony, supplemented after a time by aid from the Society.

After Bridge's death, the parish at Rye remained vacant for three years until Robert Jenney was sent there, as has already been noted. On his being transferred to Long Island in 1726, James Wetmore was sent to Rye and the parish began to enjoy the benefit of his long and useful ministry. In 1728 he reported that he had found many whole families unbaptized and many more with several adult members unbaptized, but as he reported two years later that the Quakers were causing trouble in his parish, it is possible that this situation was due to their influence and not to any negligence on the part of his predecessors. In 1729 the people of White Plains brought suit against the officers appointed to collect the ecclesiastical taxes, but it was decided in favor of the Church. Thereafter the Church settlement in Westchester continued undisturbed until the Revolution. In time the local support became sufficient so that the Society discontinued its stipends.

Long Island, except that part of it which was nearest to Manhattan, was settled largely from Connecticut, and it was there that the dissenting interest was strongest. In the most eastern part of the island, which was included in Suffolk County, no attempt was made to establish the Church at all, and it was not introduced there until a few of the inhabitants got together voluntarily and petitioned for a missionary. In King's County, on the western nose of the island, no attempt at an establishment was made, either, because the population was largely Dutch. The Act of 1693 had, however, provided for the settlement of two "sufficient Protestant ministers" in Queen's County, which lay in between the other two, and it was here that the dispute over the application of the act waged most bitterly.

The controversy centered in the village of Jamaica, where one of the ministers appointed under the act was to be located. In that town the dissenters, who constituted most of the population, had called a minister of their own and started to build a church. When the act for settling the ministry was passed, they stopped building, and the church was completed and a parsonage built by the local vestry elected under the act. This body was composed of dissenters, and in 1702 it called a dissenting minister to the parish. In the same year, the Society for the Propagation of the Gospel sent a missionary to Jamaica, but he died before he could be inducted. James Honeyman was next sent there, and remained a short time but presently became the subject of evil reports. These were eventually shown to be unfounded, but Honeyman was removed and sent by Cornbury to Newport. He was replaced by William Urquhart whom the governor formally inducted in 1704. Having done this, Cornbury ordered the dissenting minister to yield the church and parsonage to Urquhart. This was an arbitrary proceeding, since the right to their possession had never been legally determined, and it became a source of complaint on the part of the governor's enemies, but was complied with for the time being and given an *ex post facto* legality by an act of the Assembly in 1706.

Urquhart remained in possession of the property until his death, but during the vacancy which followed the dissenters again seized both church and parsonage, and some justices of the peace who fined them for taking the former were dismissed. In 1710 the local vestry called another dissenting minister, and in the same year the Church minister designated for the post, the Rev. Thomas Poyer, arrived in the colony. Robert Hunter, who was then governor, was probably as much concerned for the interests of the Church as Cornbury had been, but he was more scrupulous as to the means he used to promote them. He told Poyer that the only legal method to obtain either the property or his salary was to bring suit for them in the colonial courts, and offered to bear the costs of the action himself. Poyer, however, was not prepared to take such a measure without consulting the authorities at home. When they learned of the situation they advised him not to commence the suit until he was sure of having it tried before favorable judges, or until they had obtained an instruction from the Queen, which was presently granted, directing the governor to admit appeals to himself and Council in suits for any amount where the Church was a party, as, normally, such appeals were allowed only in cases involving one hundred pounds or more.

Its Conclusion
This hesitation caused a long delay, during which Poyer was without parsonage or salary (except his stipend from the Society), and was so unpopular that the local miller refused to grind his grain, telling him to eat it whole, as the hogs did. Eventually, however, Poyer was authorized to start a suit for his salary, and after having been lost in the lower court, the case was finally decided in favor of the Church by Chief Justice Morris in 1723, though Poyer experienced some difficulty in collecting the arrears. The right to the church building was made a separate issue, probably because the structure had been begun by the dissenters before the passage of the Act of Establishment, and a jury under Morris subsequently decided that it belonged to the Presbyterians. The Episcopalians were thereby forced to meet in the town house

for a while, but in a short time they succeeded in building another church.

At Hempstead, where the other minister appointed for Queen's County was located, the opposition to the Church was less bitter and less prolonged. This was partly because the dissenters had not been organized there before a Church minister was sent among them, and partly, it is probable, because of the moderation and prudence of the one who was sent. John Thomas, who was appointed to the post in 1704, was rebuked by Secretary Chamberlayne, early in his career, for boasting of the stubborn dissenters he had won over instead of the stubborn heathen he should have converted—a sensitivity on this point seldom displayed by the Secretaries—but he was by no means the fanatical Churchman that this rebuke might seem to imply. On the contrary, if he won over the dissenters it was by his moderation and his readiness to go as far as he could in making allowance for their prejudices, not by any vigorous insistence upon the exclusive claims of the Church. In 1705 he reported that, though he had had less trouble than his colleague at Jamaica, everything depended upon the support of the governor, but he soon established himself sufficiently in the favor of his people so that he was not molested when Cornbury was recalled. As he enjoyed a long life and was not transferred, the parish was saved from those frequent vacancies which served as occasions for renewing the dispute between Churchmen and dissenters at Jamaica.

After the settlement of the Jamaica dispute, the growth of the Church in the county was steady but quiet, and there are few striking occurrences in its subsequent history. After the death of Thomas, Jenney served for a time as missionary at Hempstead and was succeeded by Samuel Seabury, the elder, who so endeared himself to the people that they built a house for his widow after his death. His son served for a time as minister at Jamaica, until he was transferred to Westchester in 1766.

In 1724 some residents of Brookhaven, in Suffolk County, petitioned for a minister, and a few years later Alexander Campbell was sent to them. He was convicted of gross immorality, however, and was removed. His successor, Isaac Browne, during a long and devoted ministry built up a thriving parish.

The early history of the Church on Staten Island was also

Staten Island

marked with controversy, but most of the disputes were among the Churchmen themselves, not between them and the dissenters. Under the first missionary, the Rev. Aeneas Mackenzie, the progress of the Church was peaceable and encouraging. In 1715 Governor Hunter incorporated the parish by letters patent, and the next year Mackenzie reported that a church and parsonage had been built and a glebe purchased, entirely by voluntary subscription.

After Mackenzie's death this peaceful development was interrupted. In 1723 the wardens and vestry of the local church (St. Andrew's) elected Robert Weyman to be their rector, and in the same year Governor Burnet appointed William Harrison to the post and the Society sent James Wetmore there. These men were all Church ministers, and likewise men of good character who were the victims of the conflicting schemes of others rather than of any misconduct of their own, but, as the parish could support only one minister, two of them had to be disappointed. It was finally agreed that Harrison should remain on Staten Island, without any aid from the Society, and that Wetmore should be appointed assistant at Trinity, New York. Weyman was sent elsewhere.

Harrison continued an acceptable ministry on the island, and in 1735 was restored to the Society's pay-roll. He also shared in the labor of starting the church at Newark, New Jersey. His successor got into a dispute with the vestry over the right to sell wood from the parish land and resigned, but under the two ministers who followed, the Church enjoyed a long period of peaceful development only interrupted in 1762 when Lord Amherst caused his troops to camp on the glebe, which resulted in great damage to the church property.

Albany

Though Albany had not been included in the act for settling ministers, a missionary, the Rev. Thomas Barclay, was sent there in 1709, the Society's stipend being supplemented by an allowance from the English government, given because Barclay's services would benefit the soldiers who were stationed at that frontier post, and also, it is possible, in the hope that he would be able to counteract the efforts of the French missionaries to win over the Iroquois. Some work had already been done among these Indians by Dutch ministers, and Barclay, though with difficulty, succeeded in persuading the converts to accept the Church of England. Some of the Dutch were also won over by being told that the doctrine of the Church was substantially the same as theirs. In 1713 Barclay wrote that he had succeeded in inducing three of the leading families of the region—the Schuylers, the van Rensselaers, and the Livingstons—to accept his ministry. The last-named family, or part of it, subsequently became Presbyterian, however. Barclay is said by a later missionary to have suffered from a hasty temper, but he worked hard and with fair success until 1722, when he went mad.

He was not replaced until 1728 when John Miln was sent to the village, which he found "beyond expectation polite and large," with a population of about one thousand, most of whom, however, were Dutch Calvinists. Barclay had succeeded in having a church built before his collapse. He had also worked among the Mohawk Indians with some success, and Miln made a practice of visiting them four times a year until 1735 when Henry Barclay, a son of Thomas, was sent to work among them. Thereafter, missionaries were generally maintained both at Albany and at the Mohawk Castle, though for a few years during the later sixties both stations were united under the Rev. Henry Munro. Some residents of Dutchess County petitioned for a missionary in 1766, and one was presently sent to Poughkeepsie.

In 1710 Governor Hunter acquired some lands in the colony as a speculation, and endeavored to settle them with some Germans from the Palatinate, whose elector was driving many of his subjects out by his efforts to bring his dominion back to Roman Catholicism. Hunter's experiment was a tragic failure, and after a period of starvation the surviving Palatines drifted into Pennsylvania and the other colonies to the southward. In religion the settlers were divided between Lutheranism and Calvinism, and while they were in the colony the Calvinists agreed to conform to the Church, but the Lutherans refused to do so.

German Settlers

The founding of King's College (now Columbia) was largely the work of Churchmen. It remained under Church control until well after the Revolution, and the shadow of this control still persists. Talk of the project probably began with the century, but it was not until 1746 that the legislature authorized the formation of a lottery to raise money for the purpose. The money thus obtained was placed in the hands of a board of trustees of whom

King's College

a majority were Churchmen, and was supplemented by the gift of a large tract of land from Trinity Church. A condition of the latter gift was that the president of the College should always be a communicant of the Church, and that the services of the Book of Common Prayer should always be used in the chapel. According to a statement made by the vestry, the reason for this specification was that an effort had been made by some to exclude all religious teaching from the College. Whatever its motives, the gift roused some opposition to the College among the dissenters, especially the Presbyterians.

Nevertheless, the Assembly continued to show some favor to the College. In 1753 it passed an act appointing trustees and in the same year it appropriated five hundred pounds out of the excise duties for the next seven years to the College. In 1754 the College was given a royal charter. It had started operations earlier in the same year under Dr. Samuel Johnson, late of Stratford, who was probably at that time the most learned of the colonial clergy. He continued in office until 1762, when he was succeeded by the Rev. Myles Cooper, a gifted if somewhat facetious Englishman, who had been a tutor at the College the year before, and who continued as president until the Revolution drove him out and changed the name of the College from King's to Columbia.

In 1762 James Jay was sent to England to raise money for the College. When he arrived, he found the Rev. William Smith on the ground seeking funds for the institution at Philadelphia, of which he was the head. Smith was annoyed at the intrusion, but Archbishop Secker persuaded him of the advisability of joining forces with Jay, and the two of them obtained a royal "brief" under which they could have collections made in the churches of England if the rectors were willing. The King also granted £400 to King's College and £200 to the College at Philadelphia, the reason for the discrimination being that the latter had another patron in Thomas Penn, the proprietor. The joint collection was fairly successful, bringing £5,937 to each institution.

If we have lingered too long over the history of the Church in New York, our excuse must be found in its complex character. As the Church developed along different lines in each of the leading counties, it is necessary to go into some detail in order to make the subject clear. The story of Pennsylvania, though not

Pennsylvania

less important, is considerably simpler. That colony, as everyone knows, was founded by William Penn, partly as a real estate speculation and partly as a refuge for Quakers. Both objects required the exercise of general toleration in matters of religion, and such a toleration was provided for from the start. Moreover, as has already been mentioned, the freedom of the members of the Church of England to worship in their own way in the colony had been secured by a special clause in the proprietary charter.

Nevertheless, though the Church did not suffer any persecution in Pennsylvania, its relations with the proprietor were not altogether devoid of friction. Its supporters complained, though whether justly or not it is difficult to say, that Penn electioneered with the people to make them vote for Quaker candidates, and further discriminated against Churchmen by allowing the courts to refuse oaths even to those who wished to take them. Later on, they also complained of not being allowed to bear arms. On the other hand, Penn protested that the ministers of the Church preached too much against Quaker principles, "as if . . . they would stir up their people against those whose tenderness admits them into shares in the administration to turn them out," and he added, "We cannot yet be so self-denying as to let those that had no part of the heat of the day, not one third of the number and not one fourth of the estate, and not one tenth of the trouble and labour . . . give laws to us and make us dissenters, and worse than that in our own country." In later years, the colony was pretty definitely divided into a Quaker and an anti-Quaker party, with Churchmen supplying most of the leadership of the latter, but the issues between them were only secondarily religious, and related chiefly to such questions as the defense of the frontier—a matter in which scruples of the Quakers always caused a good deal of difficulty—and the support due to the proprietors, who by then had become Churchmen.

The opinion has been expressed by a recent historian of Pennsylvania, Charles P. Keith, that—"Probably from the time that the English took possession of the town of New Castle in October, 1664, stipulating that all the conquered should, as formerly, enjoy the liberty of their conscience in Church discipline, there was always some person on the western shore of Delaware River and Bay who acknowledged belonging to the Church of England." *Organization of Christ Church*

The same authority thinks that the first minister of the Church to go into the region was the Rev. John Yeo, whom we have already mentioned in connection with the founding of the Church in Maryland, and who came from that colony into the settlements along the Delaware in 1677 and held services for some months during the ensuing year. This was before the actual founding of the colony of Pennsylvania, which was not chartered until 1680, and we must skip eighteen years before we find the formal beginning of the Church in that province, for it was not until 1694-5, that the Churchmen at Philadelphia began to associate together with a view to organizing a parish. They may have been stimulated to this partly by the example and prompting of Governor Francis Nicholson and Secretary Thomas Lawrence of Maryland, but the movement probably had a local origin also. It was about this time that George Keith withdrew from the fold of orthodox Quakerism and began his progress toward the Church, and the religious unrest which resulted probably led the Churchmen to think about the desirability of making provision for their own needs. While their Church was being built, they made use for a time of the Keithian meeting-house, but few of their number, possibly only one, were converts from Quakerism.

Evan Evans

The name of the first minister of Christ Church, as the parish thus organized came to be called, is not known. It would seem that for a time the Church people were kept together through the work of I. Arrowsmith, a schoolmaster sent by Nicholson, who was probably, like most Church of England schoolmasters, in deacon's orders, and that the services of a priest were occasionally supplied from Maryland. In 1697, having completed their church building, the congregation asked the Archbishop of Canterbury to supply them with a minister, and sent Colonel Robert Quarry to England to support their petition. The request was favorably received, and the Rev. Thomas Clayton was sent among them. He lived only two years after his arrival, but during that time he worked hard and effectively—so much so that his brethren in Maryland criticized him for being overzealous in his efforts to convert the Quakers and other dissenters. On his death he was succeeded after an interval by Evan Evans who, though not the planter of the Church at Philadelphia, deserves to be regarded as its chief cultivator, for during a ministry of eighteen years he brought it to a flourishing condition.

Evans was supported, in addition to what he received in local contributions, by a stipend of fifty pounds from the Society for the Propagation of the Gospel, which also gave thirty pounds to support a parish school. In a report which he made to the Society in 1707 he also mentioned Sir Francis Nicholson as one of the chief benefactors of the Church. During the early years of his rectorate he enjoyed the services of an assistant, the Rev. John Thomas, later missionary at Hempstead, and while thus supplied he held two evening lectures a month, one on the last Sunday of the month, preparatory to the Eucharist which was to be celebrated the following week, and the other for the benefit of a group of young men who were also accustomed to meet after morning service to read the Bible and sing psalms. On the latter occasions, Evans, whenever he could be present, would read prayers and preach. The evening lectures had the advantage of attracting many young Quakers, who would begin by listening at the windows until some of them got up courage enough to come inside, where what they heard proved sufficiently appealing so that eventually they were baptized and came to Communion. Nevertheless, when Thomas resigned, Evans hesitated to ask for another assistant because, in the absence of a bishop, he feared that there would be no one to settle the inevitable disputes arising between rector and curate.

Evans had also preached at the villages in the neighborhood of Philadelphia, and had organized parishes in some of them. The second church in the colony was built in the old Swedish burying-ground at Chester. The family of James Sandelands, who had originally donated the cemetery tract, had started to build a wall around their family plot when it was suggested to them that, as the Swedish church had fallen into decay, they should turn their wall into a new church. With this suggestion they complied, their neighbors helping them, and in 1703 the structure was completed and opened for use by George Keith. The chief promoter of this enterprise was Jasper Yeates, who had also been one of the founders of Christ Church, Philadelphia. Shortly after the completion of the building, a missionary was sent by the Society to serve Chester and the neighboring communities. He left after a few years and the church was supplied only irregularly until 1728

Expansion of the Church in Pennsylvania

when Richard Backhouse began his long ministry there. He found that many who had formerly belonged to the Church had drifted back into Quakerism for want of a pastor.

The Swedes had been the first settlers along the Delaware, and their relations with the Church were always very cordial. Trinity Church, Wilmington, and Gloria Dei Church, Philadelphia (both commonly known as "Old Swedes'"), which were originally built to serve their colony, are now Episcopal churches. The Swedes were glad to accept ministers of the Church of England when these were sent to them and, on the other hand, their ministers were occasionally employed in that Church without any question being raised as to the validity of their orders. In 1705 the Society for the Propagation of the Gospel appointed one of them, the Rev. Andreas Rudman, its minister at Oxford, a village in southeastern Pennsylvania. He died in 1709 and was succeeded by a Welshman, who also served the Welsh community at Radnor. After the latter's death, both stations were supplied only intermittently.

Later History of Christ Church

In 1715 Evans paid a visit to England and made the mistake of appointing Francis Phillips, whom the Society had sent to Stratford, Connecticut, *locum tenens* in his absence. Phillips not only interfered with Robert Jenney, whom the Society had sent to Philadelphia as curate, but got himself involved in an unsavory scandal. It is impossible to say certainly whether or not the charges brought against him were true, but the preponderance of evidence seems to indicate that they were. The neighboring clergy believed them, and so did a number of the laity, but the vestry did not, and a temporary schism resulted in the parish, as those who did believe declined to attend Phillips' ministrations. In order to keep this faction from leaving the Church altogether, the neighboring clergy preached to them by turns until 1716 when the return of Evans and the departure of Phillips healed the breach.

Evans retired in 1718 and Jenney was transferred to New York the same year, so that the parish again had to be supplied by its neighbors until the Rev. John Vicary was sent by the Bishop of London in 1719. Vicary held the post until his death in 1723, when the unfortunate parish was again exposed to an ecclesiastical scandal. Vicary had been ill during the last year of his life, and the parish was supplied for a time by the Rev. William Harrison. When the latter moved to Staten Island, the vestry obtained the

Trouble with
Urmiston

services of John Urmiston, whose career in South Carolina and in Maryland has already been mentioned. The vice of drunkenness, with which Urmiston was charged in those two colonies, had by now become habitual with him, and it was not very long before the vestry was obliged to dismiss him. He departed into Maryland, whence he wrote to the Society charging John Talbot with being responsible for his removal and accusing him both of being a "Jacobite" and of having obtained episcopal consecration from the Nonjurors. He also made a complaint against Christ Church which showed that a rather high standard of Church life was maintained there. "I was not sorry," he said, "for my removal from so precarious and slavish a place, where they require two sermons every Lord's Day, prayers all the week, and homilies on festivals, besides abundance of funerals, Christenings at home, and sick to be visited."

After getting rid of Urmiston, the vestry asked Talbot to come to restore order, and then employed his friend, Dr. Richard Welton, a Nonjuror, until 1726 when Governor Keith expelled him from the colony. Bishop Gibson had delayed sending a successor to Vicary for three years, possibly because too many other matters claimed his attention at his first coming to the See of London. The shock of learning that a Nonjuror had actually been employed in the parish roused him to action, however, and in 1726 he sent the Rev. Archibald Cummings to Philadelphia as rector and Commissary, in which positions he served acceptably until 1741. In the latter part of Cummings' rectorate, the Rev. Richard Peters was called as his assistant, but after a time he resigned, because of a disagreement with the rector, and took up the practice of law, for which he had originally been trained, becoming secretary to the land office, and later Secretary of the colony. When Cummings died, the vestry petitioned London to license Peters as their rector, but his request was refused, and Robert Jenney was sent back to them instead. Jenney served as rector for twenty years, and when he died the Bishop at last agreed to accept Peters, who, by then, had become one of the leading men of the colony. During his incumbency, which lasted until the Revolution, the parish was, for the first time, granted a corporate charter.

By 1761 the number of Churchmen resident in Philadelphia had

St. Peter's
Church

increased sufficiently so that a second Church was required, and a new congregation, that of St. Peter's, was organized by the vestry of Christ Church. When the building was completed, it was decided that the two parishes should be placed upon an exactly equal footing, being subject to a united vestry and served by the same ministers with an equal claim upon them. The pews in the two churches were to rent for the same amounts, and the pewholders to have equal rights in voting for the vestry. It was at first contemplated to put all of the ministers on an equal footing also, but this policy was abandoned. The arrangement thus worked out was a mean between the system which prevailed at Boston of having the several churches entirely independent of one another, and that employed in New York, where the chapels were kept subordinate to the main parish.

St. Paul's
Church

In 1759 William McClennachan, who had deserted the Society's mission on the Kennebec, arrived in Philadelphia and induced the vestry to elect him assistant minister without the consent of the rector. He belonged to the Methodist party—probably to the Whitefieldian wing—and according to Dr. Smith, he was both a "quack doctor and a quack preacher," having come to the colonies equipped with the remedies of one Dr. Ward, which remedies he hoped to sell to the inhabitants. Because of the opposition of Smith and Jenney, he was unable to obtain a license for his post either from London or Canterbury and had to withdraw. He took with him, however, a part of the congregation, whom he organized into St. Paul's Church. He remained with them only two years, but the parish continued, though for many years its history was an uneasy one.

College of
Philadelphia

The organization of the College (originally an academy) at Philadelphia was mainly the work of Franklin, though he was assisted by Richard Peters, and others. Franklin was anxious to obtain the services of Samuel Johnson of Stratford, later of King's College, as head of the institution, but the latter declined, and in 1749 the Academy started work with the Rev. David Martin as rector. He died in 1751 and William Smith, who had lately arrived in New York and had published a pamphlet telling how he would run a college, was offered, on trial, the post of instructor in natural philosophy, logic, and kindred subjects. He seems all his life to have possessed the knack of winning the favor of influential people, and he had not been long in Philadelphia before Franklin and Peters decided to make him rector of the Academy, if the necessary funds could be obtained. These were presently forthcoming from Thomas Penn, the proprietor. Smith went to England in 1753 to obtain orders, and returned in 1754 to become head of the Academy. In 1755 it was rechartered as a college, and he became its first provost. Both Franklin and Smith were men of broad religious views, though Smith's were probably not so hazy as the former's, and they saw to it that no religious test should ever be required of either the students or faculty of the College, which was placed upon a strictly non-denominational basis. In 1762 Smith went to England to raise money for the College, with results which we have seen. He also was successful in raising some money for it in the southern colonies.

He quarreled with Franklin—or Franklin with him—after a few years, and the latter thereafter gave but cool support to the College. Their dispute was primarily political, as Smith supported the party of the proprietors, which Franklin opposed, but it was given a personal animus by Smith's support of the claim made by Franklin's co-worker, Ebenezer Kinnersley, to be the chief discoverer of electricity. Smith's political views also got him into trouble with the Quaker party and in 1758 the Assembly put him in jail for contempt in printing the defense of a judge, William Moore, whom they had impeached. The chastisement proved on the whole a blessing, for it led to a marriage with the judge's daughter which was apparently a happy one, and gained for Smith the sympathy of the proprietors and others in England who were familiar with the case.

William Smith was one of the most brilliant of the provincial clergy and he exercised a great and constructive influence upon the history of the Church both during the colonial period and in the epoch of reorganization. Like most brilliant men he was ambitious, and one cannot escape the feeling that self-interest generally played a rather important part among the motives that influenced his conduct. In his later years he became rather avaricious, and engaged in land speculations which were more successful than such ventures usually are. Nevertheless, he worked hard to advance the interests both of religion and learning on this continent, and he took a broader and more statesmanlike view of

Character of
Provost Smith

the needs of the Church in America than most of his contemporaries were able to attain. His advice was sought and valued by Archbishop Secker and by the Society, and it is probable that the shift in the latter's policy away from its over-emphasis on New England, which became increasingly apparent in the decades immediately preceding the Revolution, was due, at least in part, to Smith's repeated insistence upon the needs of the frontier.

Work Among the Germans

While Smith was in England seeking ordination, in 1753, he published a pamphlet setting forth the educational needs of the Germans who had recently come into Pennsylvania in large numbers, some of them from Hunter's abortive settlement in New York, but most of them direct from Germany, where Penn had advertised his colony extensively. They had, for the most part, gone into what was then the western part of the colony, and like most settlers, had experienced a serious cultural decline on reaching the frontier. Smith feared that they would either sink into barbarism or fall under the influence of the French and give up their nominal allegiance to England. He proposed the organization of a system of free schools in the western district where English and German settlers should learn the rudiments of education side by side, with a view to their eventual assimilation. The scheme was carried out in part by the organization in 1754 of the Society for Propagating Knowledge among the Germans of Pennsylvania, with Smith, Franklin, Peters, and other prominent colonials as trustees. The scheme was dependent upon support from England, and interest in it over there faded rapidly after the departure of its gifted advocate. It died in a few years for want of adequate support, but while it lasted, it did good work. Had it been continued, some of the primitive folkways now associated with the "Pennsylvania Dutch" might never have developed.

The Frontier

In 1758 the Society for the Propagation of the Gospel decided to do something for the Pennsylvania frontier, and sent the Rev. Thomas Barton into York and Cumberland counties. He later moved his headquarters eastward to Lancaster, but continued to serve the southwestern part of the colony until the Revolution. Dr. Smith credited him, together with two Presbyterian ministers, with having kept the people together and prevented the region from being deserted during the French and Indian War. In 1761 a missionary was sent to Carlisle.

Delaware was, of course, under the jurisdiction of the government of Pennsylvania during most of the colonial period, and the Delaware history of the Church there is really a phase of its growth in the smaller towns of the larger colony. The first mission in Delaware was organized at New Castle in 1704, and the Rev. George Ross was sent to supply it. He proved restless at first, and made an attempt to obtain a better living elsewhere, but after a while he settled down to a long and devoted ministry. In 1719 he declined an offer of the rectorate at Philadelphia because he could not obtain a successor for New Castle. In 1705 a minister was sent to Dover. In 1717 Ross went with Governor Keith on a visit to Sussex County and found that at Lewes and elsewhere there were loyal Churchmen who met together to hear services read by a lay reader and postponed the baptism of their children until a Church minister visited them. In 1722 a missionary was sent to the county. He reported that the Churchmen formed the largest religious body at Lewes. The presence of Charles Inglis at Dover has already been mentioned in connection with his removal to New York. While at Dover he endeavored with some success to curb the practice of getting the electorate drunk at political meetings. He preached near the meeting places, and persuaded some of the leading candidates to stay away. He told the Society that before he began this reform, Churchmen were the worst offenders.

The first missionary of the Church in New Jersey was the Rev. Alexander Innes, formerly chaplain at New York, and a Non- New Jersey juror, who assembled a congregation in Monmouth County at the beginning of the eighteenth century, and preached there for some time, but his work in that section was not followed up until the latter part of the century. Keith and Talbot both preached in New Jersey and Talbot settled at Burlington in 1703, whence he continued to visit the other parts of the colony whenever he could. An attempt had been made in East Jersey in 1697 to provide public support for ministers, though not specifically those of the Church, but it was defeated by the Baptists and Quakers. The next year, the proprietors, who were Quakers, appointed Jeremiah Bass as governor, with instructions to oppose such a measure. Bass later became one of the chief supporters of the Church at Burlington, but at this time he was a Baptist.

In 1705 the Society sent two missionaries, John Brooke and

Thorogood Moore, to New Jersey. They were both devoted young men, and their work had a promising beginning. Brooke catechized twelve to fifteen days a month, and visited the other days, by which method he rapidly assembled congregations in the villages which he served. Moore, however, made the mistake of supposing that the great of this world were as amenable to ecclesiastical discipline as the lowly. While in New York, on his way to New Jersey, he publicly expressed the opinion that the local clergy ought to excommunicate Cornbury for masquerading in women's clothes. After he had arrived in New Jersey, he put his theories into practice by excommunicating Lieutenant-Governor Ingoldsby, whose manner of life was only a little less notorious than his superior's. He was also suspected of being too friendly with Lewis Morris, the leader of the opposition to Cornbury. When Cornbury visited Moore's station in New Jersey and desired to receive Communion, the missionary found it necessary to visit a village twelve miles away. This was the last straw, and Moore was carried a prisoner to Fort Anne in New York. Brooke promptly went to the same place and helped his colleague to escape. They fled to Massachusetts, whence they took ship for England. The ship was lost on the way over, and they were heard from no more.

Their departure left Talbot once more the only Church minister in New Jersey. In 1709 John Bartow of Westchester visited the colony and found that many congregations might be formed if there were ministers, but that the people showed no disposition to support them. In the same year the Society sent Edward Vaughan to the colony and he was followed by Thomas Halliday a little later. The two missionaries did not like each other very well at first, and they sent back numerous complaints against one another to the secretary. Halliday seems to have suffered from a violent temper, and to have been a bit too fond of "the bottle." He also got himself mixed up in the political disputes of the colony, though, for that matter, it was practically impossible to keep out of them. In 1714 the people at Amboy (now Perth Amboy), one of his stations, carried away all of the furnishings of the church and told him to get out, as he was a "knave and a villain." On the advice of his brethren, he took this as a hint that he was not wanted, and confined his efforts to Piscataqua and

Hopewell, his other stations. Eventually, he came to terms with Vaughan, and the two agreed to rotate among the missions of the colony, except Burlington, where Talbot was still stationed. By 1718 Halliday's vices had grown upon him so much as to become a scandal, and he was obliged to leave New Jersey.

Talbot, all this time, had been serving quietly and devotedly at Burlington, and doing what he could to settle the difficulties that arose from time to time in the other parts of the colony, and at Philadelphia. In 1724 he stated that he was accustomed to read Morning and Evening Prayer daily in his church, and thought he was the only minister in America who did so. In 1718 a school-master was sent to his parish. Urmiston's charges against Talbot in 1724 climaxed a long series of accusations that he was a "Jacobite" and led to his dismissal, the specific offense alleged against him being that of "exercising jurisdiction over his brethren," which he denied doing. He stayed at Burlington, however, during the few years that remained of his life. In 1727 he was succeeded by Nathaniel Harwood.

Dismissal of Talbot

After Halliday's departure, Vaughan remained at Elizabeth, and the Rev. William Skinner was sent to Perth Amboy and Piscataqua (Piscataway). In 1722 the inhabitants of Salem, in south-western New Jersey, petitioned for a minister and John Holbrook was sent them. The county officials of Monmouth had petitioned for a missionary, in 1717, saying that libertinism was rife in the county and that the ministers of other denominations could do nothing to curb it, but they thought that a Church minister might. In spite of this flattering request nothing was done for them, nor was any more attention paid to a second petition in 1729, at which time there were no ministers of any sort in the county, except one or two Quaker teachers. It was not until 1734 that the Society sent a missionary to the county where the services of the Church had first been heard in New Jersey.

Growth of the Church in New Jersey

Vaughan and William Harrison of Staten Island organized a church at Newark in the early thirties and the mission continued to be supplied by the missionaries in New Jersey or on the island until 1751, when a resident missionary was appointed to the post. Vaughan died in 1747 and the vestry at Elizabeth employed a local youth, Thomas Bradbury Chandler, as catechist and lay reader until he was old enough to be ordained, whereupon he became

Thomas
Bradbury
Chandler

their minister and served them until a few years after the Revolution, though his Tory sympathies drove him from the county while the struggle was going on. His championship of the colonial episcopate in the sixties made him one of the more prominent of the American clergy and he was the first choice of the Society for Bishop of Nova Scotia, but was obliged to decline because of ill health. As father-in-law of Bishop Hobart, he may have had some influence in forming the ideals of later American High Churchmanship.

CHAPTER VII

"Infidels, Bond and Free"

Ｈ OW MANY infidels, bond and free, are there in your parish, and what is done for their conversion?" was one of the questions which Bishop Gibson asked of all the colonial ministers in 1724, and, we are sorry to say, most of them were not able to give the question a very satisfactory answer. The comparative indifference shown in the colonial period by all religious denominations, except the Roman Catholics and the Moravians, to the conversion of the Indians who were found upon the continent and of the negroes who were brought to it, is one of the most remarkable features of our religious history. A few devoted individuals, such as John Eliot and Eleazer Wheelock did, it is true, give their lives to the work, and societies for the promotion of such efforts were occasionally projected and even organized, but very little persistent work was done by any denomination as a whole, with the exception of the two mentioned.

General Indifference to the Conversion of the Indians and Negroes

Among the rest, though this is faint praise, the Church of England had probably as honorable a record as any other. She did not accomplish a great deal, and her efforts can hardly be said to have been proportionate to her resources, but she did keep pecking at the task more or less steadily, and in the end she achieved something. The Society for the Propagation of the Gospel generally had somebody ministering to the Mohawks—eventually with success—and it sent one or two missionaries to other tribes at different times. It also urged its regular missionaries repeatedly to do what they could for any negroes or Indians that might be in their parishes, and its proddings were seconded from time to time by the Bishops of London and the Archbishops of Canterbury. Archbishop Secker, who took a sincere interest in everything relating to the spiritual welfare of the colonies, concerned himself with

Efforts of the Church

this problem quite a bit, and corresponded with a number of leading colonials on schemes for the evangelization of the Indians, but none of the proposals discussed came to much. Even the civil authorities took an interest in the matter occasionally, and in 1715 the Commissioners of Trade and Plantations wrote to the Bishop of London that they had learned that "several nations of Indians have been desirous of Protestant missionaries to instruct them in the true religion." Their chief concern was that the missionaries sent over should be persons "of unspotted characters, and whose lives and conversations ought to be unblamable," by which they apparently meant that they should be of the right political complexion, for the Commissioners objected specifically to John Talbot, whose life and conversation, when viewed from any but a partisan standpoint, were about as unblamable as any man's could be.

Thanks to the promptings of the Society and the Bishops, a little was done for the Indians in almost every colony where they existed in any great number. As we have already seen, there is reason to believe that the earliest ministers in Virginia had succeeded in converting a few of them by the time of the colony's first Indian War. The first project for the College there contemplated the education of Indians as well as whites, and when that institution was at length established, earnest and partly successful efforts were made to get Indian youths to attend it. These endeavors were stimulated by a legacy left by Robert Boyle for the purpose of educating Indians at the College, and were energetically encouraged by Governors Nicholson and Spottswood.

In 1710 Nicholson sent Robert Hicks and John Evans as agents to inform the neighboring Indians of Boyle's legacy and to try to obtain nine or ten children for instruction. The Indians were to be assured that the children would be clothed and well treated, and that their parents might visit them whenever they wished. They should also have an Indian man with them, to wait upon them and to talk with them in Indian, so that they would not forget the language of their people while they were at the College. These provisions show a more intelligent approach to the Indian problem than was generally made by colonial officials, but it cannot be said that the Indians received the offer with enthusiasm. Their family feeling was strong, they were suspicious of the English and they were not particularly hospitable to English culture, except in the

(margin note) Work Among the Indians in Virginia

matter of firearms and rum. In the end it was only by agreeing to relinquish the tribute money that the Indians had been accustomed to pay that the governor obtained a number of children for the College. Nicholson also projected the founding of a chapel and mission house, and the employment of a missionary and interpreter among the Indians, but these plans had not been brought to fruition when he was recalled.

Spottswood took as much interest in the conversion of the Indians as his predecessor. He visited the tributary tribes and some of the more remote ones personally, and sought to persuade them to send their children to the College. In 1712 he reported that there were fourteen Indians attending, and that he expected six more from the neighboring tribes. He also established a preparatory school for them at his own expense. In 1716 Spottswood sent the Rev. Charles Griffin to the frontier to instruct the Indian children. Griffin soon assembled seventy pupils and succeeded in teaching them the Creed, the Lord's Prayer, the Ten Commandments, the existence of but one God, the names of the Three Persons, and what each had done for them. He also reported that they behaved reverently at prayers and were able to make the responses. After Spottswood's retirement, interest in the Indians, except as potential enemies, seems to have lagged, and we hear little of their presence at the College, or of missionaries being sent to them. The feeling between the two races was growing more hostile and the College was prospering as a place for educating planters' sons, who probably were not very anxious to associate on terms of equality with the aborigines.

Interest of Governor Spottswood

In South Carolina, though little was actually done for the conversion of the Indians, the problem was frequently discussed. As we have already seen, the Society had originally intended that its first missionary in the colony, Samuel Thomas, should work among the Indians, but Governor Johnson, for reasons best known to himself, sent him to Goose Creek instead. His successor at that station, the devoted Francis Le Jau, took an active interest in the welfare of the Indians. He conversed with them whenever he had the opportunity, endeavored conscientiously to understand and appreciate their ideas and standards, and frequently urged the Society to send a missionary among them. He stated that they "do make us ashamed by their life, conversation, and sense of religion

The Indian Problem in South Carolina

quite different from ours." "Ours," he said, "consists in words and appearance; theirs, in reality." He thought that if the Indians could be made to understand what was meant by the words commonly used in speaking of religion, they would appear "other than imagined," for he discovered that, as he gained their confidence and came to understand their terminology, they disclosed "surprising things" about their faith—things, apparently, which showed a closer approximation to Christianity than was generally supposed. He believed that the chief obstacle to their conversion would be the manner in which the Indian trade was carried on, as it consisted chiefly in fomenting wars among them for the purpose of getting slaves.

Commissary Johnston also took some interest in the Indian problem. In 1710 he reported that the Indian traders with whom he had conversed had told him that it would not be difficult to convert the Indians to Christianity, and he himself felt, like Le Jau, that the chief difficulty would be in the misconduct of these same traders. The next year, he got himself appointed a Commissioner for Indian Affairs, in the hope of learning more about them, but whatever knowledge he acquired thereby did not lead to any practical result. In 1714 a resident of the colony wrote to a friend of the Society that he had a son whom he designed for the ministry and that he proposed sending him among a neighboring tribe of Yamassees to learn their language and instruct them in Christianity, but it seems probable that he changed his mind, for nothing more can be learned concerning the project. In 1723 Francis Varnod, the missionary at Dorchester, South Carolina, wrote to the Secretary that he thought the conversion of the Indians a practicable object and suggested sending a discreet young man in deacon's orders to live among them. Like Le Jau, he had formed a good opinion of the Indian character. "I find," he said, ". . . that these poor pagans are endued with very good natural parts, of a temper very sedate and tranquil, and quite opposite to that hot and violent spirit of the negroes." Again, however, the matter ended in suggestion.

Other Southern Colonies

What was done for the Indians in the other southern colonies cannot be described as anything more than a gesture. Giles Rainsford, one of the Society's missionaries in North Carolina, spent a few months among the Indians there in 1714, and obtained some knowledge of their language, on the strength of which he offered himself as minister at an Indian settlement projected by Governor Spottswood of Virginia. The governor's plans never matured, however, and Rainsford's services were employed elsewhere. A later North Carolina missionary reported in 1722 that the Indians in the colony had been reduced to three hundred fighting men, with the usual complement of non-combatants, and he thought there was little chance of their conversion. In Maryland, to judge from the answers of the clergy to Bishop Gibson's questions, nothing was done for the Indians because their language was unintelligible, and they were hostile to Christianity anyway. The marriage of Thomas Bosomworth of Georgia with a squaw in 1745 doubtless showed an interest of some sort in the Indians, but one may be permitted to question whether it proceeded from a missionary spirit, though Bosomworth said it did. Samuel Frink, the minister at Augusta, made some effort to convert the Chickasaw Indians in 1766, but without success. He observed that he thought it desirable to reclaim the white people of the colony first, as he found them "almost as destitute of any sense of religion as the Indians themselves."

In Pennsylvania the only attempt to convert the Indians seems to have been that made by Thomas Barton on his first coming into the western counties. He had hopes of succeeding in the endeavor, but they were dashed when Braddock's defeat alienated the Indians from the English. Dr. Smith took an interest in the Indian question but he was not in a position to do anything himself. In New Jersey there were but few Indians, and nothing was done for them. *Pennsylvania and New Jersey*

In New England attempts to convert the Indians, with the exception of those who lived as slaves or otherwise within the limits of the regular parishes, were infrequent and spasmodic, and even when the Indians themselves expressed the desire for a missionary, they were not supplied with one. In 1727 some of the missionaries succeeded in converting Charles Augustus Ninaagret, the chief sachem of the Narragansetts. Ninaagret asked the Society to send a missionary to his people, but this was not done, though the neighboring ministers may have worked among them from time to time. In 1742 Stephen Roe, the assistant at King's Chapel, visited Maine with the governor of Massachusetts, who had gone there to make a treaty with the Indians. French missionaries had been *New England* working among these tribes, and Roe found many of the Indians wearing crucifixes, whereupon he took occasion to warn them against the sinfulness of "image worship and prayers to saints and angels." In 1745 the Society apparently had some intention of sending a missionary to the Moskito Indians, for Samuel Johnson wrote that he did not know of any minister who was willing to go there, but that Mr. Prince, the schoolmaster at Stratford, would be willing to do so. The project was evidently given up, however, for neither Prince, nor anyone else, was appointed. In 1756 the Mohican Indians asked the Society for a share in the services of the missionary at Norwich, and this was probably granted them. At the outbreak of the Revolution the Commissioners for Indian Affairs in New England were employing a minister of the Church as missionary among the Cheroche Indians in Bristol County, Rhode Island. Jacob Bailey, the devoted missionary on the Kennebec, found that the ravages of war had left only about fifty Indians (the remnant of the once powerful Norridgewolk tribe) in that region in 1765. Like Roe, he also found that they had been under French influence and were averse to Protestantism and English customs.

It was in New York that the most persistent and effective work was done among the Indians. The Iroquois, whose territory extended over most of the colony west of Albany, reaching down into Pennsylvania, and including tributaries in New England and the South, were the only important body of Indians who were consistently friendly to the English, Champlain's muskets having secured their attachment to any power that opposed the French. Their allegiance was, moreover, of vital importance, for they guarded the otherwise exposed frontier of New York, which formed the natural gateway from Canada into the English colonies. There were, therefore, excellent practical reasons for seeking to attach these people to the national faith of England, but it is not necessary to assume that this was the only motive for sending missionaries among them, or even that it was the predominant one. We have just seen that the Society was anxious to do what it could for the conversion of the Indians everywhere, even though its efforts may not always have been as energetic as could be wished, and the greater friendliness of the Iroquois offered a more

Work Among the Iroquois in New York

encouraging prospect for work among them than was to be found elsewhere.

Moreover, the Dutch ministers at Albany had already made a successful beginning among the Mohawks, who were then the easternmost of the Five Nations which made up the Iroquois Confederacy. Their work had been started when the colony belonged to the Netherlands, and was continued after the English occupation until 1702 when Lord Bellomont, the governor, forbade Godfrey Delius, the then pastor at Albany, to go on with the work. In the following year Robert Livingston, the Indian agent, submitted to the Society for the Propagation of the Gospel a plan for converting the Iroquois by sending a missionary to each of the nations. A house and stockade were to be built for each minister and Livingston further suggested that each should bring with him two boys to learn the language and act as interpreters, as well as a supply of presents to win over the Indians. He also recommended that, as the Dutch ministers at Albany had done good work among the Indians, Delius, as their present representative, should be given a stipend by the Society. With this last suggestion the Society complied, and Delius was offered a place on its rolls. He declined, partly because he still harbored resentment at the ill usage which he had received from Bellomont, and partly because he had become convinced that work among the Indians could not achieve any permanent success until the traders were prevented from supplying them with rum. At the same time he warned the Society that the Jesuits were becoming active among the Iroquois, and that something must be done soon if the tribes were not to be lost to England.

It was, however, several years before anyone was sent to take over Delius' work. Daniel Bondet, the French minister at New Rochelle, is said by his brother clergy to have done successful work among the neighboring Indians, but these, presumably, were not Iroquois. In 1709, as was stated in the preceding chapter, Thomas Barclay was sent to Albany by the Society for the purpose of ministering both to the whites and the Indians. He found that there were about thirty Indians who were communicants of the Dutch Church, but he observed that they were ignorant and not very virtuous in their way of living. Nevertheless, he set to work to bring them into the Church of England, and eventually he

Thomas Barclay

succeeded in doing so. Three years after his arrival he paid a visit to the Mohawk village, which was some distance from Albany, and rebuked the Indians for profaning the chapel there, some of them having used it for a slaughterhouse.

In 1710 the Indian chiefs had asked that a missionary should be sent to live among their people, and late in the fall of 1712 the Rev. William Andrews arrived at the Mohawk village in answer to their petition. Andrews was evidently a sincere and earnest man, but he had but little realization of the delicacy of the task that confronted him, and very little understanding of or sympathy for the people to whom he was sent. He gave no heed to the first rule of all missionary work, to present the milk of the Gospel before the strong meat, but started in at once to instruct the Indians in all of the major tenets of Christian theology, "the Doctrine of God, of the Creation, of providence, of Man's fall and restoration, of faith, repentance and the nature of the sacraments," even going so far as to project a course of lectures upon the catechism.

As might be expected, the Indians proved unresponsive to teachings which they could but dimly understand, especially as they were forced, in the beginning at least, to hear them through an interpreter. In 1715 Andrews reported that he had about twenty Indian children in his school, but that he had to bribe them with food to keep them there. He still clung to the belief, however, that a few of the Indians were sincere Christians. Eventually it would seem that the Mohawks decided to have fun with the good man, for some of them told him that they would come to his services if he would give them a draft of rum, and others expressed the opinion that baptism was all that was required to make anyone a good Christian. One man, whom he had excommunicated for drunkenness, sabbath-breaking, "cruelty in biting off a prisoner's nails," and other offenses, threatened to shoot him. He carried on, in spite of discouragements, for seven years, but eventually he became convinced that the Indians could never be converted, and resigned.

Andrews' departure was followed, two years later, by Barclay's madness, and it was some time before either Albany or the Indians had another missionary. John Miln arrived at Albany in 1728, and the next year he visited the Mohawks. He administered the communion to ten, and baptized three Indian and two English

William
Andrews

Other
Missionaries

children in the village. Thereafter, until the appointment of a missionary especially for them, he made a practice of visiting the Indians four times a year. In spite of Andrews' experience, he found them well disposed towards Christianity, and was greeted joyfully on every visit. In 1735 the Indians were once more given a missionary of their own—or mostly of their own—for Henry Barclay was sent to Fort Hunter chiefly to minister to them, though there were now a few white settlers in that region, and their number was presently increased by the coming of a group of Irish Protestants. Barclay also made a beginning in the conversion of the Oneidas, the next tribe westward.

When Barclay became rector of Trinity Church, New York City, the Rev. John Ogilvie was sent to take over his work among the Indians. Ogilvie does not seem to have undertaken his task in any very optimistic spirit, but he persisted in it for some years. He complained that, though the Indians would behave fairly well when he was present, he would no sooner leave them than they would set upon an orgy of drunkenness, and that the dissolute lives led by most of the traders made a very bad impression upon the aborigines. In 1760 he was compelled to go as chaplain with General Amherst's expedition against Canada. On his return, he became assistant at Trinity, New York.

After a vacancy of some duration, Albany and the Indian fort were again placed under the care of a single man, the Rev. Henry Munro. In his first report, Munro urged the importance of separating the two missions, and in this he was vigorously supported by Sir William Johnson, the Indian agent, who thought ministers should be stationed at Albany, Schenectady, Johnstown, and the Mohawk village. Johnson also urged the establishment of a school for the Indians similar to that which Eleazer Wheelock was building at Hanover, New Hampshire (now Dartmouth College). Archbishop Secker, to whom he made this suggestion, had at first been in favor of sending Indian youths to Wheelock's school (which had received numerous contributions from English Churchmen), with a view to their being episcopally ordained after completing the courses, but East Apthorp, the missionary at Cambridge, assured him that if this were done, all would turn out to be Presbyterians. Secker was much alarmed at such a

Sir William
Johnson

prospect, and on his advice the Society planned to set up a rival school. Nothing came of the project, however.

In 1770 Myles Cooper and Charles Inglis paid a visit to Johnson during which they were interviewed by a deputation of Mohawks who earnestly solicited a missionary, complaining that the Roman Catholic Indians of Canada, who had formerly been enemies of the English, had been allowed to have a minister, but they, who had always been friendly, had none. This petition was duly transmitted to the Society by Inglis and Cooper, and the next year that body finally succeeded in sending out a missionary. He was the Rev. John Stuart, and he had not been long at Fort Hunter before it became apparent that the Society had at last found a man who was ideally fitted for the post. He had, of course, a great advantage over other missionaries in the support of Johnson, who probably exercised a greater influence over the Indians than any other Englishman in colonial times, and he was to some extent able to build upon the foundations laid by his predecessors, but the rapidity with which he worked himself into the affections of a proud and shy people is, nevertheless, remarkable. Even before he had learned their language, Stuart was able to persuade them to repair their chapel, and, with the aid of the sachems, he had considerable success in suppressing drunkenness. When the Revolutionary War came along, the Indians promised him their protection if he would stay with them, and they did protect him until they themselves were driven out by the colonial forces.

The infidels in bonds were mostly negroes, though quite a number of Indians were also enslaved in colonial times. They presented a different problem from the free natives, and at first sight it might seem that, as they were settled among Christians and were subject to Christian masters, their conversion would have been much easier. This, in all probability, would have been the case if their masters had taken any interest in promoting such conversion but, except in a very few cases, the best that the ministers could hope for was that the masters would be indifferent to it. Normally they opposed it for various reasons. It is, obviously, a little difficult to take a benevolent interest in a man's future blessedness when you are energetically endeavoring to make him exist wholly for your benefit in this present life. Later on, when slavery had existed long enough so that people regarded it as the

John Stuart

The Negroes

natural state of the negro, the attitude of the master towards his servants might be, and frequently was, tinctured with honest benevolence, but at first, when the still savage African had to be terrorized into submission, such an attitude was difficult. Moreover, there was, at the beginning of the eighteenth century, a widely prevalent fear, based upon some provisions of mediæval canon law, that any slave who became a Christian could claim his freedom. James I had solemnly announced that this was not so in the preceding century, and various laws were passed to the same effect, but it took a long time to eradicate the belief. Difficulties of Conversion

The planters also maintained, in some cases, that slaves who had been converted were more difficult to control. This opinion was probably based largely on prejudice, for at a later time it was discovered that Christian negroes made better slaves, and piety became a virtue to be stressed upon the auction block. That development took place, however, after the negroes had become more used to servitude, when it was easier to persuade them that submission was a Christian duty.

Even when the master's permission had been obtained, and the negro converted, the problem was only half solved. As the slave was not a free agent, it was often impossible for him to lead a Christian life, even if he wished to do so. After his conversion he might be sold to a master who would deny him any religious privileges at all, or failing this, he might still be compelled to do many things which were inconsistent with his profession. Moreover, so few pleasures were allowed him that it was very hard to turn away from any that he could enjoy, even when it happened to be sinful. Especially did the ministers find it difficult to bring the negroes to observe any regularity in their sexual relations. Whatever traditional customs they had had in this, or in any other respect, had been hopelessly destroyed by the interruption of all of their habitual relationships which necessarily resulted from their transplantation, and it was difficult for them to restrain a desire which their masters were glad to see them indulge, since its products were economically valuable. Even if they did marry and endeavor to be faithful to one another, there was always the possibility that husband and wife might be sold to opposite ends of the colony.

In spite of these difficulties, however, fairly persistent efforts were made by the colonial ministers for the conversion of the negroes, and in some instances with a certain amount of success. In New York and Philadelphia the Society for the Propagation of the Gospel maintained catechists especially to instruct the negroes, and their efforts seem to have produced satisfactory results. The New York catechist was Elias Neau, a French Huguenot refugee, who, before coming to this country, had suffered imprisonment for his faith. While in his dungeon, he had comforted himself by learning the liturgy of the Church of England, and after coming to this country he conformed to that Church. Though he was a layman and a merchant, his interest in the welfare of the negroes led to his appointment as the Society's catechist in 1704. Vesey, though he held a high opinion of Neau's personal character, disapproved of this appointment, because he thought the catechist should at least be in deacon's orders, and told Neau that he had no right to officiate unless he obtained a special license from the Bishop of London. Cornbury, however, said that this was not necessary, and himself gave Neau a license.

The results of his efforts proved encouraging, though Vesey remained cool towards him, and most of the masters were not over-enthusiastic. The Dutch minister preached in favor of his instructions, and that helped him somewhat. When Jenney was sent as assistant and schoolmaster at Trinity, he for a time superseded Neau, but a number of prominent laymen petitioned for the latter's restoration, and the work was given back to him in 1719. He was finally succeeded by Wetmore in 1723, and thereafter the teaching was continued by the assistant at Trinity, until 1760, when the Bray Associates, an organization formed by admirers of Thomas Bray, founded a negro school in New York.

Some work, though not a great deal, was also done among the negroes in other parts of New York. Thomas Barclay reported from Albany in 1717 that he was having success in instructing the slaves there and Miln stated in 1730 that John Beasley, the schoolmaster at the same place, in addition to his work with the white children, had instructed twenty negroes in the catechism. Thomas Standard, who was missionary at Westchester in 1729, bought two negroes whom he hoped to instruct in Christianity but charges which were brought against his moral character forced his removal shortly afterwards, so nothing came of his plan. Robert

Charlton reported from Staten Island in 1746 that he found the practice of singing the psalms increased the attentiveness of the negroes, and their desire to learn to read. In New Jersey the Rev. Abraham Beach worked conscientiously on behalf of the negroes and was able to report a respectable number of baptisms.

The catechist at Philadelphia was the Rev. William Sturgeon, who was not appointed until 1747. As he was in priest's orders, William it was also expected that he would assist Robert Jenney at Christ Sturgeon Church, and he performed both functions in a satisfactory manner. Though he was dismissed by the Society in 1763 on charges of neglecting his duties, he vindicated himself and was reinstated. He retired in 1766, when his work was taken over by the Bray Associates, who continued to support it until 1804. In New Jersey, John Holbrook, the minister at Salem, reported in 1724 that he had asked the masters to send their negroes to him for catechizing, but it does not appear that his request met with much response. Samuel Cooke, the minister at Shrewsbury, Monmouth County, reported baptizing two negroes in 1752.

It was in the South that the need for instructing the slaves was greatest, and there it constituted a most pressing problem for Virginia every parish priest, though, for reasons already stated, many of them were able to make but a poor shift at dealing with it. When the clergy of Virginia answered Bishop Gibson's queries in 1724, most of them reported that they would catechize and instruct the slaves whenever their masters permitted, but they also indicated that this was done in only a minority of cases. In the same year a proposal was offered to encourage the conversion of the slaves by providing that every slave child who was baptized and properly instructed in the Christian religion before he was ten, should be exempt from all taxes until he was eighteen, but this suggestion did not commend itself to the legislature. In 1726 John Lang, a minister of the province, complained that even when people did bring their slaves to be baptized and instructed, they allowed them afterwards to live "in common without marriage or any other Christian decency." Jonathan Boucher, while serving in Virginia in 1765 and 1766, baptized a total of 418 slaves, but few of the clergy had such success, and only a minority of the slaves were christened before the Revolution.

In Maryland conditions were a little better. The answers to the

Maryland

1724 questionnaire there show that most of the clergy were accustomed to instruct the negroes with some regularity, and at a visitation held on the Eastern Shore in the same year, the ministers petitioned the Bishop to call upon the laity to instruct their slaves or have them instructed, a request with which Gibson complied by issuing a pastoral letter on the subject a little later. At visitations which he held on both shores in 1730, Commissary Henderson stated in his address, "There is one thing . . . in which we must confess we are blameworthy, both pastors and people, in that greater care is not taken about the instruction of the negroes." The next year, he questioned the clergy specifically as to what they had done to this end, saying that he himself read prayers on Sunday afternoons in summer, and catechized such negroes as would come, though the number was not so large as he wished. The rest of the clergy claimed to have made special efforts of some sort. Some complained that the masters would not coöperate, but others had had better success, had baptized many and had a few communicants. Some of these, however, complained that communicants were lost through their sale. The Rev. Arthur Holt, who came to Maryland in 1734, found his people, for the most part, "pretty well inclined to have their slaves be Christians," and baptized several negro infants within a short time of his arrival in the colony.

South
Carolina:
Work of
Le Jau

The same hostility to the conversion of their slaves was shown by the planters in South Carolina as elsewhere, but a few of the ministers, by patient effort, had considerable success in overcoming it. The most effective work in this respect was done by Francis Le Jau, the minister at Goose Creek. He obtained the permission of most of the masters in his parish to instruct their slaves, though some were not very cordial about it, and as a result he was able to baptize many slaves and admit a few to Communion. He had to overcome quite a bit of opposition in the process, however. One woman expressed dismay at the thought that any of her slaves might go to heaven, where, as she flattered herself, she would have to see them, and a young man refused to come to Communion if slaves were admitted to the rail. The weather also worked against Le Jau, for the extremity of the temperature in one direction or another frequently kept him from going out. Nevertheless, thanks to his efforts, his successor was able to report eighteen black in addition to seventeen white communicants in 1761.

One of the most frequent objections made to the conversion of the slaves in the early years of the century was, as has already been noted, that they would be free if they became Christians. To silence this objection the South Carolina legislature in 1712 passed an act which permitted slaves to be baptized, but provided definitely that such an action should not make them free. This removed the difficulties under that head, but it was not long before other excuses for opposing the conversion of the negroes were thought of. When the ministers of the colony sent Commissary Johnston to England in 1713 with their collection of complaints to the Society, one of their grievances was that obstacles were placed in the way of performance of their "chief duty," the conversion of the negroes. In elaborating this point, Johnston said that, under present circumstances, the conversion of the slaves was practically impossible. The slaves could be instructed only on the Lord's Day, when the minister was necessarily busy with the whites. The distance between plantations made it impossible to assemble many slaves in one place, and this would be dangerous, even if possible, because the negroes would soon learn their own strength and be tempted to revolt. Most of the masters thought Christians made poor slaves, and the legislature gave but scant encouragement to the work. Many of the planters required their slaves to keep themselves by working a garden of their own one day a week. Some would allow only Sunday for this purpose, and even if Saturday were allowed him, the slave was tempted to use the extra day.

Le Jau, as we have seen, managed to achieve satisfactory results in spite of all these difficulties, and other ministers succeeded in overcoming them to a certain extent. Ebenezer Taylor reported in 1713 that though most of the masters refused to concern themselves with the conversion of their slaves, two women of his parish had taken great pains with theirs, and a year later he stated that their efforts had led to the baptism of twenty-six. William Treadwell Bull, Johnston's successor as Commissary, reported in 1718 that every negro in his parish was baptized. Another minister reported that he had set apart Sunday afternoons for the instruction of the negroes, as they had formerly crowded the

Obstacles to Conversion of Negroes

church in such numbers as to be offensive to the whites. The negroes were grateful for his efforts, and so were their masters, who found that the slaves behaved better as a result of his instructions.

Alexander Garden, after his coming to the colony, endeavored to have a law passed requiring every master of eighty or more slaves to have one of them trained as a schoolmaster to instruct negro children, but this measure touched the pocketbooks of the planters too closely to meet with their approval. Garden therefore suggested that the Society for the Propagation of the Gospel should appoint some of the clergymen in South Carolina its agents to purchase negro boys between twelve and sixteen to be trained as catechists. His idea seemed good to the Society and it requested Garden, and two other ministers, to purchase two slave boys with whom the experiment could be tried. This particular scheme did not work out very well, as the character of the boys chosen was not so good, but Garden did succeed in establishing a successful school for negroes at Charleston.

The experiences of the missionaries in North Carolina and Georgia were substantially the same as those in the three other southern colonies. Ebenezer Taylor, who was sent into the former province from South Carolina in 1719, reported shortly after his arrival that he had baptized two negroes and could have baptized more, had not the report been circulated that those who were baptized would be freed. His early death prevented any further efforts. James Moir, who served in North Carolina for many years, claimed to have baptized three hundred whites and sixty negroes. Governor Dobbs expressed some doubt as to the justice of this claim, but whether with reason or merely because he was prejudiced against Moir is not certain. In Georgia, as we have seen, Bartholomew Zouberbuhler, who had been rector at Savannah, left money to support a schoolmaster for the negroes, and the trustees of his estate employed Cornelius Winter at this post, the duties of which he performed acceptably.

There were fewer slaves in New England than in the other colonies, but the ministers, nevertheless, did what they could for these. Timothy Cutler reported baptizing negroes at Christ Church, Boston, on several occasions, though never in large numbers. Matthias Plant reported from Newbury in 1727 that he had one negress who desired Baptism, but that her master would not permit it. In Connecticut, Christopher Newton of Ripton and Jeremiah Leaming of Norwalk reported the baptism of negroes at different times. Either there were more negroes in Rhode Island than in these other two colonies, or else more was done for them there, for we hear of more baptisms. James Honeyman, during his long ministry at Newport, took especial pains for their conversion, and with gratifying results. In 1727 he reported that there were sixty or seventy negro and Indian slaves who constantly attended public worship, and that thirteen of them were baptized. In 1742-43 he baptized five grown negroes and two negro children, and in the latter year he stated that there were one hundred negroes who attended service, and that five of them were constant communicants. At Narragansett, McSparran also worked with the negroes and persuaded several of them to desire Baptism, but he had difficulty in obtaining the consent of their masters. When Marmaduke Browne came to Newport in 1762, he opened a school for negro children, at the instance of a Society known as "The Associates of the late Dr. Bray." The next year he reported that he had thirty children of both sexes in attendance.

To sum up, it may be said that the Church of England in the colonies worked with some effect among the Mohawk Indians, and that it made spasmodic efforts for the conversion of other tribes. Among the negroes its labors were more persistent and, in spite of numerous difficulties, were attended with some success. Nevertheless, it is probable that only a very small minority of them had been reached by that or any other denomination before the Revolution.

Work of
James
Honeyman

CHAPTER VIII

THE STRUGGLE FOR THE EPISCOPATE

Early Efforts
to Obtain
Bishops

THE CAMPAIGN for resident bishops in the American plantations was carried on throughout most of the colonial period, though there were times when the issue was allowed to remain more or less quiescent. We have already alluded to Archbishop Laud's desire to bring New England into conformity with the Established Church, and it is said that in 1638 he proposed to further this end by sending over a bishop. There is also a possibility that the Commissioners sent to New England in 1664 were directed to set up bishops, but this supposition is based only upon a general rumor. In 1695, John Miller, who had been chaplain at New York, proposed that London should send a suffragan bishop to that colony to take over both the ecclesiastical and civil government, but no one took his suggestion very seriously. With the coming of the eighteenth century the struggle was placed on a broader basis, and its objectives were made more definite. During this period we can distinguish three distinct campaigns for the colonial episcopate, one initiated by the Society for the Propagation of the Gospel in the first two decades of the century, one started by the Bishop of London in the forties, and one set on foot by the colonial clergy in the sixties and seventies. In between these campaigns the issue was kept alive by occasional petitions, suggestions, and debates.

The Need for
Bishops

The reasons why bishops were needed in the colonies were obvious, and to the Churchman of the present day it would seem that they ought to have been conclusive. Whatever opinion might be held as to the theoretical necessity of bishops in a Christian Church, no one could deny that, as the Church of England was then and had always been constituted, they were essential to her complete life. The reader who has followed our narrative thus far must have become aware of how many ways there were in which her functioning in the colonies was handicapped by the lack of her leading officers. Had there been bishops in the colonies, many young men might have entered the Church who, because they were unwilling or unable to undertake the voyage to England, were forced, as things were, either to enter the service of other denominations or to continue as laymen; the many candidates who died on shipboard or in England might have been saved; and the unworthy men who thrust themselves into the ministry might have been excluded by the investigation which a resident bishop could make. Had there been bishops the immoral clergymen whose evil deeds were so often thrown in the face of the Church by her enemies would have been deposed from her ministry, and many young men whose heads were turned at finding themselves located in a strange, crude country with no one to direct them might have been kept from straying at all by a little paternal advice and authority. Had there been bishops, disputes among the clergy might have been ironed out, and disputes with the civil authorities more efficiently handled. Had there been bishops, the clergy might have been encouraged to exercise a better spiritual discipline over the laity. Had there been bishops, the Society for the Propagation of the Gospel would have had some correspondents in the colonies who were capable of taking something more than a purely local view of the Church's needs there, thus avoiding some of the mistakes and misdirections of its energies which necessarily resulted.

Why, then, were bishops not sent? Probably the best explanation is that the inherent conservatism of the English Church prevented it from evolving, until it was too late, the particular type of officer that it needed for the novel situation prevailing in the thirteen colonies, but to justify this explanation it is necessary to translate it into terms of the problem as it existed, and of the controversies that surrounded it. It was obvious that no bishop claiming any temporal powers could be introduced into the colonies unless he came riding on a cannon, and by the eighteenth century the idea of spreading religion by force had gone out of fashion in England. A bishop with power to enforce civil penalties would not only have been anathema in all of the dissenting colonies, but he would have been exceedingly unpopular in the Church colonies as well. What sort of a bishop would

Why They Were not Sent

he be, however, who had no support from the state? It was known, of course, that bishops had existed without such support in primitive times, but none had existed in England within anyone's memory (except, of course, the Nonjurors, who were not to be considered), and most people seemed to think it unlikely that they would ever exist in the colonies. The advocates of the colonial episcopate generally insisted, it is true, that they desired only bishops with purely "spiritual" powers, but their assertion was regarded as a subterfuge by their enemies, and as an impractical ideal by a good many of their friends.

What, people asked, could such bishops do that the Commissaries could not do? And when it was answered that they could ordain, depose, consecrate, confirm, and possibly excommunicate (some of the proposals would have denied the bishops any jurisdiction over the laity at all), they were not impressed. Moreover, it must be admitted that the advocates of episcopacy were not themselves very successful in solving the problem of how these bishops were to be supported. Numerous schemes were put forward, but most of them contemplated the support being derived, at least in part, from the state, and this would necessarily have detracted from the purely spiritual character of the desired episcopate.

The inertia which made these obstacles seem insurmountable might have been overcome in time had it not been for the opposition of three powerful groups to the idea of sending any bishops to the colonies at all. These groups were the English politicians, especially those of Whig leanings, the English dissenters, and the dissenters in the colonies, or rather the Congregationalists and Presbyterians there, for the Baptists and Quakers concerned themselves very little in the matter. They had suffered as much from elders as from bishops, and they saw no good reason to distinguish between them.

Political
Objections

The objections of the politicians were perhaps best summed up in a letter which Horatio Walpole, the brother of Sir Robert, wrote to Bishop Sherlock in 1750. In the first place, he said, there was no indication that the colonies desired a bishop. It was true there were some colonies which had set up the Church, and required episcopally ordained ministers, but these had never expressed to the King any desire for a bishop. That they had accepted the Commissaries without demur, merely justified the inference that they wanted that much jurisdiction and no more. All this was perfectly true, for, as we shall see, the southern colonies gave but little support to the move for an episcopate and sometimes actually opposed it. Walpole evidently did not consider the applications from individual Churchmen and clerical conventions as being of any importance. In the second place, he said, if the measure were a desirable one, it would have been adopted before. Thirdly, it would stir up controversy and threaten the peace of the country by rousing the hostility of the dissenters, who were "necessary supports to the present establishment in state"— *i. e.,* to the Hanoverian dynasty—and by reawakening the controversy between Low Churchmen and High Churchmen. This would not only prove embarrassing to the King and Council, but it might actually endanger the security of the ruling house, as Jacobitism had "rather increased than diminished since the suppression of the last unnatural rebellion in 1745." Fourthly, because of Sherlock's known views on the proper relations of Church and State, it would be suspected that, though he professed to desire only a spiritual episcopate in the colonies, his ultimate objective would be a temporal establishment. Finally, Sherlock had not shown how his bishops could be supported without causing expense to the colonies.

These are the observations of a practical man, and they show a shrewd understanding of the situation. Sherlock's efforts, and those of other supporters of the colonial episcopate, did arouse the opposition of the dissenters, and they did give rise to just the suspicion that Walpole said they would. At the same time, the letter is a perfect illustration of the general policy of "let well enough alone" that characterized the English government under the first two Georges. Both of these monarchs, being Germans, were unpopular in England, and they were accepted merely because they, or the ministers who ruled for them, maintained an order of things with which most Englishmen were satisfied. The bugbear of Jacobitism—*i. e.,* of Stuart legitimacy—haunted their reigns, and to take any steps which might produce a controversy among their followers seemed but to invite a return of the older house. Thus in these reigns the inertia which is natural to all human institutions was reënforced by specific political conditions.

The objections of the English dissenters proceeded mainly from

Early
Hanoverian
Policies

the fact that the proposed episcopate would be obnoxious to their
brethren across the water, though most of them probably added
to this a natural hostility to anything that might promote the
interests of the Established Church. There may also have been a
fear among their opponents that if purely spiritual bishops were
once settled in the colonies they would begin to enquire whether
it might not be desirable in England also.

The attitude of the Independents and Presbyterians in America
was more complicated. To begin with, they had an opposing
theory of the ministry. Though the early Puritans had been
willing to accept episcopacy in England, on condition that the
bishops did not impose too many other burdens on their consciences, their New England descendants had come to regard
the institution as definitely an evil one, and the Presbyterians had
always thought it so. In the second place, as Walpole had anticipated, they doubted the sincerity of the advocates of episcopacy
in saying that they wanted spiritual bishops only, and suspected
a design was afoot to subvert their religious freedom by the introduction of a full episcopal Establishment such as existed in England. Their fathers had suffered at the hands of such an
establishment in times past, for the bishops had been the chief
agents in carrying out the Stuart religious policies, and though
the teeth of the English prelates had been pretty well drawn since
then, the New Englanders tended to think of these officers in
terms of the traditions which had been handed down about them.

Moreover, it would not be fair to the dissenters to represent
their fears of a temporal establishment as being altogether groundless. There were certainly some of the advocates of episcopacy
who would have been very glad of such an establishment could
they have obtained it, and even supposing that the professions of
a majority of its supporters were perfectly sincere, as they probably
were, there was no certainty of their being able to control the
future development of the institution once it was introduced.

The Presbyterians, in addition to sharing the Puritan dread of
persecution, were mostly Scotch or Scotch-Irish, and so had a
national antipathy to the English Church. Furthermore, during the
later years of the century, when the colonial opposition to the
introduction of bishops became the most conspicuous feature of
the controversy, the Presbyterians and Congregationalists were

definitely committed to the party that was opposing the political designs of the British Ministry, and politics and polity got pretty well mixed up in their thinking. In their more popular productions they represented the proposals for a colonial episcopate as being a part of the same plot to enslave the colonies that had led to the Stamp Act and other offensive measures. This supposition was unfounded, for the English Ministry never favored the episcopal scheme, but the colonists were not very well informed as to the ramifications of English politics, and the general loyalty of the northern Churchmen to the home government seemed to give color to their suspicions.

The Society for the Propagation of the Gospel began to work for a colonial episcopate almost as soon as it was founded. Bray himself had set the example of advocating this measure, and the Society was also urged to it by its missionaries and other ministers in the provinces. Talbot was especially persistent in his advocacy of the subject, and visited England in 1706 to promote it. In 1705, fourteen clergymen assembled at Burlington and petitioned the Society to send over a bishop. Evan Evans, in the report which he made to the Society in 1707, to which we have referred in a previous chapter, advocated the sending of a bishop to the colonies on the ground that such an officer would be able to maintain discipline among the clergy and support them in disciplining the laity, to keep peace among the ministers, and to keep up the supply by ordaining candidates in the colonies. He also suggested that the presence of a bishop would have the effect of creating a college at his See city as young men would be drawn there by the prospect of being ordained.

In the same year that the Society received Evans' report, Bishop Compton also furnished it with some observations upon the subject of the colonial episcopate. He held that the necessity of having a bishop in the provinces was clearly demonstrated by the disordered state of their ecclesiastical affairs, but that the sending of an absolute bishop, such as ruled in the Isle of Man, would give rise to great opposition, as the colonists had for a long time enjoyed great license in religious affairs. A suffragan—*i. e.,* a bishop appointed as assistant to some bishop in England—might be more successful. The people were already used to having Commissaries with authority, in matters of discipline, similar to that

Bishop Compton's Observations

of a suffragan, and they themselves were anxious to obtain the added benefits of Confirmation, the consecration of churches, and Holy Orders. Moreover, suffragans could be more easily removed if the experiment should fail.

The S.P.G.
Plan
The policy of appointing suffragans had also been advocated by a committee of the Society in 1703. Some years later another committee elaborated the proposal by suggesting that four bishops be sent to the plantations: one to be located at Williamsburg, Virginia; one at Burlington, New Jersey; and two in the West Indies. To provide for their salaries it was suggested that the tithes offered by some of the colonial clergy should be accepted, that the bishops be granted Ordinary jurisdiction with its attending fees, that lands be purchased for them, that they should have one-tenth of all grants and escheats in the colonies, and that Her Majesty should be requested to grant them various supplementary sources of income.

Its Near
Success
This report is of importance because most of the later proposals for the introduction of the episcopate differed from it only in detail. Some of the sources of revenue which it suggested were not very practical. The Society rejected the first one and referred the third back to the committee. The second would have excited great opposition in the colonial governors, who then enjoyed most of the usual perquisites of the Ordinary. Nevertheless, the scheme formed the basis of a representation placed before Queen Anne in 1713. Previous petitions to the Queen had been unsuccessful, and a sermon in favor of the measure which was preached before the Society in 1712 by Bishop Kennett had produced no better results, but this last request met with Her Majesty's favor and a bill was prepared for submission to Parliament. The object thus almost gained was lost by Anne's death in 1715. The Society renewed its petition to George I within a very short time of his accession, but it was useless. The new King had no interest in the Church and neither did his ministers, who were Whigs.

When the prospects of obtaining a bishop had seemed bright, the Society commissioned Talbot and Governor Hunter to purchase a house for him in Burlington. It remained in the Society's possession until 1748, just as a new bid for the episcopate was being made, when it burned down, having already fallen into disrepair. Another interesting sidelight on this first campaign for a colonial bishop was the effort of the friends of Dean Swift, including Hunter, to get him the post. Had they succeeded, it is to be feared that the aims of the chief promoters of the episcopate would have been defeated, for Swift was apparently looking for a sinecure.

After the failure of the petition to George I in 1715, there was a lull in the campaign, though a few guns continued to be fired from time to time on both sides of the Atlantic. In the very year of its defeat, the Society received a legacy of £1000 from Archbishop Tenison, which was to be used to help support a bishop when one was obtained, and until then to provide a pension for the oldest missionary in the colonial service. Other bequests for the support of the episcopate were received from time to time, though the total amount was not large.

Petitions also continued to come over from various parts of the colonies with considerable frequency. In 1718 the clergymen and vestries at Philadelphia and Burlington sent over a petition for a bishop, and the next year one was signed by clergy and laymen from New York, New Jersey, Pennsylvania, and Maryland. Pigot stressed the need for a bishop in his early reports from Connecticut, where he went in 1722. When he learned of the conversions to be expected at Yale, he suggested that if a bishop could be sent to the colonies to ordain the converts, those who were legally settled in parishes could retain them, which they could not do if they had to leave for England. After his conversion, Samuel Johnson frequently spoke of the importance of introducing the episcopate, and in 1732 he suggested to Bishop Gibson the possibility of setting up a complete Church Establishment in the colonies. In 1724 the clergy of the Eastern Shore in Maryland urged the sending of a bishop. In 1725 and 1727 the clergy of New England held conventions and sent addresses to the King and the Society in favor of a bishop. In the latter year the ministers and vestries of Christ Church and King's Chapel in Boston sent a similar petition, and the Bishop of London actually proposed to send a suffragan to Maryland, but was prevented by the local courts.

In 1741, the battle was reopened in England when Thomas Secker, then Bishop of Oxford, preached a sermon before the Society in which he urged sending bishops to the colonies. The author of this sermon, who became Archbishop of Canterbury in

The Struggle Continued

Bishop Secker's Sermon

1758, was a lifelong friend of the provincial Church and one of the ablest and most politic of the advocates of the colonial episcopate. His maiden effort in that direction drew from the Rev. Andrew Eliot of New England some *Remarks Upon the Bishop of Oxford's Sermon*, which filled the first of the many pamphlets to be issued by American dissenters against the introduction of bishops. They also foreshadowed the general line of argument followed by later controversialists, expressing suspicion that the bishops would be supported by taxes laid upon all of the colonists, and that their coming would lead to the setting up of a general establishment from which no colony could escape.

Bishop Gibson had presented a memorial in favor of colonial bishops on his coming to the See in 1723, and in 1745 he offered the King and Council £1000 toward their support if any should be sent over in his lifetime, but it was not until the coming of his successor, Thomas Sherlock, in 1748, that the second campaign was really opened. Bishop Gibson, as we have seen in an earlier chapter, had taken out a royal commission investing him officially with the jurisdiction over the colonies which his predecessors had exercised by force of custom. Under this commission the hand of the Bishop and his agents had been strengthened, and the discipline of the clergy had been maintained more vigorously. Sherlock, however, had doubts about its validity, and, in any case, considered the authority granted under it inadequate, as the jurisdiction extended only to the clergy, and as no appeal was allowed from the Commissaries to the bishop. Moreover, he thought it a hardship for the colonies to be under a bishop who could never live among them, so that they must necessarily be deprived of Confirmation and Ordination unless they came to England for them. He also felt that the supervision of the colonies was too much of a burden for one man, when combined with the supervision of a large diocese in England, and desired to be relieved of it.

For these reasons, which he expressed, and possibly also because he hoped to increase the loyalty of the colonists by strengthening the English Church among them, Sherlock refused to sue for a patent as Gibson had done, and instead began at once to work for a colonial episcopate. Shortly after his elevation, he went to the King and presented the religious needs of the colony in such a

Bishop
Sherlock's
Efforts

way that His Majesty consented to have the matter laid before his ministers. As he could obtain no satisfaction from them, he again went to the King and obtained his approval for the calling of a Council which, however, took no action. In 1748 he sent a representative to visit New York and Philadelphia and sound out public opinion on the subject of bishops. That a suffragan would not have any powers which would threaten the liberties of the people, and yet could do many useful things which were impossible to a Commissary, was brought to the attention of those approached by the agent. When the matter was put in this way, most people, he said, were willing to admit that the measure might be a desirable one.

In the year 1749, Sherlock entered into a private correspondence with the Duke of Newcastle in which he urged the sending of a bishop to the colonies, at first upon the ground that he ought to be relieved of the burden of colonial jurisdiction. When Newcastle insisted that the question was too important a one to be decided upon personal grounds, Sherlock urged the importance of the measure for the good of the colonies. His arguments, however, met with little favor, and Newcastle continued to insist that the measure was inexpedient. The next year, as we have already seen, Horatio Walpole also wrote to Sherlock expostulating with him for starting something that might lead to trouble. A deputation from the committee in charge of the civil affairs of the dissenters had waited upon the King in 1749 and again in 1750 to represent to him the undesirability of the measure, and it is possible that their activity had something to do with the caution of the ministers.

In 1750 Sherlock again memorialized the King with some "Considerations . . . relating to Ecclesiastical Government in his Majesty's Dominions in America," in which he advanced the usual arguments in favor of a colonial episcopate, insisted that there was no thought of settling any bishops in the colonies with "coercive power," and sought to answer some of the other objections which might be brought against the measure. It would seem, nevertheless, that he had given up hope of the immediate attainment of his ends, for in the same year that he submitted this memorial he addressed a circular letter to the colonial clergy asking them what jurisdiction had been exercised by his predecessors

Sherlock's Memorial

and their representatives. He says in this letter, it is true, that the matter of colonial bishops was still pending, as the King had to go to Hanover before any action was taken, but it is unlikely that he would have made the enquiry had he had much hope of transferring the burden of the jurisdiction to other shoulders. As late as 1751 rumors were afloat among the dissenters in New Jersey that a bishop was about to be sent over, but there was no foundation for the report, and in May, 1752, Secretary Bearcroft wrote to one of the Massachusetts missionaries that there were now no further hopes of obtaining a bishop, and that Sherlock talked of taking out a patent for the colonies. This he never did, but he did carry on the customary jurisdiction during the rest of his career. Secker, who had more political discretion than Sherlock, seems to have shared the opinion of the Ministry that the latter's move was an untimely one, though for different reasons. At least, we presume he was referring to this when he wrote to Samuel Johnson in 1758, "The design when, some years ago it seemed to be in great forwardness, received a most mortifying check by means of an unseasonable step, which a worthy and able prelate took to promote it, and of which his opposers made their advantage."

When the campaign was reopened in the sixties, the initiative was taken by various clerical conventions on this side of the water. In the meantime, occasional pleas were made in behalf of the episcopate by individuals both here and in England. Bishop Butler, the author of the famous *Analogy,* had drafted a plan for a colonial episcopate in 1750, at the same time that Sherlock was presenting his memorial to the King. From America, Johnson continued his appeals for a bishop in letters to Canterbury and London, and Smith also urged the measure from time to time. In 1760 Henry Caner, the rector of King's Chapel, wrote to the secretary expressing the opinion that when the missionaries failed in their work it was generally due to the want of episcopal authority. Until that was supplied he thought the Bishop of London should appoint a Commissary, or, better yet, an archdeacon—so far as is known, the only suggestion for sending such an officer to America. The annexation of Canada at the close of the Seven Years' War raised some hope that the sending of a bishop to Quebec might rouse less opposition than his introduction into the older colonies. Such a measure was suggested shortly after the close of the war

Intermittent
Efforts

by the Dean of Gloucester in some *Queries humbly submitted to the friends of the Protestant Episcopacy in North America*. In 1764 Richard Peters of Philadelphia presented to the Archbishops of Canterbury and York some *Thoughts on the Present State of the Church of England in America*, in which he reverted to the old plan of sending out four suffragans. He thought that such suffragans could be appointed in the archdiocese of Canterbury by the King, under a law already existing, without having recourse to a special act of Parliament. He varied Bishop Compton's scheme further by proposing that three, instead of two, of the bishops should reside on the continent of North America.

Voluntary conventions had been held by the clergy of the various colonies from early times, but in the later part of the colonial period they tended to meet more regularly than formerly and, in the northern colonies, there was also a tendency to include two or three colonies in one convention. The clergy of Massachusetts and Rhode Island had always been accustomed to meet together, and they occasionally had some of their brethren from Connecticut with them. The ministers in New York and New Jersey began holding joint annual conventions in 1756. Pennsylvania conventions were frequently attended by clergymen from New Jersey and Maryland. In 1766 articles of organization were drawn up for a convention to include members from New York, New Jersey, and Connecticut, and other colonies were invited to join the movement. When the convention met in November of the same year it had members from Connecticut, New York, New Jersey, and Pennsylvania, but it does not appear that so representative a group was assembled more than once. *Clerical Conventions in the Colonies*

The clerical conventions had been accustomed to memorialize the Society, the bishops, or the King in behalf of a colonial episcopate whenever they thought they had an opportunity to be heard. We have already mentioned a few of their appeals. According to William Smith, the Pennsylvania clergy used to memorialize every new Bishop of London and Archbishop of Canterbury in favor of the measure. In 1765 two other conventions, that of New York and New Jersey, and that of Connecticut sent over memorials which they desired the Archbishop of Canterbury to present to the King. Secker, however, thought it unwise to do so *Their Petitions for a Bishop* at the time, as both countries were then "on fire about the Stamp Act," and the two conventions apologized the next year for their indiscretion.

Southern
Opposition

Evidently it seemed to the members of these conventions, however, that as the Churchmen in their sections had, for the most part, taken the side of the mother country in the prevailing disputes, the excitement furnished a very good reason why their requests should be favorably listened to. In 1771 both conventions renewed their petitions, and both took occasion to point out the loyalty of Churchmen to the Crown, and to suggest that political expediency, if nothing else, should dictate the strengthening of the Church in every way possible. The New York and New Jersey convention commissioned Myles Cooper, the president of King's College, to carry their petition to England personally. Cooper and Robert McKean, a New Jersey missionary, had been previously deputed by the convention to secure the support of some of the southern clergy for the measure, and had succeeded in getting a vote of approval from a thinly attended convention in Virginia. This move, however, did their cause more harm than good, for two of the Virginia clergy, Thomas Gwatkin and Samuel Henley, protested against the action of the convention and shortly afterwards the colonial House of Burgesses gave these two gentlemen and some others who had sided with them a vote of thanks for "the wise and well-timed opposition they have made to the pernicious project of a few mistaken clergymen for introducing an American bishop." Thus the fact, which should have been known to the convention, that the southerners were, on the whole, opposed to the introduction of the episcopate, was unnecessarily underlined. Subsequently an attempt was made to obtain the support of the Pennsylvania clergy to the petition, but they declined, giving as their reasons the untimeliness of the measure as indicated by the action of the House of Burgesses; the fact, already mentioned, that they had always addressed every new occupant of the Sees of Canterbury and London in favor of the episcopate, which made them feel that supporting a supplementary petition would imply a doubt of the zeal or wisdom of their superiors; and the inadvisability of a small group of clergy sending a petition directly to the throne, since, if rejected or ignored, it would not be proper to present another for some years. They also felt that the cause had probably been hurt by too many petitions anyway. Cooper sailed for England in the fall of 1771, but his mission bore no fruit. In 1774 Secretary Hind of the Society for the Propagation of the Gospel expressed to Dr. Smith the fear that the prospect of obtaining an episcopate had been "thrown . . . at a greater distance than ever by the present distracted state of the colonies."

The action of the Virginia House of Burgesses in condemning the move for episcopacy drew forth an *Address from the Clergy of New York and New Jersey to the Episcopalians in Virginia,* written by Cooper and signed by seven other ministers, which expressed great surprise that the southern Churchmen should have opposed a measure which was so consistent with their supposed principles, and in support of which the northern Episcopalians were unanimous. If this surprise were genuine, it is a striking illustration of the ignorance of the colonists of one section with respect to the sentiments of another, for from the time of Bishop Compton, if not earlier, it had been recognized that the Virginians were opposed to the introduction of any sort of jurisdiction which would impair the freedom that they enjoyed in ecclesiastical affairs. In succeeding years they had continued to whittle down the authority of their Commissaries until it was a mere shadow. Moreover, by now, the issue had become thoroughly impregnated with political implications, both for the Churchmen and for their opponents. The northern Churchmen thought they deserved a bishop because they were conspicuously loyal to the Crown, but the southern Churchmen were not conspicuously loyal to the Crown. Their sympathies for the most part were with the party of resistance, and they were probably not altogether uninfluenced by the belief of the northern leaders of this party that bishops would be just another agency of British tyranny.

Similar, though milder, political motives may have had some part in producing the coolness with which the petition was treated in Pennsylvania, for many of the leading clergymen in that colony were in favor of the early measures of resistance, though not all of them proved willing, when the time came, to go the full length of independence.

While the Episcopal conventions were campaigning for bishops, the Presbyterians and Congregationalists also organized a tri-

Remonstrance
of the
Northern
Clergy

colonial convention, partly, at least, for the purpose of opposing them. This convention was apparently inspired by the meeting of the Church of England clergy of New York, New Jersey, and Connecticut, for it included the same colonies, and held its first meeting at Elizabeth five days after the Episcopalian meeting. Its objects were supposed to include a general consultation on the interests of the two denominations in the three colonies, but the opposition to the introduction of the episcopate had a large place in its activities.

Pamphlet
Warfare

The later stages of the campaign for the episcopate were marked by an almost continuous pamphlet controversy, which may be briefly summarized. In his *Serious Address*, to which we referred in an earlier chapter, Noah Hobart took a mild swipe at the demand for bishops by saying that he did not think bishops had anything to do with the discipline of the Church of England, a view which he based on the indirect way in which their authority was exercised. This was in 1748, but the conflict did not become hot until 1763, when Jonathan Mayhew published some *Observations on the Charter and Conduct of the Society for the Propagation of the Gospel*, in which he asserted that the chief design of the Society was to root out "Presbyterianism" and establish episcopacy in the colonies. This was answered by Henry Caner in a pamphlet which was mainly devoted to personalities, and by Arthur Browne, of Portsmouth, in one which admitted the design to introduce episcopacy, denied there was any intention of driving out the Puritan religion by force, and declared that if a majority of the colonists should, happily, become Episcopalians, there would be no reason why bishops should not be supported by taxation. The most important reply to Mayhew, however, was an *Answer* published anonymously, but written by Secker, which took the familiar ground that bishops were necessary to complete the Church's ministry, that temporal bishops were not desired, and that spiritual bishops ought to be allowed as a simple matter of toleration. Mayhew answered his opponents in two pamphlets, one directed against Caner and the other against Secker. In the latter he argued that, whatever character the colonial bishops might have when first sent over, they would inevitably seek to increase their authority in every way possible. An answer to this from the pen of East Apthorp, the minister at Cambridge, closed this phase of the controversy.

The debate was reopened in 1767 with the publication of a sermon preached by John Ewer, Bishop of Llandaff, before the Society in which he stressed the need of bishops in the colonies, dwelling especially upon the hardships suffered by those who had to come to England for orders. His sermon was attacked by Charles Chauncy, a prominent Puritan minister of Boston, and William Livingston of New York, and defended by Charles Inglis, assistant minister at Trinity Church, New York. In the same year, Thomas Bradbury Chandler, the missionary at Elizabeth, published an *Appeal to the Public on Behalf of the Church of England in America*, as a result of promptings from Dr. Johnson and the convention of New York and New Jersey. In this document he repeated the plea for a purely spiritual episcopate, but in a letter which he wrote to the Bishop of London concerning the work, he said, "There are some other facts and reasons which could not be prudently mentioned in a work of this nature, as the least intimation of them would be of ill consequence in this irritable age and country, but were they known they would have a far greater tendency to engage such of our superiors . . . as are governed altogether by political motives to espouse the cause of the Church of England in America." This has been taken as an indication that Chandler was contemplating a temporal establishment, but it seems more likely that it merely refers to the argument from the greater loyalty of the northern Churchmen which was later advanced openly.

Chandler's Pamphlets

Dr. Chauncy replied to Chandler's effort by printing the *Appeal Answered*, and the latter retorted with the *Appeal Defended*. Next came Chauncy's *Reply*, and Chandler's *Appeal Further Defended*, in which he sought to reinforce the old arguments by correcting his opponent's grammar. In 1769, a letter written by Archbishop Secker to Horatio Walpole in 1750, in defense of the American episcopate, was posthumously published. This provoked a *Critical Commentary* by Francis Blackburne, Archdeacon of Cleveland, a Churchman who seems to have had a good deal of sympathy with dissenters. Chandler again entered the lists in 1774 with *A Free Examination of the Critical Commentary* in which he supported Secker, and to which he subjoined Bishop Sherlock's memorial of 1750.

In 1768 the controversy broke in the newspapers and became embittered by the catch phrases of popular politics. The scenes of this conflict were New York and Philadelphia, and the opponents of episcopacy were, in New York, the "American Whig," who was in reality William Livingston, and in Philadelphia the "Centinel," or Francis Allison, Vice-provost of the College of Philadelphia. Allison is quoted by one of the Pennsylvania missionaries as having said that he would have no objection to the coming of truly "primitive" bishops to America, and his publications were a little more moderate than Livingston's, but both men were convinced that the introduction of the episcopate was simply a part of the plot of the British government to subvert American liberty. They were answered vigorously by a writer who signed himself "Timothy Tickle" in *A Whip for the American Whig*, and more reasonably by Allison's superior, William Smith, who signed himself "The Anatomist." Thus the ecclesiastical issue was smothered by the political controversy between the colonies and the mother country which, in its ultimate outcome, was at last to make possible the sending of bishops.

An interesting side issue to the struggle for the episcopate is the question of whether or not there were bishops in the colonies who had been consecrated by the Nonjurors. It is not very important but it furnishes one of the minor mysteries of American history. The persons suspected of being in such orders were John Talbot, with whom the reader is already well acquainted, and Richard Welton, who served for a time as minister of Christ Church, Philadelphia. The evidence in favor of their having been consecrated is largely indirect. John Urmiston, the drunkard whom Talbot helped to expel from Christ Church, wrote letters to Dr. Bray, to the Secretary of the Society for the Propagation of the Gospel, and to another person, in all of which he declared that Talbot had convened the Pennsylvania clergy and demanded obedience from them as a bishop. Commissary Henderson made a similar charge in 1724, saying that Talbot had returned to the colonies in episcopal orders two years previously and that Welton had arrived more recently in the same capacity. The source of

Henderson's information is not known, however, and it is more than possible that he derived it from Urmiston.

The report thus started obtained general circulation and was repeated by Governor Burnet of New York and a number of colonial clergymen, but none of these writers pretended to have first-hand knowledge of the matter, and none of them was located either in Pennsylvania or New Jersey, whence accurate information on the subject might most naturally be expected to come. The Society attached enough weight to these reports, coupled with earlier charges of Jacobitism, to dismiss Talbot from its service, and the story is repeated by a number of historians of the period, including Lothbury in his *History of the Nonjurors*, Perceval in a work on the Apostolic Succession, and the author of a work called *Reliquiae Hernianae*. All that the modern historian can say, however, is that, though it is possible that Talbot and Welton were in episcopal orders, the supposition cannot, in the absence of reliable first-hand testimony, be regarded as proven.

Report Widely Circulated

CHAPTER IX

REVOLUTION AND REORGANIZATION

Position of the Church in the Revolution

REVOLUTIONS, like street fights, are likely to be as dangerous to the innocent bystanders as to the participants, and the position of the Church in the American Revolution was, in some sense, that of an innocent bystander. This is not to say that her members did not take sides, for many of them did, but they did not all take the same side, and it is probable that influences other than their Churchmanship governed their decision for or against the rebellion. In spite of the efforts of the opponents (and some of the advocates) of episcopacy to connect that topic with the general controversy, the real issues of the struggle were not ecclesiastical, and the Church had no direct concern in them. Most of her ministers would probably have preferred to remain neutral if they could, though clearly this was an impossibility. Nevertheless, the Church was profoundly affected by the Revolution. When it was over she was compelled to reorganize herself from the bottom up, to obtain from a foreign power the episcopate so long denied her when her members were still subjects of that power, and to find entirely new methods of supporting her services in most of the places where she held them. She was obliged to do all this, moreover, at a time when she had but a fraction of her former number of ministers, and when she was regarded with suspicion in many sections where most of her members had been hostile to the revolutionary cause.

Loyalists in the Church

It was frequently stated by the missionaries that the growth of the Church always meant the growth of loyalty to the Crown, and this statement has been repeated by some reputable historians, but it is only partly true. Had it been entirely true, two-thirds of the signers of the Declaration of Independence would not have been Churchmen. What was true, on the whole, was that where the Church expanded in sections which were generally hostile to

172

it, its adherents were likely to stand out as loyal to the Crown, because, whether they were new arrivals or converts, they would be out of sympathy with the prevailing sentiments of the colony, and would naturally look across the water for encouragement and protection. It was also true that most of the missionaries of the Society for the Propagation of the Gospel were loyalist, partly because they generally served in hostile sections, partly because any suspicion of disloyalty would have led to their immediate dismissal, and partly because they were mostly High Churchmen, and High Churchmanship was associated with attachment to the Crown. When they were suspected of disaffection of any sort, it was generally Jacobitism, not Whiggery, with which they were charged. The ministers who were locally supported showed more sympathy with colonial aspirations, and when the test came, a good many of them were at least passively friendly towards independence. To express this distinction along geographical lines is to say that the clergy in New England were nearly all loyalist, that many of those in the South (except in the colonies which were still supplied by missionaries), were revolutionary, and that those in the Middle Colonies were divided, but predominantly loyalist. There were, however, some exceptions to these rules, as we shall see later.

The laity of the Church tended to divide upon lines similar to those of the clergy, not, it is probable, because they allowed themselves to be swayed by the latter so much as because they were subject to similar influences. The Church had, by this time, acquired something of that quality of "upper-classishness" which has handicapped its work in this country ever since. When it first invaded a colony, unless it did so under the immediate protection of the governor, its adherents were likely to be drawn from the poorer inhabitants—either new settlers or persons who had not fitted too well into the life of the colony. As time went on, however, it drew to itself, especially in the larger centers, a good many of the wealthier merchants and office holders whose interests disposed them favorably towards the royal government, who liked to imitate the English gentry, and who probably desired a greater freedom in their personal lives than was allowed them by other denominations. Though these men had supported much of the earlier opposition to the imperialistic policy adopted by the British

Attitude of
the Laity

government in the sixties and seventies, they were opposed to violent measures, and most of them took the loyalist side when the issue was finally drawn, while the less prosperous classes tended to favor revolt. When the members of the upper classes did join the rebellion, however (and a few of them did so), they tended naturally to gravitate to positions of leadership in it.

Leadership of Churchmen in the Revolution

Hence we find the Church supplying a respectable number of revolutionary leaders even in colonies where a majority of its adherents were Tory. In the South, where there were few of the merchant class, its strongest members were naturally the large planters, but in the older southern colonies, where it was established by law, the Church still had the nominal allegiance of a majority of the inhabitants, since the support of a dissenting minister was an extra expense which would be borne only as the result of earnest conviction. Moreover, compared with the convictions of northern merchants, a larger proportion of the southern planters favored independence. Hence, in the South nearly all of the leaders and a majority of the rank and file of the revolutionary movement were drawn from the Church, though most of them showed but a scant regard for her welfare when she was in distress.

Plight of the Tory Clergy

Most of the ministers, as has been said, would have preferred to remain neutral in the struggle if they could, but circumstances would not allow this. A few did become Tory pamphleteers. Samuel Seabury, the future Bishop of Connecticut, wrote some *Letters of a Westchester Farmer* that provided effective Tory propaganda; Jonathan Odell, a missionary in New Jersey, directed some satiric verse against the Whigs; and Charles Inglis, the assistant rector at Trinity Church, New York, prepared an answer to Thomas Paine's *Common Sense*. Some others, who were not moved to literary expression by the struggle, did feel bound to preach sermons against rebellion, but the majority would have asked nothing better than the permission to go on quietly holding services and preaching on other questions than those of politics. Unfortunately, they could not hold service in conformity to the Prayer Book without praying for the King, and where the rebels were in control this was not likely to be permitted. To omit the royal prayers was to violate their oaths of allegiance and the vows taken at ordination to conform to the laws of the Church. Such a course might be justified if they were convinced that the revolt was right in principle, or it might be held allowable on the plea of coercion, or as a necessary means of continuing the performance of their pastoral duties, and a few of the clergy who were not in general sympathy with the revolt accepted one or the other of these last two views, and omitted the prayers. The great majority of the loyalist ministers, however, felt their oaths and their allegiance must come before everything, and were consequently obliged either to discontinue their services, to abandon their cures altogether, or to defy the rebels and go to jail. Only a minority chose the last course.

It was characteristic of the military situation prevailing throughout the war that, while the British held several of the larger cities from time to time, they were seldom able to hold any very large areas outside of them. They could, and frequently did, defeat rebel armies in the field, and when they concentrated in a city they could be dislodged only with great difficulty, but they did not have the forces necessary to hold the country as a whole against the guerrilla warfare carried on by the rebels between campaigns. Consequently the loyalist missionaries in most parts of the country were at the mercy of the rebels.

In New England, outside of Connecticut, most of the clergy were obliged to flee during the conflict, seeking refuge in New York, which was held by the British from 1776 until the close of the war, in Canada, or in England. When the struggle ended there were but four missionaries in Massachusetts, one of whom had come from Nova Scotia during the war, one in New Hampshire, and none in Rhode Island or Maine. In Boston, a considerable portion of the laity seem to have been in favor of the Revolution, though only one of the ministers was. It was in the tower of Christ Church that the lanterns were set which warned Paul Revere and his fellow-rider that the British troops were marching to Lexington and Concord, and because of what he considered the disloyal sentiments of the vestry, the rector, Mather Byles, resigned, and accepted the post of minister at Portsmouth. He was unable to get there, however, because that town had also fallen into the hands of the rebels. When the British evacuated Boston, Byles fled to Halifax, as did Henry Caner, rector of King's Chapel. William Walter, rector of Trinity Church, fled to New York. Some of the leading members of King's Chapel, being

The Situation in New England

loyalists, were also obliged to leave town, and the Chapel eventually passed into the hands of the Unitarians. Christ Church and Trinity, however, had pro-Revolutionary vestries, and the assistant at the latter, Samuel Parker, was sufficiently in favor of independence to carry on without prayers for the King. For a time he preached at Christ Church, also, to prevent its acquisition by the French, which Congress at one time intended.

Outside of Boston, the church at Cambridge was the first to be closed, the minister there being forced to flee shortly after the Battle of Lexington. Some of the other ministers were suffered to continue for a time, but were eventually silenced or expelled, with the exception of Edward Bass, the missionary at Newbury, who consented to omit the prayers for the King, and to observe the fasts appointed by Congress. In Rhode Island and Maine the missionaries were also presently expelled. In New Hampshire, Ranna Cossit continued to serve at Claremont, but was not allowed to visit other parts of the colony. Most of the ministers left before they were seriously molested, except William Clark, the missionary at Dedham, who was imprisoned for a time at Boston.

The troubles in Connecticut began when the colonial militia returned from service with Washington at Boston. Richard Mansfield, the missionary at Derby, who had preached against rebellion, and sent a petition on behalf of loyalists to General Tryon in New York, which was intercepted, was forced to flee to Long Island where he could be protected by loyal troops. He returned at the end of the war. At Newtown the aged minister, John Beach, then in his seventy-eighth year, was imprisoned, as were some of the local "selectmen" also, in an effort to make them support the rebel "association." As they persisted in their refusal to do so, they were released under heavy bonds not to bear arms or engage in seditious actions. Beach continued to hold services and pray for the King throughout the war, declaring that he would persist until the rebels cut his tongue out. Samuel Peters, the minister at Hebron, was attacked by two mobs, and finally fled to England. He came back after the war, and divided his time between trying to become Bishop of Vermont and endeavoring to make good his title to a land grant which he had purchased in England. Abraham Jarvis, who was to become the second

Connecticut

Bishop of Connecticut, is said by his grandson to have escaped the hand of a rebel assassin only because the latter was unable to pick a quarrel with him and would not kill him in cold blooc. This story comes to us too indirectly to be regarded as certain, however. Most of Jarvis' relatives were Tories, and, according to the same authority, two of his nephews served in the British Army. Their father was shot by rebels at his own door, and another brother escaped from the "vigilance committee" only by hiding in a wood bin.

The Church in Connecticut suffered from its friends as well as its enemies, for General Tryon raided the state in 1779, burning Norwalk, Fairfield, and some other villages destroying their churches in the process. He carried the missionaries at the two places mentioned, Jeremiah Leaming and John Sayre, back to New York with him. A few other ministers also left the state, but a majority remained at their posts. In 1782, the last year of the war, they sent word to the Society that they continued to officiate as formerly, and that they were now living in greater security than they had been (active hostilities ceased after Yorktown, of course), but that they received very little from the people because of the heavy taxes with which the latter were burdened. In spite of its difficulties, the Church there was flourishing, and many outsiders had conformed to it. *General Tryon's Raid*

The fact that New York City was held by the British throughout the greater part of the war caused it to become a city of refuge for loyalists from all of the neighboring states, and from the remoter parts of its own state. A considerable number of loyalist missionaries consequently gathered there during most of the conflict. Some of these later departed for England or Canada, and a number were given chaplaincies in the royal army, but some remained without other support than the stipends which the Society continued to pay them. They were, it is true, allowed rations of food and fuel by the military authorities, and apparently were also given a small allowance in money, but there is reason to suspect that the quality of the food was not always the best, for one missionary reported that he and his family would eat it "if our stomachs could accommodate themselves to worms and many other impurities which we (without any necessity for it) find in our bread." Other refugees report that supplies were plentiful but *Tory Refugees in New York* very dear and, as the incomes of most were small, it is probable that they suffered some hardship. Walter, who had means of his own, was able to relieve some of his colleagues while he remained at New York, and the Society also raised a fund for their benefit.

New York
City Before
the British
Occupation

During the year that preceded the British occupation of New York after the outbreak of hostilities, the Church there was subjected to some interference. Myles Cooper, the president of King's College, fled the country at the beginning of the war and did not return. Samuel Auchmuty, the rector of Trinity Church, retired for a time to New Brunswick, New Jersey, and left his assistant, Inglis, in charge. Washington attended Trinity when he was in town and one of his generals told Inglis to omit the prayers for the King. The latter did not do so, however, and the general later apologized. This was before the Declaration of Independence. After that event, Inglis departed for Long Island, where he remained until General Howe entered the city in September. Shortly after the British occupation, one-fourth of the city was destroyed in a conflagration which most contemporaries thought was started by rebels. Trinity Church was burned down in this fire, but the College and St. Paul's Chapel were saved.

Auchmuty also returned after the British came in, but he died a short time later, and Inglis became rector. Thereafter, except for the presence of the refugees, the affairs of the Church within the city were carried on more or less as usual. The regular services were held, the parish school was kept open, its buildings being exempted from billets by the commandant, and the negroes were regularly catechized. As the Dutch Church was used for a hospital, the Dutch-speaking portion of the congregation was permitted to use St. George's Chapel. The English-speaking portion had previously hired a Presbyterian minister and become hostile to the Episcopal Church. Most of them were now with the rebels.

The Rest of
the State

On Staten Island and Long Island the presence of British troops also made it possible to keep up the services of the Church during part of the time, though both places were exposed to occasional raids from the neighboring states. In some places on Long Island the royal troops proved nearly as disturbing as the rebels. At Huntington they used the church for a barracks. At Hempstead the parish school was used for a guardroom, and the minister's house and farm were also used and damaged by the troops.

Leonard Cutting, the minister, wrote to the Society, "Where the army is, oppression (such as, in England, you can have no conception of) universally prevails." At Jamaica, on the other hand, things were so peaceable that the parish raised eight hundred pounds by a lottery, which it invested in a glebe. At Brooklyn the war was actually the cause of introducing the services of the Church, for James Sayre, who had been driven away from Fredericksburg in Dutchess County, began preaching in the Dutch Church three Sundays out of four.

The rest of the state was generally in control of the rebels and most of the ministers were driven out sooner or later. Seabury, who, as we have seen, had written some pamphlets against the rebellion, was carried into Connecticut early in the war by some irregulars and kept prisoner for a time, his family being subjected to some indignities during his absence. When Westchester County fell into the hands of the colonial forces, he and Wetmore were both expelled. He supported himself by practicing medicine in New York until 1778, when he became chaplain in a loyalist regiment. Sooner or later most of the other ministers were also herded into New York City. Munro, at Albany, resigned early in the war to become a chaplain. Stuart, after the flight of his Indians, was held prisoner at Schenectady for three years, when he was sent to Canada after giving bonds to procure the release of an American colonel in exchange.

The only minister in New York who was definitely pro-Revolutionary was Samuel Provoost, who had been assistant at Trinity for a time, but resigned in 1769 because his sentiments were already too disloyal for the vestry. During the war he served in the army. A considerable number of the parishioners of Trinity had been in sympathy with the Revolution, and had left the city before the arrival of the British. As soon as Inglis and the royal troops had departed, after the treaty of peace in 1783, the loyalist vestry elected Benjamin Moore, who had been assistant minister, their rector. When the revolutionists returned to the city, they had this election annulled and elected Provoost instead. He subsequently became the first Bishop of New York.

In Pennsylvania a number of the leading clergymen supported the revolutionary movement in its early stages. When the Continental Congress recommended a general fast in 1775, Richard

Pennsylvania

Peters, the rector of Christ Church, observed it, on the advice of his vestry. This, however, was not a proof of decided Whig leanings, as a number of the Tory ministers felt justified in doing the same, to keep peace in their parishes, since Congress had not yet openly declared rebellion. Peters resigned on September 23, 1775, because of ill health, and Jacob Duché, his chief assistant, was elected rector. Duché was a strong Whig, and served as first chaplain of the Continental Congress. After the Declaration of Independence, Duché called a meeting of his vestry which voted to omit the prayers for the King for the sake of "the peace and well-being of the Churches." When the British occupied the city in 1777, however, he became a loyalist, and when they were forced to evacuate the city he fled to England.

The other assistant at Christ and St. Peter's was William White, a young man who had been appointed to the position in 1772, and who was a brother-in-law of Robert Morris, the financier of the Revolution. White had felt some hesitancy about the propriety of revolt, but when most of his countrymen seemed in favor of it he felt it his duty to follow them, and adhered unflinchingly to his decision thereafter. He became chaplain of the Continental Congress when it was running away from Philadelphia during one of the darkest moments of the war. When the city was retaken, he was elected rector of Christ Church, but accepted only with the understanding that he should resign if Duché was later able to return. He continued at his post during the war, and was, at one time, the only Episcopalian minister in the state.

William White

William Smith, the Provost of the College of Philadelphia, had participated in the early resistance to British imperialism, and had served on one or two committees of correspondence. He had been opposed to declaring independence, and had written some pamphlets against it, signed "Cato," but accepted it after it was declared. He also preached a funeral sermon on General Montgomery, killed in the siege of Quebec, which was considered insufficiently patriotic by the rebels, and when the British were advancing on Philadelphia he was placed under surveillance by Congress as a suspicious character. He fled with the rebels, however, and did not return until they did. In 1779, the charter of the College was annulled by the state legislature, and its property transferred to the newly organized University of Pennsylvania,

William Smith

the pretext for this move being that the College had abandoned its non-denominational character, though this seems to have been untrue. Smith thereupon moved to Maryland and settled down at Chester, whose rector had become a refugee, and where he presently organized a new institution which he called Washington College, after the general, who was one of its patrons. The other Pennsylvania ministers were all eventually expelled from the state, though Barton remained at Lancaster until 1778. In 1779 John Andrews, who had been a loyalist, came into the colony from Maryland, and decided that necessity justified his acceptance of the revolutionary government.

In New Jersey all of the ministers, except Robert Blackwell at Gloucester, closed their churches after they had been threatened New Jersey with prosecution and one of them, William Ayers, had been dragged from the pulpit for saying the prayers for the King. Blackwell, who was in sympathy with the revolt, omitted the prayers. Some of the missionaries fled from the colony, but Uzal Ogden, William Ayers, William Frazer and Abraham Beach remained at their posts, and in 1782, when the war seemed about over, and they felt that something must be done to check the decay of religion and morals, they resumed their services without the crucial prayers.

In the South, as has already been said, a larger proportion of the ministers were sympathetic to the Revolution, though those The South actively favoring it were probably not in a majority except in South Carolina, where only five of the twenty clergy were loyalist. In Virginia and Maryland those definitely in favor of the revolt are estimated to have been about one-third of the clergy, but it is evident that not all of the remaining two-thirds were strongly loyalist, for a Virginia convention voted to omit the prayers for the King after the Declaration of Independence. The few ministers in Georgia and North Carolina, with the exception of the rector of Savannah, who was an absentee, were supported by the Society for the Propagation of the Gospel. It is not surprising, therefore, that the only revolutionary ministers in these two colonies were the Rev. Charles Pettigrew, who married the daughter of a colonel in the Continental Army, and the Rev. William Percy, the head of Bethesda College.

Of the Virginia rebels, the two most prominent were James

Madison, the first bishop of the diocese, and David Griffith, who was elected to that office but not consecrated. In South Carolina, Robert Smith, the future bishop, and another minister were banished for their revolutionary sympathies when the state was under British control. Henry Purcell, of the same state, served as chaplain and judge advocate in the Continental Army. Thomas John Claggett, the first Bishop of Maryland, was friendly to the revolt, though he had some scruples about repudiating his former oaths.

It might be supposed, from what has been said so far, that the Revolution would have left the Episcopal Church in the northern states in a much weaker condition than in the southern, but actually the situation was nearly the opposite. If we should draw a heavy line across the northern and eastern borders of Connecticut, and another across the southern border of Maryland, we would enclose between them the area within which the Church recuperated most rapidly from the effects of the Revolution. Outside of this area the recovery was, on the whole, more rapid in the states to the northward than it was in those to the southward, and within it the state in which the Church was in the strongest position at the close of the war was Connecticut, where, as we have seen, the loyalism of the clergy was the most unanimous. It would seem evident, therefore, that, while the Tory sympathies of the northern clergy undoubtedly increased the prejudices against the Episcopal Church, other factors must also be taken into consideration if we wish to explain its undoubted decline after the Revolution. To attempt to account for that decline solely on the basis of the Church's loyalist tendencies, as some writers have done, is to fall into the common error of over-simplifying a complex problem.

Some of the other causes of the Church's decline suggest themselves at once when we consider how her position was affected by the change in the political status of the country. As the charter of the Society for the Propagation of the Gospel permitted it to work only within the "foreign plantations" (*i. e.,* colonies) of the British Empire, its support was necessarily withdrawn from the American Episcopal Church as soon as the independence of the United States was recognized. In Connecticut most of the parishes, and in the other states some of them, were able to raise sufficient support locally to make it possible for their ministers to

Situation at the Close of the War

Causes of the Church's Decline

struggle along, but in a great many places the people were unable or unwilling to do this, and consequently the Society's missionaries would have been obliged to leave these communities even if their political views had been unexceptionable.

Moreover, whatever consciousness of unity had been imparted to the colonial Church by its general dependence upon England, by the shadowy jurisdiction of the Bishop of London, and by the frequent communication of its leading ministers with the English ecclesiastical authorities, was lost to it after the Revolution, and, at the same time, the need for American bishops, which had been chronic in colonial times, now became acute, for it would never do, even if it were permitted, for the Church to have constant recourse to a foreign power for the replenishment of her ministry. To many, however, it seemed that this need would be a long time in being filled. Actually, bishops were obtained within a few years after the close of the Revolution, but even so the delay was sufficient to give some of the more active and better-supplied denominations an opportunity of gaining ground against the Church.

These difficulties, however, confronted the Church everywhere throughout the country, and some of them operated more strongly in the North than in the South. Why, then, was the decline of the Church in the South so strongly marked? The immediate reason, of course, was that the Church was disestablished—that is, deprived of all public support—in all of the southern states either during the Revolution or immediately after it. This circumstance, itself, requires an explanation, however, and it is also obvious that it could not of itself, since no rival establishment was set up, account for the widespread defection from the Episcopal Church which followed. Deeper reasons for this defection must be sought. *Causes Operating Especially in the South*

In the imagination of most northerners the South is commonly thought of as having been populated chiefly by wealthy and aristocratic planters and their negro slaves. The incompleteness of this picture at once becomes apparent when we reflect that, though it took a great many more slaves than masters to operate a plantation, yet the negroes were never in a majority in more than one or two of the southern states. Of what then was the rest of the white population composed? It was composed partly of small planters and farmers in the mountainous uplands, partly of white *Opposition of the Lower Classes* servants, indentured or hired, and partly of artisans, free laborers and petty merchants—in short, of the elements which compose the proletariat and lower middle class in all societies. For such people, life is always a harsh struggle, and in the South it was rendered especially so by the competition of slave labor. They envied the comfort and luxury of the wealthy planters and smarted under their contempt. Naturally, therefore, they hated them. Until the attack of the abolitionists had welded the South into political unity, they always opposed the planters in politics, and once they were free to do so they opposed them in religion also. Moreover, they found the other denominations more congenial to their tastes than the Episcopal Church would have been even if it had not labored under the disadvantage of being the Church of the aristocracy. The preaching of the other ministers was probably more earnest and certainly more emotional than that of the Episcopalians. However much they might differ in other respects, Baptists, Presbyterians, Methodists, and irregulars all agreed in teaching a conversion theology—*i. e.,* a theology which proclaimed the need of a radical change from a life of sin to a life of sanctity —and such a theology has always had a tremendous appeal to the emotionally deprived. Finally, there had been, throughout the eighteenth century, a substantial immigration into all the southern colonies of people from New England, the European continent, Scotland, and Ireland, who had always belonged to other religious bodies than the Church of England, some of whom spoke a different language from that of the Prayer Book.

Growth of
Dissent

In our study of the colonial Church in the South we have already had occasion to notice a rapid growth of dissent in the decades preceding the Revolution, and in one or two colonies we found reason to believe that the dissenters were already in a majority, though prevented by property qualifications and other restrictions from gaining control of the government. It is obvious, however, that as long as the Episcopal Church was established in that region, so that everyone had to contribute to its support, many whose natural sympathies were with other forms of Christianity would remain in nominal allegiance to it in order to avoid the added expense of supporting a dissenting minister. When the Revolutionary upheaval gave them an opportunity, such people naturally sided with the dissenters in demanding disestablishment, and when that was obtained, they as naturally transferred their support to religious denominations that suited them better. In Virginia they weakened the Church further by depriving it of its glebes.

In obtaining disestablishment they were helped by the political philosophy which was used to rationalize the revolutionary movement, and by the widespread prevalence of a non-Christian and sometimes anti-Christian religious philosophy among the educated classes. The principal tenets of eighteenth century political liberalism were religious freedom, free speech, freedom of the press, economic individualism ("laissez-faire"), and democratic, or at least republican government. These were the ideals, therefore, which were used to inspire the revolutionary armies and to guide the debates of Congress. To the wealthier leaders of the movement many of them were probably not much more than convenient catch phrases, which might prove dangerous if the people were allowed to take them too seriously, and as soon as the war was over, a struggle, eventually successful, was begun for the establishment of a government that would adequately protect the rights of property from the inroads of crazy idealists and hungry debtors. In the meantime, however, some concessions had to be made to the demands of the poorer classes that their aspirations be given some practical satisfaction, and about the easiest concession which the wealthy could make was to permit the disestablishment of the Church. At the worst, this was better than exposing themselves to economic loss, and to those who were in sympathy with the Deistic view that no religious differences mattered much, so long as everyone worshipped a Supreme Being, the sacrifice was not even painful. Except for the Deists, the planter class continued in nominal allegiance to the Church, but for some time the support which most of them gave it was less than half-hearted, and the infusion of a new religious force, that of the Evangelicals, was required before Episcopalianism again became very active in the South.

While recognizing, however, that the Episcopal Church experienced a serious decline following the American Revolution, we should avoid exaggerating this decline. Too much has been said and written about the deadness of the Church at this period. Had it been dead, it could not, in a little more than six years after the

The Revolutionary Philosophy

Decline of the Church not to be Exaggerated

close of the war, have developed diocesan organizations in a majority of the states, united these into a national body along lines for which it had no immediate precedent, and obtained from England and Scotland the number of bishops necessary to guarantee a continuance of the succession. In view of the difficulties which confronted it, and the lack of experience of Churchmen in united action, the achievements of the Church in those years are, in fact, remarkable.

Beginnings of Reorganization

Even during the war some beginnings had been made towards diocesan organizations in two of the states, though for the time being they proved abortive. Shortly after the Declaration of Independence, as we have seen, a convention met in Virginia and voted to omit the prayers for the King from the liturgy. Before the war was over, however, the legislature had surrounded the Church with so many restrictions that in 1784 the clergy could do no more than meet and petition for the repeal of the restraining laws. In Maryland the clergy had been deprived of public support early in the struggle as the result of a clause in the state bill of rights which called for religious freedom. Shortly after this they were required to take oaths of allegiance to the new government, and some of them, holding this to be inconsistent with their ordination vows, left the state. In 1779 the legislature passed an act providing for the election of vestries in existing parishes, and turning the Church property over to them, but it left the clergy dependent on voluntary contributions, except for what support they could derive from their glebes. In 1780, thanks to the exertions of William Smith and some others, a convention was assembled, composed of three clergymen and a number of laymen. This convention petitioned the Assembly for the public support of religion, but subsequently withdrew the petition because of the troublous state of the times. It also voted to call the body which it repre-

Name of the Church

sented the Protestant Episcopal Church. This was the first use of the present name of the Church by an official organization, but the phrase was not a new one. It had sometimes been used in the colonial period to describe the ecclesiastical position of the Church of England, and was employed by the Rev. Thomas Barton in a petition which he addressed to the Pennsylvania legislature in behalf of his fellow clergy in 1778. The name was subsequently adopted for the whole Church more by common consent than because anyone especially advocated it. The word Protestant, though originally applied only to the Lutherans, had by then come to mean any form of Western Christianity not owning allegiance to the Pope, and as episcopacy was the most conspicuous feature which distinguished our Church from the other non-Roman Catholic bodies, this seemed the most natural way to describe it. The only alternative suggested, and that only by one or two, was "Reformed Episcopal Church," which, historically, would have implied a Calvinistic origin, though it was probably not so intended.

After the war was over, a more general reorganization was set on foot, which was to result eventually in the formation of the general constitution which has formed the basis of the Church's national life ever since. This movement had a more or less spontaneous origin in several states, and many people contributed to its advancement, but its most important leader, the coördinator of its various elements, was William White, whom we have recently met as the revolutionary rector of Christ Church, Philadelphia. White, who was thirty-six at the close of the Revolution, having been born in 1747, was the son of a wealthy landowner and man of affairs in Philadelphia, who had held various public offices both in Pennsylvania and Maryland. His father-in-law was a former mayor of Philadelphia, and his sister's husband was Robert Morris, the financier of the Revolution. Thus he was one who could claim the right to leadership by inheritance and association as well as on the strength of his own abilities. He had been educated at the College of Philadelphia and had studied theology under William Smith and under his own predecessors at Christ Church, Richard Peters and Jacob Duché. Having directed his steps toward the ministry from an early period, he went to England as soon as he was old enough to be ordained and, on his return to America in 1772, was elected assistant-minister of Christ Church, becoming rector during the Revolution, and serving as Chaplain of the Continental Congress throughout the war. Though he had embraced the cause of independence from a sense of duty, he was of too moderate a temper to carry over his political sentiments into his personal or ecclesiastical relationships and continued, whenever possible, a friendly intercourse with his fellow clergymen on the Tory side. As he was about the only outstanding Whig minister

Leadership of White

who displayed such moderation, he naturally became the one to whom the leaders of both sides turned with their ideas and suggestions after the war was over, and he was enough of a statesman to make the most of this position, and to coördinate his own ideas with the suggestions which he received from others, until an effective union was developed.

In exercising this leadership White was helped further by the central position and importance of the parish of which he was rector and by the general moderation of his religious views. White's theological position has been frequently misunderstood, not because it was at all obscure or uncertain, but because it could not be made to fit very well under any of the party labels that were prevalent in his later life. His own views, as he himself tells us, underwent very little change after he had reached maturity, but those about him were not so stedfast, and by the middle years of his life, the party which had formed the natural background for his opinions had largely disappeared and been replaced by one with which he had very little sympathy. He belonged, in fact, to the older school of Low Churchmanship, which preceded the Evangelicals. The members of this school were orthodox in their theology, unlike the latitudinarians, who represented the extreme phase of their party, but they were disposed to tolerate a fairly wide variety of opinions so long as there was no departure from essentials. They believed in the Apostolic origin of the episcopate, but in the absence of a specific command for its continuance they were unwilling to condemn as altogether invalid the ministries of those denominations which had been compelled to sacrifice it, and they were not disposed to rate the authority of bishops too highly, even within the Church. They were disposed to emphasize, perhaps too much, the rational and intellectual side of Christianity but they never yielded its supernatural claims altogether in favor of mere rationalism. If they were, as a rule, somewhat lacking in fire, they were strong in judiciousness and moderation, and they were capable of appreciating the value of a comprehensive Church.

It was under the leadership of men who held views such as these that the central movement in the process of union was carried on, which fact accounts for a certain receptiveness to innovation, and willingness to tone down some of the distinctive traditions of the Church that characterized that movement. Eventually, the need of including the High Churchmen, and especially those of Connecticut, within the union compelled the adoption of a more conservative attitude, but the handiwork of the Low Church organizers can still be seen in the fabric of our Church in such things as the inclusion of laymen in ecclesiastical councils, the slight authority given to bishops over independent parishes, the curtailment of their authority in other respects by standing committees and diocesan conventions, the omission of the Athanasian Creed from the Prayer Book, the permission to omit the sign of the cross in Baptism, and to substitute the "place of departed spirits" for "hell" in the Apostles' Creed.

Geographically, the union movement was primarily the work of the middle states, though in saying this we must, for the moment, include Maryland in that category, for it was there that William Smith, perhaps the second most important leader of the movement, was then resident, and that state was represented in all of the early conventions. In New England, outside of Connecticut, the Episcopalians were receptive to unity, and under the leadership of Samuel Parker they coöperated in some of the earlier phases of the movement, but after the consecration of Bishop Seabury in Connecticut they tended to hold aloof until they were sure that the validity of his orders would be accepted by the rest of the states. Had it not been, a schism would have been created in the Church, and the rest of New England would naturally have allied itself with Connecticut. That state had, as we have seen, retained a larger complement of ministers than any other after the Revolution (fourteen out of twenty), and it had, moreover, a strong independent tradition which was strengthened by its having become, in consequence of the flight of the Tory clergymen elsewhere, the chief heir of colonial High Churchmanship. Connecticut Churchmen were as desirous as any others of seeing the Church united along national lines, but they sought to attain that end in their own way. Because of the importance which they attached to episcopacy, it seemed to them improper to undertake the reorganization of the Church until bishops had been obtained. Their first move, therefore, was to try to supply this need for themselves, after which they probably thought that they would be in a position to take the lead in reorganizing the Church generally. It so happened, however, that by the time they had obtained a bishop, the process

Leadership of the Middle Colonies in the Reorganization of the Church of organization had gone far enough elsewhere so that it could not be turned into new lines, and in the end their chief function in the movement was to act as a check on its more radical tendencies.

Attitude of the South

In the South, the prevailing type of Churchmanship tended towards the opposite extreme. As we have seen, southern Episcopalians had cared but little for the obtaining of American bishops in colonial times, and while they now recognized the necessity of doing so, they desired to curtail their power in every way possible. Moreover, the Church in the South was greatly weakened by the shock of disestablishment and, in Virginia especially, it was surrounded with numerous restrictions by the legislature. Virginia and South Carolina were represented in some of the preliminary conventions, but the only clergyman in either state who took an active interest in the process of unification in its early stages was David Griffith, the rector of Fairfax Parish, Virginia.

White's Pamphlet

The first public suggestion of a plan of union and reorganization was made by White in 1782, in a pamphlet called *The Case of the Episcopal Churches in the United States Considered*. At the time that this was published, the active hostilities of the Revolution had ceased for some time but no satisfactory terms of peace had yet been reached, and some proposals which were thought to represent the farthest point likely to be conceded by the British government had lately been rejected by Congress. It seemed likely, therefore, that a long time would ensue during which the United States would be practically independent without having their freedom recognized by the mother country, as had been the case with the Dutch Republic after its revolt from Spain, which was the only modern precedent that people had to judge by.

If this had happened, it is obvious that the obtaining of bishops from England would have been impossible, and also that it would no longer have been possible for candidates to be ordained to the lower grades of the ministry there. The Church in this country would have been in danger of disintegrating for want of organization and leadership. White, therefore, proposed that until the episcopate could be obtained (and only until then), the Church should be organized in a federal system of three grades, the ministers of the smallest unit (co-extensive with the state) to have collectively the power of ordination. The Church was to make a formal declaration of its preference for episcopacy, and of its intention of obtaining it as soon as possible, but in the meantime White felt that the necessity of the case would fully justify the resort to presbyterial ordination, and he cited expressions from Cranmer, Hooker, Usher, and other leading English divines to support this view.

As it turned out, a treaty of peace was finally arranged within a very short time after the publication of this pamphlet, and before it had been widely circulated, so that the considerations which led to its chief proposal were never fully understood, and it created a temporary distrust of White among those who regarded episcopacy as essential to the Church. Nevertheless, it made an important contribution to the movement for reorganization, and two of its suggestions had an important effect upon the future constitution of the Episcopal Church. The procedure of completing a federal constitution before obtaining the episcopate was, in fact, the one followed outside of Connecticut, and besides having the advantage of uniting the Church before its various parts had become so crystallized as to make fusion difficult, it proved more successful than the Connecticut plan in obtaining the episcopal succession from England. The other proposal was the inclusion of lay representatives in the governing body of the Church, which was here for the first time publicly advanced as a principle, though a practical example of it had already been furnished in Maryland. This policy was soon adopted in every state except Connecticut, and eventually there, and has become an important feature of our ecclesiastical constitution. Moreover, perhaps precisely because its main argument was objectionable to many, the pamphlet led to a widespread discussion of the problems involved in the reorganization of the Church, and it naturally gave to its author a prominent place in this discussion. Shortly after its publication, he began to receive letters on the subject from clergymen of all parties, commencing with some from Charles Inglis in May, 1783, just before Inglis left New York, and continuing in such numbers as to constitute White a sort of unofficial committee of correspondence on the affairs of the Church, before any official committees had been appointed.

Its Importance

In August, 1783, the Maryland Episcopalians held a second convention under the presidency of William Smith. Earlier in the year Smith and the Rev. Thomas Gates, another clergyman of

The Second Maryland Convention

the state, had petitioned for permission to introduce a law that would open the way for a revision of the liturgy, but the desired measure had not been passed. When the Convention met it adopted a declaration of rights for the "Protestant Episcopal Church," asserting her continuity with the Church of England in the colonies and her consequent title to the property held by that Church in Maryland, her right to "preserve herself as an entire Church," her need of a threefold ministry (bishops, priests, and deacons), and the propriety of amending her liturgy to meet new conditions. It also elected Dr. Smith to be bishop as soon as he could obtain consecration from England. The declaration of rights was submitted to Governor William Paca, a Churchman and a former pupil of Smith's at the College of Philadelphia, with the suggestion that he obtain legislative sanction for it if he thought such sanction necessary. Paca replied that the approval of the legislature was not required, as "every denomination of clergy are to be deemed adequate judges of their own spiritual rights and of the ministerial commission and authority necessary to the due administration of the ordinances of religion among themselves"—in other words, the internal arrangements of the Church were no business of the State's.

In November, 1783, White suggested to his vestry a meeting of committees from the vestries of the three churches in Philadelphia to confer with the city clergy on the formation of a representative body for the Church in Pennsylvania. These committees, when they assembled, thought that plans for organization should have the concurrence of all Episcopalians in the United States, and as a step in that direction, a meeting of clergy and laity from various parts of Pennsylvania was called for May 24, 1784. This convention adopted a set of fundamental principles to the effect that the Episcopal Church in the United States should be independent of all foreign authority, that it had full powers to regulate its own affairs, that it should maintain the "Doctrines of the Gospel" as proposed by the Church of England and conform to the worship of that Church as far as possible, that it should have a threefold ministry, that canons should be made by representatives of the clergy and laity jointly, and that no powers should be delegated to a general ecclesiastical government except such as could not be conveniently exercised by state conventions. It also resolved that a standing

The Pennsylvania Declaration of Principles

committee be appointed to correspond with committees of other states with a view to the formation of a general constitution.

Between the calling of this convention and its assembling, another meeting had been held which also took an important step toward the organization of General Convention. In January, 1784, Abraham Beach, the rector of New Brunswick, New Jersey, had written to White expressing his alarm at the silence which seemed to prevail as to measures for the revival of the Church. He thought the first thing to do was to secure a meeting of as many of the clergy as possible, and, as the affairs of the Corporation for the Relief of Widows and Orphans of Clergymen in Pennsylvania, New York, and New Jersey were badly in need of attention, he suggested that a meeting of that corporation be called in the spring, and that an attempt be made to get together as many of the clergy who were not members as possible at the same time. In a later letter he suggested including respectable laymen also. White promptly accepted this proposal and the meeting was held at New Brunswick on May 11th. The corporation merely voted to hold another meeting in the fall, but the clergy and laymen who were present held a separate meeting in which they appointed a committee to wait upon the clergy of Connecticut and ask their concurrence in plans for the rehabilitation of the Church. Other committees were appointed in the three states represented to correspond with each other and with other persons "for the purpose of forming a continental representation of the Episcopal Church."

While these beginnings were being made in the Middle States, the Connecticut clergy had been taking steps for the restoration of the Church in the way that seemed best to them. Shortly after the treaty of peace, ten of them held a secret meeting in which they voted to ask either Jeremiah Leaming or Samuel Seabury to become their bishop, promising obedience to whichever should be consecrated. The delegation which was sent to New York, where both of these men were then living, offered the post first to Leaming, who declined from motives of self-distrust, and then to Seabury, who felt it his duty to accept. Seabury sailed for England armed with a letter from the Connecticut clergy to the Archbishops, in which they gave as one of their reasons for desiring a bishop the dangerous proposal lately made by White at Philadelphia, and with three letters of recommendation from Leaming,

The Meeting at New Brunswick

Seabury Elected Bishop of Connecticut

Inglis, and Moore in New York. Seabury was instructed to seek consecration in England, if possible, but if not, to try to obtain it from the Nonjuring bishops in Scotland. In England the Archbishops said they were unable to ordain him because they had no right to send a bishop to Connecticut without the consent of that state, because he would probably not be received there, because no definite provision had been made for his support, and because the oaths of allegiance could not be dropped without, at least, the consent of the King in Council, and this could not be obtained unless the State of Connecticut should signify its willingness to have a bishop reside within its jurisdiction. Later on they also objected to the fact that his election had not been concurred in by the laity and that there was no definitely organized diocese over which he could exercise jurisdiction. Finding, after repeated attempts, that these objections could not be removed, Seabury at length applied to the Scottish bishops, who were not dependent on the government, and was consecrated by Bishops Kilgour, Petrie and Skinner late in 1784, the service taking place in a chapel on the top floor of Skinner's home.

His
Consecration

At the time of his consecration, Seabury entered into a concordat with the Scotch bishops in which he agreed to accept the whole doctrine of the Gospel, to regard bishops as independent of lay control, and to accommodate the worship and discipline of the Church in Connecticut as nearly as possible to that of Scotland. The two Churches were also declared to be in full communion with one another and pledged to brotherly intercourse. The chief significance of this document is that it led to the inclusion of some features of the Scottish liturgy in our Communion Service. On his return to the United States, Seabury was readily accepted as bishop in Connecticut, but he met with opposition elsewhere. Though there could be no serious doubt as to the validity of his orders, he was objectionable personally to many because of his stand during the Revolution, and others objected to his having obtained consecration from a Church which they regarded as schismatic from the Church of England.

When the committee from the New Brunswick meeting visited Connecticut in June, 1784, Seabury was still trying to obtain consecration in England and the local clergy, while expressing sympathy with the desire for union, were unwilling to take any action until they had a bishop. In Massachusetts and Rhode Island, however, a joint convention, held in the fall of 1784, ratified the principles of the Pennsylvania state convention with two minor qualifications.

The next general meeting was held in New York in October of the same year under the presidency of William Smith. The Middle States and Maryland all sent delegations of ministers and laymen, and clergymen from Massachusetts, Rhode Island, and Connecticut also participated. David Griffith was present from Virginia, but was unable to take an active part because the clergy there were still surrounded by legal restrictions. The convention recommended certain principles of union to the states, the most important being that there should be a General Convention of clerical and lay deputies, that the doctrines and as much as possible of the liturgy of the Church of England should be retained, and that the first meeting of the proposed General Convention should be held in Philadelphia during September, 1785. Meeting in New York, 1784

That convention, when it met, contained representatives from all of the Middle States, and from Maryland, Virginia, and South Carolina as well, but none from New England. The Massachusetts Episcopalians found the distance too great, and those of Connecticut absented themselves because the principles set forth at New York had failed to provide for the presidency of a bishop. The convention, after electing White president, proceeded to appoint a committee of which William Smith was the chairman, to draft a constitution, revise the liturgy, and formulate a plan for obtaining the episcopate. The work of revising the liturgy was continued by the committee—chiefly by White and Smith—after the convention adjourned, though on lines which it had approved, but the constitution and the plan for securing bishops were completed and approved by the convention. The plan took especial care to avoid the objections which had been made to Seabury's consecration. The General Convention was to address the English bishops and request them to confer episcopal orders on such men as might be chosen by the state conventions, the state conventions were advised to take special pains to make it clear that the candidates were elected with the concurrence of the laity, and the deputies present were desired to request their civil rulers to certify The Convention of 1785 that the application was not contrary to the constitutions and laws of their several states.

Three states, New York, Pennsylvania, and Virginia, complied with these suggestions and elected bishops. In Pennsylvania the choice, of course, fell on White. Virginia elected Griffith and New York chose Samuel Provoost, rector of Trinity. Maryland, as we have seen, had elected William Smith two years earlier. The New York choice, though inevitable, was not altogether a fortunate one. Provoost had been an enthusiastic revolutionist and he was not able to forget political differences in dealing with ecclesiastical affairs. His opposition to Seabury amounted almost to a mania, and it took all of White's adroitness and diplomacy to keep him from precipitating an open break with Connecticut. The application to the civil rulers was successful, not only in the states, but with Congress also, both the president of that body, R. H. Lee, and the Secretary for Foreign Affairs, John Jay, supplying the desired certificates, while John Adams, our minister to Great Britain, also exerted himself in behalf of the measure. Jay and Lee were Episcopalians, but the coöperation of Adams was an example of the general spirit of religious toleration which ruled the times.

The political obstacles having thus been overcome, an ecclesiastical one threatened to arise, and that as a result of the Convention's own action. White and Smith, continuing the work of revision begun at the Convention of 1785, had issued a "Proposed Book," which, while professing a desire to adhere to the basic usages of the Church of England, represented, in fact, a strong expression of the Protestant tradition of the Church, omitting the Athanasian and the Nicene Creeds, the "descent into hell" from the Apostles' Creed, and all expressions implying baptismal regeneration. It also permitted the omission of the Sign of the Cross in Baptism, and made other changes which were obnoxious to the more conservative members of the Church. Some of these changes probably went beyond what the revisers themselves desired, and were included to conciliate the extremists, for both the Pennsylvania and the Maryland conventions, with the concurrence of White and Smith, subsequently voted to restore the Nicene Creed. To the Archbishops the book seemed to come very close to a departure in essentials from the teaching of the English Church, and they felt doubtful as to the wisdom of consecrating American bishops until some of the omissions were restored. Nevertheless, they secured the passage of a bill through Parliament permitting the consecration, trusting that an accommodation on the disputed points would follow.

At the Convention of 1786 the opponents of Bishop Seabury made an effort to secure action that would cast doubt on the validity of his consecration. The motions for this purpose were made by the Rev. Robert Smith of South Carolina and were supported by South Carolina, New York, and New Jersey. The first motion was to require the clergy present to show their letters of orders or tell by whom they were ordained, the object being to challenge those ordained by Seabury. Debate on this proposal was shut off by a moving of the previous question by William Smith, seconded by White, and the motion was defeated. The next motion was that the Convention resolve to do nothing that would imply the validity of ordinations performed by Dr. Seabury. This was defeated in the same manner. White himself, however, proposed a resolution, which was unanimously adopted, recommending that the states represented should refuse to admit to pastoral charge any clergyman professing canonical subjection to a bishop in any state or country not represented, and a resolution was also passed advising the states not to admit into their jurisdiction anyone who should be ordained by a bishop residing in America while the application to the English bishops was pending. The reason for this apparently contradictory proceeding was that, on the one hand, the leaders of the Convention were anxious to avoid any declaration against Seabury which would be an obstacle to eventual union, while, on the other hand, they were disturbed by the fact that Seabury ordained men for states outside of his own without reference to the local conventions, and that he apparently required from such men a promise of some sort of obedience to him until bishops should be obtained for their respective states. They also felt that the application to the English bishops might be jeopardized if too definite a recognition were given to Seabury while it was pending.

The Convention of 1786: Attack on Seabury

After thus suspending the Seabury question, and dealing with a few minor matters, the Convention adjourned until fall when it reassembled in Wilmington, Delaware, where it received a communication from the Archbishops specifying the conditions of

Communication from the Archbishops

consecration and stating their objections to the Proposed Book and the proposed constitution, and a later note saying that the act authorizing the consecration had been passed by Parliament. The Convention sought to meet the objections of the Archbishops in part by voting to retain the Nicene Creed and the "descent into hell" in the Apostles', but it persisted in rejecting the Athanasian Creed and retaining an article of the constitution subjecting bishops to trial by their diocesan conventions, to which objections had also been made. Before adjourning, the deputies signed testimonials for Provoost, White, and Griffith, but refused to sign those of William Smith because of a charge, brought by the Rev. John Andrews, that he had been drunk at the preceding Convention. This is the only occasion on which such a charge was ever made against Dr. Smith, and were it not for the respectability of the witness and the readiness with which his testimony was accepted by men who were certainly Smith's friends, we should be disposed to reject it. As it is, it seems necessary to conclude that there were, at least, good grounds for suspicion.

Of the three whose testimonials were signed, two, White and Provoost, sailed at once for England and were consecrated the ensuing February, but Griffith, because of the passive resistance of the Virginia Standing Committee, under the leadership of the Rev. James Madison, was unable to obtain either the necessary funds for the voyage, or the calling of a diocesan convention to sign his testimonials. Thus, when the new bishops returned to America in the spring, there were three bishops in the country— the number necessary for a consecration—but only two of them were of the English succession. This situation might, under favorable conditions, have promoted the cause of union, but actually it proved embarrassing, for it forced to the front the question of Seabury's orders. Provoost, to whom the horrid words Tory and Nonjuror were enough to invalidate any consecration, would do nothing that involved coöperation with his brother bishop in Connecticut, and White considered himself under an implied promise to the Archbishops not to act with Seabury until there was a canonical number of bishops of the English line in America—an attitude which he may have taken partly to keep Provoost from forcing the issue on more fundamental grounds.

The two years that elapsed between the return of the bishops

Consecration
of White and
Provoost

and the assembling of the next Convention were occupied in efforts to unite the two lines and to complete the English succession by obtaining the consecration of Griffith. Seabury, now that two states had organizations which he could regard as complete, showed his desire to promote the cause of union by writing to White and Provoost to suggest a conference of the three on ecclesiastical affairs. Provoost failed to answer this letter. White replied and expressed his desire for unity, but declined to attend such a conference, probably because he thought that the fusion must be effected by a representative convention, not by the individual bishops.

This cold reception apparently led the Connecticut clergy to fear that Seabury's orders would not be recognized by the rest of the Church, for they proceeded to elect Abraham Jarvis to go to Scotland for consecration in case such recognition should be withheld. Jeremiah Leaming wrote anxious letters to White, in which he suggested that Joseph Priestley, the famous Unitarian scientist, and a friend of White's, was plotting to divide the Church in order to advance the cause of Unitarianism. White himself apparently foresaw that the problem would be fully solved only when the English succession was completed, for he bent his chief efforts towards obtaining the consecration of Griffith, though without success.

When the Convention finally met, on July 28, 1789, the states had already been brought into a closer political union by the adoption of the Federal Constitution, and that fact may have strengthened the cause of union in the Church. At any rate, everyone there—Bishop Provoost being happily absent—was anxious to promote unification, and in order to clear up any "misapprehensions," it was unanimously resolved "that it is the opinion of this Convention that the consecration of the Right Rev. Dr. Seabury to the episcopal office is valid." On receiving a request from Massachusetts that the three bishops should unite in the consecration of Edward Bass, bishop-elect of that state—a request which was designed to bring the two lines together—the Convention, on motion of William Smith, unanimously resolved that a complete order of bishops, derived from England and Scotland, now existed in the United States, that they were fully competent to perform every duty of the episcopal office, and that they were

The Convention of 1789: First Meeting

requested to unite in the consecration desired. If White and Provoost felt any delicacy respecting their obligations to the English bishops, the Convention undertook to address the latter and seek to have the difficulty removed.

New England Joins the Convention

After some further legislation, of which the most important was the adoption of a constitutional provision that the bishops should constitute a separate house as soon as there were three or more in union with the Convention, the meeting adjourned to September 29th, to give time for the communication of its proceedings to be presented to Seabury. This was done by White, who also solicited Seabury's attendance at the adjourned Convention and expressed his personal conviction of the validity of the latter's orders, and his willingness to unite in the proposed consecration if the obligation which he felt to the English bishops should be removed by them. To this Seabury replied at once, saying that he would most willingly attend the Convention. When that body reassembled in Philadelphia, not only Seabury and the Connecticut delegation, but deputies from Massachusetts and New Hampshire were also present. After some alterations had been made, they all signed the constitution, and White and Seabury separated themselves from the rest of the Convention, to become the first House of Bishops, making this the first complete General Convention in the sense in which that title has ever since been used. Having thus completed its organization the Convention proceeded to revise the liturgy on somewhat more conservative lines than those of 1785.

Concessions to Connecticut

In the union thus effected, some concessions were made to the Connecticut Churchmen. The Bishops became a separate house, with the right of initiating legislation as well as revising it (though they did not obtain an absolute veto until some time later), and some of the omissions of the Proposed Book were restored, including the Nicene Creed and the Sign of the Cross in Baptism (though with permission to omit it), but the Athanasian Creed was still omitted and all of the essential features of the previously developed organization were retained, including lay representation and the trial of bishops by their own conventions, two provisions to which strenuous objections had been made in Connecticut. It was provided, however, that a diocese need not send lay delegates to General Convention if it preferred not to, and for a time Connecticut did not. Seabury felt that the results of the Convention were in some measure a defeat for his party. In a letter which he wrote to White the following spring he complained that, in the matter of the Creeds, there appeared to have been "too great an aim at victory" among his opponents at the Convention and that he could see no reason for not restoring the Athanasian Creed, with a permissive rubric, except "that it would not have afforded matter of complete triumph." When, through a misunderstanding between the two houses, the "descent into hell" in the Apostles' Creed was placed in brackets with a rubric permitting its omission, he felt that this was the last straw, and doubted for a time if he could accept the Book. In the end, however, his zeal for the welfare of the Church overcame his personal feelings, and he did his best, eventually with success, to bring the revised Prayer Book into general use in Connecticut.

Before an answer could be received to letters sent to the Archbishops requesting their approval of the uniting of White and Provoost with Seabury in the performance of episcopal acts, Virginia, where Griffith's death had vacated the post of bishop-elect, chose James Madison, president of the College of William and Mary, instead and sent him to England for consecration. Before he left he wrote to Seabury concerning the possibility of his being consecrated in this country, but the letter was apparently intended merely as a polite gesture, for he did not wait to receive an answer before sailing. His return solved the difficulties respecting the succession, and the four bishops united in consecrating Thomas John Claggett to be the first Bishop of Maryland in 1792. Edward Bass, Bishop of Massachusetts, was not consecrated until five years later, the Massachusetts convention having become somewhat lethargic after 1789.

Consecration of James Madison

It had been agreed between White and Seabury at the Convention of 1789 that the senior bishop present should preside over the House of Bishops. At the next Convention, because of the objections of Provoost and Madison, this rule was modified, and the presidency placed in rotation, but in 1795 the rule of seniority was restored and continued until the organization of the National Council in 1919. As Seabury died in 1796, White presided over the Convention of 1798 and every Convention thereafter until his death in 1836.

CHAPTER X

Recuperation

IN CONTRAST to the periods which immediately preceded and followed it, the epoch of our history which extends approximately from 1789, when the organization of the Episcopal Church was completed, to 1811, when the consecration of Bishops Hobart and Griswold may be said to have started the period of rapid expansion, is so quiet that at first sight it almost seems that nothing was being done. The very brilliance of the succeeding period, should, however, serve to warn us against taking such a view. No man can build on air, and the great achievements of the later leaders would have been impossible had there not been a certain amount of quiet repairing of the shattered foundations of the Church in the years preceding.

The period can, perhaps, best be compared to that stage which sometimes follows the crisis of a long sickness when the patient is no longer in imminent danger but when day follows tedious day without any sign of recovery. To the patient and his friends it often seems as if he never would recover, but the experienced physician assures them that the sick man is "doing as well as can be expected," for he knows, in spite of appearances, that the patient is gradually regaining his shattered strength.

So it was with the Church during the period which we are discussing. The crisis precipitated by the Revolution had passed with the organization of General Convention and the obtaining of the episcopate, but the Church was still exhausted and a period of quiet recuperation was required. While it seemed on the surface that nothing was happening, some old parishes were being reopened, those that had kept open were growing stronger, the people were getting used to the necessity of self-support, the presence of bishops and the functioning of diocesan conventions, and new leaders were growing up who were accustomed to the

Church as it now was, and were accordingly capable of thinking in terms of present possibilities rather than of past powers.

Within eight years after the completion of the English succession, the episcopate was extended to three states besides the four which had obtained bishops from Great Britain. As we have seen, Bishop Claggett was consecrated in 1792, and he was followed by Robert Smith, Bishop of South Carolina, in 1795, and Edward Bass, Bishop of Massachusetts and Rhode Island, in 1797. As Bishop White exercised some jurisdiction over New Jersey and Delaware, there were ten states with at least a partial claim on the services of a bishop. The election of Bishop Smith was the occasion of an incident which illustrates the strong jealousy of the episcopate prevailing in some sections. Shortly before that election took place Henry Purcell and two other South Carolinians sent a circular letter to the rectors and vestries of the state asserting that they were a select committee appointed by seven churches to ask the coöperation of the other Episcopalians in the state in sending one of their clergy immediately northward to obtain power solely to ordain and confirm, but not to have any of the usual attributes of episcopal authority, even in the dilute form in which they then existed in the country. The reason given for making this move was that the House of Deputies had announced in 1792 its intention of considering at the next Convention the granting of an absolute negative to the House of Bishops, and the signers of the circular were confident that the passage of such a measure would lead to the secession of Virginia and South Carolina from the General Convention. As a result of this circular a convention assembled and elected Robert Smith bishop. When, however, Bishop White, acting on instructions from the House of Bishops, asked Smith if the sentiments expressed in the letter had been approved by the state convention, he was told that they had not, and on this understanding the consecration was allowed to proceed.

In the meantime, Purcell had delivered himself of an anonymous pamphlet entitled *Strictures on the Love of Power in the Prelacy,* in which, after attacking all bishops generally, he made a particular attack upon the American bishops, excepting White, and especially upon Bishop Seabury, who was supposed to be in favor of the veto power. As Purcell represented South Carolina in the House of Deputies, the attention of that body was called to this

Extension of the Episcopate

Purcell Incident

pamphlet by the Rev. John Andrews, Vice-provost of the University of Pennsylvania, and it was declared to contain "very offensive and censurable matter." Purcell would, in fact, have been expelled from the Convention, had not the Bishops intervened to ask for clemency after he had, with many tears, signed a recantation in the presence of Bishop White and William Smith, president of the lower house. After the Convention had adjourned, Purcell showed the insincerity of his repentance by sending to Dr. Andrews a letter charging him with slandering the author and apparently implying that either a threat of violence or a challenge to a duel was to be conveyed by the bearer. As a result of this Purcell was hailed before the Mayor of Philadelphia and bound over to keep the peace.

Other States Seek Bishops
Two or three other states made efforts to obtain bishops in these early years, but were prevented by various circumstances. In 1794 a convention in North Carolina elected the Rev. Charles Pettigrew bishop, but he was unable to reach the General Convention before its adjournment, and the application for consecration was not subsequently renewed, though Pettigrew lived until 1807. It was some years, in fact, before the Church in that state actually secured a delegation to General Convention, and much longer before it had a bishop. In the year 1795 the Rev. Samuel Peters, former missionary at Hebron, Connecticut, applied for consecration as Bishop of Vermont, but was refused it on the ground that Vermont had not acceded to the Constitution of the General Church. There had been only one clergyman in Vermont at the time of Peters' election and he had left shortly after. As a result of this incident a canon was passed providing that no bishop should be consecrated for a state unless there were at least six presbyters resident within it. Because of this canon the House of Deputies at the next Convention declined to sign the testimonials of Uzal Ogden who had been elected Bishop of New Jersey. Though more than six clergy had voted in his election, a majority of them were held not to be canonically resident, as they were only employed on a temporary basis by their vestries, and it is possible that a desire to discourage this type of tenure had something to do with the refusal to confirm the election, though it was also charged by his opponents that Ogden was insufficiently attached to the teachings of the Church.

During the period of organization and afterwards, some efforts were made to reunite the Methodists, or followers of John Wesley, who were then just beginning to develop as a separate denomination, with the Episcopal Church, from which most of them had originally come. Shortly after the close of the Revolution, when a serious want of ministers was felt in this country, Wesley appointed the Rev. Thomas Coke, a presbyter of the Church of England, to act as "superintendent" of the Methodists here, with power to ordain ministers. Coke was to "lay hands" upon the Rev. Francis Asbury, the actual leader of the American Methodists, who then received a similar authority. In 1784, not long after this event, Coke and Asbury were interviewed by two Episcopalian clergymen, the Rev. John Andrews and the Rev. William West, who urged them not to separate from the Episcopal Church, and suggested that when a regular succession had been obtained special bishops might be consecrated for the Methodists. Both of the superintendents rejected this proposal and when Andrews again urged it in a private interview with Coke, the latter replied that as the "new system" was now in successful operation he saw no advantage for the Methodists in obtaining a more traditional succession.

When William White went to England to obtain consecration in 1787, he sought an interview with John Wesley on the position of the American Methodists, but, though he had a letter of introduction from the Rev. Joseph Pilmore, one of Wesley's followers who remained in the Episcopal Church, he received so cool a reply to his request that he did not renew it. He did, however, have an interview with Charles Wesley, who expressed disapproval of the separation.

In 1791, an overture was made from the other side, for Thomas Coke, who had so definitely rejected the proposals of Andrews and West in 1784, had suffered a change of heart as the result of subsequent developments. As he had been the first of the superintendents to be named by Wesley, he had expected to become the principal leader of the Methodist Church, but the prestige already acquired by Asbury, his tremendous energy and unflagging devotion to his work, and his superior administrative ability made him the dominant member of the partnership and in time not only was Coke largely eclipsed but even the influence of John Wesley was

Relations with the Methodists

Coke's Proposal

considerably weakened. Under these circumstances Coke sought to strengthen his position by forming an alliance with the Episcopal Church, and he wrote to White and Seabury suggesting an arrangement not unlike that which he had rejected earlier. As the chief obstacle to reunion, he thought, would be the unwillingness of the present ordained ministers to give up the right of administering the sacraments, though they might submit to being reordained, and the reluctance of the lay preachers, whose literary qualifications were limited, to let their future ordination depend upon the present bishops of the Episcopal Church, he hinted to White and definitely suggested to Seabury that he and Asbury should both be consecrated bishops, though he did not undertake to state exactly what relationship they should then have to the Episcopal Church.

Seabury returned no answer to the letter sent to him, but White sent a non-committal reply, which was the only thing he thought proper since he personally had no authority to act in the matter. Had the proposal been more cordially received it might, perhaps, have resulted in bringing a few Methodists into the Episcopal Church, but it is hardly possible that it could have effected a general union, for Asbury, whose influence was by then all-powerful, would certainly have opposed it. Moreover, a condition which Coke himself regarded as essential to the plan, the coöperation of Wesley, was rendered impossible by that gentleman's death, news of which reached this country between the sending of Coke's letter and his receipt of White's answer. Coke subsequently had one or two interviews with White, but nothing of importance transpired during them and he presently returned to England, having despaired of regaining his influence among the American Methodists.

The issue of this and the previous attempts at union convinced most of those who were acquainted with the situation that the object, however desirable, was impossible of attainment. At the General Convention of 1792, however, Bishop Madison of Virginia was still anxious to promote the cause, if possible, and he persuaded his fellow bishops to propose to the lower house a joint declaration that the Episcopal Church was willing to modify such features of her system as she considered properly subject to human alteration if by so doing she could effect a union with any other

Bishop
Madison's
Proposed
Declaration

Christian denomination. It was also proposed that the state conventions should be advised to enter into such conferences with other religious groups as they thought desirable, and report the results to the next General Convention. This resolution was strongly opposed by a majority of the House of Deputies, however, and in order to avoid an open breach between the two houses the Bishops were given leave to withdraw it, which they did.

In 1797 overtures for union were made by the Lutheran Consistory in the state of New York to the Episcopal diocese of that state, and a committee was appointed by the diocesan convention to confer on the subject and to bring the matter before the next General Convention if necessary, but nothing came of it. The meeting of General Convention was postponed until 1799 because of an epidemic of yellow fever in 1798 when it should have met, and the state convention did not meet again until 1801, when it was preoccupied with the resignation of Bishop Provoost, and in the general uncertainty, the opportunity for union with the Lutherans was lost sight of.

Overtures from the Lutherans

The bishops of the first generation in the American Episcopal Church (those who were consecrated during the period of organization or shortly after), are generally supposed to have been highly inactive, and this view is, on the whole, correct. It is not correct, however, to assume that the inactivity was necessarily due to laziness or indifference on the part of the bishops. In some cases it may have been, but in others it certainly was not, and there were other reasons why the early bishops should have preferred not to be too vigorous in the exercise of their office. We have just seen, in the Purcell incident, with how much suspicion episcopacy was regarded in South Carolina. Other states were not quite so extreme in their views, but there was probably none, outside of Connecticut, where the office was not looked upon with a certain amount of distrust by most professed Episcopalians. Bishops were a novelty in this country, and it was also, so far as the experience of Englishmen and Americans went, a novelty to have them entirely deprived of temporal power. As experiments always make people uneasy, the feeling was everywhere latent that if a careful watch were not kept on the bishops, they might acquire an amount of power which would seriously curtail the liberties of the lower orders of clergy and the laity.

The Early Bishops

For this reason the office was at first surrounded with a good
Distrust of the many restrictions, some of which still remain. The Maryland con-
Episcopate vention of 1784 had declared, "According to what we conceive to
be of true Apostolic Institution, the duty and office of a bishop
differs in nothing from that of other priests, except in the power
of ordination and confirmation, and the right of presidency in
ecclesiastical meetings or synods," and this principle governed the
provisions made for the episcopate in nearly all of the states. Some,
indeed, denied the bishop even the right of presidency in their
conventions, giving him only an *ex officio* seat, though the obvious
inconvenience of such an arrangement led to its early abandonment. All of the states subjected their bishops to trial by their
own conventions, though most of them required that a member
of the episcopal order should preside at such trials and pronounce
the sentence. Some did not, however, require the presence of a
bishop for the trial and sentencing of members of the lower orders.
In the few matters in which he was allowed to exercise jurisdiction, moreover, such as the approval of candidates for ordination,
the bishop was generally required to act only with the concurrence
of the diocesan convention or of its permanent representative, the
Standing Committee. This latter institution, which is peculiar to
our branch of the Church, had its origin in the need of providing
some interim authority for the convention before bishops had been
obtained, and its continuance thereafter, though it has persisted
down to the present day, is explicable only by the desire which
was felt to place a curb upon the episcopal authority.

Under these circumstances, it is easy to see why the bishops
Moderation should have been very cautious in asserting their authority. They
Necessary had been chosen to do the two things for which their office, according to the usage of the Church, was absolutely essential: to
ordain and to confirm. Little else was allowed them. Indeed, they
found it inexpedient even to visit parishes for Confirmation unless
they were definitely invited. All of the various administrative functions which make the work of a bishop so important to the proper
functioning of a diocese today were denied them. There were, as
yet, no diocesan missions, or other institutions, no diocesan funds,
and no diocesan organizations or diocesan branches of national
organizations. The power of settling disputes between parishes
and their rectors had not yet been granted to the bishops, nor had

they been given the right to be consulted in the appointment of a rector. All of the less tangible influence which comes to a bishop from the prestige of his office had also to be slowly developed. For the present, the vital thing was that nothing should happen which would frighten or disgust the people with the episcopate, and in this negative respect, at least, the conduct of the early bishops was unexceptionable. They claimed no authority which was not given them, and by their moderation and restraint they eventually obtained privileges which undoubtedly would have been denied them had they been requested, so that the next generation of bishops was able to take over an office which had come to be trusted and respected, and to develop possibilities in it which would have shocked the people of an earlier time.

Connecticut represented a partial exception to this situation, and there Seabury, and his successor, Abraham Jarvis, were able to exercise a jurisdiction somewhat resembling that of later bishops, though backed by far fewer resources. Elsewhere, most of the bishops seem to have done what they could, or at least what was expected of them, but we must make some exceptions even to this limited commendation. Bishop Madison, after some earnest efforts at reviving the Church in Virginia, gave up in despair, and became entirely absorbed in his duties as president of the College of William and Mary. According to an early historian of the diocese of South Carolina, Bishop Smith did not perform any confirmations, but this may have been the result of the jealousy of his office prevailing in that state and not to indifference on his part. He probably performed some ordinations. In Maryland, Bishop Claggett carried on his work fairly regularly, except when he was incapacitated with the gout, and the condition of his diocese was generally pretty good.

In Massachusetts, Bishop Bass performed a number of ordinations and some confirmations. As there were but few active parishes left in the state, his duties cannot have been great, however. He was also Bishop of Rhode Island, but it does not appear that he did much work there. He died in 1804, and Samuel Parker, who was the real leader of the Church in Massachusetts, succeeded him, but died within less than a year after his consecration. Thereafter, the state, like all the rest of New England except Connecticut, was without a bishop until the organization of the Eastern

Work of Seabury and Jarvis

Diocese in 1811. There must have been some growth in the meantime, however. Bishop Griswold, at a later date, estimated the number of clergy in the four states comprising the Eastern Diocese to have been about fifteen at the time of its organization, and most of these were in Massachusetts and Rhode Island.

Bishop Provoost of New York made regular visitations for Confirmation and the consecration of churches in the district around New York City and on Long Island, which were the only parts of the state where the Church was then active, except at Albany. He also performed a respectable number of ordinations. In 1801 he resigned his jurisdiction, because of ill health, and went to live on his farm in the Bowery. He was succeeded by Benjamin Moore, who, as we have seen, had been the Tory choice for rector of Trinity after the Revolution, and who had served as assistant there after his demotion. Under Moore, the Church expanded along the Hudson between Westchester and Albany, and a start was made on missionary work in the western part of the state, which was beginning to be filled up with settlers from New England. In 1811 Moore was stricken with paralysis, which incapacitated him for active work, and John Henry Hobart was chosen as his assistant. Because of the spectacular growth of the Episcopal Church in New York during Hobart's episcopate, it has been customary to represent the preceding period as one of deadness, but actually the revival of the Church began under Bishop Provoost, and its growth was continuous throughout the episcopate of Bishop Moore. During the latter part of this period, however, the energetic influence of Hobart was already being felt in the diocese, for he had become an assistant at Trinity in 1800, and he took an important place in the affairs of the diocese from the start. He published some devotional manuals calculated to raise the standards of personal religion within the state, he engaged in a pamphlet controversy with the Presbyterians which will be noticed later, and, with the coöperation and advice of Bishop Moore, he organized a number of societies designed to stimulate the laity to greater efforts in supporting missionary work, promoting theological education, and distributing Bibles and Prayer Books.

Bishop White was the only one of the early bishops to live very far into the later period, and his career illustrates the fact that the greater activity of the later bishops was due at least as much to a

Margin notes:

Bishops Provoost and Moore in New York

Bishop White in Pennsylvania

change in circumstances as to a change in personalities, for he performed much more extensive visitations in his later years than he did at the beginning of his episcopate. The regular reports of his activities to the diocesan convention do not begin, or, at least, were not printed, until 1811. Before this he apparently visited any towns which asked him to come, but he would not have covered a large area in doing so, for the Church was pretty well restricted to the southeastern part of the state. He probably also made some visitations in southern New Jersey and Delaware. In 1811 he reported that parochial duties had prevented his visiting other parishes, but thereafter he made regular visitations. In 1813 he visited York and Lancaster, as well as some towns farther east. In 1814 he reported the confirmation of 465 persons, a record for these early years, but 275 of these were in Philadelphia, and the rest in towns of Pennsylvania and New Jersey not far from Philadelphia. For some years Lancaster county represented the western limit of his activities, for York was not revisited until 1822. In 1824 he got as far north as Wilkes Barre, and the next year he projected a visit to Pittsburgh and the other missions that had grown up beyond the Alleghenies. This purpose was defeated by an accident in which he suffered a fractured wrist, but before that happened he had already reached Lewistown, near the center of the state. In 1826 he succeeded in completing his western tour. He visited Pittsburgh and some other towns near the western border of the state and went on to Wheeling, Virginia, which Bishop Moore, of that state, had asked him to visit. The total distance covered in this trip was 830 miles and the number confirmed 503, a respectable achievement for a man of seventy-three at a time when the horse was the fastest means of locomotion, and when conditions in a large part of the state were still primitive. In 1827 White made a tour of 400 miles in the northeastern part of the state. In that year he was given an assistant, Henry Ustick Onderdonk, who had no parochial connection, and thereafter White left the care of the remoter parts of the state to him.

White, like all of the early bishops, except Madison, who was a college president, was the rector of a large parish as well as head of the diocese, for he retained his position at Christ Church until his death. Besides his diocesan and parochial activities, he also took an important part in the civic affairs of Philadelphia,

His Western Tour

His Civic
Leadership

being a founder and leader of a number of charitable and religious organizations, including the Philadelphia Bible Society, the first such society in the country. These activities probably benefited the Church indirectly by enhancing its prestige. He also coöperated with some of the clergy of his diocese in 1812 in organizing the Society for the Advancement of Christianity in Pennsylvania. The chief function of this society was the support of missionaries in the remoter parts of the state, and its principal leader was Jackson Kemper, later first Missionary Bishop of the Northwest, but then, and for many years, assistant at Christ Church. He was also the companion of White on his western tour in 1826.

CHAPTER XI

REVIVAL AND EXPANSION

THE MOST convenient date to mark the beginning of the period of active expansion in the history of the Episcopal Church, that is, the period during which it began to pass the limits of its colonial activity and enter new territory, is 1811, for that date saw the consecration of the two bishops who were to be the first and probably the most important leaders of the new epoch, John Henry Hobart of New York, and Alexander Viets Griswold of the Eastern Diocese. It must be borne in mind, however, that the division thus fixed is, like all historical divisions, an indefinite one. As we have seen, some beginning of expansion was made, at least in New York, before this date, and in many other places the movement cannot be said to have begun until somewhat later. In the older states of the South, moreover, the period should probably be described as one of active revival rather than expansion, for, inasmuch as the Church never did recover the predominance in those states which it had enjoyed in colonial times, it is not altogether accurate to speak of it as expanding there.

Consecration of Hobart and Griswold

The selection of the Hobart-Griswold consecration as the starting point of the period has a further advantage in that the two subjects of the consecration were outstanding representatives of the two types of Churchmanship which were to dominate the era: High Churchmanship and Evangelicalism. Of the former Hobart was not only the outstanding leader, but to some extent the remolder also, for he infused the movement with the ardor of his own spirit, giving it a warmth and vitality which it had not possessed since the days of its great seventeenth-century leaders, and he also injected into it a note of personal piety which may in some measure have been borrowed from its rivals. Hobart was the outstanding opponent of the Evangelicals, but it is a rare controversialist who is not influenced to some extent by the other side,

"Hobart Churchmanship"

and Hobart's watchword of "Evangelical truth and Apostolic order" would at least suggest the possibility that such an influence existed. At any rate, so great was Hobart's influence upon his fellow High Churchmen that the theological position which they held was known for some time, in this country, as "Hobart Churchmanship."

Griswold
and the
Evangelicals

Griswold was much less of a party leader than Hobart, and, indeed, he disliked to think of himself as a party man at all, but nevertheless it was generally recognized by his contemporaries that he could be counted upon to act with the Evangelical party, or, at least, with its more conservative and churchly section, and under his leadership the Eastern Diocese acquired a moderately Evangelical character. This party, which was to exercise a great influence upon the revival and expansion of the Episcopal Church, had its origin, like Methodism, in the preaching and teaching of John and Charles Wesley and their followers. The Wesleys were both of them clergymen of the Church of England, and they both remained within it, at least officially, all their days. Charles Wesley, indeed, was strongly attached to the Church. John, who was the principal leader of the movement, was less so, but he was opposed for various reasons to any separation of the English Methodists from the Established Church. He was, however, convinced of the principle that presbyters had as good a claim to the power of ordination as bishops, and after the Revolution he put this theory into practice, as we have seen, by ordaining superintendents (later called bishops), for the Methodists in this country. This move caused, or rather, completed the separation of the American Methodists from the Episcopal Church, and eventually a separation took place in England also.

The more conservative members of the movement, however, remained within the Church of England and the Episcopal Church in this country. Even a few of those whose names are associated more or less prominently with the founding of American Methodism refused to join the separation, and continued all their lives within the Episcopal Church. Joseph Pilmore, who had come to this country as a lay preacher among the Methodists, was one of the first candidates ordained by Bishop Seabury, and became rector of St. Paul's Church, Philadelphia. The Rev. Devereux Jarratt, a Virginia clergyman, ordained near the close of the colonial era, who labored valiantly in the difficult period following the Revolution, at first encouraged the Methodists, but dissociated himself from them when their trend away from the Church became evident.

Most of the later Evangelicals, however, had had no direct contact with the Methodists, but were followers of the more conservative phase of the movement. Theologically, they agreed with all of the leading denominations of Protestants in teaching that men were saved only by an active, personal faith in Christ, and that good actions were of no account except as they furnished evidence of such a faith. They agreed with the Calvinists in stressing the necessity of conversion, by which they meant conscious acceptance of and submission to Christ, but they disagreed with them by rejecting the doctrine of predestination.

Evangelical Principles and Methods

These two last points, taken together, resulted in those peculiarities of method which, much more than any technicalities of theology, gave to the Evangelicals their distinctive character. Since conversion was necessary, and since, while it was certainly dependent on and primarily the result of divine grace, it was not absolutely predetermined, but could be obtained by all who freely and earnestly sought it, it followed that it was the duty of the pastor to do everything in his power to make people seek it and to bring them to the state of mind in which they would be most likely to receive it. The Wesleys had found that the most effective means to this end was preaching of an emotional sort, supplemented by classes for religious instruction, usually in the Bible, by evening "lectures," which were simply a specialized form of sermon, and by "prayer meetings," or informal assemblies at which not only the minister, but such of the people as felt moved to do so, engaged in extemporaneous prayer. The Evangelicals took over these devices, and superimposed them upon the regular devotional system of the Church as represented in the Prayer Book. They adhered strictly to that book in their regular Sunday services, except that they claimed the right to add an extemporaneous prayer before or after the sermon, but the most vital part of their devotional life was expressed in the informal exercises already mentioned, and in their sermons. Some of their special meetings were held on Sunday evenings, after the regular services for the day were over, but most of them had to be held on weekdays, and it was the boast of the more advanced Evangelicals that they had some sort of religious exercise in their churches nearly every night.

Attitude Towards the Sacraments

A conversion theology necessarily stresses the internal and personal aspects of religious life, rather than the institutional and external. It was inevitable, therefore, that the sacraments and orders of the Church should not seem vitally important to the Evangelicals. They objected to the phrase "baptismal regeneration," which was frequently used by the High Churchmen, because they held that a man could be regenerated only by a personal conversion, and they generally insisted that Confirmation should be postponed until after the individual had been converted. The Eucharist they regarded chiefly as a service of commemoration, valuable to the devout, but not a regular means of transmitting supernatural grace. Towards the ministry they took the traditional attitude of Low Churchmen, holding episcopacy to be of Apostolic origin, and consequently preferable to any other form of ecclesiastical organization, but not absolutely essential to a valid ministry. In their preaching they sought to stress the fundamental truths of the Gospel, as they understood them, rather than the distinctive claims and doctrines of the Church. Because of this emphasis on "Gospel preaching," they got into the habit of referring to themselves as "evangelical men," and it was from this phrase that their party name was derived.

Missionary Spirit

Any vital religious movement tends to develop a strong missionary spirit, and this was conspicuously true of the Evangelicals. They were notably active in the organization of the Church's missionary work, both along diocesan and national lines, and they supplied a large proportion of the recruits for service in the various missionary fields. The theological seminary in Virginia, which was under their control, displayed from the start a strong missionary zeal which has characterized it down to the present day. They also showed their religious spirit in the field of social service by organizing charitable enterprises of all sorts, and by supporting most of the conspicuous social reforms of the day.

In their moral standards the Evangelicals tended to resemble the Puritans, condemning all forms of self-indulgence and looking with disapproval upon all of the lighter social amusements, such as dancing, card-playing, and theater-going. They also shared the Puritan consciousness of the supernatural in everyday life, often seeing the direct operation of the Divine Hand in events which would generally be regarded as fortuitous. Their conversion was naturally looked upon as a definitely supernatural visitation, and thereafter every misfortune was regarded as a specific arrangement of God for their discipline and every fortunate circumstance as a sign of His special favor. Something of this consciousness is, no doubt, the heritage of every Christian, but with the Evangelicals it was stronger and more vivid than is usually the case.

The High Churchman was not less conscious of the Divine Presence than the Evangelical, but he was more inclined to regard it as being expressed according to regular laws. Even its supernatural manifestations, he thought, had been regularized in the sacraments and other institutions of the Church. He did not, if he was a Hobart High Churchman, at least, underestimate the importance of personal devotion, but neither did he believe in the necessity of a definite conversion experience, and he did believe that only those whose spiritual development took place within the Church, and through the use of her sacraments, could regard themselves as walking in the "covenanted" way of salvation. He maintained that Christ had founded a definite institution, the Church, to carry on His work, that He had supplied it with a definite, threefold ministry of bishops, priests, and deacons, and that only to those who submitted to the Church thus constituted and accepted its ministrations was salvation definitely promised. He would not say that God, in His mercy, might not save others also, but no others could claim the benefit of any promises.

High Churchmanship

For this reason the High Churchman thought it his duty, while not neglecting the fundamental teachings of the Gospel, to lay a good deal of emphasis upon the exclusive claim of the Church to be the institution through which the Gospel promises would be realized. Hence that phrase of Hobart's about "Evangelical truth and Apostolic order," and hence also a remark he used to make in defense of his support of societies for distributing the Bible and Prayer Book together, rather than the Bible alone, that in so doing the Church was distributed together with the Scriptures. In other words, he believed that the Gospel could not be properly proclaimed except by the institution to which he held that it had originally been intrusted by Our Lord.

The differences between the two parties were carried out into

The Church
and Society:
High Church
View

a number of matters of detail and even affected to some extent their relations with civil society. After the Revolution the High Churchmen tended to favor making the separation of Church and State as complete as possible, refusing to take part in organizations or enterprises that might have even remotely a political bearing. This was the opposite of the position taken by the party in England, but the reversal was an understandable one. Where the Church was supported by the State it was natural for those who took the highest view of the claims of the Church to favor such a relationship more vigorously than others. Where the Church was completely separated from the State, it was as natural for the same party to try to emphasize its dignity and independence by carrying the separation as far as possible.

Evangelical
View

Prominent Evangelicals, while they did not as a rule participate actively in politics, were much more ready than the High Churchmen to take part in civic enterprises and to give their support to quasi-political reform movements. They championed the temperance movement in its earlier, voluntary phase, but many of them withdrew from it when it moved on to favor legal prohibition. Most of the northern leaders were privately opposed to slavery, but few of them publicly espoused the abolition movement, though many, both in the North and South, supported the American Colonization Society, which, officially neutral on the slavery question, was regarded by some of its adherents as providing a possible means of gradual abolition.

As they represented the more Protestant tradition of the Church, the Evangelicals felt a greater kinship with Protestants of other denominations than did the High Churchmen, who were fond of representing the Church as standing midway between Protestant errors and Roman corruptions. The Evangelicals, therefore, generally participated in the inter-denominational Bible societies, Tract societies, and Sunday school unions which were a prominent feature of the religious life of the time, whereas the High Churchmen preferred to form similar organizations composed exclusively of Episcopalians. The more extreme among the Evangelicals also liked to unite with the members of other denominations in their services, and resented the canons and rubrics which hindered them from doing so. It was also characteristic of this party that its members tended to unite in voluntary clerical associations, sometimes called "convocations." In a diocese where the Evangelicals were predominant, these associations would include nearly all of the clergy, and they would sometimes meet at strategic points for the holding of protracted revivals. High Churchmen, probably because they feared the tendencies of the associations, were opposed to any clerical organizations of an unofficial character.

Between the extremes of these parties there were many gradations, and there were many devout Episcopalians of the middle ground who could not be identified with any party. Moreover, the differences between them, in spite of their numerous ramifications, were not, after all, so very fundamental, and until the situation was complicated by the Oxford Movement, their disputes were not generally so bitter as to hamper seriously the efficiency of the Church. Nevertheless, their presence must have been felt in some measure by any Episcopalian of the period who took much interest in the affairs of his Church, and they exerted some influence on most of the major events of the time.

Of the two men who were consecrated bishops in 1811, Hobart, as we have seen, was the outstanding leader of the High Church party. Though he was younger than Griswold, both in age and in ministerial service, he was already better known to the Church at large. Born in Philadelphia in the first year of the Revolution, he had grown up under the spiritual care of Bishop White, and was always regarded by White with something of the affection of a father for a favorite son. He was educated at the College of Philadelphia and at the College of New Jersey, now Princeton, graduating from the latter institution in 1793. He studied theology under Bishop White, but he was of too ardent a temper to be satisfied with White's moderate Churchmanship, and as a result of his own reflection and study, and possibly also of the influence of his father-in-law, Thomas Bradbury Chandler, he early became a pronounced High Churchman. He possessed a tremendous capacity for friendship and the ability to yield a whole-hearted devotion to any cause that he might espouse. He gave himself unstintedly to the Church and, as his constitution was not as vigorous as it might have been, he probably brought himself to an early grave by his exertions in her behalf. At the same time, Hobart possessed the faults which are usually associated with

Character of Hobart

warm tempers. He was sensitive and impulsive, and intolerant of all opposition to his policies. He sometimes allowed himself to be drawn into prolonged controversies over trivial points, and he was seldom able to keep a note of personal resentment from creeping into his controversial writings. On the other hand, his hostility was generally short-lived, and when he quarreled with his friends the dispute was likely to end in a frank confession of error on his part.

His Early
Career

Hobart was ordained deacon by Bishop White in 1798, and after serving his diaconate at various stations in Pennsylvania and New Jersey and on Long Island, he was called as assistant minister at Trinity Church, New York City, in 1800 and ordained to the priesthood by Bishop Provoost shortly afterwards. He began almost at once to rise into prominence in the diocese and in the general Church. He was elected secretary of the diocesan convention in 1801 and sent as delegate to the General Convention in 1804. The latter year also saw the appearance of two books bearing his name: *A Companion to the Altar* and *A Companion of the Festivals and Fasts*. The former was a series of exercises and instructions for use preparatory to Communion and during it, and the latter was a series of meditations and instructions for use in connection with the holy days for which Collects, Gospels, and Epistles were provided in the Prayer Book. Both works were frankly based upon some older English manuals of devotion, but Hobart modified much and added much, and infused the whole with his own warmth of spirit and vigorous piety. To some of the older High Churchmen, it seemed that they were a little tainted with "enthusiasm," and they probably brought entirely new standards of personal devotion to many members of the Church. *A Companion to the Altar* remained for many years the standard, if not the only, Eucharistic manual among American Episcopalians.

To *A Companion of the Festivals and Fasts* Hobart prefaced some "Preliminary Instructions Concerning the Church" in which he advanced the usual thesis of his party that the Church was a divinely formed society whose officers (bishops, priests, and deacons) had their commission from Christ through the Apostles, and that all men were morally obliged to belong to this society. In conclusion he said, "The obligation of communion with the

Church is founded on its being a society established by God to which He has annexed all the privileges and blessings of the Gospel Covenant. . . . Though we presume to judge no man, leaving all judgment to that Being who is alone qualified to make allowance for the ignorance, invincible prejudices, imperfect reasonings, and mistaken judgments of His frail creatures, yet it must not from hence be concluded that it is a matter of indifference whether Christians communicate with the Church or not, or that there is doubt upon the subject of schism, whether it be a sin or not."

Naturally, this strong statement of the claims of a Church which included but a small fraction of the total number of American Christians produced resentment among outsiders, and it was presently attacked by the Rev. Dr. Linn, a Presbyterian clergyman who had undertaken to furnish some papers upon religious subjects for the *Albany Centinel*. His strictures were replied to by an Episcopalian layman, Thomas Yardley How, a close personal friend of Hobart's, and a controversy was precipitated which was soon joined by Hobart himself, by Frederick Beasley, the rector of St. Peter's Church, Albany, and by Bishop Moore of New York, all writing, as was the custom of the time, under various pseudonyms, such as "Layman," "Cyprian," "Detector," and "Vindex," while Dr. Linn continued to support the Presbyterian side, signing himself variously as "The Miscellanist," "Umpire," "Inquirer,'" and "Clemens." Eventually even Bishop White was drawn into the controversy, for an allusion of Linn to his *Case of the Episcopal Churches* caused him to write a letter explaining the special circumstances under which this pamphlet was written, though not retracting its basic position.

[marginal note: Controversy with the Presbyterians]

After the newspaper controversy had subsided, Hobart, in 1806, published the various letters under the title of *A Collection of Essays on the Subject of Episcopacy*. This had the effect of reviving the dispute, for the *Essays* were very ably but severely reviewed in the *Christian Magazine* by its editor, the Rev. John M. Mason, one of the outstanding Presbyterian ministers of the day, and Hobart replied in another series of letters, which he published as *An Apology for Apostolic Order and Its Advocates*. This was in turn reviewed by Dr. Mason, and the controversy was then closed. In this later phase of the debate it would seem

[marginal note: Dr. Mason]

that the Presbyterians had rather the advantage, for Dr. Mason was both more learned and more logical than his younger opponent. The importance of such controversies, however, has little to do with the question of which side gains the dialectical victory. Their value, if they have any, lies in the fact that they draw attention to the claims of the less known party, and in this particular instance the very desultoriness of Hobart's reasoning may have been an asset, for it caused him to drag in the doctrine of predestination, the rejection of which by most Episcopalians gave the Church its strongest appeal to the many who at this period were finding the tenets of orthodox Calvinism too severe.

Difficulty of
Assembling
Bishops for
Consecration

When the time came for the consecration of Hobart and Griswold to the episcopate, some difficulty was experienced in obtaining the number of bishops necessary to perform the rite. Bishop Moore, whose paralysis was the occasion for Hobart's election, was confined to his room, and Bishop Madison was unwilling to leave the College of William and Mary. Bishop Claggett, who was just recovering from an attack of the gout, tried to come to the General Convention, which met at New Haven, but suffered a relapse and was unable to do so. Bishops White and Jarvis were, therefore, the only members of their order at the Convention. Bishop Provoost was still alive, but, besides having retired, he was partially paralyzed and was just recovering from an attack of jaundice, so that he was unwilling to go as far as New Haven. He did, however, finally consent to assist at the consecration if it were held in New York, and so the two bishops and the two candidates went there for the ceremony, which was performed in Trinity Church on May 29, 1811.

Cave Jones
Affair

Hobart had been elected assistant-bishop of New York by a large majority of the diocesan convention, but the choice was not quite unanimous, and after the election had occurred, his opponents made a futile attempt to prevent his consecration. The dispute was a personal rather than a party one, for the participants were all of them men who had, or thought they had, been slighted by Hobart, or who were in a position which caused them to feel more or less embarrassed by his advancement. The leader of the attack was the Rev. Cave Jones, one of Hobart's fellow assistants at Trinity Church. Between the election and the consecration, Jones published a *Solemn Appeal to the Church*, in which he set forth a long list of grievances against Hobart which, he thought, made that person unworthy of being elevated to the episcopate. Most of the injuries were purely imaginary, and the rest were trivial instances of the effect of Hobart's impulsiveness upon a proud and sensitive nature.

The pamphlet had no effect upon the consecration, but the controversy was continued afterwards, Jones being supported by Richard Channing Moore, the rector of St. Stephen's Church, New York, and Henry I. Feltus, rector of St. Ann's, Brooklyn, two Evangelical clergymen of whom Hobart had once or twice spoken severely; by Abraham Beach, who was then the senior assistant at Trinity; and by a number of the laity under the leadership of John Jay and his family. Beach had no especial grievance against Hobart, but he felt some embarrassment at having a subordinate in the parish made bishop. The vestry of Trinity Church supported Hobart, and when Jones refused to resign, they appealed to Bishop Moore, under a canon passed by General Convention in 1804, to sever the pastoral relationship. When Moore did this, the Jones faction, possibly through the influence of Jay, persuaded Bishop Provoost to write to the diocesan convention to the effect that he had decided his resignation was invalid, and would, therefore, expect to be consulted on diocesan affairs, though he could do no active work. The Convention, however, refused to restore his jurisdiction, and the dispute between Jones and Trinity was eventually referred to five judges of the state supreme court who ruled that Jones must accept the separation, but granted him a money compensation. After his withdrawal the dispute subsided rapidly. Dr. Beach was retired on a pension and Dr. Moore was presently elected Bishop of Virginia, and departed from New York. Hobart preached his consecration sermon and declared himself satisfied with Moore's declaration of his intention to adhere to the doctrines and discipline of the Church, though, as he had apparently never done anything else, it is difficult to see why the matter had to be emphasized. Feltus soon fell under the spell of Hobart's personality and became one of his most ardent followers.

After his consecration Hobart continued his efforts to set forth the principles of the Church as he understood them, adopting for this purpose the English custom of delivering occasional

Supporters of Jones

Hobart's
"Charges"
and
"Pastoral
Letters"

"charges" to the clergy and laity of the diocese. The titles of some of these are, in themselves, an indication of his ecclesiastical position. In 1818 he delivered one on *The Corruptions of the Church of Rome Contrasted with Certain Protestant Errors,* and he followed this the next year with one entitled *The Churchman: The Principles of the Churchman Stated and Explained in Distinction from the Corruptions of the Church of Rome and the Errors of Certain Protestant Sects.* In 1826 he delivered one called *The High Churchman Vindicated,* and in 1829 he published one on *The Duty of the Clergy with Respect to Inculcating the Doctrine of the Trinity.* He also published a number of "pastoral letters," which generally dealt with subjects of a more immediate and transitory nature than the charges. Besides these occasional pronouncements, Hobart delivered an address at every convention in which he gave an account of the state of the Church, reported the number of episcopal acts which he had performed, and sometimes touched upon other topics which seemed to him to require comment. This custom was not a new one, but it had been observed irregularly by the earlier bishops.

Controversies

Hobart's opposition to interdenominational Bible societies involved him in a number of controversies during his episcopate, because these societies were very popular with all varieties of Protestants at that time, and with a section of the Episcopal Church. The most serious of these disputes occurred in 1823, when some strictures of Hobart on the American Bible Society were attacked in a pamphlet by William Jay, a son of John Jay. Hobart replied, and a prolonged debate ensued between the two of them.

Near the close of his episcopate, Hobart got into a dispute with a few of his clergy in the City of New York who had organized a society known as the Protestant Episcopal Clerical Association. The objects of the association were simply personal intercourse and mutual improvement, but as a majority, though not all, of its members were Evangelicals, Hobart distrusted it, and issued a pastoral letter against it. As the members had no desire to make their association an instrument of party, they promptly disbanded, but they felt obliged to defend themselves from the charges of the pastoral, and so another pamphlet war ensued.

These controversies are mentioned merely because they serve to illustrate Hobart's religious position and the zeal with which he held it. The subjects with which they dealt were not, after all, of great importance, and the impression which they tend to create of dissension within the diocese is an erroneous one. An overwhelming majority, both of the clergy and the laity throughout the state of New York, were in sympathy with most of Hobart's policies and warmly attached to him personally. With the exception of the Jay family, the few who were not in sympathy with him rarely ventured upon public opposition. The Clerical Association was not intended as an opposition measure at all, and its members were much surprised when Hobart so interpreted it.

Valuable as Hobart's various presentations of Church principles may well have been, it was not in them but in his tireless efforts for the building up of his diocese that his greatest services lay. New York at this time presented a situation which has been rather too rare in our Church history: a splendid opportunity for development with a man in charge who was ideally fitted to take advantage of it, and with at least tolerably adequate resources at his back. The part of New York state which lies west of the Hudson had remained entirely unsettled in colonial times, except for one or two trading posts and forts. With the coming of the nineteenth century this region began to be filled up with settlers who were poured into it by the first wave of westward migration from New England. This movement was approaching its highest momentum when Hobart became bishop, and it continued at a high rate throughout his episcopate.

His Work as a Diocesan

In ·a weak diocese not even the ablest and most energetic of bishops, as Hobart certainly was, could have ·done much to take advantage of the opportunity thus presented, for at that time there was no possibility of obtaining help from outside. As we have seen, however, the Church had been growing quietly but steadily in New York during the period of alleged deadness, and in the older part of the state it was now in a fairly strong position. Trinity, thanks to the large landed endowment which it had inherited from colonial times, and which, in spite of occasional manifestations of jealousy by the legislature, it had succeeded in preserving since, was the richest parish in the Episcopal Church and, probably, in any American denomination. Under the prudent management of Provoost and Moore, its resources

Financial Support

had increased and from the first it used its surplus generously in helping weaker parishes. When Hobart came into practical control of the parish after Bishop Moore's illness and Dr. Beach's retirement, these gifts were increased to such an extent that the finances of the parish were impaired, and a curtailment had to follow. Under Hobart's stirring influence the laity of the city and state were roused from the habits of inactivity which had been produced by the colonial Establishment, and they generously supported the missionary society and other organizations which were called into being.

Before Hobart's election the Church had expanded along the Hudson, and a few missionaries, of whom the most notable were Davenport Phelps and Daniel Nash, later known as "Father Nash," had been sent to serve the western counties, but the work there was definitely in its infancy. In 1815, Hobart wrote to the lieutenant-governor protesting against a proposed law which would have forbidden ministers to perform marriages outside of the counties where they resided, on the ground that there were many counties where no Episcopal minister was resident, and this, too, though the number of clergymen in the state had doubled since his consecration. By the time of his death in 1830 there was probably not an important community in the state that did not have its Episcopal parish and resident clergyman, and in Rochester and Buffalo there were two parishes.

In 1812, at the end of his first year as bishop, Hobart reported the confirmation of five hundred persons and the visitation of parishes in Oneida, Onondaga, Cayuga, Ontario, and Otsego counties, all of which are in central or western New York. Four churches had been consecrated, including St. Peter's, Auburn, in Cayuga County. In 1813 he reported eleven hundred confirmations. Seven hundred and eighty of these were in New York City, but the rest had been confirmed in a visitation to the towns along the Hudson, and the counties of the "Southern Tier." Every year thereafter saw the visitation of a large part of the state, and almost every year saw the consecration of one or more new churches. The visitations were not merely occasions for Confirmation or consecration, but they brought, both to the pastor and his people, inspiration, advice, and, if necessary, material help. In between them, moreover, Hobart was in constant correspondence with his clergy, who turned to him for help and advice in every problem from the wearing of a surplice or dealing with anti-Masons to saving their churches from foreclosure. They never turned in vain. Somehow, somewhere, Hobart found means to help them in every difficulty.

In order to obtain support for his work, and to arouse the laity to a sense of their obligations to the Church, Hobart organized a large number of societies for the pursuit of various churchly ends. Some of these he had formed, or helped to form, before his elevation to the episcopate. Thus the Protestant Episcopal Society for the Promotion of Religion and Learning in the State of New York was organized under his leadership and that of Bishop Moore in 1802, its objects being to help in educating theological students, and to aid in missionary work. This was followed in 1806 by the New York Protestant Episcopal Theological Education Society, devoted more exclusively to the training of candidates for Holy Orders, by the New York Bible and Common Prayer Book Society in 1809, the Protestant Episcopal Tract Society in 1810, and the Young Men's Auxiliary Bible and Common Prayer Book Society in 1816. Subsequently he organized a diocesan missionary society, and the New York Protestant Episcopal Sunday School Society. All of these societies were originally only statewide, though some of them later became affiliated with national institutions. Hobart's distrust of the Evangelicals made him somewhat hesitant about participating in general Church organizations unless he was sure of being able to control them. He also organized a publishing house, the Protestant Episcopal Press, which flourished for a number of years, and he became the proprietor of the *Churchman's Magazine*, formerly published at New Haven, and moved it to New York.

Hobart combined the direction of the largest parish in the country with the duties of the episcopate, for he became rector of Trinity after the death of Bishop Moore, in 1815, having been in practical charge of the parish since 1811. After his own death, in 1830, the two positions were separated, the Rev. Benjamin Treadwell Onderdonk, a brother of the Assistant Bishop of Pennsylvania, succeeding Hobart as bishop, while the Rev. William Berrian succeeded him as rector. Under Bishop Onderdonk the diocese continued to prosper, though, as the course of empire

Organized Societies

Bishop Onderdonk

had now proceeded farther westward; its growth was less spectacular. By 1838 it had become strong enough to be divided, and the Diocese of Western New York was organized, making the first instance of the formation of a diocese which was not bounded by state lines, except for an abortive attempt which had been made in the 1790's to combine western New Hampshire and eastern Vermont into one diocese. The first Bishop of Western New York was William Heathcote De Lancey, a descendant of that Colonel Heathcote who figured so prominently in our account of colonial New York and Connecticut.

Organization
of Eastern
Diocese

The Eastern Diocese, over which Griswold was to preside, included the states of Massachusetts (to which Maine was still attached), Rhode Island, New Hampshire, and Vermont. It was organized in 1811 as the result of overtures which had been made to the other states by Massachusetts in 1809. Its exact character was never clearly determined, but it was commonly described as a "federated diocese," a type of institution of which the only other example in our history was the short-lived Southwestern Diocese which was organized in imitation of this one but proved unsuccessful. Essentially, it was a device to obtain the services of a bishop for several states without giving any one state a special claim upon him. The constituent states retained their own diocesan organizations and functioned independently in all matters not relating to the episcopate, including the sending of delegates to the General Convention. It was, in fact, several years before that body gave an official recognition to the Eastern Diocese as such, except to list Griswold as its bishop in the journals. When his testimonials were presented in 1811, the House of Bishops required proof that his election had been concurred in by each of the individual states before they would consent to his consecration. When Maine finally became separated from Massachusetts, it immediately organized itself as a separate diocese, yet retained the services of the bishop.

Early Career
of Griswold

Griswold himself was about ten years older than Hobart, having been born in Simsbury, Connecticut, in 1766. His mother's family, the Viets, were of German extraction and had been Presbyterians until they were brought into the Church by his uncle, Roger Viets, who was converted while at Yale, and became a missionary of the Society for the Propagation of the Gospel. The

Griswolds, who were of English origin, had always been Churchmen. The future bishop was prevented by the Revolutionary
War and an early marriage from obtaining a college education,
but he enjoyed a satisfactory equivalent in the tuition of Roger
Viets, a man of learning, and in private study. He became a candidate for Holy Orders in 1794 and was ordained deacon and
priest by Bishop Seabury the next year. After serving for some
time as rector of three small parishes in Litchfield County, Connecticut, he accepted a call to Bristol, Rhode Island, in 1804. This
had been a strong parish in colonial times, but the Revolution
and the long vacancy in the rectorship which followed had
reduced it to a point where it had only twenty-five families and
twenty communicants. Under Griswold's skilful ministrations it
rapidly revived and soon surpassed even its colonial strength.

It was probably this pastoral success that led to Griswold's election as bishop of the new diocese, for he had done nothing to
make himself conspicuous outside of his own field of work. He
had participated in the early measures for the organization of the
Eastern Diocese, but he was contemplating a return to Connecticut at the time of the first convention, and only attended it because an accident had prevented a visit to his prospective parish.
His election came as a surprise to him, for he himself had favored
Hobart for the post, and it was only after considerable hesitation
that he accepted the office.

In character Griswold was in many respects the opposite of
Hobart. He was outwardly cool and deliberate where Hobart was
impulsive and emotional, and while Hobart's restless energy
pushed him ahead in any movement in which he participated,
Griswold's shyness and self-distrust prevented him from accepting
leadership until it was thrust upon him. He was less gifted than
Hobart in social qualities, and though he was not without a certain quiet charm, his bashfulness and reserve prevented him,
except among his intimates, from being the delightful companion
that Hobart could be. The general affection with which he came
to be regarded arose rather from a gradual appreciation of his
kindness, tact, and simple-hearted devotion to the cause he served,
than from any more glamorous appeal to popularity. It was, perhaps, only in their whole-souled devotion to duty that the two
men can be said to have resembled one another, though Griswold,

His
Character

like many quiet men, seems to have been all on fire within, and in his preaching was inclined, like most of the Evangelicals, to emotionalism, frequently moving his hearers to tears.

Though, as has been said, there had been some recuperation within the states included in the Eastern Diocese before its organization, the church was still in a precarious condition in most of them. The Boston churches, with the exception of King's Chapel, which was irrevocably lost, had been brought back to a healthy condition, Bristol had been revived by Griswold himself, and Newport was flourishing under the able leadership of Theodore Dehon, subsequently Bishop of South Carolina, but, on the other hand, the Church at Portland seemed about to expire, that at Marblehead was very weak, that at Taunton was just beginning to show signs of life, that at Bridgewater was merely a name, and many parishes had been lost sight of altogether. According to a later statement of Griswold's, there were at that time thirteen church buildings in Massachusetts, "three of them of but little value," four in Rhode Island, five in New Hampshire, two in Maine, of which that at Portland "was without a parish," and none in Vermont. To serve these churches there were, according to various estimates, fifteen or sixteen clergymen in the four states.

Moreover, the future prospects of the diocese seemed much less encouraging than those which were presented in New York. The westward migration, which was filling up a large section of that state, was draining New England and taking from it precisely those younger and more restless spirits who would be most likely to turn to a Church which departed from the prevailing traditions of the region. Yet this very circumstance, while it increased the difficulty of the work, made it also vitally important, for if a portion of these emigrants could be won over before they left, they would form nuclei of the Church in the territories to which they went. At the same time, the diocese had much more feeble resources for carrying out its task than did New York. The strongest parishes, those at Boston, were not only much less wealthy than Trinity Church, New York, but they were also much less generous, and were inclined to show but little interest in the affairs of the Church beyond their own boundaries.

There was, however, one circumstance which operated in favor of the growth of the Church in New England. The breakdown of Puritanism, whose early stages we noticed in colonial times, was proceeding at an accelerated pace, and the religious opinions of many were becoming increasingly unsettled. The bitter prejudices against episcopacy were gradually dying out, and the pious, temperate, and somewhat Puritanical character of its present representative hastened their demise. To this situation and to the herculean labors of Bishop Griswold must be attributed the remarkable growth which came to the Church during the thirty years of his episcopate. In 1811-12 he made his first visitation of the diocese, and the people of a great many parishes in western Massachusetts and in the other states had their first sight of a bishop. On this tour he confirmed 1,212 persons, ordained one deacon and two priests, consecrated two churches, and admitted five candidates for orders. In 1831 he reported 530 confirmations at forty-seven services, and in 1833 he spoke of having preached 123 times outside of his own parish. These are not exceptional years, but are mentioned simply as typical examples of his yearly work. Though he continued, until the last few years of his life, to serve as rector at Bristol and later at Salem, it was his custom to visit all of the parishes in his diocese annually, traveling by stage-coach or horseback among the towns of New England from Rhode Island to Maine. That he did not work himself into an early grave, as Hobart did, was not because he worked less, but because he had inherited a constitution of unusual vigor.

In 1839, four years before his death, he summarized the results of his work by contrasting the state of the diocese then with what it had been in 1811. In Massachusetts, seven of the thirteen churches had been rebuilt, and the total number had been increased to thirty-eight. Rhode Island's four churches had become seventeen, and one was being built. In New Hampshire the five churches had increased to nine, and for the two in Maine there were now five. Vermont, which had been without a church building in 1811, had become strong enough to separate from the Eastern Diocese in 1832 and elect its own bishop, having at that time twelve churches, with four more being built.

At the time of Griswold's consecration it had been thought that the life of one man would not be long enough to set the individual dioceses upon their feet, and that the federation would have to continue longer. Griswold, however, lived to be seventy-seven and his work was so successful that only the un-willingness of the several states to relinquish his supervision pre-vented the dissolution of the diocese before his death. Vermont did withdraw in 1832, choosing John Henry Hopkins as its bishop. Massachusetts elected an assistant bishop, Manton H. Eastburn, in 1842, who became bishop of that diocese on Griswold's death in 1843. After that event, Rhode Island elected John Prentiss Kewley Henshaw its bishop and he also exercised jurisdiction in Maine until George Burgess became bishop there in 1847. New Hamp-shire elected a bishop, Carlton Chase, in 1843.

Griswold, as might be expected from his background, had been inclined to High Churchmanship in the early days of his min-istry. At least, he tells us that, following the example of those whom he thought wiser than himself, he was accustomed to lay a good deal of stress on the distinctive principles of the Church. In time he decided that this was unwise, and began instead to emphasize the fundamental truths of the Gospel. In other words, he adopted the Evangelical ideal, and, though he tried to avoid partisanship, he administered the diocese more or less along Evangelical lines. He was not as prolific of organizations as Ho-bart, but he, or those under him, created a number to support the work of the diocese. Missionary societies of one sort or another were organized in all of the states. Massachusetts, in 1836, made its missionary work a function of its convention, and elected a diocesan Board of Missions in imitation of the General Board, an example which was followed by most of the dioceses of the country sooner or later. In Rhode Island the missionary work was supported through the Clerical Association or Convocation. Prayer Book, tract, and Sunday school societies were also organ-ized, and many of the clergy coöperated with the interdenomi-national Bible societies, of which Griswold approved. He deliv-ered occasional "Charges," but not so many as Hobart, and upon subjects of a less controversial nature. Before he became Presiding Bishop in 1836 he prided himself upon never interfering in mat-ters that lay outside of his own diocese, but he was, nevertheless, a prime mover in one of the most important actions of the Gen-eral Church at this period, the organization of the Domestic and Foreign Missionary Society, of which more will be said later.

The revival of the Church in the South began about the same

Griswold's
Methods

time as the expansion in the North, the bishops of the second
generation coming there within a few years of Hobart and Griswold. In Virginia the most important leaders of the revival were
William H. Wilmer, William Meade, and Richard Channing
Moore. Wilmer was rector of St. Paul's Church, Alexandria, from
1812 to 1827, but he served the whole diocese by visiting vacant
parishes, within a circuit of fifty miles, encouraging young men
to study for the ministry, and exerting an important leadership
on the standing committee. Meade also officiated at Alexandria for
a time, but his most important early work was done around
his home in the northwestern county of Frederick. Both men
united in seeking to secure a successor to Bishop Madison, after
his death in 1812, and, in 1814, managed to bring about the election of Moore, who was then rector of St. Stephen's Church, New
York. These men were pronounced Evangelicals, and in their
efforts to reanimate the Church they followed the lines of their
party, holding frequent revivals and "protracted meetings," though
these were probably of a less ecstatic nature than those held by
other denominations. They also organized missionary societies and
clerical associations to support the work of the diocese. To compensate for the shortage of ministers the rectors of parishes which
were supplied made a practice of visiting those which were vacant
whenever they could. Moore also made an extensive use of candidates for Holy Orders, permitting them to preach, in spite of a
canon of 1804 forbidding the practice. The Evangelical influence
in the diocese led to the insistence upon much more rigid standards
of personal conduct and a higher tone of spiritual life than had
been customary in colonial times, but, as is generally the case,
such an insistence was welcomed more often than it was objected
to by the laity, and on visiting parishes which were apparently
dead, the Bishop and his clergy were frequently surprised at the
eagerness with which the people rallied to the standard of the
Church.

Under such leadership, the diocese rapidly regained its vitality,
and in a few years it had become one of the strongest in the
country. Meade was unanimously elected assistant bishop in 1828,
but with a provision that he should not succeed upon the death
of Bishop Moore unless he were chosen by the diocese to do so.
This condition met with the disapproval of the General Convention, and though that body consented to Meade's consecration,

Revival of
the Church in
Virginia:
Meade and
Moore

it passed a canon to forbid such an arrangement in the future. When Moore died in 1841, Meade was named his successor without any difficulty. Moore also acted as Bishop of North Carolina from 1819-23, and he performed some episcopal services in Maryland between the period from the death of Bishop Kemp in 1827 to the consecration of Bishop Stone in 1830.

South Carolina

In South Carolina the revival of the Church was equally rapid, and had probably begun somewhat earlier. That state differed from its neighbors in sharing with the more important northern states the advantage of having a large urban center to provide a base of operations in the restoration of the Church, for Charleston, though its prestige was declining, was still an important city. As has been intimated, Bishop Smith's episcopate was not a very active one, but with the coming of Nathaniel Bowen as rector of St. Michael's, Charleston, a more vigorous spirit was felt in the diocese. In 1804 Bowen succeeded in bringing about a revival of the diocesan convention, which had been suspended since 1798 because of the jealousy of the vestries. In 1809, with the coöperation of his successor, Theodore Dehon, he organized the Society for the Advancement of Christianity in South Carolina, which, like the later society of the same name in Pennsylvania, was designated to assist candidates for Holy Orders in obtaining an education and to support diocesan missionaries.

Theodore Dehon

Bowen was called to become the first rector of Grace Church, New York, in 1809, and Dehon, who had had a successful rectorate at Newport, was chosen to succeed him. After visiting in Charleston for a few months he accepted the call, and began to carry on the good work begun by Dr. Bowen.

One of the objections of the laity to the diocesan convention was the *ex officio* membership of the clergy, and to overcome their prejudice against this by stressing the religious character of the gatherings, Dehon secured the adoption of a rule that they should always be opened with the Eucharist. In his parish he succeeded in reviving the custom of public baptism, though he carefully avoided any open controversy on the subject. His leadership in the diocese was acknowledged by his election as president of the Standing Committee in 1811, and in the following year he was chosen bishop. Though he lived less than five years after his consecration, he left the diocese in a vigorous and healthy condition when he died. Besides performing the regular duties of the episcopate and carrying on the work of his parish, he kept up a familiar intercourse with his clergy, and helped in the vacant parishes, often instructing the candidates for Confirmation himself. He projected a parish for the poor of Charleston, in which the pews should be rented by wealthy patrons but left open for general use—one of the first proposals for a "free Church" in this country. He also interested himself in the charitable institutions of the city, often holding services in the orphan asylum and the poorhouse. He served for a time on the board of managers of the Charleston Bible Society, but resigned, along with the other Episcopal clergymen who had participated in it, when tendencies began to develop which seemed likely to endanger its non-sectarian character. When he died in 1817, Dr. Bowen was called back into South Carolina to succeed him, and the diocese was insured a continuance of prosperity under that able and devoted prelate. The Churchmanship of South Carolina was much less definitely Evangelical than that of Virginia, and, indeed, cannot be readily identified as belonging to any party. Dehon was, perhaps, mildly Evangelical and Bowen might possibly be described as a moderate High Churchman, but neither was in any sense a party man. It is not surprising, therefore, that under their leadership the diocese was conspicuous for its support of the general institutions of the Church, regardless of which party happened to control them.

In Maryland the revival of the Church was less rapid than in Virginia and South Carolina, but it began earlier and continued steadily throughout this and a good part of the preceding period, though as late as 1817 it was reported that parts of the diocese were still decayed. Claggett became incapacitated by ill health in 1814 and James Kemp was elected his assistant, succeeding to the full jurisdiction on Claggett's death in 1816. Though he also became Provost of the University of Maryland in 1815, and so continued throughout his life, he was, nevertheless, conscientious in the performance of his episcopal duties. He was killed in a stage-coach accident in 1827, and there was a vacancy of three years in the episcopate before he was succeeded by William Murray Stone in 1830. Under Kemp and Stone the diocese acquired a

Maryland

generally High Church tendency which prepared it for the
Anglo-Catholicism of Bishop Whittingham.

North
Carolina

North Carolina, after its abortive attempt to secure the consecration of Charles Pettigrew, lapsed into an inactivity from which
it did not begin to rouse itself until 1817, when it held a convention and adopted a diocesan organization. At that time there
were three clergymen in the state. In 1818 the convention organized a diocesan missionary society, and the next year it placed
itself under the jurisdiction of Bishop Moore of Virginia, where
it remained until 1823, when it obtained its first bishop, John
Stark Ravenscroft. Under him the diocese grew steadily, but the
Church never became as strong in North Carolina as in its neighbors to the north and south. Ravenscroft was a High Churchman,
and his successor, Bishop Ives, was even more so, but the conversion of the latter to Roman Catholicism in 1853 threw the diocese
back into the Evangelical fold.

New Jersey

New Jersey continued under outside jurisdiction, part of the
time from Pennsylvania and part of the time from New York,
until 1815, when it chose the Rev. John Croes, rector at New
Brunswick, to be its bishop. During his episcopate, which lasted
until 1832, and that of his successor, George Washington Doane,
the Church attained a strong position in the state. Delaware
shifted its supervision from Bishop White to Bishop Claggett in
1804 and back again to Bishop White, together with Bishop
Henry Onderdonk, in 1831. In 1816, because of the depressed
state of the Church in Delaware, the diocese requested that one
of the only two clergymen there—the Rev. Robert Clay and the
Rev. William Wickes—visit every congregation in the state twice
a year. The diocese did not obtain a bishop of its own until
1841, when Alfred Lee was elected.

Controversy
in Pennsyl-
vania

In the preceding chapter, we carried the story of the growth
of the Church in Pennsylvania down to the election of the
assistant bishop in 1827. That election was, unfortunately, attended with a good deal of controversy. The Evangelicals and
High Churchmen were more nearly balanced in Pennsylvania
than in the other states and the conflict between them was consequently sharper. Though Bishop White had been a Low Churchman, in the older sense of the term, he had no sympathy whatever with the Evangelicals, and they were, perhaps, the only group

to whom he ever tended to be seriously unfair. Habitually reticent in all personal matters himself, he could not understand the freedom with which they discussed the intimate details of their spiritual life, and, observing the note of self-praise which undoubtedly sometimes entered into such discussions, he was unable to sense the earnest spirituality which at least as often lay behind them. He was offended, too, by the rather cavalier manner in which the more extreme members of the party dealt with the rubrics and canons of the Church. Though his own opinions had not undergone any marked change, he tended in his later years to act more and more with the High Churchmen, by way of reaction from the Evangelicals, and this tendency was probably strengthened by his strong personal affection for Bishop Hobart. Not only did he criticize the Evangelicals severely on a number of occasions, but after 1825 he adopted the practice, in revising the diocesan journals for publication, of deleting from the parochial reports the general observations upon the spiritual condition of their parishes which the members of that party were accustomed to make, but which he regarded as being either false or irrelevant.

On their part, the Evangelicals did what they could to oppose him, though generally in an indirect manner, for his personal prestige was so great as to make direct opposition unwise. They organized missionary societies of their own, instead of coöperating with the diocesan society, and carried on work over which the Bishop could exercise but little control. They also sent such candidates for Holy Orders as were attached to their party to the Virginia Seminary, which was under Evangelical leadership, instead of to the General Seminary in New York, which White supported.

The controversy reached a climax when White, under the impression that his clergy desired him to do so, asked for the election of an assistant bishop. At the special convention held for this purpose in 1826 the "friends of the Bishop," including the High Churchmen and a few survivors of the Bishop's own party, nominated the Rev. Bird Wilson, a professor at General Seminary and a former pupil of White's. The Evangelicals nominated William Meade, who had not yet been elected assistant bishop of Virginia. Neither side could obtain a majority of both clergy and laity, however, and so the election was postponed until the

Disputed Election

regular convention of 1827. In the meantime a good deal of elec-
tioneering was carried on, and both candidates withdrew because
of the bitterness that was being displayed. The Evangelicals then
proposed to back the Rev. James Milnor, rector of St. George's
Church, New York, but he also declined to run. At the convention of 1827, the High Churchmen found themselves with a
majority of the laity, and a majority of one among the clergy.
After Wilson's withdrawal they had intended to back John Henry
Hopkins, the rector at Pittsburgh, but as he would not vote for
himself, it was necessary to look outside of the state, and they
finally decided upon Henry Ustick Onderdonk, then rector of a
church in New York, and a close personal friend of Hobart's.
Onderdonk was accordingly elected, but a great deal of bitterness
resulted, especially because some clergymen whom the minority
thought entitled to seats in the convention had been excluded.
The dispute subsided after a time, but the rancor between the
parties remained and eventually contributed to Onderdonk's undoing. In the meantime, however, he devoted himself assiduously
to his duties and the diocese was undoubtedly strengthened by
his work.

It has been found necessary to go into some detail in discussing
Importance of the Period the growth of the Episcopal Church in the older states during the
period covered in this chapter because it is the period during
which the Church attained the relative position among American
religious groups which it has held ever since, not only in respect
to numbers, but as to the character and location of its members
as well, for by 1830 it had already become predominantly an urban
and upper-class denomination. The general religious upheaval of
the country, which began in colonial times and which led to a
realignment of the main divisions of American Protestantism,
came to an end in the decade from 1830-40. Since then, though
there have been occasional conversions one way or another, there
has been no general shift from one denomination to another. The
only religious bodies which have experienced a conspicuous
change in their proportionate strength in later years have been
those which have grown by immigration.

As the Episcopal Church became accustomed to the idea of
Theological Education national unity and felt a return of health and strength in most
of its members, it naturally began to see the advisability of pro-

viding for some of its needs along national rather than diocesan lines. One of the most conspicuous of such needs was the provision of theological training for the many young men who must be induced to enter the Church's ministry if she were to meet the opportunities presented to her by a rapidly growing country. In colonial times most of the colleges of the country had maintained theological professors under whom candidates for the ministry could obtain the necessary instruction, though if the college were not under Episcopalian control it would be necessary to supplement this work with some study under a minister of the Church. After the Revolution, as the character of the colleges became less theological, this supplementary instruction became more important and a sort of apprentice system developed, the candidate placing himself under some more or less learned minister for the purpose of being instructed in theology. In 1801 the House of Deputies of General Convention made an effort to standardize this system by asking the bishops to prepare a course of theological instruction, and at the next General Convention, that of 1804, a course of study prepared by Bishop White was officially adopted.

It was not long, however, before the desirability of creating a definite institution for theological education began to be felt, and the first move in this direction was made at the General Convention of 1814 when Christopher E. Gadsden of the diocese of South Carolina introduced a resolution to found a general theological seminary for the whole Church. The measure was lost that year, only South Carolina, Virginia, Massachusetts, Rhode Island, and a portion of the lay delegation from Maryland supporting it. A resolution, originating in the House of Bishops, was, however, adopted requesting the bishop or other ecclesiastical authority in each diocese to enquire into and consider the advisability of establishing a general seminary, and to report at the next convention. *General Seminary Proposed, 1814*

The reason why the measure was defeated at this time was that many of the leaders of the Church thought that the end could be better obtained by diocesan seminaries. In 1817, however, it was decided to go through with the measure of founding a general seminary, and a committee composed of three bishops, White, Hobart, and Croes; three clergymen, Charles Wharton, William Harris, and Thomas Y. How, who had been ordained since the *Committee Appointed, 1817* epistolary controversy referred to earlier; and three laymen, William Meredith, Rufus King, and Charles F. Mercer, were appointed to make the necessary arrangements. None of the episcopal members of the committee was much in favor of the project, for White and Hobart preferred diocesan seminaries and Croes had doubts about the desirability of any seminary, but they proceeded nevertheless to carry out the task assigned them as well as they were able, appointing Nathaniel Bowen and William H. Wilmer, later replaced by Thomas Church Brownell, as agents to raise money in the Middle and Southern States respectively.

Instruction
Begun, 1819

In 1818 they appointed two more agents, Dr. How and Samuel Farmar Jarvis, a son of Bishop Jarvis, to raise money in New England and resolved to start the seminary as soon as they had enough money to pay the professors. It was at first intended that there should be three of these, Dr. Wharton, Dr. Jarvis, and Samuel H. Turner, a gifted young protegé of Bishop White's from Pennsylvania, but as the funds were not sufficient for this purpose the number was reduced to two, and in the spring of 1819 the General Theological Seminary began its existence in New York City with Jarvis and Turner for its faculty, and with a student body of six, two of whom, Manton Eastburn and George Washington Doane, subsequently became bishops. Jarvis resigned shortly afterward to become rector of St. Paul's Church, Boston, which had been organized by his admirers, and Turner was left as the only professor.

Though Hobart had coöperated in organizing the Seminary, he showed little interest in it after it was founded, and it met with a cold reception in New York. With the coming of winter, the Seminary's treatment proved literally cold, for it was forbidden the privilege of meeting in a little room it had been using in St. John's Chapel, unless it would supply its own firewood, so that in the end meetings were held afternoons in a room where Lawson Carter, one of the students, kept a girls' school during the mornings. In 1820 the General Convention moved the Seminary to New Haven, Connecticut, where the presence of Dr. Brownell, its former agent, as bishop promised a more friendly reception. Hobart was glad to get rid of the Seminary, for he wanted to found a diocesan seminary, and promptly did so. While at New Haven, the General Seminary "was patronized by many of the leading Churchmen, especially in South Carolina and New York City;" in spite of the fact that Hobart objected to the soliciting of contributions for it in his diocese. John Pintard, a New York merchant, gave a large number of books to form the basis of its library. The Seminary also had its faculty doubled, the Rev. Bird Wilson becoming the second professor, and added $29,690 to its endowment.

In 1821 another New York layman, Jacob Sherred, died and left $60,000 to go either to a general seminary, if established in New York, or to a seminary established by that diocese. A disagreement naturally arose as to whether the General Seminary, if it returned to New York, or the diocesan seminary already functioning there would have the best claim to the legacy, and a special General Convention was called to settle the dispute. As the best legal opinion favored the claims of the diocesan seminary, it was found necessary to yield to a compromise which was, in reality, a surrender to New York. The two institutions were to be united and the faculties of both to be retained. The trustees, except for the bishops, who were *ex officio* members of the Board, were to be elected by the dioceses in proportion to the numbers of their clergy and the size of their contributions to the Seminary. This gave New York almost, if not quite, a majority of the total Board, and, as that body would naturally meet in New York City, there was little doubt that the diocese could muster a working majority at any meeting. Such an arrangement imparted a partisan character to the Seminary, which it was a long time in losing, and cost the support of some of the Evangelicals, but it resulted in the active coöperation of the most energetic, and, next to White, the most influential of the bishops, for Hobart promptly forgot his former opinions and decided that the founding of diocesan seminaries showed a lack of loyalty to the Church. In 1829 the Seminary was left $100,000 by Frederick Kohne of Pennsylvania and South Carolina, but its use of the legacy was delayed for some time by a life interest which had been bequeathed to the testator's widow. In the meantime, the finances of the institution became precarious, for the existence of the bequest caused other contributors to lose interest. Its first building was erected in 1827.

Even before the delivery of General Seminary to New York, the Diocese of Virginia began to seek some local provision for the education of its candidates, endeavoring, in 1820, to secure the

The Sherred Legacy

The Virginia Seminary

appointment of a theological professor at William and Mary. When this project failed, efforts were begun to found a separate diocesan institution. In 1824 the Virginia Seminary opened in Alexandria with the Rev. Reuel Keith and the Rev. William H. Wilmer as its first professors. It has continued its useful career ever since, earning especial honor by the number of its graduates who have gone into the mission field. As might be expected from the Seminary's origin, its ecclesiastical tradition has been Evangelical.

Two other eastern dioceses, Maryland and Massachusetts, made efforts to found seminaries at this period, but without success. The Maryland attempt, which was begun in 1822, was given up the year following at the insistence of Bishop Kemp, who was opposed to any institution that would compete with General Seminary. In Massachusetts two attempts were made. In 1830 a committee was appointed to consider the expediency of establishing a diocesan seminary and at the next convention it reported that, as the Rev. John Henry Hopkins, who had been instructing theological students in western Pennsylvania, had come as assistant at Trinity Church, Boston, with the hope of continuing his work there, it recommended the founding of a seminary at Cambridge under his leadership. Some beginning of the work was, in fact, actually made, but Hopkins felt that he was not receiving sufficient encouragement, and was induced to accept the episcopate in Vermont in 1832. In 1835 the project was revived. The year following the committee appointed to consider it reported the raising of $32,000, and more was pledged at the convention, but these bright prospects were destroyed by the panic of 1837 and the ensuing depression.

There were some changes in the outward arrangements of Church life which took place at this period, the effects of which can still be seen in our ecclesiastical habits. The interior arrangement of the church building was not much altered until after the Oxford Movement, though a growing emphasis upon the Eucharist led to an increase of the practice of placing the Communion Table between the pulpit and the congregation. The outward appearance of the church was altered, however, by the shift from Greek to Gothic, or pseudo-Gothic, as the standard pattern of Church architecture. This change began in the twenties and thirties, but it was some years before the true principles of

Efforts to
Found a
Seminary in
Massachusetts

Gothic style came to be well enough understood to make possible the production of respectable examples.

A more important development was the Sunday School Movement. This had its origin in the work of Robert Raikes, an English Churchman, at the close of the eighteenth century and spread rapidly among all denominations in England and America in the early years of the nineteenth. At first the schools were designed for the purpose of giving religious instruction and teaching the elements of reading and writing to the children of the poor, for whom state schools had not yet been provided. It was not long, however, before they were changed into a means of giving religious instruction to all the children of the parish, and thus took over the rector's traditional duty of catechizing the young people in his cure. The first Sunday school to be organized definitely under the auspices of an Episcopal church was started by two assistant ministers of Christ Church, Philadelphia, in 1814. Supplementary to the Sunday schools, but not originally connected with them, were the Bible classes for adolescents of both sexes and, in some cases, for adults also. These originated among the Evangelicals, but in course of time they came to be adopted by other types of Churchmen also. *Sunday Schools*

The multiplication of parish organizations of all sorts was a characteristic of the period, and there were few parishes, whether High or Low, which were without their complement of Sunday school societies, Bible, or Bible and Prayer Book societies, Tract societies, and female missionary societies. The last named were, perhaps, the most important, for they supplied a good deal of the support that was given to the missionary activities of the dioceses and, subsequently, of the general Church, raising money by their needlework and other products which they assembled and sold at fairs. In the western country, where there was a shortage of women, and, consequently, of female handiwork, these fairs probably had a real economic value and the amount of money raised by them was often quite large. *Parochial Societies*

The early nineteenth century was an era of cheap printing such as must excite the envy of everyone with an itching pen, and this fact, combined with the high postage rates, which restricted most of the periodicals to a sectional circulation, led to a great multiplication of journals of all sorts, religious or otherwise. Of those *Periodicals* associated with the Episcopal Church, the most important, because of continuous publication and general circulation, were the *Churchman's Magazine*, founded in 1804, and controlled for a time by Hobart, of which the present *Churchman* is the successor, and the *Southern Churchman*, founded in 1835. Other periodicals, less long-lived, were *The Banner of the Church*, published by G. W. Doane, when he was at Boston; *The Church Register*, published at Philadelphia; and *The Protestant Episcopalian* and its successor, *The Banner of the Cross*, published in the same city. Two influential periodicals, founded later in the century and published for many years, but now discontinued, were the *Church Journal* and the *Church Review,* both of New York. Most important of all was the *Spirit of Missions*, the Church's official missionary organ, started in 1836 and published continuously ever since, though its name was changed to *Forth* in 1940.

Church Schools

The foundation of Church boarding schools, both for boys and girls, was also a characteristic feature of the period, a reaction, probably, from the secular tendencies that were appearing in other parts of the educational field. The movement had its beginning, apparently, with the organization of the Flushing Institute, a boys' school at Flushing, Long Island, by William Augustus Muhlenberg in 1827. This school, though run on paternalistic lines, was successful as long as Muhlenberg remained at its head. He subsequently attached a college to it, which he called St. Paul's, and which was run in the same manner. His example was soon followed by a number of other prominent Churchmen, including Bishop Hopkins and Bishop Doane. Most of the schools were shipwrecked, sooner or later, upon the rocks of finance, but Bishop Doane's St. Mary's Hall, a girls' school at Burlington, New Jersey, has survived, though its founder was nearly ruined by his efforts to carry it through the depression of 1837-40.

Church Colleges

Two Church colleges were also founded in the East at this period, in addition to the short-lived St. Paul's. Geneva, later Hobart College, was chartered in 1822 in connection with an attempt of Hobart's to found a branch theological seminary at Geneva, New York. The seminary was discontinued in 1826, but the college has continued to serve the Church down to the present time. Washington, later Trinity, College was founded at Hartford, Connecticut, after an alliance of the Episcopalians with the

Democrats had overcome the reluctance of the legislature to charter a college which might compete with Yale. Prior to its foundation, the Diocese of Connecticut had operated an Academy at Cheshire whose upper classes seem to have given very nearly the equivalent of a college education.

The age was one for action rather than study, but the Church nevertheless possessed a number of distinguished scholars during this period. The combination of scholarship with parochial work seems, indeed, to have been a more common practice then than now. Bishop White, in addition to his other activities, was the author of a number of able works upon various theological subjects. The most important of those published were his *Comparative Views of the Controversy Between the Calvinists and the Arminians* and *Lectures on the Catechism*. He was thoroughly familiar with the great English divines, and with the earlier Church Fathers, though he had but little regard for those who came after the third century. Bishop Hopkins was a yet more thorough student of Patristics and was probably responsible in some measure for reviving the study of the Fathers in this country. He was also an authority on canon law and a number of other subjects, being, in fact, one of the most versatile men of his day. Before entering the ministry he had been manager of a large iron smelter and had become a successful lawyer. As an artist of some ability he had prepared the plates for Alexander Wilson's *Ornithology*, one of the first large publishing enterprises carried out in this country. At a later time, he and his son sought to recoup the family finances by taking up the new art of lithography. He also had a hand in the Gothic Revival, having published a volume of designs for that style of architecture.

Another scholar deserving mention is Francis Lister Hawks, for some time rector of St. Thomas' Church, New York, who began the systematic study of American Church History and made some invaluable transcripts of such of the records of the Society for the Propagation of the Gospel and the Bishop of London as had any bearing upon the history of the colonial Church. His work was carried on, in the succeeding period, by Bishop William Stevens Perry, to whose labors all subsequent historians of the American Episcopal Church must feel themselves indebted.

Of the men who were on the faculty of General Theological

Scholars of the Church

Seminary, the two most distinguished scholars were probably Samuel H. Turner and Clement Clark Moore. Dr. Turner had, at one time or another, taught all of the subjects in the curriculum, but his specialty was the Old Testament, and in this field, though not himself a "Higher Critic," he was one of those who were responsible for introducing to the American public the German scholars who had developed this science. Dr. Moore, who was a son of Bishop Benjamin Moore, and the donor of the land upon which the Seminary was built, though a layman, was probably the outstanding Hebrew scholar of his day in America. He is best known to later generations, however, as the author of *A Visit from St. Nicholas*.

Preponderance of Women in the Church

It is probable that women have always been in a majority among those who were actively interested in religion, but in the nineteenth century this preponderance began to assume alarming proportions. The earliest complaints of the tendency came from the Evangelicals, and it seems probable that the highly emotional character of their movement was one of the causes of it. Whatever may have been the faults of the older High Churchmanship, it possessed, at least, a sturdy masculinity that was lacking in later religious parties. An age in which it was possible for a popular religious author to write, "Supposing the degree of piety the same, the woman always exhibits it in a more engaging view than the man," was obviously not a time in which we would look for the development of a virile faith, and there was, in fact, a sentimental quality to all of the religious movements which were characteristic of the nineteenth century that is, perhaps, not unrelated to the present paucity of male attendants at our services.

CHAPTER XII

Missions and Missionaries

THE DISTINCTION between missionary and non-missionary work within the Church is necessarily an arbitrary one, since, in the broadest sense of the term, all of the Church's work is missionary. For a good many years, the official usage of the Episcopal Church has been to apply the term "missionary" to all activity which is not self-supporting, but this is not very satisfactory, as it conveys the implication that work which is self-supporting cannot be missionary. Since some distinction is necessary, however, and since the growth of the Church in the older parts of the country has been discussed in the preceding chapter, missionary work, for the present purpose, may be defined as the work of the Church in entirely new territory, domestic or foreign, regardless of who pays for it. Meaning of the Word "Missionary"

The earliest domestic missionaries of the Episcopal Church, if we use the term in the sense proposed, were, in fact, men who relied upon whatever support they could obtain in the regions to which they went, not upon the assistance of any regularly organized missionary society, diocesan or national. Thus, Daniel Nash, the pioneer missionary of the Church in western New York, lived for many years upon the scanty contributions which the struggling settlers were able to give him, before he entered the employ of the diocesan missionary society, solely, as he said, to obtain an adequate support for his family. Early Missionaries to the West

Nash ended his days in New York state, but some of these early missionaries, like the pioneers they served, followed the frontier steadily westward. The Rev. Palmer Dyer, for instance, left his parish in Syracuse, New York, when that place had become a thriving village, to do his part in building up the Church in the "Far West," settling at Peoria, Illinois, when there was but one other Episcopal clergyman in the state, and no resident minister or organized religious society of any sort in the county. Ezekiel Gilbert Gear, who also began his work in western New York, wandered even farther, for after leaving New York state, where he had worked in the villages of Onondaga and Ithaca, he served in Ohio, Wisconsin, and Illinois, and eventually became the first missionary of the Church in Minnesota. There were many other such men who could be named, if space permitted, though, unfortunately, there were never nearly so many as were needed. We might mention Henry Caswall among them, because he wrote an interesting book on *America and the American Church*, which tells us a good deal about missionary life in the early nineteenth century. He was an Englishman who came to this country in 1828 and gave himself for some years to the work of the Church in the West. After serving in Ohio and Indiana, and acting as professor in a theological seminary founded by Bishop Bosworth Smith at Lexington, Kentucky, he traveled north to continue his labors in Canada. During part of the time that he worked in this country he was helped by the Domestic and Foreign Missionary Society.

The most prominent of these early missionaries, however, was Philander Chase, the first Bishop of Ohio and Illinois. Chase, who was a native of New Hampshire, a brother of Senator Dudley Chase of Vermont and uncle of Salmon Portland Chase, Lincoln's Secretary of the Treasury, began his labors in western New York. Ordained deacon by Bishop Provoost in 1798, he served for a time as an itinerant missionary, first in the neighborhood of Troy, New York, and later at Oneida Castle, Utica, and Auburn. From 1803 to 1805 he was rector of the Church at Poughkeepsie and taught a school there. In the latter year, on the recommendations of Hobart, Chase became the first rector of Christ Church, New Orleans. Ill health forced him to return north in 1811, and he became rector of Christ Church, Hartford, Connecticut. His spirit was too restless for the work of a quiet eastern parish, however, and in 1817 he went as missionary to Ohio, without any assured means of support, except a small private income. At the time of his coming to that state there was only one other Episcopal minister there, the Rev. Roger Searle. In January, 1818, the two of them, with representatives of the laity, held a convention and organized the diocese. In June of the same year, when the number of resident

Philander Chase and His Mission to Ohio

ministers had increased to four, a second convention was held, and Chase was elected bishop.

There was, at this time, no general missionary society of the Church and the older dioceses had not yet sufficiently mastered their own problems to be able to lend much aid to, or even to take much interest in, the work of the West. It was, therefore, necessary for Ohio to struggle along as best it could on its own resources. One of its early missionaries, Dr. Joseph Doddridge, was able to support himself by his labors as a physician, and another, the Rev. Thomas A. Osborne, had a professorship at Cincinnati College, but the rest were compelled to rely upon what support their parishioners could give them, or to eke out their income, as did Chase, by teaching school. In 1821 they organized a diocesan missionary society, which may have given them some help.

In 1823, when Chase was feeling greatly discouraged at the lack of interest in his work that was shown in the East, his son called his attention to an article in a British periodical, in which his labors were very highly spoken of. This incident determined Chase to seek help from England, and on further reflection, he decided that such help could best take the form of founding a theological seminary to furnish him the ministers he so much needed. General Seminary was, it is true, already in existence, but, apart from the sometimes prohibitive expense of sending candidates East, it was early observed that those who were sent tended to settle in eastern parishes after graduation. Accordingly, Chase sailed for England in 1823 to appeal for funds to found a western seminary.

He Seeks Help From England

This application was disapproved by most of Chase's fellow bishops, because they thought it unwise to appeal to England for any funds for the American Church, and it was bitterly opposed by Hobart as conflicting with the interests of General Seminary to which he was now whole-heartedly devoted. Hobart wrote to the other bishops and stirred their latent opposition into an active one. In his correspondence with them and with Chase, he hopelessly confused their ground of opposition with his own, representing to Chase that they agreed with him in objecting to the measure as opposed to the interests of General Seminary, though only one of them, Bishop Brownell, took this view, and though a

Opposition of Hobart

resolution had been adopted by General Convention in 1820, when the General Seminary had been moved to New Haven, expressly reserving to the several dioceses the right to found seminaries of their own. This resolution which, at the time, had had Hobart's warm approval, was not repealed when the Seminary returned to New York. Moreover, in a letter to White, Hobart professed to agree with the general opposition to all solicitations in England, though his own later conduct was quite inconsistent with this profession.

Founding of Kenyon College

Hobart and Chase both sailed for England at about the same time, but Hobart carried his opposition to the length of refusing to travel on the same packet with Chase, lest it should seem that he approved of the latter's mission. He also wrote Chase that he was sailing for England solely for the benefit of his health, though at the time of his departure he had a commission from the trustees of General Theological Seminary to solicit funds for that institution abroad. In this project he was not very successful, for he only appears to have remitted $946.67 to the trustees, but he did succeed in making a great deal of trouble for Chase, and for a time it seemed that the latter's visit would be a failure. Chase, however, was armed with a letter of introduction from Henry Clay to Lord Gambier, whom Clay had met while negotiating the Treaty of Ghent in 1814-15, and, through a casual meeting with George Wharton Marriott, an English High Church clergyman, he had the good fortune to obtain an introduction to Lord Kenyon, a leading nobleman of that party. Through these two noblemen he met other people of wealth and distinction and eventually from them and from Lord Bexley, Lady Rosse, and Miss Macfarlane, the daughter of a former Bishop of Inverness, he obtained enough money so that he felt justified in starting the seminary on his return to Ohio in 1824. To broaden its support he attached to it a college which before long began to overshadow the seminary. The institutions perpetuated the names of their aristocratic benefactors, the College being called Kenyon, the seminary Bexley Hall, and the village which grew up around them, Gambier. The chapel was named in honor of Lady Rosse.

Chase was, if possible, even less capable of tolerating opposition than Hobart was, and he had not the latter's personal charm with which to cover this intolerance. He had gone to England in spite of the opposition of most of his brother bishops, and when he started work upon his college he soon made it evident that he did not intend to pay much attention to anyone else's advice. Instead of founding the institution in a settled community, where local pride would have insured it some support, he built it in the wilderness on the theory that living would be cheaper there, and the students would be kept out of temptation, though in both respects he was disappointed. He caused the bishop to be made *ex officio* president of the College in its charter; he assumed a paternalistic attitude towards the faculty, most of whom were, it is true, very young men, and he was very much opposed to any intervention from the board of trustees. It must be admitted that he had some justification for this attitude, since everyone was quite willing to let him do all of the work, and the College, in fact, received very little help from Ohio. He did, however, obtain increased help from the East after his visit to England, for Hobart's opposition had insured him the support of at least a portion of the Evangelicals. Benjamin Allen and Gregory Townsend Bedell, the rectors of St. Paul's and St. Andrew's churches in Philadelphia, and James Milnor, the rector of St. George's Church, New York, gave him especially cordial support in raising money for the College and in circulating a pamphlet of his called a *Plea for the West*—a title which was borrowed by Lyman Beecher some years later.

Chase's absolutism caused a rebellion in 1831 on the part of the professors, who objected to the bishop's insistence on the right to exercise episcopal as well as presidential authority within the College, to veto all acts of the faculty, and even to direct their personal lives. They also disliked his policy of leaving the discipline of the College in charge of Mrs. Chase when he was away. When the trustees supported the faculty, Chase appealed to the diocesan convention, and when that body also failed him, he resigned both the presidency and his episcopal jurisdiction in Ohio, insisting that the two were inseparable.

The convention, after a languid attempt to induce Chase to reconsider, accepted his resignation and elected Charles Pettit McIlvaine to take his place. These proceedings gave rise to a lengthy debate at the General Convention which met the next year, and though the deputies finally agreed to recognize a *de*

Rebellion of the Faculty, and Chase's Resignation

facto vacancy and sign McIlvaine's testimonials, they attached a clause to their resolution condemning Chase for "dereliction" in resigning. The Bishops, in agreeing to the consecration, expressed their disapproval of episcopal resignations in general, and a canon was finally passed requiring the consent of two-thirds of the diocese and of General Convention for such resignations.

In spite of the ill feeling which he stirred up, Chase had always worked assiduously to promote the interests of his diocese, and thanks to this exertion and to the rapid growth in the population of the state, it was in a vigorous condition at the time of his resignation. Under McIlvaine, who was one of the outstanding preachers of his day, an active growth continued and the diocese rapidly became a strong one, while its bishop became one of the most conspicuous leaders of the Evangelical party. After a short time, McIlvaine had the same difficulties at Kenyon that Chase had had, but he held on, and eventually secured a settlement of the dispute which left him in substantial control of the College while relieving him of the active duties of the presidency.

Chase in Illinois

Chase, after leaving Ohio, went into Michigan, which was organized as a diocese shortly afterward, and admitted into union with the General Convention in 1832, the first case of a territory being so admitted. In 1835 he was elected Bishop of Illinois at its primary convention, and again he assumed the burdens of a pioneer bishop. He visited England a second time shortly after his election to raise funds for his new work, but with only moderate success. The diocese also received some help, though not much, from the Domestic and Foreign Missionary Society, and Chase himself was granted a salary by that body in 1836, but this action was held to be unconstitutional, because he was not subject to the Society's jurisdiction, and it was discontinued the year following. In 1839 Chase visited the South and succeeded in raising some money towards a second college which he proposed to found. It was chartered in 1847, taking the name of Jubilee College, and was located in the center of a 3,000-acre tract of land, subsequently procured by the State of Illinois for preservation as a state park.

The organization of a general missionary society was the most important single event in the history of the Episcopal Church in the early nineteenth century. This institution was organized by the General Convention in 1820, under the title of the Domestic and Foreign Missionary Society of the Protestant Episcopal Church, a title which is still the legal designation of the missionary agency of the Church. The measure was the result of the interest and suggestions of many people, but one of the original sponsors of the movement was Bishop Griswold, who had published a charge and pastoral letter in 1816 advocating a greater interest in missionary work and noting the general revival of missionary interest among Protestants, and the work that was being done by the missionary societies of other denominations. Subsequently he had entered into a correspondence with the English Church Missionary Society, which was probably one of the reasons why that Society donated two hundred pounds to the American organization shortly after it was started.

Organization of the Domestic and Foreign Missionary Society, 1820

The constitution of the new society provided at first for a contributors' membership, as was customary in such societies at the time. A gift of three dollars made one an annual member, thirty dollars secured a life membership, and fifty dollars constituted the donor a "patron" with the privilege of a seat on the board of directors. This last provision was abandoned in a short time because the number of patrons increased so rapidly that the board became too cumbersome. The Presiding Bishop of the Church was *ex officio* president, making Bishop White the first person to hold this office, and all of the other bishops were *ex officio* vice-presidents and directors. Twenty-four other directors were to be chosen by ballot at each triennial meeting. Among those who showed their interest in the missionary work of the Church by becoming "patrons" of the Society during the first three years of its life were the following clergymen whom we have already met in one place or another: Frederick Beasley, S. H. Turner, James Milnor, J. P. K. Henshaw, Jackson Kemper, and Benjamin Allen, and two laymen whom everyone knows: John Jay and Francis Scott Key. In the succeeding triennium four bishops, White, Griswold, R. C. Moore, and Brownell, added their names to the list.

Though the interests of the Society, as its name suggests, were about equally divided between the domestic and the foreign field, and though the contributions to the two fields tended to be equal after the first few years, it was some time before the foreign program could actually be undertaken, and a great many years before the foreign missions of the Church could be said to have progressed

Work in the West

beyond their infancy. For the first half of its existence, at least, the most important work of the Society was done in the domestic field, which generally meant the new territories of the West, though some missionaries were also sent to Maine and to the far South.

At the time that the Society was organized there was, according to a statement made in the Ohio convention of 1820, no minister of the Episcopal Church in Indiana, Tennessee, Illinois, or Missouri, and it is probable that there was none in any of the organized territories either. Some beginning had been made, however, in Kentucky, and in Louisiana, where, as we have seen, Christ Church, New Orleans, was started under Philander Chase in 1805. After its organization was completed, the Society sent Amos G. Baldwin to investigate conditions in the West and see what could be done there. His explorations seem to have been confined to Kentucky, where he found a parish organized at Lexington, and one in process of organization at Paris, under the Rev. William Wall, who also officiated at Cynthiana and Georgetown. He himself, being delayed for some time at Washington, Kentucky, held service six times there and found a number of people who had been brought up in the Episcopal Church and were still attached to it.

Early Efforts
In 1823 the Society sent the Rev. Melish I. Motte to St. Augustine, Florida, where work had been begun by the Rev. Andrew Fowler in 1821, but he found the prospects so discouraging, and the expenses so great, that he returned in less than a year and left the service of the Society. In 1823 Henry H. Pfeiffer was sent to Indiana, where he remained two years, and reported the existence of great spiritual necessities and an excellent opportunity for a missionary at Vincennes. During the same period, Thomas Horrel was sent to Jackson, Missouri, where he remained for a year and then went to St. Louis. A church had been organized here by a clergyman named Ward some years previously but had declined when Ward left at the end of eighteen months. Horrel soon revived it and began raising money for a church building. He remained at this post several years, developing a flourishing parish. When he came, St. Louis had a population of five or six thousand, and was growing rapidly. Richard F. Cadle was sent about the same time to Detroit, then numbering two thousand inhabitants, where he held services in the territorial council house by permission of Governor Cass. He found there a fairly large number of

Churchmen, and built up a strong parish. Norman Nash was sent to establish a school at Green Bay, Wisconsin (then a part of Michigan Territory), where the Oneida Indians had recently been moved from New York. The project failed at that time, apparently because Nash laid his plans upon too large a scale.

At the meeting of the Society in 1826 it was decided to extend aid to the dioceses of Ohio and Delaware and to count as mission *Indian School* stations all states and territories not yet organized into dioceses, Indian settlements not located in organized dioceses, and some place on the west coast of Africa to be selected by the executive committee. From 1826 to 1829 the Society made a second attempt to begin a mission in Florida, sending Addison Searle to Pensacola, Horatio N. Gray to Tallahassee, and Raymond A. Henderson to St. Augustine. The school at Green Bay was also revived under Cadle, who carried it on fairly successfully for a number of years, with government aid. In 1834, however, he got into trouble over an excessive bit of discipline administered to one of the boys, and though he was exonerated by the Society, after an investigation conducted by Kemper and Milnor, he resigned and returned for a time to parish work, but in a few years he was back with the Society and serving as itinerant in Wisconsin. In 1828 Bishop Hobart visited the Indians at Green Bay and, on his way, consecrated the church at Detroit and confirmed twelve. In 1830 Bishop Brownell made a visitation on behalf of the Society, covering parts of Ohio, Kentucky, Louisiana, Mississippi, Georgia and South Carolina, the apparently strange arrangement of the states being accounted for by the fact that he followed the water route down the Ohio and Mississippi and back along the Gulf of Mexico and the Atlantic Coast. He evidently made another visit to the South some years later, for his presence is recorded at the diocesan conventions of Alabama in July, 1834, and January, 1835.

After the Society had been functioning long enough to acquire a definite policy, it adopted in the domestic sphere the rule, which *Policies of the* had been followed by the Society for the Propagation of the Gospel *Society* in colonial times, of requiring some measure of local support for its missionaries, under ordinary circumstances, and of not contributing toward the building of churches, though, like all wisely managed organizations, it occasionally violated its own rules. It also followed the policy of trying to bring the total stipends of its missionaries up to five hundred dollars a year. This, though not lavish, represented a fairly adequate support at the time, and was more than was received by the rectors of some of the smaller settled parishes. Living expenses in the West, however, for one who could not produce his own food, were generally higher than in the East and the work was harder, so that, as there was still a marked shortage of clergy to supply even the older parishes, the Society generally had more difficulty in finding men than in finding the money to pay them. As a rule missionaries were not sent to the actual frontier, but to the region behind it, where stable settlements had already begun to develop, and even there many splendid missionary opportunities had to be neglected for want of ministers. Had the Church been willing to lower drastically the educational requirements for its regular clergy, to make a more extensive use of lay workers, or to develop a system of itinerancy, its growth in the West would have been much more rapid and its present strength probably greater, but though there were some timid gestures in that direction, no serious attempt to adapt the Church's system to the special needs of a rapidly growing country was ever made, and the constant calls of the western leaders for men were but feebly answered.

In its earliest years the Society obtained its support mainly from Pennsylvania and South Carolina and, to a less extent, from the rest of the South and New England, for Hobart was not cordial towards its efforts to raise money in New York. His successor, however, was more friendly, and after 1830 New York took the lead, as it should have done, among the states supporting the Society, South Carolina being second. The total contributions increased steadily and fairly rapidly, except during years of depression, until the middle of the century when partisan bitterness stirred up by the Oxford Movement and the Ritualistic controversy caused a lessening of the Society's support.

In 1835 the organization of the Society was completely remodeled, the new constitution providing that every member of the Episcopal Church should be regarded as a member of the Society, whose affairs were henceforth to be controlled by a "Board of Missions," composed of all the bishops and thirty other members elected by the General Convention. This body was to function through two executive committees, one for domestic and one for

Reorganization of the Society, 1835

foreign missions, and each committee was to employ a secretary and general agent at an adequate salary to raise money and manage its affairs generally. The most significant feature of this new arrangement, at least in principle, was the making of the Society co-extensive with the Church, but its practical importance has sometimes been exaggerated. Though the support of the Society increased after the arrangement, until checked by the depression of 1837-40, it had been increasing steadily before, and the rate of increase was not greatly accelerated. Some advance might, in any case, have been expected from the better organization of the Society's executive.

The General Convention of 1835, besides approving of the above arrangement, passed a canon to provide for the election of "missionary bishops" at home and abroad. The reader who has followed the labors of Hobart, Griswold, Chase, and their contemporaries may feel that they, if anyone, should be entitled to the designation of "missionary bishops," but officially a bishop is a missionary only if he is elected by General Convention instead of the territory over which he has jurisdiction, and is supported by the general Missionary Society and subject to its control. Before 1835 we had no bishops of this sort. The first two elected under the new canon were Francis Lister Hawks, who was to be Bishop of Louisiana, Arkansas, and Florida, and Jackson Kemper, who was to be Bishop of Missouri and Indiana. Hawks declined, but Kemper accepted, and was consecrated on September 25, 1835.

"Missionary Bishops" Provided For

Before this time, bishops had been obtained in Kentucky and Tennessee by election, Kentucky having chosen Benjamin Bosworth Smith to that office in 1832 and Tennessee, in 1833, having named James Hervey Otey, who also exercised jurisdiction in other parts of the Southwest. In 1834, an attempt had been made to unite the states of Alabama, Mississippi, and Louisiana as the "Southwestern Diocese," in imitation of the Eastern Diocese, but the project was given up when the General Convention of 1835 repealed the canon authorizing it in favor of the scheme of electing missionary bishops.

Jackson Kemper, whose consecration made him our first missionary bishop, in the official sense, was one of the most important figures in the early history of our Church in the West, and by his tireless labors he did much to supply the want of subordinate

Jackson Kemper

ministers. The official title of his jurisdiction gives a very inadequate idea of the extent of his activities. He subsequently added the supervision of Wisconsin to his other work, and he frequently made visitations in other states at the request of the Missionary Society or of his brother bishops. As we have seen, Kemper had served for years as assistant minister at Christ Church. He had resigned in 1831, however, and was rector of St. Paul's Church, Norwalk, Connecticut, at the time of his election. While at Philadelphia he had made a visit for the Society for the Advancement of Christianity in Pennsylvania to the western part of the state in 1812, and had gone into western Virginia, where a meeting with the Dr. Doddridge previously mentioned had called his attention to needs farther west. He made another tour on behalf of the same organization in 1814, going as far as northern Ohio, and he accompanied Bishop White on his western visitation in 1826. In 1834, as we have seen, he went with James Milnor to settle the difficulties of the mission at Green Bay.

Bishop
Kemper's
Visitations

Kemper went west shortly after his consecration, accompanied by the Rev. Samuel Roosevelt Johnson, who was to serve the Church for a number of years in Indiana, where, at the time, there was only one other missionary. Kemper himself became the rector of the church at St. Louis, securing the services of the Rev. Peter Minaud as assistant. He spent the winter of 1835 in Illinois, supplying for Bishop Chase, who was in England. In 1837 he organized a college in Missouri to which his friends, in his absence, gave the name of Kemper College. Their action was unfortunate, for it caused the bishop to feel some embarrassment in appealing for funds for the institution. It was closed in 1845. In 1838 Kemper made a visitation of the states along the Mississippi, the Gulf, and the southern Atlantic Coast, as Bishop Brownell had done in 1830, though, as the number of stations had increased, Kemper's tour was probably more arduous. It had originally been projected in conjunction with Bishop Otey of Tennessee, but the latter was prevented by illness from going.

Wisconsin, where Cadle had succeeded in opening a number of stations, had originally been attached to Michigan, but when Samuel Allen McCoskry was elected bishop for the latter state in 1836, Wisconsin objected to his jurisdiction and asked to be placed under Kemper, a request which was eventually granted. Iowa was also added to his jurisdiction about this time, Dubuque having previously been made a mission station at his suggestion.

General Seminary, in its earlier years, was not very prolific in the number of graduates which it sent into the mission field, but after the student body fell under the influence of the Oxford Movement in the late thirties, a stronger missionary spirit began to develop. In 1840 a number of students who had been influenced by this movement started discussing the possibility of organizing a semi-monastic group to carry on missionary work somewhere in the West under Kemper. Eventually four of them, James Warley Miles, William Adams, James Lloyd Breck, and John Henry Hobart, Jr., the son of Bishop Hobart, decided to go through with it, if their respective bishops would permit them to do so. Miles' bishop, Christopher Gadsden of South Carolina, would not, but the rest obtained the necessary permission, and in 1841 the three of them settled at Prairieville, now Waukesha, Wisconsin, where they built St. John's Church in the Wilderness. The next year they moved to Nashotah, Wisconsin, where land had been purchased for them. They were to be supported, to the extent of salaries of $250 apiece, by the Missionary Society, and Cadle at first consented to become their "Superior." He resigned in a short time, however, and Breck was reluctantly forced to take command. Though they took no vows, and called their establishment an "associate mission," it was their intention to give it more or less of a monastic character. They were to wear a sort of habit and be under a rule of obedience, and it was expected that they would not marry while connected with the mission. They assumed responsibility for the work of the Church in a large area about their mission which included several different races and types of settlement, and, as an incidental feature of their work, they undertook the training of a few theological students.

To one of them, Adams, the teaching program proved the only congenial feature of the work. He resigned from the mission in 1843, and when he returned two years later it was with the understanding that he was to serve as a teacher only. In 1848 he married Bishop Kemper's daughter, Elizabeth. So thoroughly did that young lady succeed in altering his principles that in 1850, when he published a textbook on moral theology entitled *The Elements of Christian Science*, he took the position that it was morally wrong

Founding of Nashotah

It Becomes a Theological Seminary

not to marry. By 1850 Hobart had also withdrawn from the mission and it had so far lost its original character that Breck, who alone still cherished the early ideal, resigned and went with two young followers to found a similar station in Minnesota, where Ezekiel G. Gear was then the only Episcopal minister. Nashotah passed under the control of the Rev. Azel D. Cole, Adams being unwilling to assume executive responsibility, and under the two of them it developed into an educational institution pure and simple. Breck himself, incidentally, married twice in the course of his later career.

Kemper was relieved of his jurisdiction in Missouri in 1844 when Cicero Stephen Hawks was elected bishop of that state. In 1849 George Upfold became Bishop of Indiana. Kemper, however, had by then taken over the care of Minnesota and in 1856 he was given jurisdiction over Kansas. In 1859 he resigned his missionary jurisdiction because of age, but remained Bishop of Wisconsin, which had become an independent diocese, until his death in 1870. In 1859 Henry Benjamin Whipple was elected Bishop of Minnesota and the unorganized area of the West was divided into two missionary jurisdictions, one of the Northwest and one of the Southwest. Joseph Cruikshank Talbot became bishop of the former and Henry Champlin Lay of the latter. Talbot, whose jurisdiction included several million square miles, used to refer to himself, with some justification, as "Bishop of All Outdoors."

While Kemper was carrying on his extensive work in the Northwest, the Southwest was by no means neglected. In 1838 Leonidas Polk was elected Missionary Bishop of Arkansas, with the proviso that he should perform episcopal functions in other vacant southern dioceses also. In 1841 he became Bishop of Louisiana. In 1844 Nicholas Hamner Cobbs was elected Bishop of Alabama, and George W. Freeman was appointed by the General Convention to be Bishop of Arkansas and to exercise jurisdiction over the Indian Territory (where, however, we had no missionaries) and the Republic of Texas. Freeman was subsequently given a general jurisdiction for the Southwest. Francis L. Hawks was also elected Bishop of Mississippi in 1844, having gone to that state to escape prosecution by his creditors in New York. Charges arising out of his financial embarrassments, which were the result of the failure of a boys' school he had founded, were interposed

Other
Missionary
Bishops

to prevent his consecration, and, though the Deputies declared him exonerated, they referred the matter back to the diocesan convention for further action. Before that was taken, Hawks declared that he would not accept the election anyway, and Mississippi did not finally obtain a bishop until 1850 when William Mercer Green was elected. Texas, which had become a state in the meantime, was admitted into union with General Convention in the same year.

Breck, after he went into Minnesota, established an associate mission on a larger scale than Nashotah, having at one time twelve co-workers of both sexes. He still had trouble with the propensity of his colleagues for marriage and eventually, as has been mentioned, succumbed to that temptation himself. His mission, which had its headquarters at Christ Church, St. Paul, served a large part of the state and was largely responsible for building up the Church there. Breck founded two branch missions among the Chippeway Indians and took personal charge of this part of the work himself, leaving the white mission under the direction of Dr. van Ingen. In 1857 he began the foundation of a theological seminary at Faribault, which he named for Bishop Seabury. This institution proved successful and continued at Faribault until a short time ago when it was merged with the Western Theological Seminary and moved to Evanston, Illinois. *Breck in Minnesota*

Missionary work was begun in California in 1850, in the year that it became a state, the Rev. Dr. J. L. H. Ver Mehr and the Rev. Flavel Mines' being sent there. In 1853 California applied for admission to General Convention, but as it had failed to ratify the General Constitution its petition could not be granted. The House of Deputies did, however, recommend the appointment of a bishop and several presbyters for the state, and, in accordance with this suggestion, William Ingraham Kip was elected by the upper house and duly consecrated for the post. After overcoming some local opposition, he succeeded in winning election as diocesan. Five missionaries, in addition to the two already there, were sent to help him within the next two years. In 1867 he was joined by Breck, who went to the Coast in that year to found his third associate mission. In 1853 a bishop, Thomas F. Scott, had also been sent to Oregon Territory, which then included the present state of Oregon and a large part of Idaho. Two presbyters were sent to work under him. *California*

The increasing number of young men under the influence of the
Oxford Movement who went into the domestic mission field, and
the refusal of the Society or its bishops to discriminate against
them, cost it in some measure the support of the Evangelicals,
who were angered when they found the western deputies voting
with the Anglo-Catholics at the General Convention of 1847. At
the next Convention, 1850, the committee on the Missionary Society reported an alarming decline in receipts, and in 1851 some
Evangelicals at Philadelphia organized The Missionary Society
for the West, which was to raise money that should be spent
through the Domestic Committee but with the contributing society
reserving the privilege to say on whom or how it should be spent.
In 1859 a still more radical measure was undertaken with the
organization of the American Church Missionary Society, which
proposed to carry on work entirely under its own direction, both
at home and abroad. One incidental result of its activities was the
commencement of our work in Latin America. It was named in
imitation of the English Church Missionary Society, which had
generally been under Evangelical control. After the strife of parties had begun to subside, it became an auxiliary of the Domestic
and Foreign Missionary Society.

It was inevitable that the foreign missionary work of the Church
should grow much more slowly than the domestic. The domestic
work was carried on in a rapidly growing section, among Christians of our own race, and, for the most part, in communities
where there were at least some Episcopalians to provide a certain
amount of local support from the start. In the foreign field everything had to be begun by the Society.

It was, in fact, some time before the foreign work could be got
under way at all. Shortly after its organization the Society projected a mission to Africa, where the American Colonization
Society was settling such negroes as its philanthropic supporters
were able to bring out of slavery, but various circumstances forced
the repeated postponement of the enterprise, and in the end our
first foreign missionaries were sent, not to Africa, but to Greece.
The revolt of that country from the Turkish Empire, which led
to its independence in 1829, had excited the sympathy of the
whole Western World, and of our young republic in particular,
and this sympathy led the Rev. John J. Robertson to volunteer for

Theological Disputes Hurt the Society

The Foreign Field

Greece

service there. His object, of course, was not to convert the Greeks, who were Christians already, but to provide them with opportunities for education which their long subjection and present poverty had prevented. He founded a school at Smyrna, where he was joined two years later by the Rev. J. H. Hill and wife, and another clergyman. The school was subsequently moved to Athens, where it was continued, under the Hills and their successors, for many years, winning expressions of gratitude from the leaders of the Greek people.

The African mission was at last started in 1835 when James M. Thomson, a negro, was appointed as the first Episcopal missionary. He was not in orders and served only as a teacher, though a parish had been organized by the Episcopalian residents of Monrovia the year before his coming. He died in 1838, but his wife remained in the employ of the Society until her death in 1864. In 1836 the Rev. Thomas S. Savage, M.D., was sent out, and remained in Africa for ten years, then returning to the United States to enter parish work. With him in the same year went the Rev. John Payne, who, in 1851, was consecrated first Bishop of Liberia, or, as his title originally read, of West Africa. He was supported by a number of other workers.

Our next foreign field was China, which was just then coming within the orbit of expanding Europe. Our first missionaries there, the Rev. Henry Lockwood and the Rev. Francis R. Hanson, were appointed in 1835, but they were requested to spend six months in the study of medicine before leaving for their stations. They went first to Canton, but later moved to Batavia, in Java, where there seemed to be better opportunities of doing useful work while learning the Chinese language. Hanson left the mission in 1837 and Lockwood in 1839. The Rev. William J. Boone had been sent to join the missionaries at Batavia in 1837 and in 1840 he moved the mission back to China. In 1844 he was consecrated bishop, being the first bishop consecrated for strictly foreign missionary service within the Anglican communion. In 1845 he settled the mission at Shanghai, where he was joined by the Rev. Cleveland Keith in 1851, by the Rev. Robert Nelson in 1852, and by the Rev. C. M. Williams and the Rev. John Liggins in 1856. In 1859 the last two were sent as the first Protestant missionaries to Japan. Liggins was soon forced to leave because of ill health, but Williams continued and became first Bishop of Japan in 1866. In 1859 Boone was joined by the Rev. S. I. J. Schereschewsky, who devoted himself for many years to translating the Bible into Chinese.

Missionary Spirit

With the consecration of Bishop Boone and Bishop Payne, the work in the two largest of our early mission fields may be said to have gotten fairly under way. The effort which started that work was a phase of the general revival of missionary interest among Protestants which marked the early nineteenth century. This revival was partly the result of a growing sense of spiritual responsibility and partly of the general urge for the spreading of European culture which characterized the century. There was about all of the early work, probably, something of the spirit of "From Greenland's Icy Mountains," but the smugness of the early missionaries and their sponsors is often exaggerated. The instructions provided for the first missionaries to China, furnished by Bishop White, and the instructions supplied to Bishop Boone by Bishop Meade reminded them that they were going to a civilized country and stressed the importance of an appreciative attitude toward Chinese culture.

An attempt was also made at this period to establish a mission in Persia, then as now under Mohammedan control. The Rev. Horatio Southgate was sent there in 1835 to explore the field and continued at the work for some years. In 1844 he was consecrated bishop at the same time as Boone, an unwise move, since the Christians in Persia were under the jurisdiction of Orthodox bishops. He resigned in a few years because of disagreements with the Society and returned to America where he became rector of the Church of the Advent, Boston, one of the early centers of Anglo-Catholicism in this country. A mission was also started in Crete, but it was short-lived.

The Indians

There was only a very slight amount of work done by the Church among the American Indians at this period. The work among the Oneidas in New York, which had been interrupted by the Revolution, was vigorously revived under Hobart, and Eleazer Williams, who was himself part Indian, being descended from a white woman who was captured in an Indian raid in colonial times and married to her captor, was sent to take charge of it, first as catechist and then as presbyter. He went with the Indians to Wisconsin and continued to work among them until someone persuaded him that it would be more profitable to capitalize his striking facial resemblance to the Bourbons by posing as the Lost Dauphin. Thereafter the work had to be carried on by less romantic characters. We have already traced, in part, the fortunes of the school at Green Bay. It was at length abandoned, but a mission was kept up at the Duck Creek Reservation, near Green Bay, under the Rev. Solomon Davis, whose faithful labors extended over many years. This was our only Indian mission until Breck began his work among the Chippeways.

Work among the negroes was carried on more extensively and successfully, but not, for the most part, under the Missionary The Negroes Society, though the Domestic Committee did set up a special fund for their benefit. Most of the work was done in the organized dioceses and by regular ministers, though special negro churches were organized in Philadelphia, New York, and some other northern cities, and at least fourteen free negroes were ordained to the ministry before the Civil War. All of the southern bishops laid stress on work among the negroes, and most of the southern rectors engaged in it. The prejudices against the conversion of this race which had prevailed in colonial times died out in the nineteenth century when it began to be discovered that Christian slaves were more docile than others, but some southern clergymen, in urging the support of this work, felt it necessary, for the purpose of quieting these prejudices still further, to stress their approval of the institution of slavery. The Episcopal Church had fair success among the negroes on the plantations, where the masters could supervise their religious life, but in the towns, where they had more opportunity to choose their own churches, they generally preferred other denominations. By the middle of the century most of the negroes had been converted by some denomination or other and the defenders of slavery began to describe that institution as one of the greatest missionary enterprises of the age.

CHAPTER XIII

The Oxford Movement and After

Changes in
the Church

A CHURCHMAN of today, even if he came from a parish which was fairly conservative in the matter of ritual and ornament, would probably feel scarcely more at home in a church of his own communion at the beginning of the nineteenth century than he would in one of another denomination. The actual service of the Prayer Book would be familiar, for, though it has been altered, the changes have not been fundamental, but in nearly all of the things which gave it its setting he would see a difference. The furnishings of the church would be different, as one can see for himself if he goes into one of the old churches which have been kept as they were a century or more ago. There would be no altar with solid sides, designed to resemble stone, even when it is not built of stone. In its place, there would be a communion *table*, with recognizable legs, and this, moreover, would not, as at present, he placed squarely against the last end of the church. It might be set behind the pulpit, out in front of it, or even at the opposite end of the church. The priest, in celebrating, would stand at the "north," or right end of this table, half-facing the people. It would have no colored "hangings," but only the "fair linen cloth" required by the rubric. There would be no candles and no cross or crucifix. The pulpit would probably be more prominent than at present, and might even hide the communion table.

When the service began, no vested choir would come marching in. If there were a choir of any sort, it would be up in the gallery out of sight. The only vestments worn by the priest would be a long, white surplice while officiating, and a black gown while preaching. Before ascending the pulpit, he would probably disappear behind a screen somewhere to change from one of these garments to the other. It would be much less likely that the service one happened to attend was the Eucharist, because that was less often celebrated. If it was, it would be celebrated with the least possible ceremonial and with the priest standing at the north end of the table, so that he could half face the congregation, and perform the manual acts in their sight, as the rubric then directed. If there were a choir at all, it would not be vested and would probably be seated in the gallery, not between the Congregation and the Communion Table.

These differences, which would go so far towards making the familiar service unfamiliar, are the direct, though incidental, result of the work performed by a group of young scholars, and one older one, at Oxford University in the eighteen thirties. It was not the primary object of these men to introduce changes in ceremonial. In the beginning it was not their object to introduce such changes at all. But the changes came about as the result of the Movement which those men started, and they are the consequences of that Movement which present themselves most conspicuously to the average layman. They also serve to symbolize it in another way, for, just as they have affected the usages of many Episcopal churches that are in no way associated with it, so there are many Churchmen who would not care to be considered its followers but who, nevertheless, think differently about the Church and its teaching than they would if the changes had not occurred. On the other hand, just as there are many professed followers of the Movement today who use ceremonial of which its founders never dreamed, so there are many such persons who hold theological opinions quite different from those originally maintained by the school, either because they have gone much further in the direction in which it first started, or because, while retaining something of its basic position, they have adopted many ideas originally put forward by other groups. In other words, the Oxford Movement has so thoroughly permeated the life of our Church, and has influenced and been influenced by other tendencies and forces to such a degree, that the extent of its influence can no longer be measured by the use of the party names associated with it.

The Movement is generally regarded as having originated in a plea for a more pronounced Churchmanship made by John Keble, a Fellow of Oxford, in a sermon which he preached at the opening of the Assize in 1833, but it found its most important expression in

Effects of the Oxford Movement

The Tracts for the Times

a series of pamphlets called *Tracts for the Times* which were written by Keble and some of his associates in that and the years following. The principal authors of these papers, besides Keble, were Hurrell Froude, who died in 1836, when the movement was still in its infancy; Edward Bouverie Pusey, a Professor in Oxford, older than the other writers and already a distinguished scholar; and John Henry Newman, who rapidly became the leader of the group, and who wrote the most striking of the tracts.

English Churchmanship at this time was in a rather decayed condition. The reviving influence exerted by Hobart upon American High Churchmanship had not extended to the Old World, and the party in England had lost a good deal of its original vigor. Evangelicalism, though less decadent, had also lost some of its early fire, and, in any case, it was not disposed to lay much emphasis upon the distinctive claims of the Church. As a result of this lassitude, there was serious talk of disestablishment, and it was felt that only a vigorous restatement of Church principles could avert this threat.

The Tracta-
rian Position
This was the original object of the *Tracts*, and, in fact, the earlier numbers of the series were merely a restatement of the position of seventeenth-century High Churchmanship, but as the discussion progressed, some of the writers, and especially Newman, began to go beyond this position. Newman was evidently moving towards that theory of development in religious belief which was to become the theme of one of his best-known works, and this led him into a gradually increasing emphasis upon the tradition of the Catholic Church until he finally reached the conclusion that the Bible could be properly interpreted only in the light of this tradition. Such a position was obviously in conflict with the principle of the sufficiency and self-interpretative quality of Scripture which, if any doctrine can be so called, was the fundamental tenet of the Reformation and had hitherto been accepted, at least tacitly, by High Churchman as well as Low.

If the Tractarian view, which was simply the traditional Catholic view, was to be accepted instead of the Protestant one, it was obvious that a complete reappraisal of the position of the Anglican communion would be called for. The tendency of the Reformation, and of the churches which were subjected to it, was to dismiss the centuries which had intervened since the close of the

Scriptural Revelation as centuries of growing corruption, from which Christianity, or a part of it, had been purified by the Protestant Revolt. Actually, most of the older Protestant denominations accepted the results of Christian development up to Nicea, but they believed they did so only because the Nicene theology could be proved from the Bible. If, however, Anglicans were again to accept the theory that tradition was the key to Scripture, it was obvious that ages of Christian thought which had previously been contemptuously slighted must be respectfully reconsidered, and that much which had been dismissed as corruption might have to be regarded as legitimate development. In Tract Thirty-eight, which was in the form of a philosophic dialogue, Newman made his protagonist say, "I receive the Church as a messenger from Christ, rich in treasures old and new, rich with the accumulated wealth of ages. . . . As I will not consent to be deprived of the records of the Reformation, so neither will I part with those of former times." The full implications of this statement were not developed in that tract, nor, indeed, in any of them, but the hint was significant of things to come.

While, however, it is probably correct to regard this view of the importance of tradition as being the root of most of the later developments of the movement, it was not the point upon which the early controversy concerning the Tracts was waged most bitterly. Even the earlier numbers had caused a good deal of uneasiness among the Evangelicals and when, as the series continued, the writers began to speak of the need for a "second Reformation," to wave aside "the prejudice which has been excited in the minds of Protestants against the principle . . . of anathematizing," to hold that the Tridentine doctrine of Purgatory might be within the bounds of permissible opinion, and to reproduce a large part of the Roman Breviary with the comment that "There is so much of excellence and beauty in the services of the Breviary that, were it skilfully set before the Protestant by Roman controversialists as the book of devotions received in their communion, it would undoubtedly raise a prejudice in their favor," many of the older High Churchmen also began to feel a trifle nervous. Even the statement of the Tractarians that their purpose was to claim "whatever is good and true in those Devotions . . . for the Church Catholic" did not prove entirely reassuring.

Evangelical Opposition

It was not, however, until the publication of Tract Ninety that the storm actually broke and it became evident that what had gone before was but a premonitory rumbling. This Tract, which was written by Newman, was an attempt to show that the Catholic position, as it had been developed among the Tractarians, was sanctioned by the Thirty-Nine Articles. These Articles have been so badly battered in the years since this pamphlet was written that it is difficult to understand the respect with which they were then generally regarded. At the time of the organization of the Episcopal Church in this country, Bishop White and some others had, it is true, thought that it would be a good idea to revise them, but the majority had not shared this opinion and they had, after a few years, been adopted with but slight alteration. Generally speaking, both High and Low Churchmen felt that the Articles gave a sufficient sanction to their respective positions, as, indeed, they probably did, and were much attached to them. In England, all clergymen were, and still are, required to sign them at their ordination. When Newman tried to put his new wine into these old bottles, it seemed to many that he was straining them to the breaking point. They objected especially to his contention that the Articles did not condemn all doctrines of purgatory, that they gave no sanction to the right of private judgment in interpreting Scripture, and that they left one free to believe in the infallibility of some kinds of general councils. Above all, his opponents, and especially the Evangelicals, objected to his insistence that good works might have a rôle, even if a minor one, in our justification, a view, indeed, which Newman could reconcile with the Articles only by ignoring the first half of Article XI. Justification by faith only had been one of the great watchwords of the Reformation, and it lay at the very root of the Evangelical system. It was, therefore, at the rejection of this doctrine that the Evangelicals leveled their heaviest artillery.

As a result of the furor aroused by this Tract, the publication of the series was stopped and Newman retired for a period of reflection which finally led him into the Roman Catholic Church. The Movement, however, continued, and spread throughout the Anglican communion under various titles of which the most common were "The Oxford Movement," "Tractarianism," and "Puseyism." Like all things Anglican, the Movement was never sharply defined, and there was no specific statement of principles to which all of its adherents felt obliged to give assent. Proceeding, however, from the basic principle of Catholic tradition as the true interpreter of Scripture, it developed certain features which served to mark it off as a distinct party, though there was a good deal of shading along the margins, and in time many people came to approve certain features of the Movement without accepting its whole program.

Most of the adherents of the Movement agreed to define Catholic tradition, in the terms of the famous "canon" of St. Vincent de Lerins, as that which had been believed "everywhere, always and by all," and for practical purposes they interpreted this as referring to the generally received tradition of the Christian Church before the division of East and West. They regarded the seven General Councils, held before that division, as being infallible insofar as they expressed the general tradition. The legitimate heirs of the undivided Church, they thought, were the three great communions, Eastern Orthodox, Roman Catholic, and Anglican, and some minor groups which, like these three, had maintained the succession of bishops without interruption and remained substantially orthodox in doctrine. Such religious bodies they regarded as being branches of the one Catholic Church, and through their insistence upon the right of the Anglican Communion to be called "Catholic" in this sense, they acquired the designation of "Anglo-Catholic," which in time became the title most commonly applied to them. The application of the adjective "Catholic" to the Church of England was not a new thing, but it had not previously been used so often, nor had it, since the Reformation, been applied in a sense that was definitely antithetical to "Protestant."

Most of the Anglo-Catholics, though there were some exceptions, did not regard as *necessary of belief* any doctrine which could not be shown to have obtained general acceptance before the division of the Church, and ordinarily they regarded its affirmation by a General Council as the best test of such acceptance. Some of them, however, were disposed to regard doctrines which had developed in the Western Church during the Middle Ages, such as the belief in purgatory and the Immaculate Conception of the Virgin Mary, as falling within the bounds of *permissible*

Theological Position

opinion which the pious were justified in accepting if it appealed to them.

In regard to religious institutions and ceremonies, the Anglo-Catholics early showed a strong tendency to return to the customs of the Middle Ages. The Movement had not been long under way before proposals began to be made for the revival of monasticism, and, though it was a long time before a successful order was actually founded, experiments in that direction were constantly being made. The first leaders of the party were opposed to introducing actual changes in ceremonial, partly because they realized that this would increase the bitterness of the opposition, and partly because they feared that any proposals for liturgical revision would give the Evangelicals an opportunity to demand changes in the opposite direction. They showed themselves, however, as in their publication of the Breviary, sympathetic to many liturgical customs of the Middle Ages which had been rejected at the Reformation. When, in the next generation, some of the bolder spirits of the party began to translate these sympathies into action, the opposition to the Movement was, as the older leaders had foreseen, both intensified and extended, for the ritual changes which resulted brought the implications of the Movement home to many, especially of the laity, by whom its theological position had been but little considered. Even at the beginning, the Tractarians introduced some changes in the internal arrangements of the churches, such as placing the altar against the east wall and reducing the conspicuousness of the pulpit, but these were, in any case, a natural corollary of the revival of Gothic architecture for the external construction of the churches.

The revival of interest in and respect for mediæval usages was a natural consequence of the emphasis of the Anglo-Catholics upon the continuous tradition of the Church, but it also fitted in with the general interest in the Middle Ages that was one of the features of nineteenth-century culture, and which had already shown itself in literature, through the Romantic Movement, and in architecture, through the Gothic Revival. In the field of history, or, at least, of pseudo-history, this interest was to be forced into an unnatural union with nationalism and democracy, and issue in what may be called the Anglo-Saxon Legend, or the theory that the democratic institutions of modern England were the result

Usages and
Ceremonies

Cultural
Overtones

of the triumph of a supposedly primitive Anglo-Saxon democracy in its long struggle with foreign oppression as represented by the Normans. Under more or less Anglo-Catholic auspices a corresponding theory developed in Church history which represented the Church of England as having been from early times a distinct branch of the Church Catholic, deriving its origin from the undivided Church of primitive times, but properly independent in its own sphere and subjected for a time to the supremacy of the Popes only through the pusillanimity of its rulers. On this theory, the Henrician Reformation became simply a proper declaration of the Church's independence of Rome, and the more Protestant tendencies displayed in the later stages of the revolt were attributed to the influence of foreign reformers.

One of the most important practical consequences of the Oxford Movement was the renewed vitality and fresh direction which it gave to the devotional life of that portion of the Church which was affected by it. Following the general tendency of their party, the Anglo-Catholics revived the traditional classification of the Seven Sacraments, and insisted that the devotions of Churchmen should be centered around these rites. They emphasized, even more than older High Churchmen, the doctrine of Baptismal Regeneration, and in their view of the Eucharist they tended to express a strong belief in the Real Presence, sometimes even approaching the Roman Catholic theory of Transubstantiation. They celebrated the Communion much more often than had been customary, and gave it a larger place in their religious life. Of the remaining five sacraments, three, Confirmation, Matrimony, and Orders, had been in constant use without being called sacraments. The other two, Penance, in the form of auricular confession, and Holy Unction were both revived sooner or later.

As a result of this program, a rich devotional life developed among the followers of the Movement, and a spirit of religious service showed itself which led many ministers to go into fields that the older High Churchmen had generally neglected. In England they went into the cities to do religious work among the poor. In this country many of their young men went to work in the West, where previously the Evangelicals had supplied most of the missionaries.

In recent years new forces have begun to operate within the

fold of Anglo-Catholicism, and new tendencies have developed. A "Liberal Catholic" movement has grown up which is only just becoming articulate, and there are probably many Anglo-Catholics not identified with this new group who have, nevertheless, been more or less influenced by some aspects of Liberalism. There is also a growing section of the party which is interested in the social implications of Catholicism. To these modern Anglo-Catholics the foregoing description is only partially applicable, but it is believed to give a fairly accurate representation of the older phases of the movement. As has been said before, however, it must be remembered that the party has never produced any definite formularies accepted by all its adherents, and there have always been many along its fringes who accepted only part of its program. There have also been extremists on the other side who, shirking the considerable exercise of scholarship which was necessary to work out a distinctly Anglican position, have followed the easier course of simply adopting all of Roman Catholicism except the Pope, but these have been important merely as they seemed to give color to the charges of its opponents that Anglo-Catholicism was "Romanism" in disguise.

The Movement in America

In this country the controversy resulting from the Oxford Movement did not assume great proportions until 1843, or about two years after the publication of Tract Ninety. While the Tracts were still being published some discussion pro and con appeared in the Church papers and other mediums, but the general tendency of those in positions of responsibility was to minimize the controversy as much as possible. The Tracts did, however, win some followers among the students of General Theological Seminary, which became the earliest, and remained for a long time, the most important center of Anglo-Catholicism in this country. Most of the faculty, at this time, kept aloof from the Movement, but one of the younger professors, the Rev. William Rollinson Whittingham, who taught Ecclesiastical History, became an early convert, and, as he enjoyed the popularity which belongs by right to the newest member of any faculty, he soon had a number of followers among the students. When these men graduated and went into parishes, they naturally began to impress their views on those around them. In 1839, Bishop Henry Onderdonk observed with gratification the placing of a cross on the spire of St. Paul's Church, Washington

County, Pennsylvania, and in 1841 Bishop Griswold noted with different sentiments alterations in the internal arrangements of St. Stephen's Church, Providence, and the church at Nantucket, which he regarded as reminiscent of the Dark Ages. In the following year, he complained that Nantucket, whose rector, the Rev. F. W. I. Pollard, was a recent graduate of General, had made further changes which he considered still worse. 1841, as we have seen, was the year in which Nashotah was organized under definitely Anglo-Catholic auspices. In the same year Bishop McIlvaine published a book called *Oxford Divinity Compared with that of the Romish and Anglican Churches*, in which, while acquitting the Tractarians of any deliberate intention of "Romanizing" the Church of England, he contended that this was the inevitable tendency of their teaching, basing his argument chiefly upon their willingness to admit "good works" into the scheme of salvation. Nevertheless, when J. P. K. Henshaw, shortly to become Bishop of Rhode Island, published his memoirs of Bishop R. C. Moore, in 1842, he was able to say, "The excitement of the Tract controversy is now rapidly subsiding."

Opposition to It

A few months sufficed to show the premature character of this prophecy. Dr. Whittingham had been elected Bishop of Maryland in 1840, and had accordingly left General Seminary but his successor, the Rev. John D. Ogilby, held substantially the same position as Whittingham, and the interest of the students in the Oxford Movement tended to increase rather than diminish. This interest was, from the first, regarded with a certain amount of suspicion by the ecclesiastical authorities of the Church, and with the ordination of Arthur Carey in the diocese of New York in 1843, a definite crisis developed. Carey, whose brilliance, earnestness, and charm were acknowledged even by his bitterest opponents, had been a leader among the Tractarian students at General Seminary, and came to accept some of the most advanced views of his party. He had been associated, while at the Seminary, with St. Peter's Church, New York City, whose rector, the Rev. Hugh Smith, though aware of his sympathy with the Oxford theology, thought highly of him and was glad to have him as a teacher in his Sunday school.

The Carey Ordination, 1843

Before the final signing of Carey's testimonials, however, Dr. Smith heard reports which led him to believe that the young man's opinions were more extreme than he thought. He accordingly had a long conversation with the candidate, in the course of which he elicited the information that, should he be denied admission to our ministry, Carey *might possibly* enter that of the Roman Catholic Church, though in the present state of his views he thought it unlikely; that he did not regard the differences between the two communions as embracing any "points of faith" in the technical sense of that phrase; that he was not prepared to pronounce the doctrine of Transubstantiation absurd or impossible, but regarded it "as *taught within the last hundred years as possibly* meaning no more than what we mean by the Real Presence, which we most assuredly hold"; that he did not feel sure the Tridentine doctrine of purgatory was entirely untenable, though he did reject the doctrine as popularly received in the Roman communion; that he was not prepared to say that the Church of Rome was no longer "an integral or pure branch of the Church of Christ," or to say whether she or the Anglican Church was at present more pure; that, while he objected to the practice of withholding the Cup from the laity, he did not regard it as invalidating the Roman Catholic Eucharist; that he regarded many features of the English Reformation as unjustifiable, though he admitted that some reformation was then necessary; that, while he would not himself undertake to prove doctrine from passages in the Apocrypha, he could not condemn the Roman Catholic Church for calling it Holy Scripture; and that he did not consider the promise of conformity in the Ordination service as committing him to an acceptance of the Thirty-Nine Articles.

Protested by Smith and Anthon

As a result of this conversation, Dr. Smith refused to sign Carey's testimonials and presented a statement of his reasons for refusing to Bishop Benjamin Onderdonk. He also consulted his friend, the Rev. Henry Anthon, the rector of St. Mark's Church, who agreed with him as to the propriety of his conduct. Carey, however, obtained the necessary testimonials from the Rev. William Berrian, rector of Trinity Church. Bishop Onderdonk then asked Doctors Smith and Anthon to assist at an examination of Carey before himself and six of the leading presbyters of the diocese, including, besides Berrian, John McVickar, a professor at Columbia College, Samuel Seabury (a grandson of Bishop Seabury), editor of *The Churchman*, Joseph H. Price, rector of St.

Stephen's Church, Benjamin I. Haight, rector of All Saints' Church and a professor at General, and another New York rector, Edward Y. Higbee. The examination, though long and painful, being conducted chiefly by the two protestors, did not elicit anything as to Carey's opinions not already known. When it was over, Bishop Onderdonk asked each of the presbyters individually for his opinion. Smith and Anthon, of course, were dissatisfied, but all of the others expressed the opinion that the candidate's answers were satisfactory. The Bishop reserved decision for a time, during which he considered a further protest from Smith and Anthon, but he finally decided to go through with the ordination.

After so thorough a hearing had been given to the charges against Carey, and the question had been decided by the only person who had any authority to do so, it might be supposed that the matter would have been allowed to drop, but the two accusers thought it their duty to read a formal protest during the Ordination service. When they had done so, the Bishop replied that, as the matter had already been adjudicated, he would proceed with the ordination, which he did. All parties to the proceedings subsequently sought to justify themselves, and before the storm had subsided Carey was dead. His health had never been vigorous, and he died while on a voyage to Havana, where he had gone in hope of recuperation.

The excitement caused by the Carey case served to heighten the popular suspicion that General Seminary was rapidly becoming a Roman Catholic mission. To satisfy Doctors Smith and Anthon, some special questions, designed to detect any subversive tendencies, had been introduced into the examination of the senior class, for though Carey had graduated the year before, there were other suspects in the class, especially one B. B. J. McMaster, who subsequently did become a Roman Catholic. The Board of Trustees also appointed a committee to investigate the condition of the Seminary, and, on hearing its report, voted twenty-six to twenty-five to inform the House of Bishops at the General Convention of 1844 that the Seminary had never been "in a more healthful condition." As the majority also resolved not to give the Bishops the details of the investigation, the minority decided to make a report of its own indicating that the condition of the Seminary was not at its healthiest.

General
Seminary
Investigated

The Bishops'
Queries

Having received these two reports, in 1844, the Bishops prepared a series of questions to be answered by all of the professors, designed to determine what theological ideas were being implanted in the students' minds. This document was concocted in a most amazing manner, every question relating to Catholic teaching being balanced by one concerned with some feature of Calvinism or German Rationalism. The latter group were, possibly, intended for Professor Turner, whose use of German critics exposed him to a certain amount of suspicion, but the questions relating to Calvinism must certainly have been aimed in the air. The purpose of the whole arrangement can only have been to disguise the true object of the inquiry, which was obviously to find out if Professor Ogilby, the only Tractarian on the faculty, was teaching doctrines not admitted by the Episcopal Church. The older professors answered the questions briefly and somewhat testily, but Ogilby took great pains to make his position clear, and certainly succeeded in indicating that he had not made any dangerous approach toward Roman Catholicism. Bishop McIlvaine, however, apparently suspected that Ogilby was making some mental reservations, for he obtained permission to address further questions to him individually. Ogilby emerged unscathed from this cross-examination and the Bishops proceeded to acquit the Seminary of teaching strange doctrines.

The Oxford
Movement
Attacked in
General
Convention

An unsuccessful attempt was made at this same convention to obtain a specific condemnation of the Oxford Movement. After a resolution had been introduced and withdrawn condemning the use of any name but "Protestant Episcopal Church," or the omission of that name in printed documents relating to the Church, another was offered attacking the Tractarian theology and asking the Bishops to take action against it. This was defeated, and in its place the Deputies resolved that they considered "the Liturgy, Offices and Articles of the Church sufficient exponents of her sense of the essential doctrines of Holy Scripture," and the canons an adequate means of maintaining discipline. They also resolved that they did not consider General Convention the proper place for censuring the errors of individuals, or regard the Church as responsible for such errors, even if the individuals were among her members.

The Convention of 1844 also passed a canon allowing a bishop to resign his jurisdiction directly to the House of Bishops, without the consent of his diocese, and another one providing a mode of procedure for the trial of a bishop before the same House. This second canon culminated a movement which began with an amendment to the constitution introduced by Bishop Doane in 1838 and passed in 1841, providing that a bishop should be tried by a court composed only of bishops, and that the mode of trying him should be provided by General Convention. A method of procedure, prepared by Bishop Hopkins, was passed in 1841, and the measure of 1844 was a revision of this. The whole arrangement had originated with the High Churchmen, and was designed to enhance the prestige of the bishops and secure them from the jealousy of their own conventions. By one of the ironies of history, however, the procedure was used by the Evangelicals, within a decade of its passage, to bring to trial two High Church bishops, neither of whom would have been prosecuted by his own diocese.

One of the changes made in the trial procedure in 1844 was a provision allowing a bishop to avoid a formal trial by confessing his guilt. This, together with the canon on resignations, was designed to cover the case of the Right Rev. Henry Ustick Onderdonk, Bishop of Pennsylvania, who had been presented by his diocesan convention for drunkenness. He admitted the offense, but explained that he had begun the use of spiritous liquors on the advice of his physician, in an effort to alleviate a chronic stomach disorder, and had given up their use when he became aware of their effect. His case would seem to be one that called for clemency, but the prevailing spirit of the time was not mercy. The bitterness excited by his election had been intensified by his friendliness to the Oxford Movement, and the Evangelicals, who were now in control, refused to accept his resignation, which he offered, in hopes that they could force him to stand trial. After the passage of the canons alluded to, Onderdonk resigned his jurisdiction to the House of Bishops, and also confessed to them the guilt of intemperance. His brethren, however, proved no more merciful than his diocese, and he was indefinitely suspended from his office. This sentence was removed in 1856, on Onderdonk's profession of repentance, after a pamphlet controversy in which Bishop Hopkins opposed the removal, and Horace Binney, of Philadelphia, one of the most prominent lawyers of his day, supported

Suspension of Bishop Henry Onderdonk

it. Onderdonk's jurisdiction was never restored, Alonzo Potter, a leading Evangelical, having become bishop after his resignation.

Trial of Bishop Benjamin Onderdonk

The first bishop to be subjected to a formal trial under the new amendment and canon was Henry Onderdonk's brother, Benjamin Treadwell Onderdonk of New York. Shortly after the Carey ordination, Bishop Onderdonk's enemies, of whom the leader was the Rev. James C. Richmond, an erratic clergyman of Evangelical sympathies, who was known to his contemporaries as "crazy Richmond," began to collect various charges which they thought reflected seriously upon the Bishop's moral character. When the diocesan convention refused to heed their accusations, they succeeded in persuading three Evangelical bishops, Meade of Virginia, Otey of Tennessee, and Elliott of Georgia, to present Onderdonk to the House of Bishops. Some of the charges dug up by the investigators were not even accepted by the presentors, though their attitude toward the evidence was not a very critical one. The charges as presented related to drunkenness and improper familiarities with women, which were not, however, alleged to have extended to any overt act of adultery. The charge of drunkenness was not sustained by any competent witness at all. The worst of the other charges, and the only one which implied a criminal intention, was not supported by the presentors' own witness. The remaining counts in the presentment, if allowance is made for the exaggeration to be expected from the sort of women who would consent to appear in such a case, indicated no more than that the Bishop, as is frequently the case with elderly men of a certain type, was in the habit of handling people while conversing with them. Such a habit is, no doubt, socially obnoxious, but it is hardly criminal. One of the alleged offenses had taken place seven years before the trial, and the most recent, two and one-half years before. The defense was able to show, moreover, that until they were approached by Mr. Richmond, the witnesses had not acted towards the Bishop with the reserve that they might have been expected to display if they really believed that they had received improper advances from him. Nevertheless, the Bishop was found guilty, and sentenced to indefinite suspension, a punishment from which he was never released.

His Condemnation

It is impossible not to see in this verdict the influence of the bitter party feeling which prevailed at the time, especially as the voting throughout the trial was pretty much along party lines, all of the Evangelicals voting to condemn Bishop Onderdonk and most, though not all, of the High Churchmen voting to acquit him. Most of the witnesses also appear to have had their impressions of the Bishop's conduct affected by their Churchmanship. Allowance must be made, however, for the inexperience of the bishops in cases of this sort, for the peculiar nineteenth-century sensitivity upon all matters relating to sex, and for the bad management of the defense by Bishop Onderdonk's counsel, Robert Graham, a man who was not a Churchman, and who had won his reputation at the bar in the defense of notorious criminals.

The third bishop to come under the action of the Canon of 1844, and the second to be subjected to a formal trial, or what passed for one, was George Washington Doane, of New Jersey, who was brought to trial first in 1852 and again in 1853, on charges of financial irregularities arising out of the difficulties he had met with while trying to establish St. Mary's Hall in Burlington, New Jersey. The chief presentor was again Bishop Meade, supported this time by Bishops McIlvaine of Ohio and Burgess of Maine. The diocese of New Jersey had previously investigated most of the charges, and decided that they did not show a criminal intention. In 1852 the House of Bishops decided to accept the decision of the diocesan convention and drop further proceedings. As this action was clearly uncanonical, the case was reopened in 1853. After a good deal of maneuvering, the Court accepted a declaration of Bishop Doane's in which he confessed to having misapplied trust funds under the impression that he could replace them, and admitted a good many other financial irregularities, but denied that he had meant to do anything wrong. On the basis of this curious document, the Court again voted to drop all proceedings. From the point of view of canon law, this trial was a farce, but it is possible that substantial justice resulted. Doane's mismanagement of his financial affairs was shocking, but it was obviously the result of incompetence rather than criminality and little would have been gained by raking over all his affairs. The much greater clemency shown to him than to the Onderdonks indicates a partial subsidence of party feeling and probably a general conviction that the business of presenting bishops was being carried too far. It is also possible that the other bishops were

Trial of Bishop Doane

better able to sympathize with financial incompetence than with sexual impropriety, or drunkenness.

The Problem of Providing Episcopal Supervision for New York

We have anticipated our story a little, in order to include Bishop Doane's case in the sequence of episcopal trials. The sentence of indefinite suspension which was inflicted on the two Onderdonks was a defective one from a canonical point of view, for it left open the question of whether or not the respondent was permanently deprived of his jurisdiction. In Pennsylvania, where the jurisdiction had been previously resigned, this did not matter much, but in New York it raised a serious problem. Benjamin Onderdonk was unwilling to make an implied confession of guilt by resigning, and his diocese, which remained loyal to him, was unwilling to take any action which might lessen the possibility of his restoration. The General Convention of 1847 passed a canon to prevent such difficulties in the future by requiring the Bishops, when imposing the sentence of suspension, to fix the time or conditions under which it should terminate. All the Convention would do for New York, however, was to provide that a diocese whose bishop was disqualified by judicial sentence, or for other reasons, might employ the services of a neighboring bishop or a missionary bishop. As such an arrangement was hardly adequate for the largest diocese in the country, the Convention of 1850 passed a canon allowing a diocese whose bishop was under sentence of indefinite suspension to elect a provisional bishop, who should exercise full jurisdiction until and unless the suspended bishop was restored, in which case the provisional bishop would become an assistant bishop. New York regarded this measure as unsatisfactory and voted against it, but, as it was the only solution offered, took advantage of it in 1852 and elected Jonathan Mayhew Wainwright provisional bishop.

Controversy in Maryland

The General Convention of 1850 also passed a canon relating to the bishop's right and duty of visitation. The election of Dr. Whittingham as Bishop of Maryland had, naturally, made that diocese a center of Anglo-Catholicism, and many young converts to the movement went there after ordination, so that they might have the opportunity of serving under a Catholic-minded bishop. Whittingham, like most of the early Tractarians, was conservative in the matter of ritual, and, in order to check the innovations of some of his young followers, on the one hand, and to bring the rest of the diocese up to his own position on the other, he was induced, as his principles amply justified him in doing, to make what then seemed a strong assertion of his episcopal authority. In the matter of visitations, specifically, he claimed the right of administering the Eucharist on all such occasions, with or without the rector'ᐧ consent, of appropriating the collections, and of pronouncing Absolution and Benediction in the services of Morning and Evening Prayer. These claims were objected to by a part of the diocese, and one clergyman, the Rev. Joseph Trapnell, was brought to trial for opposing them. The case was decided against him in the diocesan court, and since there was no method of bringing a formal appeal, some of the Maryland parishes memorialized the General Convention, asking it to take some action in the premises.

As a result of this appeal, the Convention of 1850 passed the canon alluded to, which stated that it was the duty of a bishop to visit every parish in his diocese regularly "for the purpose of examining the state of his church, inspecting the behavior of his clergy, ministering the Word, and, if he think fit, the Sacrament of the Lord's Supper . . . and administering the Apostolic Rite of Confirmation." It was "deemed proper that such visitation be made once in three years, at least." The parish visited must pay the bishop's expenses, and the other clergy must arrange to supply his own parish, if he had one. Thus a part of the Maryland dispute was settled in favor of the bishop. The remaining points were left open, with a hint as to the desirability of mutual accommodation.

It is probable that some of the provisions of this canon were directed, not at the situation in Maryland, but in Massachusetts, where a dispute had arisen between Bishop Eastburn and the Church of the Advent. That church had been organized by William Croswell in 1844 as an Anglo-Catholic parish. Bishop Eastburn, who was a bitter opponent of the Oxford Movement, refused to visit the new parish unless its services and the internal arrangements of the building were brought into conformity with the prevailing usage. This the rector and vestry refused to do, and so the parish remained unvisited.

Dispute in Massachusetts

The crucial provision of the canon of 1850, that which called for a visitation once every three years, was cast in such a form that it amounted merely to an expression of opinion by the Convention. To this Eastburn gave little heed, and after a prolonged attempt to effect a reconciliation locally, the Church of the Advent memorialized the General Convention of 1856, asking it to adopt a more mandatory regulation on the subject. This request was granted, and it was further provided that a parish not visited once in three years must apply to the Presiding Bishop for a Council of Reconciliation, which should be composed of the bishops of five neighboring dioceses.

We cannot, however, so quickly leave the year 1853, which was a dramatic and, in some respects, an important year in our history. The second trial of Bishop Doane was probably the least striking of the three major events of that year. The next to be considered was the deposition of Bishop Levi Silliman Ives, of North Carolina, who had announced his conversion to Roman Catholicism at the close of the preceding year. There had always been occasional conversions from our Church to the Roman Catholic and *vice-versa*, as there always are between denominations which have any contact with one another. After the conversion of Newman there was an increase in the number of conversions from our side which, while not especially striking when compared with the total number of our clergy, was marked when compared with the previous infrequency of such changes. Most of the converts were drawn from among the younger Tractarians, and Bishop Ives was the first in this country who had attained a prominent place in the Episcopal Church before leaving it. He had been brought up a Presbyterian but had come into the Episcopal Church as a young man, and after graduating from General Seminary had fallen under the influence of Bishop Hobart, whose son-in-law he became. With the coming of the Oxford Movement he moved over from Hobart Churchmanship to Tractarianism, and sought to introduce Anglo-Catholic usages into North Carolina, founding a religious order at Valle Crucis, which was, however, disbanded in 1849. In a Pastoral Letter on the Priestly Office, in 1849, and in a series of sermons, he was understood to teach the necessity of auricular confession, though he later explained that he had not meant quite that, and he was believed to have expressed privately his acceptance of the doctrine of Transubstantiation and his opinion that the Episcopal Church was guilty of schism. After a series

Bishop
L. S. Ives

of disputes and explanations, he furnished a committee of the diocesan convention of 1851 with a recantation in which he attributed his previous opinion to a dream of uniting the two communions, resulting from an excited state of mind induced by the condition of his bodily health.

This recantation reassured the diocese for a time, and when in 1852 Ives asked for a leave of six months and an advance of one thousand dollars on his salary to travel for his health, it was granted him. Before leaving this country, he deposited with Archbishop Hughes a renunciation of Protestantism and an expression of his determination to enter the Roman Catholic Church, but he did not notify his diocese of his decision until he had reached Rome, whence he wrote on December 22, 1852, announcing his conversion and resigning his diocese. This resignation, being addressed to the diocesan convention and not to the House of Bishops, was uncanonical, and in 1853 a canon was passed by General Convention providing that any minister abandoning our communion without availing himself of the provision for resignation, should be declared automatically deposed by his bishop, or, if he was a bishop, by the Presiding Bishop with the consent of the House. Under this canon, Bishop Ives was declared to have been deposed, and the Rev. Thomas Atkinson, who had been previously elected by the diocese, was consecrated Bishop of North Carolina. Ives, some time after his conversion, became a pioneer leader of Roman Catholic charities in this country. Within the Episcopal Church his conversion caused a good deal of excitement, but it produced no permanent results of any significance.

He Becomes a Roman Catholic

The third and most important event of the year 1853 was the presentation of the so-called "Muhlenberg Memorial" to the House of Bishops. William Augustus Muhlenberg, who was the originator of this document, was one of those who had been greatly influenced by the Oxford Movement without accepting its basic position. He is quoted by his biographer as saying, "I was far out on the bridge . . . that crosses the gulf between us and Rome. I had passed through the mists of vulgar Protestant prejudices when I saw before me 'The Mystery of Abomination.' I flew back, not to rest on the pier of High Churchism, from which this bridge of Puseyism springs, but on the solid rock of Evangelical truth, as republished by the Reformers." As a result of this experience he

The "Muhlenberg Memorial," 1853

evolved a system which he called "Evangelical Catholicism." It consisted, apparently, in engrafting Anglo-Catholic usages upon a moderately Evangelical theology. We have already mentioned the school and college which he founded at Flushing. He gave this up in 1844 and started the Church of the Holy Communion in New York City, one of the first churches in the country not to have rented pews. There he employed a fairly elaborate ritual, partly traditional, partly of his own devising. He also founded the first successful Sisterhood in our country, and he was a pioneer in Church social work, founding St. Luke's Hospital in 1850 and "St. Johnland," a charitable community on Long Island, in 1870.

Its Proposals

The Memorial, which was signed by Muhlenberg and a good many other prominent presbyters, after mentioning the decline of religion that the subscribers thought was taking place, stated that its object was to submit to the bishops "the practicality, under your auspices, of some ecclesiastical system, broader and more comprehensive than that which you now administer, surrounding and including the Protestant Episcopal Church as it now is, leaving that Church untouched, identical with that Church in all its great principles, yet providing for as much freedom in opinion, discipline, and worship, as is compatible with the essential faith and order of the Gospel." The Memorial did not undertake to explain how this end could be attained, but in a pamphlet which he published shortly afterwards Muhlenberg suggested that the bishops, acting on their inherent episcopal authority, and without any other sanction, should ordain men for the ministry outside of the Church. These men were to declare their belief in the Holy Scriptures as the Word of God, the Apostolic and Nicene Creeds, the divine institution of the two great sacraments, and the "doctrines of grace" substantially as set forth in the Thirty-Nine Articles. They were to use the Lord's Prayer, one of the creeds, the Gloria Patri, and certain other specified prayers in their Sunday services, and to follow the Prayer Book more or less closely in the canon of the Eucharist. They would be required to report once every three years to the bishop who had ordained them, but the details of their discipline were to be worked out as circumstances might require.

It is surprising that this proposal, involving, as it did, an almost unprecedented extension of episcopal authority, received its most unqualified support from Evangelicals rather than High Church- Its Supporters men. There were a number of the latter party among the signers of the Memorial, but their names are found mostly among those who, while agreeing with the general object of the Memorial, were unable to approve of all its recommendations. It is probable that most of the signers were concerned with the practical problem rather than with theories of polity, and that they adopted this appeal to the inherent powers of episcopacy in the hope that it would win them support from the Anglo-Catholics, as to some extent it did. Muhlenberg, in defending the proposal, stressed chiefly the obvious failure of the Church with its present ministry and usages to reach the common people, a failure which, he held, ought not to be regarded complacently by any Church claiming to be Catholic.

There is no doubt that Muhlenberg had laid his finger upon the most glaring weakness of the Church, but it would seem that the Its Weaknesses particular solution which he offered involved difficulties which would almost certainly have been insurmountable. Even supposing that such a course of action on the part of the bishops would not have caused a furor within the Church, as it certainly would have, the problem of organizing and disciplining a body of ministers "surrounding and including the Protestant Episcopal Church," yet remaining outside of it, would have been tremendous. Moreover, there is no evidence of the existence of any large number of popular preachers who were so anxious for episcopal ordination that they would have accepted it upon these terms. A few years later, Muhlenberg seems to have seen that his suggestion was not likely to be accepted, for in a pamphlet entitled *What the Memorialists Want*, published in 1856, he implied that all they asked for was a greater degree of liturgical freedom within the Church.

The House of Bishops, when it received the Memorial, appointed a committee, which included Bishop Alonzo Potter of Memorial Pennsylvania, one of the most statesmanlike of the Evangelical Papers Bishops, to consider its suggestions and report at the next Convention. In order to ascertain the mind of the Church upon the subject, Bishop Potter sought the opinion of all the leading bishops and other clergymen of the Episcopal Church and of some representative men from other denominations. Their answers were pub-

lished in a volume called *Memorial Papers* in 1857. They constitute
a thorough-going analysis of the Church's system as it was then
working, and are rich in suggestions for change, some of which
were adopted many years later, and some of which are still being
agitated. Most of the contributors were in favor of the general
aims of the Memorial, but thought its chief proposal too radical.

Results of
Memorial

In the end not much was done about the matter. At the Convention of 1856, Bishop Potter's committee recommended the adoption of the practice of extemporaneous preaching (the prevailing
custom was for ministers to read sermons), and its use occasionally
outside of church buildings, the use of traveling evangelists, the
ministry of women in some sort of sisterhood, a greater attention
to the instruction of the young and their employment as teachers
in Sunday schools, a more rigorous training of candidates for the
ministry, better reading of the services, more participation of the
congregations in the services, an increase of the ministry, efforts
to promote Christian unity, the separation of the Litany and Morning Prayer from the Communion Service (formerly, all were
read on Communion Sundays), and the adoption of some special
prayers which the committee had prepared.

Few of these suggestions were adopted at the time, but the
House of Bishops did resolve that the Morning Prayer, Litany,
and Communion might be separated, that on special occasions
ministers might use any parts of Scripture or the Prayer Book, at
discretion, and that individual bishops might provide special
prayers for use in their dioceses, though these must not be allowed
to supplant the Book of Common Prayer in congregations capable
of its use. They also declared their willingness to appoint a committee of conference with any Christian body that might desire
it, but with the understanding that no such committee should
have power to mature plans of union or expound doctrine or discipline. Even these resolutions, some of which merely sanctioned
existing customs, were too strong for the House of Deputies, and
in 1859 they asked the Bishops to withdraw them, on the ground
that they had disturbed the minds of many Churchmen, and were
believed to be unconstitutional. The Bishops avoided acting on this
request by pleading the lateness of the session.

This disagreement illustrates the growing friction between the
two houses which showed itself at this period. In the early years of

General Convention disagreements between the Bishops and Deputies were rare, and if the resolution of one house was unacceptable to the other, it was generally withdrawn. During the middle years of the century, however, such disagreements became almost the rule, and there was an increase in the length and asperity of the debates within the separate houses as well. There was also, as might be expected, a steady increase in the amount of business to be transacted by the Convention.

Friction in General Convention

CHAPTER XIV

CIVIL WAR AND PARTY STRIFE

BY REMAINING officially neutral in the antislavery struggle, the Episcopal Church avoided the sectional schisms which occurred in some denominations. Division of opinion among its members was not on sectional lines. Though many northern clergy were privately opposed to slavery, only three, E. M. P. Wells, Evan M. Johnson, and John McNamara, are known to have taken an active part in the struggle against it, while others followed the example of Bishop Hopkins in defending it. On the other hand, while some southern ministers agreed with Bishop George W. Freeman in approving slavery in principle, a number of leaders of the Church in the South, including Bishops Meade and Polk, though opposed to radical abolitionism, were in favor of gradual emancipation.

When the war came, the southern dioceses quite properly organized themselves into a union embracing the Confederate States, and revised the Prayer Book so as to adapt it to the political changes. Had the rebellion been successful, the division would necessarily have continued, since it is an accepted principle of the Anglican Communion that the churches in separate countries should be independent. It was important, however, that nothing should be done in the North which would prevent the reunion of the Church in the event the political secession proved a failure.

At the General Convention of 1862 this fact was clearly understood by the majority, and it was just as clearly their wish to avoid any action that would suggest the existence of a schism, or tend to perpetuate the bitterness between the two sections once the war was over, though, at the same time, they were anxious to express their loyalty to the Union. The Convention was opened with a belligerent sermon by Bishop McCoskry, but when the House of Deputies organized, the committee on arrangements, under the

A Split Avoided

The General Convention of 1862

Rev. Francis Vinton, reported that it had provided seats for all of the dioceses, absent as well as present. Some attempt was made, however, to get the Convention to condemn the rebellion, resolutions to this effect being introduced by Mr. F. R. Brunot of Pennsylvania, who had just made a visit to the battlefields, and Judge Murray Hoffman of New York. The debate on the subject was conducted mainly by the lay delegates, though a few of the clergy participated, Vinton, in spite of his earlier action, supporting the resolutions, and the Rev. Doctors W. C. Mead and Milo Mahan opposing them. The laymen appear to have divided along political rather than ecclesiastical lines. The important mid-term elections were approaching and a strong condemnation of the rebellion by General Convention would be, in effect, an endorsement of the Republican administration. So far as their political affiliations are traceable, the supporters of the resolutions seem to have been persons interested in the welfare of the Republican Party, and the opposition included such prominent Democrats as Judge Ezekiel Chambers of Maryland and Horatio Seymour of New York.

Eventually, the resolutions were tabled by a large majority, and a committee of nine was appointed to draft some resolutions which would express the sense of the House. They reported a series which affirmed the loyalty of the Episcopal Church, and its belief that a great evil would result to both the Church and the country if secession were persisted in. While stedfastly refusing to employ towards the seceders "any terms of condemnation or reproach," they expressed repentance for the sins which had brought this judgment on the country, stated the hope of the Deputies as individuals and citizens that the cause of union would triumph, and declared their readiness to use any special prayers which the bishops might think proper under the circumstances. After more debate and the introduction of a number of substitutes, many of which seem to have been designed chiefly to delay the proceedings, these resolutions were passed by the House of Deputies. *The Committee of Nine*

The Bishops merely passed a resolution, in which the lower house concurred, setting apart a day of fasting, humiliation, and prayer for the ills of the nation. They did, however, issue a belligerent Pastoral Letter. As Bishop Brownell, the Presiding Bishop, *The Pastoral Letter*

292 A HISTORY OF THE AMERICAN EPISCOPAL CHURCH

was unable to attend the Convention, Bishops Hopkins and McIlvaine, the two senior bishops present, were asked to prepare pastoral letters. That of Bishop Hopkins, as might be expected, avoided political pronouncements, but that of Bishop McIlvaine was strongly pro-Union. The House adopted the latter. According to Bishop Hopkins' son, who was then editing the *Church Journal*, this action was taken as the result of considerable pressure from Secretaries Seward and Chase, two Episcopal members of the Lincoln Cabinet. The Convention refused to elect a new Board of Missions, because of the impracticality of choosing southern members, and the old Board was continued.

When the next General Convention met in 1865, the war was over and the South was crushed. It was of the greatest importance that the representatives of the victorious section should avoid assuming a note of triumph or reproach that would antagonize the vanquished. Most of the northern delegates came to the Convention with a clear realization of this fact. When the House of Deputies assembled, the roll of all the states was called in alphabetical order, Alabama thus coming first. No southern delegates were present at the first roll call, but representatives from Texas and North Carolina appeared during the first day. All of the "Border States" were represented, though some of their deputies were late in arriving. The Rev. James Craik, of Kentucky, who had been President of the House of Deputies in 1862, was re-elected to that office. On the second day of the session Rev. William Cooper Mead and the Rev. Mark Antony DeWolfe Howe, subsequently Bishop of Central Pennsylvania, offered resolutions expressing gratitude for the restoration of peace and hope for the return of the South. Those of Dr. Howe were regarded as sounding too much of a note of triumph, and at the suggestion of Mr. Welsh of Pennsylvania both resolutions were withdrawn, pending action of the House of Bishops.

On the third day, after the appearance of the deputies from Tennessee, the Rev. George David Cummins introduced a resolution, which he said he hoped would be adopted without discussion, expressing gratitude for the presence of the representatives from Texas, North Carolina, and Tennessee. There was, however, a small group of radicals in the Convention who were unwilling that the Church should be reunited without some gesture of

The General Convention of 1865

Irenic Resolution

triumph from the North. These objected to the resolution and a motion to lay it on the table was lost only by a tie vote, a large number of the conservatives fearing that further discussion might provoke bitterness. After two clerical delegates had spoken in its favor, however, the measure was passed by an almost unanimous vote.

The Convention also passed a resolution expressing its conviction that it was improper for the clergy to bear arms. This was probably prompted by the case of Bishop Polk of Louisiana who had served in the war as a Confederate General and had been killed in action, but his name was not mentioned in the debate on the resolution, and the election of Bishop Quintard of Tennessee, who had also served in the Confederate Army, was confirmed with only two dissenting votes. A more difficult case was that of Bishop Richard Hooker Wilmer of Alabama, who had been consecrated by the southern bishops during the war, though his election, of course, had not been confirmed either by the General Convention or by the bishops and standing committees of a majority of the dioceses in the whole Church, as the constitution requires. After some discussion, it was resolved to approve his consecration on the condition that Bishop Wilmer would give a promise of conformity to the doctrine and discipline of the Protestant Episcopal Church, and would furnish proof of the validity of his consecration. This arrangement, which was based upon the theory that Wilmer had been consecrated for a foreign country, was proposed by Hamilton Fish, subsequently Secretary of State in Grant's Cabinet, and supported by Judge Chambers.

As Bishop Brownell had died early in the year, the Presiding Bishop in 1865 was Bishop Hopkins, who had always been a southern sympathizer. Bishop Atkinson, of North Carolina, appeared at the opening of the Convention and took his seat in the House of Bishops without comment. With the concurrence of the Deputies, the Bishops resolved to set apart a day of thanksgiving for "the return of peace to the country and unity to the Church." As Bishop Wilmer had issued a Pastoral Letter expressing bitter feelings against the North, the assembled bishops expressed their "fraternal regrets" at his action and their "assured confidence that no further occasion for such regrets" would occur. They decided not to issue a Pastoral Letter themselves that year, but authorized

Proceedings of the House of Bishops

Bishop McIlvaine to publish one condemning the *Essays and Reviews* recently published by some liberal Churchmen in England. As a result of the care exercised at this Convention to avoid giving offense, all of the southern states were represented at the General Convention of 1868.

One or two other incidents of the Civil War might be mentioned before leaving it. In 1861 Bishop Hopkins published a book called the *Bible View of Slavery*, in which he set forth the various occasions on which the Bible sanctioned slavery. In 1863 this was reprinted, with Hopkins' consent, by some Philadelphia Churchmen and used as a campaign document by the Pennsylvania Democrats. Regarding this as, in some measure, an invasion of his jurisdiction, Bishop Alonzo Potter published a Protest which was, in turn, used as a Republican campaign document. Hopkins replied in a pamphlet and subsequently in a longer work which he called *A Scriptural, Ecclesiastical and Historical View of Slavery*, in which he supplemented his earlier argument by showing that slavery had frequently been sanctioned by the Christian Church.

Bishop McIlvaine went to England early in the war, at the request of Secretary Seward, in an effort to win over English public opinion which, at least among the governing classes, was generally hostile to the Union cause. He also served on the Christian Commission, an interdenominational body which supplemented the work of the regular chaplains in maintaining the religious life of the Union army. Bishop Thomas M. Clark served during the war as a prominent member of the Sanitary Commission, a semi-official body which did what could be done to correct the unhealthy conditions prevailing in military camps and hospitals, and to alleviate the lot of the common soldiers in other ways. Bishop Whittingham of Maryland was one of the leaders in the movement to keep that state loyal to the Union.

The peaceful reunion of the Church after the Civil War had scarcely been completed when its harmony was torn by what was undoubtedly the bitterest conflict in its history. As we have seen, the older Tractarians, though they took an appreciative attitude toward mediæval ceremonial, were unprepared, for reasons of expediency, to introduce any movement for liturgical changes in their own way. When the party had entered on its second genera-

Margin notes:

Controversy Between Bishops Hopkins and Potter

Services of Bishops McIlvaine and Clark

Ritualistic Controversy

tion, however, many of its younger adherents began to feel that the enrichment of the Church's services which they desired was worth the conflict they knew it would produce. During the fifties, therefore, a few clergymen in England and America began the introduction of ritualistic practices which were not in accord with prevailing customs, and which were not specifically sanctioned by the Prayer Book. In defense of these innovations it was asserted that the Prayer Book itself contained no ceremonial rules, except the bare minimum necessary to go through its services, and that there had been no intention on the part of those who originally prepared it to prohibit the customary usages which were prevalent at the time of the Reformation, and continued for many years after. As long, therefore, as no ritual specifically forbidden was introduced, it was held that the revival of the lapsed ceremonial was entirely legal.

Technically this contention was probably correct, though there was some tendency to strain the rubrics and canons a bit in apply- *Legality of* ing it, but it was obvious that the effect of the ritualistic revival *Ritualism* upon most Churchmen had very little to do with its formal legality. What the average layman, and, for that matter, the average clergyman, also, saw was that usages which they had been accustomed to regard as peculiar to Roman Catholicism were being introduced into a Church which they were used to regarding as Protestant, and were changing the appearance of services they had known and loved since childhood. That they should, therefore, have lost their heads for a time is not altogether surprising. The most bitter opponents of this, as of the earlier phases of the Oxford Movement, were the Evangelicals, but they were supported by many conservative Churchmen of all sorts, including many of the older Tractarians, though these only appear to have joined in active opposition when they became convinced that Ritualism was seriously threatening the peace and even the unity of the Church. The position of the Evangelicals was weakened by the fact that, at the same time that they sought fresh canons to restrain the Ritualists, they were also asking for a relaxation of the canons and rubrics in favor of themselves. They objected especially to the necessity of speaking of regeneration in the Baptismal Office and to a canon recently passed which forbade any minister of the Church to officiate within another minister's "parish," without his consent. This was simply an imitation of the primitive and mediæval canons against "intrusion," but the effort to adapt it to this country, where there are no definite parish boundaries, was not altogether a happy one. For the purposes of the canon, a parish was defined as including the whole community in which a church was situated and if there was more than one church, the community was regarded as a joint parish, so that a visiting clergyman had to obtain the consent of all the ministers before officiating. In practice the canon was used chiefly to prevent the Evangelicals from joining in the services of other denominations.

Tyng Case

In 1868 the Rev. Stephen H. Tyng, Jr., was brought to trial under this canon, in the Diocese of New York, and sentenced to receive admonition for violating it. Though the penalty was not a very severe one, the fact that Tyng's father, the successor of Milnor at St. George's, was one of the most prominent of the Evangelicals, gave the case a good deal of notoriety, and its outcome not only made that party more anxious than ever for the repeal of the canon, but probably, also, by way of reaction, increased their desire to curb their opponents.

Bishop
Hopkins'
Opinion

At first, many of the older High Churchmen refused to support the Evangelicals. In 1867, Morgan Dix, rector of Trinity Church, William Croswell Doane, a son of the late Bishop of New Jersey and himself the future Bishop of Albany, and some other High Church clergymen asked the Presiding Bishop, John Henry Hopkins, to express his opinion upon the question of Ritualism which, they said, "is extensively agitating the Church of England and has already begun to make itself felt in our own Church." Hopkins met their request by publishing a treatise on *The Law of Ritualism* in which, after citing the Old Testament and primitive Christian precedents for ritual, he asserted that, as the use prevailing in the second year of Edward VI was, by statute, the legal use of England, most of the practices of the Ritualists were not only permitted but required by English canon law. Reasoning from the widely accepted opinion that as much of English canon law as had not been repealed was still in force in our Church, he argued *a fortiori* that the practices must at least be permitted here. This argument was not quite complete, for, as was brought out in later discussions, some of the practices of the Ritualists were forbidden by the English Canons of 1603, which, on the principle stated, must also be in force in the Protestant Episcopal Church.

At the General Convention of 1868 a serious attempt was made to obtain canons condemnatory of Ritualism, but the only resolutions on this subject which passed the House of Deputies were one asking the bishops to consider the possibility of changing the rubrics to make the ceremonial law of the Church more precise, and another recommending that changes in ritual should not be introduced in any parish without the approval of the Ordinary of the diocese. The bishops appointed a committee to report at the next Convention on the desirability of any further provision for ritual uniformity, and issued a Pastoral Letter against Ritualism. They refused to consider the possibility of any change in the rubrics, however. An unsuccessful attempt was also made by the Evangelicals to obtain a relaxation of the canon on intrusion. *General Convention of 1868*

At the Convention of 1871 the bishops' committee reported a canon which prohibited by name all of the ritualistic practices that they could think of, including incense, crucifixes, processional crosses, lights on or about the Holy Table, "except when necessary," elevation, the mixing of water with the wine, "as part of the service, or in the presence of the congregation," bowings or genuflexions, except at the Holy Name, and many other usages. They also proposed to forbid the introduction of a choral service or vested choir by any minister without the explicit consent of his vestry and the tacit consent of his bishop, and to regulate the vestments of all the clergy. The Bishops hesitated to present this straitjacket to the House of Deputies on their own responsibility, and so they asked for the appointment of a joint committee to consider the matter. This committee scrapped the proposed canon and recommended instead a declaratory canon to the effect that the ritual law of the Church was to be found in the Book of Common Prayer and appended offices, such of the English canons of 1603 as were in force in the states in 1789, and the canons of General Convention and the several dioceses. This measure passed the House of Bishops but failed, though by a narrow margin, in the House of Deputies. *General Convention of 1871*

The debate on this measure was chiefly important as it brought into prominence the Rev. James De Koven, President of Racine College, Wisconsin, who was the only avowed ritualist in the *James De Koven*

House of Deputies, and probably the only really brilliant orator that that House ever produced. No man could be better fitted to defend an unpopular cause. His forensic ability and high personal integrity invariably commanded the respect of his opponents, and his skill in debate made him almost a party in himself. His greatest argument, however, was to be delivered in the next convention, not in this one. In the present discussion he pointed out that very few of the canons of 1603 were ever in force in the American colonies anyway, and that if they were to be salvaged from desuetude now every clergyman would, among other things, be compelled to wear a plain night cap.

It was also proposed at the Convention of 1871 to amend the canon on the use of the Prayer Book by adding a statement that "this rule shall be understood to prohibit all additions to and omissions from the prescribed order of said Book." This amendment passed both houses, but the Bishops refused to concur in a further proviso attached to it by the Deputies, and the whole thing was tabled. The Bishops, acting in Council, did, however, express the opinion that the word "regenerate" in the Baptismal Office did not imply a moral change.

The Evangelicals were greatly disappointed by their failure to obtain any definite action against Ritualism at this Convention, and some of them began to despair of the Protestantism of the Episcopal Church altogether. Of this group the most prominent member was the Right Rev. George David Cummins, Assistant Bishop of Kentucky. Cummins, whose honorable contribution to the reunion of the Church after the Civil War we have already noted, had had a brilliant career as a preacher which had brought him into prominence at an early age. A consistent Evangelical, he was greatly distressed by the ritualistic practices that Bishop Smith tolerated in some of the parishes in Kentucky, and he also became involved in one or two disputes with Bishop Whitehouse of Illinois, who was especially bitter against the Evangelicals and who twice tried to prevent Cummins from preaching in his diocese. Cummins appears to have received the first suggestion of a separation from the Episcopal Church from Mason Gallagher in 1869, but at that time he thought the measure premature.

In 1872 Bishop Smith went to live at Hoboken, New Jersey, for his health, and the diocese of Kentucky adopted the unprecedented

Right Rev.
George David
Cummins

measure of asking him to exercise jurisdiction *in absentia* instead of allowing it to devolve on the assistant bishop. This naturally aroused Cummins' resentment, but the last straw was furnished by the criticism aroused by his receiving Communion and preaching in a non-Episcopalian Church in New York City on October 12, 1873. No canonical proceedings were taken against him for this act, but the controversy which it caused made him feel that his liberty within the Protestant Episcopal Church was too restricted. On November 10, 1873, he wrote to Bishop Smith, who was Presiding Bishop as well as his immediate superior, expressing his intention of leaving the Church, because of the conscientious difficulties he felt about visiting ritualistic parishes in Kentucky, his loss of hope that the "system of error" prevailing in the Anglican Communion would ever be eradicated, and the storm aroused by his communing with members of other denominations.

Withdrawal of Bishop Cummins and Others From the Church

He was followed in his departure from our communion by a number of the more radical Evangelicals, and on December 2, 1873, the seceders met at New York and organized the Reformed Episcopal Church. Curiously enough, they found the "Proposed Book" prepared by White and Smith in 1785 so perfectly fitted to their needs that they adopted it without revision as their official Prayer Book. One of the leading members of the new Church was the Rev. Charles Edward Cheney, whom Cummins presently ordained as their second bishop. He had been a presbyter of the Diocese of Illinois and had been deposed by Bishop Whitehouse for omitting the word "regenerate" in the Baptismal Service, but the sentence was reversed by a civil court.

This event was in the mind of everyone at the General Convention of 1874, and it soon became evident that the majority was resolved not to adjourn without passing some canon on ritual that would be satisfactory enough to the Evangelicals to prevent any further secession. The House of Deputies, at the preceding Convention, had been wearied by the long-windedness of certain lay delegates, and when the discussion of Ritualism came up this time, a resolution was proposed limiting each speaker to thirty minutes. De Koven, who had evidently come with a prepared speech, objected to this rule, and the delegate who proposed it declared that he was always glad to hear from Dr. De Koven and would be happy to move an exception in that gentleman's favor

The General Convention of 1874

when the time came. With this understanding the resolution was passed.

The canon finally adopted by this Convention provided that if a bishop had reason to believe that use was being made within his jurisdiction of ceremonies or practices symbolizing false or doubtful doctrine, he must summon his Standing Committee to investigate the rumor. If it proved true, he must first admonish the offending minister and, if he proved recalcitrant, bring him to trial for a violation of his ordination vows. As examples of the practices meant, the canon referred specifically to the Elevation of the Elements in the Eucharist or other acts of adoration towards them, the displaying of a crucifix in the church, and the use of incense. The complexity of this canon was the result of the desire of its sponsors to indicate that, though their immediate object was the prohibition of certain liturgical practices, their ultimate purpose was to prevent the presentation of doctrines which they considered inconsistent with the teaching of the Church.

De Koven's
Speech

The debate on the canon centered mainly on the question of Eucharistic Adoration, which was about the only ritualistic practice then advocated involving an important doctrinal issue. De Koven's speech, when he delivered it, amply justified the concession in regard to time which had been made to him. Not only was it a brilliant forensic effort, but it put the argument upon an entirely new basis. Heretofore both sides had shown a tendency to seek the greatest possible freedom for themselves while placing the greatest possible restraint upon their opponents. De Koven, however, placed his defense squarely upon the plea of comprehensiveness. He intimated that he was willing to see the bishops make any allowance they could for conscientious scruples concerning Baptismal Regeneration. He observed that, with respect to the Eucharist, Zwinglianism had been openly advocated in the Church, and that he, for one, had no desire to drive it out. He felt, however, that a similar tolerance should be shown to extreme opinions in the other direction. He quoted Dr. S. F. Jarvis, a distinguished canonist, as having said, in a sermon before the Board of Missions, that both those who believed in a real change in the Eucharist, "by which the very elements themselves, though they retain their original properties, are corporally united with and transformed into Christ," and those who held to a purely spiritual presence must be tolerated in the Church. And he concluded by saying that the Church should strive to meet the challenge of the times and not dissipate its strength in fighting over unessentials.

This view of the comprehensiveness of the Church was not a new one, as De Koven's quotation from Dr. Jarvis indicates, but it had been lost sight of in the bitterness of the controversy stirred up by the Oxford Movement. It was reasserted, independently, by John Cotton Smith in a paper read at the first meeting of the Church Congress, held shortly before the Convention, but De Koven's presentation was more widely circulated and attracted more attention.

Eventually the settlement of the controversy suggested by these men proved to be the one that was found most consistent with the genius of the Episcopal Church, but it required some time for the ideas which they presented to take hold of men's minds, and the canon which De Koven opposed was passed by a substantial majority, the Evangelicals being supported not only by the more conservative High Churchmen, but even by some of the older Tractarians, such as Bishop Coxe of Western New York and the Rev. William Dexter Wilson of Cornell University, author of *The Church Identified,* a popular presentation of the Tractarian position. The attitude of such men was probably caused partly by a fear of further schism and partly by a distrust of the ritualistic attitude towards the Eucharist, which was thought to imply a belief in the corporeal Presence. *(Ritual Canon Passed)*

The Ritualists suffered another defeat at this Convention when the Deputies refused to confirm the election of the Rev. George F. Seymour as Bishop of Illinois. Seymour was a professor at General Seminary, and the most serious charges against him were that he had once refused to concur with the rest of the faculty in a resolution designed to curb advanced views on the Eucharist and Confession among the students, though it was not alleged that he himself held such views, and that, when acting as Dean, he had permitted Father Grafton, a representative of the Confraternity of the Blessed Sacrament, to present "his peculiar views of the Holy Eucharist" to some Seminary students in a private room. Seymour had declared that the incident had occurred without his knowledge and no proof to the contrary was ever offered, but the mere suspicion of his connivance in Grafton's action was consid- *(Seymour Case)* ered enough to justify his exclusion from the episcopate. There appears, indeed, to have been some doubt as to Seymour's personal honesty in the minds of the delegates, but the basis of this distrust is unknown.

After Seymour's rejection, the Diocese of Illinois chose James De Koven as bishop. This was an even more direct challenge to the anti-Ritualists, for not only was De Koven the outstanding champion of Ritualism, but his personal integrity and worth were above the suspicion of even the most hostile minds. His rejection could be only on the ground that no one who held his views was worthy of elevation to the episcopate, and on this ground he was, in fact, rejected, the action being taken by a majority of the standing committees during the interim of General Convention.

As so often happens, this extreme gesture of intolerance marked the beginning of a reaction, and a decline in partisan bitterness may be seen as beginning at this point. The older High Churchmen and Tractarians gradually got over the fright occasioned by the withdrawal of Bishop Cummins and his followers, and the more liberal wing of the Evangelical party began to see the inconsistency of seeking to broaden the Church in one direction at the same time they were trying to narrow it in another. This change of attitude may be marked very clearly in the case of Dr. William Reed Huntington, a liberal Evangelical, who subsequently became rector of Grace Church, New York. At the General Convention of 1871, Huntington had urged the specific prohibition of ritualistic practices on the ground that doing so would emphasize what he evidently suspected, that the Ritualists were not honorable men and had very little respect for their ordination vows. In 1874 he supported the ritual canon and opposed the consecration of Seymour. But when De Koven was elected he advocated his confirmation. He explained this on the ground that he had more confidence in De Koven's personal integrity than he had in Dr. Seymour's, but in view of his stand in 1871, it would seem that his own opinions had changed also.

In 1878, four years after his rejection by the General Convention as Bishop of Illinois, Dr. Seymour became Bishop of Springfield, a diocese that had been called into being by the division of the Diocese of Illinois, his election having been confirmed without difficulty. In 1889, Father Grafton, with whom the mere suspicion

Feelings
Begin to
Soften

of an association had proven so damaging to Seymour in 1874, was consecrated Bishop of Fond du Lac.

While the foregoing conflict was going on, a number of developments took place which should be noticed before we proceed to the consideration of a later period. The fact that General Seminary came to be regarded as a center of Anglo-Catholicism cost it considerable support, and before the Civil War it had become largely dependent upon contributions from the Diocese of New York, most of its endowment having been dissipated by poor management or necessity. It seemed only fair, therefore, that the control of New York over the Seminary should be increased, and in 1859 a committee was appointed to consider the desirability of severing the Seminary's connection with General Convention altogether. The Civil War prevented this committee from reporting in 1862, but in 1865 it recommended increasing the control of New York over the institution by raising the number of clergy and the size of the contributions required to elect a trustee. These changes were approved by the Convention but they were not accepted by the trustees and so never became a part of the Seminary's constitution. By 1868, when the non-concurrence of the trustees was reported to General Convention, the financial condition of the Seminary had improved, and though some alteration in the mode of election was made in 1877, the trustees were continued essentially upon the old basis until 1883, when the proposals of 1865 were reversed, and the Seminary was brought into a much closer relationship with General Convention. The amendment then adopted provided for fifty elected members of the Board, half of whom were to be chosen by General Convention and half by the several dioceses upon the basis of their previous contributions. All of the bishops and the Dean of the Seminary were to be *ex officio* trustees. The Dean at this time was the Very Rev. Eugene Augustus Hoffman, and under his administration the Seminary rapidly attained a high degree of economic prosperity, largely through the generous gifts of himself and his family.

While the General Seminary was undergoing these various vicissitudes, two new seminaries were being founded. Philadelphia Divinity School, begun as a diocesan training school in 1860, became a fully organized seminary in 1861, with the Very Rev. George Emlen Hare as dean. Originally Evangelical, it later came

Difficulties of General Seminary

Two New Seminaries

under the influence of the Liberal Movement. Bishop Potter and others who were active in forming this seminary also organized, in 1863, the Divinity Students' Aid Society, later renamed the Evangelical Education Society, to assist students for the ministry. The Episcopal Theological School was organized at Cambridge, in 1867, under the deanship of the Very Rev. Francis Wharton, who was soon succeeded by the Very Rev. John Seeley Stone. It was financed by a gift of $100,000 from Benjamin Tyler Reed, who desired an institution that would be a stronghold of Evangelical principles. Its two leading professors, A.V.G. Allen and Peter Henry Steenstra, were liberals who took the lead in introducing the science of Higher Criticism and other features of the Liberal Movement into America.

Though the Church in the South was impoverished by war, it courageously undertook the founding of a Church university at Sewanee, Tennessee. The University of the South had been projected by Bishops Polk and Otey. Their work, interrupted by the war, was revived by Bishop Quintard in 1867. The collegiate department was opened in 1871 and the theological seminary in 1876. A medical school was added in 1892 and a law school in 1893.

Monasticism

A new attempt at introducing monasticism into the American Episcopal Church was made in 1865 when two American priests, Father Grafton and Father Prescott, were professed in the English Society of Saint John the Evangelist. After remaining in England for several years, they returned to this country but subsequently withdrew from the Society because of a disagreement as to their proper relations with the American bishops. The Order continued its work in America, however, and other priests were sent over.

Free Churches

There was a growing tendency throughout this period towards the use of "free churches" as distinct from those with rented pews. The earliest free churches were established as city missions for work among the poor in the larger cities, and were supported by the dioceses or by missionary societies. It would appear that the first free churches which were self-supporting were Muhlenberg's Church of the Holy Communion in New York and the Church of the Advent in Boston, both of which were founded in 1844. The movement spread rapidly after the Civil War, being generally supported by the Anglo-Catholics. In 1877 an effort was made to secure the passage of a canon forbidding the consecration of churches with rented pews, but the General Convention resolved that it was inexpedient to act upon the subject at that time.

There was also a movement on foot for the organization of smaller dioceses. The tradition that a diocese should· cover a whole state had been broken by the organization of the Diocese of Western New York in 1838, but it was some time before any other states were divided, and the general tendency to have dioceses cover a large area continued. As Church membership increased, this led to the severance of the bishop from any parochial connection and there were some to whom such a separation seemed undesirable. It was also felt that the organization of small dioceses would allow for more intensive work and, perhaps, for a greater variety of usages also. This movement did lead to the division of a number of large dioceses, but the efforts of its sponsors to obtain specific canonical sanction for it were unsuccessful.

Small
Dioceses

CHAPTER XV

A BROADER UNITY

Later
Development
of Ritualism

THE General Convention of 1874 should probably be regarded as marking the high point of the conflict which necessarily resulted from the introduction, through the Oxford Movement, of a new force into the life of the Church. The ritual canon which was passed in that year was obviously unenforceable, and no serious attempt seems to have been made to enforce it. The use of ritual has continued to spread steadily until, in some respects at least, it has come fairly close to fulfilling the prophecy made by Bishop Hopkins in 1867 that "Ritualism will grow into favor by degrees until it becomes the prevailing system." It cannot actually be said to have done this, for as the ritualistic system has spread it has come to be divided along lines that are not always easy to understand. Some practices, such as the use of a solid altar with at least two candles upon it and the employment of vested choirs, have become general, while other customs, such as the use of incense, which would not seem to be necessarily more radical, are still regarded as being as characteristic of extreme Anglo-Catholicism as are Eucharistic Adoration, the Invocation of Saints, and other practices which do have a definite doctrinal significance.

While, however, the distinction thus drawn is not altogether understandable in some of its details, it serves as a whole to illustrate the new attitude towards Ritualism which began to develop after 1874. In the earlier stages of the controversy, as in the debate over the older Tractarianism, it was assumed by the champions of both sides that the Church must either be wholly Catholic or wholly Protestant, so that the dispute took on the aspect of a life and death struggle between the two parties. When, however, De Koven and Smith made their pleas for comprehensiveness in 1874, they opened men's minds to the possibility that the two traditions might be able to live together in a working unity,

306

chafing each other, no doubt, but also learning from one another and enriching one another.

This possibility was strengthened by a development that was taking place at the same time in the Protestant wing of the Church. This development was known in various phases as the Liberal Movement and the Broad Church Movement, but it should probably be described as a tendency rather than a movement, for it lacked the definiteness of aim and principle that one generally associates with the latter term. Those who were under its influence often differed widely in their positive beliefs, but they agreed with one another in their desire to make the Church as comprehensive as possible and in their tendency to minimize the importance of definite dogma, though to varying degrees. They tended also to take a sympathetic attitude towards the prevailing tendencies of contemporary thought, such as the belief in evolution, and they were responsible for introducing the so-called "Higher Criticism" of the Bible into the Church, though not all of them were willing to accept its results. By "Higher Criticism," it should be observed, is meant the scientific investigation of the original sources of the Biblical narratives with a view to ascertaining their relation to the actual events described and their consequent reliability. It necessarily conflicted with the old belief in the verbal inspiration of Scripture, though not inconsistent with less definite theories of inspiration, and it was at first regarded by many as likely to undermine the Christian Faith. *Rise of Liberalism*

Like the Oxford Movement, Liberalism had its origin in England, and its transplantation to this country proved a longer process than the introduction of Tractarianism. It had certain affinities with some earlier liberalizing tendencies of the English Church, including eighteenth-century Latitudinarianism, which had also sought to minimize doctrinal differences and to achieve a rationalistic approach to Christianity. In its modern phase it obtained its first public expression with the publication in 1855 of a volume of *Essays and Reviews* by a group of English Churchmen. The essays represented various viewpoints and it was expressly stated in the preface that each writer should be held responsible for his own contribution only, but the collection showed a general tendency to take a scientific attitude towards Christianity and to try to fit it into the general scheme of historical *The Essays and Reviews; 1855* development. Some of the essayists indicated their acceptance of the results of Higher Criticism, and this fact caused the collection to be bitterly attacked by many conservative Churchmen, for that particular approach to the Bible was still largely confined to Germany. The publication seems, however, to have been not altogether unacceptable to the powers which controlled the English Church, for Frederick Temple, who edited the series and contributed one of the more conservative essays, was made Bishop of London some years later and subsequently elevated to the Archbishopric of Canterbury. In this country the *Essays* were condemned in a Pastoral Letter, written by Bishop McIlvaine with the sanction of the House of Bishops, which declared that Rationalism had no place in the Church.

Bishop Colenso

A few years later the liberal tendency was given a yet stronger expression in England with the publication, in 1861, of a *Commentary on Romans* and in 1862 of the first volume of a work called *The Pentateuch and Joshua Critically Explained*, both by the Right Rev. John William Colenso, Bishop of Natal in Africa. In these works the author, besides adopting the methods of Higher Criticism, voiced some liberal views on theology, indicating his disbelief in eternal punishment, asserting that Christ's Atonement was effected by reconciling us to God through a supreme display of love and not by means of vicarious punishment, and denying the literal inerrancy of Scripture. For these and other opinions that were supposed to be contrary to the official teaching of the Church of England Colenso was brought to trial before the Most Rev. Robert Gray, Metropolitan of South Africa, and deposed. There was, however, some question about Bishop Gray's jurisdiction in the case, so Colenso defied the sentence and was supported by the civil authorities in doing so.

The First Lambeth Conference

The opinion of the Church appears generally to have been in favor of the Metropolitan's action. The General Convention of the American Episcopal Church in 1865 approved it and when all the bishops in communion with the Church of England were invited to attend the first Lambeth Conference it was generally understood that their chief object in assembling was to do likewise. As Colenso was being supported by the British government, however, the bishops of the Established Church felt that his condemnation by the conference might prove embarrassing to themselves, and so they carefully arranged an *agenda* in which there was no place for the South African question to come up. A discussion of the subject was finally forced upon the meeting by the colonial bishops and by Bishop Hopkins from the United States, but the conference declined to take any action. The assembly was chiefly important as being the first of the frequent conferences of Anglican bishops which have been held at Lambeth since then, and which have helped to strengthen the sense of unity within the Anglican communion.

Though Bishop Colenso and the Essayists undoubtedly had some sympathizers in the United States, Liberalism did not exert an important influence upon the history of the American Episcopal Church until the last quarter of the nineteenth century, possibly because the minds of most Churchmen in the preceding quarter century were taken up by the bitter conflict over ritual. One of the first expressions of its influence was the organization of the American Church Congress, which held its first session in 1874. It was an imitation of an English institution of the same name which had been founded some years previously. Its object was to obtain a free discussion of issues which were before the Church, in an assembly which was not, like General Convention, compelled to take definite action. For this reason, it naturally sought the participation of men from all parties, but its original sponsors were most of them Liberals. Its first session was held in New York shortly before the meeting of General Convention, and Bishop Horatio Potter was asked to preside. He declined, expressing a strong disapproval of the Congress. Nevertheless, it was able to secure the support of a representative group of clergymen, including, besides Liberals such as Bishop Clark of Rhode Island, Phillips Brooks, William Reed Huntington, and Edward A. Washburn, some older Evangelicals such as Alexander H. Vinton and Heman Dyer; conservative High Churchmen, such as Bishop Williams of Connecticut; Tractarians like Professor W. D. Wilson of Cornell; and two prominent missionary bishops— Bishop Whipple of Minnesota and Bishop Hare of the Indian Jurisdiction of Niobrara. The papers delivered at its first meeting dealt with the timely topic of the "Limits of Legislation as to Doctrine and Ritual" and one of the speakers, the Rev. John Cotton

The American
Church
Congress

Smith, as has already been noted, anticipated De Koven's more brilliant plea for comprehensiveness.

Phillips
Brooks

Liberalism of any kind is necessarily individualistic, and the liberalism which developed in the Church at this time found its chief expression, even more than earlier movements, in the personalities of a few great leaders. Its most famous representative was unquestionably the Rev. Phillips Brooks, rector of Trinity Church, Boston, and subsequently Bishop of Massachusetts. A native of Massachusetts, Brooks had obtained his theological education at the Virginia Seminary, and had begun his ministry in Philadelphia where he served as rector, first of the Church of the Advent, and later of the Church of the Holy Trinity. His brilliance as a preacher brought him into prominence almost from the first, but his greatest celebrity was attained after his removal to Boston, where he was called in 1869. While there he became one of the most famous and influential American preachers of any denomination, in an age of great preachers.

Brooks had been brought up under Evangelical influences, his early religious training having been supervised by two of the most prominent of the older Evangelicals, the Rev. John S. Stone and the Rev. Alexander H. Vinton, successive rectors at St. Paul's Church, Boston. As his mind matured, however, he became more in sympathy with the trend of contemporary thought and developed a more liberal theology. In his personal views, though he was averse to any definite dogmatic formulations, he does not seem to have departed very far from orthodox Christianity but he was disposed to show his sympathy and fellowship with Liberals of all degrees, even inviting two prominent Unitarian clergymen to be present and receive Communion at the consecration of Trinity Church, which was rebuilt under his rectorship. When he was elected Bishop of Massachusetts in 1892, this proceeding was made a ground for objecting to his consecration by Bishop Seymour of Springfield, whose own election as Bishop of Illinois had been opposed for a different reason in 1874. Brooks' election was, however, confirmed without difficulty, the confirmation being supported not only by the Liberals and the Evangelicals, but by a majority of the High Churchmen and Anglo-Catholics also, including Bishop William Croswell Doane of Albany, a son of the second Bishop of New Jersey, and the Rev. Arthur C. A. Hall, curate of the Church of the Advent, who had opposed Brooks' election in the diocesan convention but could see no valid reason why he should not be consecrated after he had been elected. Father Hall, who was a member of the Society of St. John the Evangelist, was recalled to England by his Order as a measure of discipline for his stand upon this question. He subsequently withdrew from the Society and returned to this country where he became Bishop of Vermont.

Less famous than Brooks outside of the Church, but probably exerting a more lasting influence within it, were Bishop Henry Codman Potter of New York and Rev. William Reed Huntington, rector of Grace Church, New York. Potter was a son of Bishop Alonzo Potter of Pennsylvania and a nephew of Bishop Horatio Potter, his own predecessor in the See of New York. Before his election as bishop, he had served for fifteen years as rector of Grace Church, where he had succeeded the Rev. Thomas House Taylor in 1868. Under his leadership Grace Parish developed into an early example of what came to be called an "institutional church," that is, a Church which supplemented its religious activity with a number of social institutions. Like so many new things in the Church, this type of parish probably had its origin in the work of William Augustus Muhlenberg, who, as we have seen in an earlier chapter, surrounded his Church of the Holy Communion with various charitable enterprises. The general interest in social work which developed at the turn of the century caused the institutional parish to become common in our larger cities, and its popularity has only begun to decline in recent years. One of its earliest exponents, after Muhlenberg, was the Rev. W. S. Rainsford, rector of St. George's Church, New York City.

In 1883 Henry Potter was elected assistant bishop of New York, and, even before his uncle's death in 1887, he was in active charge of the diocese. He had been the choice of the Low Churchmen, in opposition to the Rev. Morgan Dix, the rector of Trinity Church, but he made a scrupulous effort to be thoroughly nonpartisan and his administration of the diocese was marked by a breadth and tolerance that were unusual for the time. In 1884 he had to deal with the case of the Rev. R. Heber Newton, the rector of All Soul's Church, who had delivered and published some sermons in which he advocated the Higher Criticism of the

Bishop Henry
C. Potter

Bible. For this he was presented to Bishop Horatio Potter by two clergymen in 1883, and the case shortly fell from that Bishop's hands into those of his nephew. Henry Potter requested that Newton desist from giving lectures on Higher Criticism in his parish, for the sake of peace, while admitting that he probably had no authority to compel him to do so. Newton complied with this request, though reluctantly, and the Bishop proceeded to pigeon-hole the presentment.

The Briggs Case

In 1899 he gave a more definite sanction to Higher Criticism by ordaining to the Priesthood the Rev. Charles Augustus Briggs, professor of Biblical Theology at Union Theological Seminary. Professor Briggs had been a pioneer exponent in this country of the new methods of Biblical criticism, and had been deposed from the Presbyterian ministry as a result. Having always entertained a certain admiration for the Episcopal Church, he applied to Bishop Potter for ordination. Though a number of English Anglo-Catholics had lately indicated their acceptance of Higher Criticism in a collection of essays called *Lux Mundi*, edited by Canon Charles Gore, most of their party in this country were still opposed to the science, and the proposed ordination of one of its chief exponents excited a good deal of criticism. Nevertheless, he was ordained, and the incident may be regarded as having settled for the American Episcopal Church a point which had already been determined in England: That the literal inerrancy of Scripture was not an official teaching of this Church and that its ministers were at liberty to undertake a critical study of the Bible, provided their doing so did not lead them to deny doctrines that were supposed to be officially approved. The subsequent heresy trials of this period, which we will notice presently, though they involved questions of Higher Criticism, did not turn upon the merits of that science *per se*, but upon certain theological opinions at which the accused ministers had arrived by means of it.

Influence of *Lux Mundi*

This does not mean that all controversy on the subject ended with the Briggs ordination. The development of the science within the Episcopal Church continued to meet with strong opposition and for some time Cambridge was the only seminary in which it was admitted. Two of the professors of that institution, Nash and Steenstra, were among the earliest Higher Critics of the

Episcopal Church. The position taken by Anglo-Catholics under the influence of *Lux Mundi*, that a belief in the verbal inspiration of the Bible was not necessary to the acceptance of Catholic tradition, however, gave Higher Criticism a bi-partisan support which made possible its acceptance without the bitter conflict that has attended its progress in some other denominations.

Bishop Potter was not the type of man who is broad in one direction only. In the same year in which he pigeon-holed the charges against Newton, he exposed himself to criticism from another quarter by professing Father James O. S. Huntington as the first member of the Order of the Holy Cross. The year following, he handled the case of the Rev. Arthur Ritchie, rector of St. Ignatius' Church, much as he had that of Dr. Newton. Father Ritchie was an advanced Ritualist who had already exposed himself to the censure of the Right Rev. William E. McLaren, the Anglo-Catholic Bishop of Chicago. In New York his introduction of ceremonies not permitted by the Prayer Book induced Bishop Potter to refuse to visit St. Ignatius'. A correspondence ensued in which Ritchie agreed to give up the practices if the bishop would waive the canonical question of his right to forbid them, and to this Potter agreed. In the present age of liturgical freedom, it may not seem that such a proceeding displayed any great latitude of mind, but it was more of a concession than would have been made by most bishops at that time. It is worth noting that Father Ritchie's position was criticized both by Bishop Seymour and by Father Grafton.

Father Huntington and the Order of the Holy Cross

When Potter was elected bishop, he was succeeded at Grace Church by William Reed Huntington, who previously had been rector at Worcester. In his later years Huntington acquired the title of "First Presbyter of the Church," largely because of his leadership in the Prayer Book revision which was carried out during the eighties, though there were a number of other grounds on which he might have claimed the title. He was one of the most influential advocates of this Church's participation in the movement for Christian unity which began to show itself at that period, and he was also a leader in the development of new Church institutions which was a characteristic of the day. He developed the institutional side of Grace Church even more than had Dr. Potter, and he was the chief advocate of the revival of the Order of

William Reed Huntington

Deaconesses. He also served on the fabric committee of the Cathedral of St. John the Divine, first projected by Bishop Horatio Potter, though in this position his inexperience, according to his biographer, the Rev. J. W. Suter, caused a number of mistakes which had to be rectified at considerable expense later.

Heresy
Trials

Huntington and Potter were Liberals of a conservative stamp, whose essential orthodoxy was never questioned by anyone, but there were some other Liberals of the period who felt themselves compelled to advocate opinions that were held to be contrary to the official teaching of the Church. One of these, the Rev. Howard MacQueary, published in 1890 a book called *The Evolution of Man and Christianity,* in which he claimed the right to interpret the articles in the Creeds relating to the Resurrection and the Virgin Birth in a different way from that in which they have been generally understood. He was suspended by Bishop Bedell of Ohio and resigned his ministry. A more famous case involving a similar issue was that of the Rev. Algernon Sidney Crapsey, rector of St. Andrew's Church, Rochester, who, in the course of some parochial lectures in 1905, expressed his disbelief in the Virgin Birth. In spite of the efforts of Bishop Walker of western New York, he was brought to trial and convicted of teaching doctrines contrary to those of the Protestant Episcopal Church. He was suspended from his ministry, and when the verdict of the diocesan court was upheld by the newly created Provincial Court of Review, he resigned his office altogether.

Growth of
Anglo-
Catholicism

The development of Liberalism within the Church did not interrupt the advance of Anglo-Catholicism. In some respects it probably fostered it, softening the opposition with its theory of comprehensiveness, and, in its more radical forms, giving the conservative members of the Church something else to worry about besides the threat of a movement towards Roman Catholicism. Ritualism, as we have seen, continued to spread, and as some of the more conservative ritualistic practices came into general use, the more radical representatives of the movement became more daring, reviving an increasing number of mediæval customs, imitating those of modern Roman Catholicism and even, sometimes, making liturgical experiments on their own account. Religious brotherhoods and sisterhoods, especially the latter, increased steadily, though not very rapidly. Repeated efforts were made to secure their sanction by General Convention, but for a long time these did not meet with much success, though a number of committees were appointed on the subject. A canon governing religious communities was not passed until 1913. By then, they had become so settled a feature of Church life that it was a question of regulating rather than of encouraging them. To provide a means of discussing various aspects of the Catholic viewpoint, an Anglo-Catholic Congress was created, resembling the Church Congress.

As the Anglo-Catholics tended to regard the terms "Protestant" and "Catholic" as antithetical, the spread of their movement naturally led to a certain amount of dissatisfaction with the present name of the Church. Proposals to change the name have been offered at nearly every General Convention since 1877, but none has been adopted. In 1910 a motion to omit the word "Protestant" from the title page of the Book of Common Prayer and identify the Episcopal Church as a "portion" of "the Holy Catholic Church" was lost in the House of Deputies only by a technicality, a plurality of both orders favoring it, but a number of dioceses being divided, and consequently, according to the rules of the House, being counted in the negative. No proposal for a complete legal change of name has, however, ever come to nearly so close a vote. Such a change would be exceedingly difficult, as nearly all of the agencies of the Church, local as well as national, have the phrase "Protestant Episcopal" in their charters. There has, moreover, been no agreement as to what name should be adopted if the present one were rejected. Those which have been most often proposed are "The American Church," "The Church in America," "The American Catholic Church," "The American Episcopal Church," and "The Episcopal Church." *(Proposed Changes in the Name of the Church)*

A natural corollary to the broadening of the idea of the Church which took place at this period was the development of an increased interest in the possibility of union with other denominations, an interest which corresponded with a general concern with the problem of Christian unity that began to manifest itself at that period. In dealing with this problem, it was necessary to consider both of the two major types of Christianity, Catholic and Protestant, for if the Episcopal Church is to play an important rôle in the reunion of Christendom, assuming that such a development takes place, it will probably be because of its ability to look *(Interest in Christian Reunion)* in both directions and to maintain some contact with both traditions. In Western Christianity the most important representative of the Catholic tradition is the Roman Catholic Church, but at present a working compromise with this body does not appear to represent a practicable ideal. Efforts towards Catholic reunion have, therefore, for the present to be concentrated upon coöperation with the Eastern Church, and with such western groups as retain the episcopal succession and other features of the Catholic tradition without submitting to the Pope.

Committee on the Swedish Church

As early as 1856 a committee was appointed by General Convention to examine into the validity of the orders of the Swedish Church. As we have seen, Swedish ministers had been accepted in the colonial Church without question, but their numbers had hardly been sufficient to establish a general rule, and no definite action had been taken to bring the two Churches into communion. The committee of 1856 entered into correspondence with the King of Sweden, but apparently never made a final report. Another committee appointed on the same subject in 1892 functioned until 1901, when it reported that, as the enquiry had not been requested by the denomination concerned, it was causing a certain amount of irritation and impairing the cordial relations of the two Churches. As a result of overtures made by the Lambeth Conference, there has been inter-communion between them since 1920.

The Resolution of 1865

In 1865 a resolution was passed expressing sympathy with the efforts of a party in the Italian Church to bring about a reformation, and another was adopted, by the House of Deputies, to the effect "That all those branches of the Apostolic Church which accept the Holy Scriptures and the Niceo-Constantinopolitan Creed, and which reject the usurpations and innovations of the Bishop of Rome are called . . . to renew those primitive relations which the Roman schism has interrupted." This resolution was not exactly calculated to improve our relations with the Roman Catholic Church, but it did represent a gesture towards unity with other Catholics. In 1874 the House of Bishops appointed a committee to keep up a "fraternal correspondence" with the "Old Catholics," a group which had withdrawn from the Roman Catholic Church after the Council of the Vatican.

The first important move towards a revival of interest in reunion on the Protestant side was made by Dr. Huntington in

1870, when he published "an essay towards unity" which he called *The Church Idea*. In this work, after setting forth his ideal of the Christian Church, he proposed a "quadrilateral," or four-fold platform which he thought should be made the basis of proposals for unity by the Anglican communion. Its four points were the Holy Scriptures as the Word of God, the Apostles' and Nicene Creeds as the rule of Faith, the two sacraments of Baptism and Holy Communion, and the episcopate as the keystone of governmental unity. The theory of the Church thus put forward was not a new one, but its reduction to four points made it a convenient basis for popular discussion and official action. The "quadrilateral" was accepted in substance in a declaration adopted by the House of Bishops in 1886, at a meeting of the General Convention in Chicago. Their declaration was reaffirmed with some modifications by the next Lambeth Conference, and was thenceforth known as the "Chicago-Lambeth Declaration." It was adopted by the House of Deputies in 1892. Its chief difficulty as a working basis for reunion is that it ranks as essential the major points in which the Episcopal Church differs from most Protestant denominations.

Dr. Huntington's Platform

In 1880 the House of Bishops appointed a committee to consider the validity of the Moravian episcopate. At the next convention this committee reported that it could not act because the question was before a committee of the Lambeth Conference. At the Convention of 1886 a number of memorials were presented urging action favorable to Church unity. One of these was signed by over a thousand clergymen. The House of Deputies adopted a resolution offered by Phillips Brooks extending cordial greetings to the General Assembly of the Congregational Church which was also meeting in Chicago, but the Bishops refused to concur, on the surprising ground that they were then maturing plans for Church unity. Since that time it has, however, become customary for General Convention to send greetings to any important Christian assembly that happens to meet in the vicinity during its sessions. The deliberations of the Bishops resulted in the declaration containing the quadrilateral.

At the General Convention of 1904 a Joint Committee on Christian Unity was appointed and instructed to seek the coöperation of other Christian bodies on matters of common interest, such as

Committee on Christian Unity, 1904

Sabbath observance, the sanctity of marriage, and religious education. In 1907 this committee was authorized to appoint a member
to represent itself, but not the Church as a whole, at the Inter-
Church Conference on Federation which was to be held the following year. That conference resulted in the organization of the
National Federation of Churches, to secure the coöperation of
such denominations as would participate upon points of mutual
concern. At the next General Convention the Committees on
Christian Unity and on Social Service were both authorized to
send representatives to the Council of the Federation. In 1913
this authorization was repeated, but a proviso was attached expressing the opinion that the sort of unity desired by Christ was
the union of all His followers in one body.

This period also saw a reawakening of the Church's concern

The Social
Christian
Movement

with the field of social morality. As a result of the separation of
Church and State under the Constitution, it had come to be generally assumed that Christian bodies should concern themselves
exclusively with matters of personal religion and private morality,
and ignore political, economic, and social questions. As the progress of the industrial revolution forced new and pressing socio-
economic problems on public attention, it became evident that this
arbitrary limitation of the Christian message could not be maintained. The resumption of Christian social teaching is generally
believed to have had its origin in 1848, when Charles Kingsley
and Frederick Maurice, two priests of the Church of England,
drafted the program of Christian Socialism. The first evidence of
awakening social conscience in the American Episcopal Church
was shown at the General Convention of 1862, when nineteen
bishops, ten presbyters, and ten laymen signed a petition to the
President on Indian rights, drafted by Bishop Whipple and circulated by Bishop Alonzo Potter. At the first Church Congress,
in 1874, a paper on the relations of capital and labor was read by
W. D. Wilson. Between 1876 and 1881, three New York clergymen, Richard Heber Newton, J. H. Rylance, and Edward A.
Washburn, wrote books dealing with social issues. In 1889, Richard
T. Ely, a layman of the Church, published some more radical
essays on the *Social Aspects of Christianity*. A periodical devoted
to Christian Socialism was started about this time by W. P. D.
Bliss, rector of the Church of the Carpenter, Boston, and Philo

W. Sprague, rector of St. John's Church, Charlestown, wrote a book in support of the cause.

The Church Association for the Advancement of the Interests of Labor was formed in 1887, through the efforts of Father Huntington, with his father, Bishop Frederick Dan Huntington, as president. Its second president was Bishop Henry Codman Potter. In 1891, the Christian Social Union was formed, also under Bishop Huntington's presidency. It disbanded in 1911, when a permanent secretary was named for the Church's commission of social service, but, in the same year, a more radical body, the Church Socialist League, was formed under the leadership of Bishop Frank Spencer Spaulding and Bernard Iddings Bell. It was dissolved during the anti-radical hysteria of the First World War, but its work was resumed in 1919 by the still active Church League for industrial Democracy, under the leadership of William B. Spofford. *Growth of a Social Outlook in the Church*

The first of the new social ideals to attract the attention of General Convention was that of world peace. In 1892 the Convention adopted a petition to be addressed to the Christian rulers of the world in favor of the use of peaceful arbitration for the settlement of international disputes. In 1898 a joint resolution was addressed to the Czar of Russia expressing gratification at his calling of the first Hague Conference, and voicing a hope that it would lead to a reduction of armaments and the establishment of an international court. A resolution for the same purpose, introduced by Mr. Stotsenberg, a lay delegate from Indiana, had branded war as "cruel, inhuman, and un-Christian," but this language was too strong for the Convention, and a milder form was substituted. In 1904 the General Convention, sitting in Boston, addressed a communication to the International Peace Congress, which was meeting in the same city, expressing sympathy with its work. At the next Convention a resolution of thankfulness for the second Hague Conference was passed, and prayers were offered for its success. In 1916, less than a year before the entry of the United States into the World War, a joint committee was appointed to further the ends of peace and to coöperate with the World Alliance for Promoting International Peace through the Churches. *Resolutions on World Peace*

The labor problem was later in arousing the official concern of the Church. In 1901 a Joint Committee on Capital and Labor was appointed to study the aims of the labor movement, investigate particular disputes, and act as an arbitrator if requested. In *Committee on Capital and Labor*

1904 it made a report which contained a number of vague generalizations but did recommend specific legislation against child labor. In 1910 its title was changed to Committee on Christian Social Service.

The Divorce Problem

Marriage and divorce present a social problem that, because of its close relation to personal morality, has always been considered as lying within the field of action permitted to the Church. In the Episcopal Church the traditional policy has always been to oppose all divorce except for adultery, and to oppose remarriage, except in the case of the innocent party to such a divorce. In 1868 this policy had been enacted into a canon, but no definite procedure had been provided for its enforcement. As public opinion became alarmed at the increase of divorce in the last quarter of the nineteenth century, efforts were made to obtain a more adequate canon on the subject. In 1886 both houses took action, but they could not agree upon the details of the canon and so the question was referred to the next Convention. The Deputies resolved not to abandon the question until a satisfactory canon was passed, as they felt that they could thus make a contribution towards saving "American civilization, decaying already at its roots." Nevertheless, no canon was agreed upon until 1904, when one was passed affirming the old principle and providing a process of enforcement.

Revision of the Prayer Book and Constitution

One important indication of the growing harmony in the Church after 1874 was the success of the Prayer Book revision that was brought to a conclusion in 1892. By then the Prayer Book of 1789 had been in use for slightly over a century, and until the revision was commenced no important changes had been made in it. In the first part of the century the attachment of Churchmen of all parties to the book had prevented any strong demand for revision. In the middle years, Muhlenberg and a few others had asked for greater liturgical freedom, but with the increasing intensity of party feeling, it was evident to most of the leaders of the Church that any effort at revision would only precipitate a bitter conflict. After the crisis had passed, and party feeling began to cool off, demands for liturgical change increased until the General Convention of 1880, on motion of Dr. Huntington, appointed a joint committee to consider the propriety of revising the Prayer Book with a view to liturgical enrichment and increased flexibility. Huntington was not only the chief sponsor of the measure, but he proved to be the most active member of the committee, which presented a complete revision to the Convention of 1886 in the form of a "Book Annexed" to its report. When this book was recommitted, however, as not meeting the wishes of the Convention, he withdrew and the work was completed by others. It was finally approved in 1892 and remained in general use until 1928, so that it should be familiar to most readers. It did not involve any fundamental change from the Book of 1789, but it was enriched with some additional prayers and canticles, and made slightly more flexible.

In the same year that it gave its final approval to the new Prayer Book, General Convention appointed a committee to revise the constitution. The first report of this committee was not approved and the revision was not fully completed until 1904, though most of the amendments were approved three years earlier. The chief changes were to recognize the office of Presiding Bishop which had theretofore existed simply by a rule of the upper house, to provide for the creation of provinces, and to authorize the House of Bishops to set up missionary jurisdictions on its own responsibility.

The desire for change which manifested itself in these revisions was shown also in the creation of various new agencies for carrying on the work of the Church. In the formation of these institutions there appeared generally to be a twofold motive: to revive some institution that had existed in other ages or branches of the Catholic Church, but had been discontinued in the Episcopal Church, and to provide a means of meeting the new problems that confronted the Church. Ever since the Muhlenberg Memorial there had been agitation in the Church for the creation of some agency to utilize the services of women, though the Church had, in fact, been using their services all along. Gradually the agitation crystallized into a demand for the revival of the primitive order of deaconesses, and of sisterhoods. The latter was too definitely Catholic a measure to win official approval for some time, but the deaconesses obtained the powerful support of Dr. Huntington and a canon establishing their order was passed in 1889. They were to be unmarried women of good character over twenty-five years of age. They were not to work in a diocese except with the

The Order of Deaconesses

permission of the bishop, or in a parish without the consent of the rector. When not connected with a parish, they were to be at the command of the bishop in whose diocese they were located. A deaconess might resign from the order at any time, but unless her resignation was dictated by weighty reasons, she could not be reinstated later.

A number of unofficial organizations were also created during this period. The Brotherhood of St. Andrew was organized in this country to enlist men in the work of the Church, and the Girls' Friendly Society, first organized in England, was brought into the United States in 1877. Its original object was to help girls of the working class, but it developed into a social and religious organization for young women of the Church. The Order of the Daughters of the King was organized in 1885 from a senior Bible class in the Church of the Holy Sepulchre, New York City. The Church Mission of Help, which was started in New York in 1911, and has since spread into sixteen dioceses, was organized to provide skilled assistance for girls between sixteen and twenty-five whose personal problems were too great for them to solve alone.

The provision in the revised constitution authorizing the creation of provinces was the result of an agitation for some subdivision of the Church larger than dioceses, which had begun almost as soon as dioceses began to be organized in areas less extensive than a whole state. The new provision was not given effective expression, however, until 1907 when a canon was passed dividing the Episcopal Church in the United States and its possessions into eight provinces. The name given to the new unit would seem to imply a desire to imitate the large divisions which existed in the English Church and in the primitive Church, but the American provinces have very little resemblance to any others. They are governed by an elective synod to which few powers have as yet been entrusted, and they have no regular presiding officer. Except as providing a basis for the Provincial Court of Review, they have no important function.

More significant, perhaps, than the creation of the provinces, was the movement for building cathedrals. The first regularly organized cathedral in the American Episcopal Church was founded by Bishop Whipple in the Diocese of Minnesota. In the latter part of the century a number of dioceses built or started to

Other Organizations

Cathedral Building

build cathedrals on a more or less elaborate scale. The best-known and probably the most important are those at New York and Washington, neither of which is yet completed.

With the development of more complicated methods of print- ing and a cheaper mail service, the numerous small Church papers **Periodicals** mentioned in an earlier chapter tended to die out, though their function was to some extent taken over by the development of official diocesan papers. Of the larger periodicals, *The Churchman* continued to carry on though, in its reaction from Catholi- cism, it moved more and more towards a broad Church position. The *Southern Churchman*, which, like *The Churchman*, had been founded earlier in the century, continued to represent the older Evangelical point of view. *The Living Church,* published first at Chicago and later at Milwaukee, was founded to represent the Anglo-Catholic interests. Its editor, Mr. Frederic C. Morehouse, also served the Church in many other ways as a prominent layman. All of these periodicals performed the function of reporting the current news of the Church and commenting upon the events re- ported. *The Living Church Annual,* which absorbed a number of older Church almanacs, continued the work, begun by *Sword's Pocket Almanac* in 1816, of recording the statistical history of the Church. During the decade of the nineties it was published as a quarterly.

The increase in the work among negroes and in the negro min- istry which followed the Civil War caused the Church to be **Provision for** seriously confronted with the race problem. A number of **Suffragans** memorials were presented to General Convention from time to time by colored Church workers, complaining of discriminations against them in the southern dioceses, and, on the other hand, the white Churchmen of the South frequently urged the creation of a negro episcopate and even of a separate negro Church. When their proposals were turned down with the statement that the Church recognized no racial distinctions, they began an agitation for the creation of "suffragan bishops," a term applied to assistant bishops without the right of succession. This proposal was also turned down as long as it was based primarily upon the racial issue, but eventually the desire of some of the larger northern dioceses to have assistants who were not assured of succession made it possible to create the office without appearing to have the negroes chiefly in mind, and an amendment for the purpose, put forward in 1907, was finally approved in 1910. The suffragans were to have seats but not votes in the House of Bishops, and were to be eligible for election as diocesan bishops or coadjutors, the latter term having been applied in the revised constitution to assistant bishops of the older type. The new office has been widely used by dioceses desiring to elect an assistant bishop without committing themselves to making him their diocesan, but it has also served the purpose intended by its original sponsors in making possible the election of negro bishops.

Two seminaries were added to the Church during this period.

New Seminaries

Berkeley Divinity School, originally located at Middletown, but recently moved to New Haven, was founded by Bishop Williams to serve as a center for Connecticut Churchmanship. Under its present Dean, the Rev. William Palmer Ladd, it has come to be identified with a program of liberal social teaching. Western Theological Seminary was founded at Chicago by Bishop Mc-Laren as the result of a gift made especially for that purpose. It has lately been merged with the Seabury Divinity School, and the combined institution, known as Seabury-Western, is located at Evanston, Illinois.

CHAPTER XVI

The Struggle for the West and for Other Lands

WERE it not for the desirability of adhering to a more or less chronological order, the story of the Church's missionary expansion since the organization of the Domestic and Foreign Missionary Society might be told in a single chapter, or in successive chapters, for it has been a continuous process, only indirectly affected by outside forces. New parties and movements may, of course, send new types of men into the mission field. They may increase or diminish the support given to the work by the Church at large, as they tend to emphasize or neglect the missionary spirit, or to stir up or allay party strife, but they affect the basic character of the work very little. The fundamental purpose, to proclaim the Gospel through the Church, remains the same, and though differing theories of Churchmanship may in some measure affect missionary methods, these are determined to a much greater extent by the practical conditions under which the work has to be carried on.

For the sake of convenience we stopped our relation of missionary history in Chapter Twelve at the beginning of the Civil War. That conflict necessarily brought a serious falling-off in the receipts of the Society, and this diminution was increased by the effects of religious partisanship. In 1862, when the strain of the war was not yet at its worst, the Domestic Committee reported that its receipts had decreased from $63,303 to $35,223 since 1860, but it had been informed that the Evangelical American Church Missionary Society had received $12,500 and employed twenty-eight missionaries in the domestic field during the current year. For three of the war years the Foreign Committee was unable to send any money at all to China, so that much of the work there had to be abandoned, and other fields also suffered seriously.

The end of the war, though it led to a gradual recovery in the

Continuous Activity in the Mission Field

Effects of the Civil War

New Work
Among
Negroes

Society's finances, also added something to the missionary responsibilities of the Church. In the first place, the general ruin which
followed in the South caused a number of parishes that had formerly been self-supporting to feel the need of assistance from
the Missionary Society. In the second place, the creation of an
immense body of free citizens, almost entirely illiterate and completely unaccustomed to independent action, furnished a problem
which the combined resources of all the social agencies in the
country proved inadequate to solve. An attempt on the part of the
Church to solve the problem resulted in the creation of a Freedman's Commission by the General Convention in 1865, with J.
Brinton Smith as Secretary and General Agent, and Robert B.
Minturn as Treasurer. The latter died shortly after the organization of the Commission and was replaced by Stewart Brown.
The year after its creation the Commission reported receipts of
$26,108, and expenditures of $24,723. After a preliminary survey,
it had started special schools at Richmond, Newbern, Norfolk,
Talcott, and Petersburg in Virginia; Wilmington and Raleigh in
North Carolina; Sumter and Winnsboro in South Carolina, and
Louisville in Kentucky. It had also taken over a school founded
by Dr. Lacey in Okolona, Mississippi, and had aided an orphanage
founded by Mrs. Canfield in Memphis.

Growth in
the West

As the year 1866 was the thirtieth anniversary of the organization of the Board of Missions, the Domestic Committee, in its
report, gave a summary of the results that had been achieved in
the intervening years. Ohio in 1836 had already become a fairly
strong diocese, having forty-seven regular ministers besides four
missionaries. In 1866 there were 102 ministers and two missionaries. A small allowance to that state had been made regularly in
the interim and it was the opinion of the committee that "no
other appropriations of the same magnitude have yielded more
abundant spiritual or material returns." In Illinois, where there had
been only six ministers besides Bishop Chase in 1836, there were,
sixty years later, one hundred parishes and nearly one hundred
ministers. Indiana had had three missionaries and four other
ministers in 1836. Church representation increased until it included forty parishes and thirty ministers. Michigan, which had
had only three missionaries and no other officiating minister, now
boasted sixty-eight parishes and sixty-four ministers. Wisconsin in

1836 had only two ministers and three stations. In 1866 it was served by seventy parish ministers and eight missionaries. Minnesota, where there had been only one minister when Breck went there in 1853, had grown, under the leadership of Bishop Whipple, who was elected in 1859, until it had fifty parishes and twenty-seven ministers, seven of whom were employed by the Society.

The first two missionaries to go to Iowa were sent there in 1839. In 1866 there were thirty-seven ministers serving forty-six parishes in that state. In Missouri the number of ministers had increased from four to thirty in thirty years. Kansas and Nebraska, an unknown region to the Society in 1836, now had, between them, twenty ministers. Tennessee's supply of clergymen had grown from ten to nearly thirty. Kentucky, with twenty-one ministers, had been fairly well developed in 1836. The number of its clergymen had since increased to thirty-five. The first missionaries to California, Mines and Ver Mehr, had been sent there during the Gold Rush of 1849. When Bishop Kip went there in 1853 there were eight ministers. In 1866 there were thirty, and it was said that more could be supported if they could be obtained. The first service in the area covered by Oregon and Washington had been held in 1847, and the first missionary sent there in 1851. Now there were eleven parishes and nine ministers in the two territories.

In the region between the Old West and the Pacific the work of the Church was just beginning in 1866. In Colorado there were seven parishes and five ministers, only one of whom was supported by the Society. In Nevada there were seven parishes but only two ministers, neither of whom was aided by the Society. Idaho and Dakota had one minister each. If any work was being done in the other parts of this region, the Domestic Committee did not know about it. *The New West*

As the foregoing review shows, the Old West had become well settled by this time and the Church there had become largely self-supporting, though a few missionaries were to be maintained by the Society in those states for some time to come. The West with which this chapter is chiefly concerned is that vast region of plain, desert, and mountain which lies between the Mississippi Valley and the Pacific Slope. This was the West of the romantic age, whose cowboys, miners, and desperadoes play so important a part in that popular fiction which is our modern substitute for folklore. It was, during most of the period, a region of great crudity, and yet, as time went on, it became an area of striking cultural contrasts also, for the wealth that was to be found in cattle-raising in the heyday of the industry brought to the plains many people of means and education from the East and from Europe.

In 1866 George Maxwell Randall, who had been consecrated Bishop of Colorado, Montana, Idaho, and Wyoming, the year before, said of the last-named portion of his jurisdiction, "I can only report . . . that after diligent enquiry and research I have been unable to discover any such territory in these 'parts.' " Wyoming, in fact, did not have any official existence until 1868 when it was first set apart as a territory of the United States. In that year Bishop Randall reported that he had found the region on his way west in the spring and remarked that it had been a wilderness until the Union Pacific was built. Since then, Cheyenne had become a flourishing, if disorderly, city, and a missionary, the Rev. J. W. Cook, had settled there. The bishop also mentioned holding service at Trinidad, Colorado, in a dance hall connected with a saloon, whose proprietor had not only offered the use of the hall but, as a special inducement, had promised to close his bar during the services. The fiddler's platform was used as a pulpit and a washstand became a reading desk.

Twenty-two years later, when much of the region was still primitive, the Right Rev. Ethelbert Talbot, "the Bishop" of *The Virginian*, was to write of arriving at a small Wyoming town one Saturday afternoon and attending a lecture on "Jerusalem and the Holy Land" delivered for the benefit of the local church by Miss Kent, "a member of a distinguished Scottish family." During the lecture, he said, "the cultivated speaker appealed several times to persons in her audience who had traveled over the same sacred grounds and could confirm her impressions." He also observed that he found Sir Robert Peel, a grandson of the English statesman, living on a nearby ranch. In New Mexico, late in the seventies, General Lew Wallace was to sit quietly writing his famous novel of ancient Rome and Jerusalem, oblivious of the fact that "Billy the Kid," a notorious local bad man, had sworn to shoot him at sight.

Glamour, however, is generally the product of distance, either in space or time, and for the missionaries the West was mainly a region of hard work, made inspiring only by that sense of apostleship which is the heritage of their calling. The shortage of men which had so hampered the work of the Church in the Old West pursued it still, and many a Macedonian Cry had to go unanswered because there was no one to heed it, but, thanks to the existence of the Missionary Society, and to a longer experience in collective action, the work was more systematically organized and more generally supported. The Church had by now consciously adopted the practice of using the episcopate as a missionary agency, and the General Convention of 1865, at which Bishop Randall was elected, divided the Far West, exclusive of California, into five missionary jurisdictions: Oregon and Washington; Arkansas and Indian Territory; Colorado, Montana, Idaho, and Wyoming; Nevada, Utah, Arizona, and New Mexico; and Nebraska and Dakota. The first two of these jurisdictions were already being served by Bishops Scott and Lay. Randall was elected to the third, Mark Antony De Wolfe Howe to the fourth, and Robert Hooper Clarkson to the fifth. Howe declined to serve and Ozi William Whitaker was chosen to replace him at the next Convention. His jurisdiction, however, only included Nevada and Arizona, for at a special session in 1866 the House of Bishops had constituted Montana, Utah, and Idaho a separate jurisdiction under Daniel Sylvester Tuttle, and had attached New Mexico to Colorado and Wyoming under Bishop Randall.

Organization of the Work

It was, of course, impossible for these men to cover their large jurisdictions in more than a superficial manner, and they had great difficulty in obtaining missionaries to help them. In 1871 Bishop Randall wrote, "From the outset my greatest trial has been to obtain ministers ready to go to this land and stay there long enough to 'possess it.'" Appeals which he had made for five months after his consecration had obtained him one deacon. After spying about the country he returned to the East and, as the result of six months' effort, he obtained one other, but when he returned to his jurisdiction he met the first deacon coming east. At the time of writing, however, he had a few more. To correct this shortage of ministers by arranging for a local supply, efforts were made to establish colleges and theological schools in most of the

Shortage of Ministers

jurisdictions. Bishop Clarkson, shortly after his election, reported the founding of a number of educational institutions, including the Nebraska College and Divinity School and the Omaha Collegiate Institute, and Bishop Randall in 1871 reported the founding of a collegiate school for boys at Golden, Colorado. Most of these institutions were short-lived.

Finances

The financial support given to the work, though less seriously deficient than the supply of men, was also far from adequate. In 1868 the financial embarrassments of the Missionary Society were so serious as to draw a resolution of sympathy from the House of Deputies. Its condition began to improve thereafter, and its receipts increased more or less steadily, but the increase was never rapid enough to keep up with the increased demands upon it, and many of the missionary jurisdictions had to be kept upon a short allowance. Bishop Randall in 1871 reported that he had received $106,000 for his work from all sources since his consecration, for which he could then show properties appraised at $114,600, even without allowing for the increase in real estate values. The annual allowance of the Board of Missions for paying missionaries in his three territories, however, was only $3,500, or, for each territory, less than half the amount that was currently appropriated for Maine. By way of contrast, he observed that the Presbyterians were paying $1,500 to one of their missionaries in Wyoming.

Local Set-backs

The leaders of the western work also had to contend with the inevitable period of economic distress and stationary or even decreasing population which followed the first boom in any new state or territory. In 1871 Bishop Tuttle reported that Idaho and Montana had reached this difficult state of transition from rapid growth to stable settlement, and that the work of the Church had been seriously hampered. For a time he had had no minister in Montana, but the Rev. W. H. Stoy had lately gone to Deer Lodge, and he hoped soon to obtain a missionary for Virginia City. There was only one minister in Idaho. The Mormon state of Utah, on the other hand, was receiving an influx of Gentiles as the result of the discovery of silver, and the parish at Salt Lake City, founded by the Rev. George W. Foote, since gone to California, was strong enough to elect Tuttle its rector and pay him a salary of $2,000, which he used in procuring assistance. By 1875 the reaction had set in in Utah also, and the Gentile immigration had been checked, but converts were still being made from Mormonism.

The depression which was general throughout the United States in 1875 was intensified in Nebraska and Dakota by a plague of locusts, and Bishop Clarkson reported that the building of churches had largely ceased, and the schools he had founded were seriously distressed, though he hoped they would be able to weather the crisis. In 1880, Bishop Wingfield of Northern California wrote that the "good times" of rapid growth which that state had known in the past were "gone forever," and that in the future "California must be content to go as other states." The year 1887, when Bishop Ethelbert Talbot first went to Wyoming, was a disastrous one for that territory. During a severe winter seventy-five per cent. of the cattle died from cold and hunger, and when spring came it was found that the bottom had fallen out of the cattle market, due to the rapid development of the industry elsewhere, so that the stock which survived could be sold for only about half the former price. The industry never became as profitable as it had been, and a few years later the silver market also collapsed, so that much of Bishop Talbot's episcopate was cast in hard times.

Nevada, whose growth had been based almost entirely upon silver, declined more rapidly and permanently than any other western state. In 1890, the Right Rev. Abiel Leonard, Bishop of Nevada and Utah, wrote, "The census shows that the decline of the population in Nevada has been going on steadily during the past decade and there are today scarcely as many people in the entire state as there are in the city of Salt Lake." As its easy divorce laws proved, in time, to be almost the only means of drawing trade to the state, a moral difficulty was added to the economic one.

Nevertheless, the Church grew steadily throughout most of the western region, though its growth was not always very even, local variations of leadership, personnel, or environment often making its advance much more rapid at one time and place than at another. In 1871, the Right Rev. Henry N. Pierce, who had succeeded Bishop Lay as Bishop of Arkansas and Indian Territory, reported that three parishes had become self-supporting within his jurisdiction since the last General Convention, when

Steady Growth

there was only one. Four churches had been consecrated, and two were being built. In the same year, Bishop Clarkson reported that there were six ministers working among the white people in Dakota Territory, where five years ago there had been only one, the Rev. Melandthon Hoyt, a pioneer of long standing. Besides these six there were three white and five Indian clergymen in the Indian jurisdiction of Niobrara, which was temporarily under his charge. In 1880 Bishop Whitaker reported that in the past ten years the number of churches in Nevada had increased from three to ten and the number of ministers from one to seven. This was before the state began its rapid decline, but in the same report in which he mentioned this decline, in 1890, Bishop Leonard, Bishop Whitaker's successor, said that the Church was growing in the three principal cities of the state.

The census of 1890 officially recorded the passing of the frontier.

Statistics of 1890: The Central West

Thenceforth there was to be no fringe of settlement in the United States, for the whole country belonged in the "settled area," though in some parts the settlement was still thin. In the same year, as shown by *The Living Church Quarterly*, the Episcopal Church had 48,569 communicants in the region lying between the Mississippi River and the states and territories on the Pacific Coast. These communicants were divided among eight dioceses and eight missionary jurisdictions, exclusive of the Indian Territory (Oklahoma) with fifty communicants, which was under the Bishop of Arkansas. Of the total number, the dioceses included 38,039, and the missionary jurisdictions 10,530. Five of the dioceses, Missouri, Texas, Iowa, Minnesota, and Kansas, had been organized before the Civil War, and in the four first named, the Church had already obtained a substantial growth by 1866. The dioceses which had been organized since the Civil War were Nebraska in 1868, Arkansas in 1871, and Colorado in 1887. A ninth missionary jurisdiction, The Platte, had been created in western Nebraska in 1889, but its statistics had not yet been separated from those of the diocese. Four of the dioceses, Arkansas, Missouri, Iowa, and Minnesota, included the four states which lie immediately west of the Mississippi, where the Church might be expected to develop first. From them, there was a pronounced westward thrust in the central part of the region, represented by Kansas, Nebraska, and Colorado, and balanced, in part, by the diocese of Texas in the South. The remoter sections of that state had, however, been separated from the diocese to form the missionary jurisdictions of Northern and Western Texas. Louisiana is not counted with these states as comprising the Central West, because, though the bulk of its area is west of the Mississippi, a majority of its Church population resides in the cities of New Orleans and Baton Rouge, on the eastern bank of the Mississippi.

On the Pacific Coast in 1890 there were 11,197 communicants of the Episcopal Church divided among two dioceses, California and Oregon, and two missionary jurisdictions, Northern California and Washington. The diocese of California had been organized in 1850 to include the whole state, but as a large part of the northern section was incapable of self-support, the diocese asked to be relieved of it, and, as the result of an amendment to the constitution finally approved in 1874, it was cut off and made a missionary jurisdiction under the Right Rev. John Henry Ducachet Wingfield. The principle upon which this action was based, *i. e.,* that the Church as a whole should assume responsibility for the larger missionary areas, even though they occurred in a state where the Church was elsewhere fairly strong, has led in the separation of a good many missionary districts from organized dioceses since it was adopted. As the total number of communicants in the Episcopal Church in the continental United States in 1890 was 484,020, the number on the Pacific Coast represented two per cent of the strength of the Church, and those in the interior region represented ten per cent.

The Pacific States

Much of the West remained a frontier region for the Church long after it had ceased to be a frontier for population, and in some places this is still the situation. During the quarter century following 1890, the work in that region was carried on under substantially the same conditions as before. The population of the West continued to grow rapidly, as did that of the whole United States. In a few of the states of the interior the population growth lagged behind that of the country as a whole, but in others it was ahead. By 1915 the total number of Episcopal communicants in the region between the Mississippi and the Pacific States was 105,531. Of these 75,302 were divided among fourteen independent dioceses and 30,229 were located within the same number

The Central West in 1915

of missionary districts. Three of the missionary jurisdictions of 1890—Montana, where Bishop Tuttle and his successor, Bishop Brewer, had carried on an important work; West Texas, where the Church had been built up by Bishop R. W. B. Elliott and Bishop J. S. Johnston; and North Texas, under Bishop Garrett—had become independent dioceses, the last named adopting the designation of the Diocese of Dallas. Neither of the two new Texas dioceses, however, included all of the missionary districts from which they had been formed. The "Panhandle" and some of the sterile central portion of the state, included in the old jurisdiction of North Texas, had been continued as a missionary district under the same title, and some of the southwestern counties, formerly belonging in West Texas, had been attached to New Mexico. The other new dioceses were the result of the division of two old ones, the former diocese of Minnesota having been divided into Minnesota and Duluth, and that of Missouri into Missouri and West Missouri. The increase in the number of missionary districts had been caused by the division of those which had included more than one state in 1890, and the creation of some others out of portions of organized dioceses, Salina having been separated from Kansas, and Western Colorado from Colorado. Indian Territory, which had been opened to white settlement in the interval, had developed two new missionary districts, Oklahoma and Eastern Oklahoma.

On the Pacific Coast the number of communicants had increased to 42,384, of whom 35,772 were in five dioceses and 6,612 in three missionary districts. Northern California had become self-supporting and had adopted the name of Diocese of Sacramento. The old Diocese of California had been divided into California and Los Angeles, and a new missionary district, that of San Joaquin, had been set up across the mountains. The states of Oregon and Washington had also been divided, the western and more populous sections becoming the dioceses of Oregon and Olympia, respectively, and the eastern portions being formed into the missionary districts of Eastern Oregon and Spokane.

As the total number of communicants in the Episcopal Church in the continental United States in 1915 was 1,010,874, the number on the Pacific Coast now represented four per cent of the strength of the Church and the interior contained ten per cent. To produce

The Pacific States in 1915

this result, the number of communicants in the interior had been a little more than doubled, and that on the Pacific had been multiplied about three and three-fourths times. The more rapid growth in the latter region is probably accounted for partly by a greater growth in population there and partly by the larger number of urban centers. The growth of the Church as a whole, it may be observed, had kept well ahead of that of the total population during the twenty-five years, for it had more than doubled by 1915, whereas the population had not yet done so even by 1920, when the next census was taken.

The American Empire, if our scattered possessions deserve so grandiloquent a title, was for the most part acquired in the second half of the nineteenth century. The Territory of Alaska was purchased from Russia in 1867, partly as an acknowledgment of that country's supposed friendliness to us during the Civil War. In 1898, as a result of the Spanish-American War and the imperialistic sentiments which attended it, we annexed the remnants of the Spanish Empire, with the exception of Cuba, to which we gave a nominal independence. The most important territories thus acquired were the island of Puerto Rico in the Caribbean Sea and the Philippine Islands, off the coast of Southeastern Asia. In the same year we annexed the Hawaiian Islands in the middle of the Pacific Ocean, as the result of a request made some time before by the Americans and other foreigners who had gained control of the local government. The Panama Canal Zone was added in 1903, and the Virgin Islands were purchased from Denmark in 1917. Alaska, where the Russian and Eskimo population were soon supplanted by settlers from the United States, furnished a situation which, except as it was conditioned by the climate, was not unlike that to be found in the more extensive and less populous of the western jurisdictions, but the other colonies, having predominantly non-European populations with varying degrees of civilization, presented many problems hitherto more often encountered in the foreign field.

The American Empire

Work in Alaska was begun by the Rev. Octavius Parker, in 1886. In 1887, the Rev. John W. Chapman started his lifelong labors at Anvik on the Yukon River. The Missionary Society had provided him with a saw-mill and a boiler engine with which to build himself a station, and he himself acquired the aid of a

Alaska

native youth of about sixteen whom he planned to use as an interpreter, and whom he later adopted as his son. By 1895 he had been joined at Anvik by Miss Bertha W. Sabine, who ran a school there, and by Dr. Mary V. Glenton, a medical missionary, who was trying to found a maternity hospital. Two other missionaries, the Rev. E. H. Edson and Dr. John B. Driggs, ran a school in another part of the territory. In the same year the Right Rev. Peter Trimble Rowe was consecrated Bishop of Alaska, and under his capable and devoted direction the work grew rapidly. By 1900 the Church had mission stations at Sitka, Skagway, Juneau, Cape Nome, and Rampart, and hospitals at Skagway, Circle City, Rampart, and Nome. In 1905 Bishop Rowe reported that the Church had seven hospitals in Alaska and that a new mission had been opened at Seward. The mission at Tanana was coöperating with the government in an effort to introduce the breeding of reindeer. Schools for the natives were maintained at eight stations. In the opinion of the leaders of the work, it was more important to educate these people "in ways of living, in the care of the sick, and in the ordinary sanitary precautions that make for health" than in reading and writing, though these were not neglected. As the native population was rapidly declining, a fear was expressed that unless effective action was taken very soon there would be no natives left to educate in anything. In 1915 Alaska reported 1,021 communicants. For many years Bishop Rowe was ably assisted in his work by his devoted Archdeacon, the Ven. Hudson Stuck.

The acquisition of our principal island possessions led to more immediate action on the part of the Episcopal Church than did the purchase of Alaska. The General Convention of 1898 appointed a Committee on the Increased Responsibilities of the Church, and as a result of its suggestions, some action was immediately taken with respect to all of the new territories. Two missionaries, the Rev. George B. Pratt and the Rev. Frederick Caunt, were sent to Puerto Rico and one, the Rev. James L. Smiley, was sent to the Philippines. There was also an Episcopalian army chaplain in each of these colonies who coöperated with the missionaries. Puerto Rico was placed under the jurisdiction of the Bishop of Chicago and, subsequently, of the Bishop of Sacramento. By 1900, it had been visited, on behalf of

Puerto Rico and the Philippines

Moreland, by Bishop Whipple of Minnesota. The Philippines were placed under the jurisdiction of the Bishop of Shanghai, and visited by him. In 1902 the Right Rev. James Heartt Van Buren was consecrated Bishop of Puerto Rico. In his report of 1910 he observed that, as few Americans who came to the island regarded it as a permanent home, the work there must be directed more and more towards the native population. In 1915, 486 communicants were reported from the island. The Right Rev. Charles Henry Brent was consecrated Bishop of the Philippine Islands in 1901, and in the years before the War he built an extensive work there, both among the native population and within the American colony at Manila. Of the missions to the natives, the most important and effective was probably that of St. Mary the Virgin under the Rev. J. A. Staunton, Jr., at Sagada. In 1915 the Philippines reported 1,130 communicants, but this represented a decrease of seventy from the preceding year.

Work in the Hawaiian Islands had been begun by the Church of England some years before their annexation by the United States. After that event, the work there was transferred to the American Episcopal Church, and in 1902 the Right Rev. Henry B. Restarick was consecrated as the first American Bishop of Honolulu, with jurisdiction in the islands and in the American colony of Samoa. Lying, as they do, at the "Crossroads of the Pacific," these islands have a very mixed population. The native races appear to be dying out and the largest single element in the population at present is Japanese. There are also a large number of Chinese and an upper class of Americans and Europeans. At the time of Bishop Restarick's consecration the number of communicants was 412. By 1910 it had increased to 1,410 and 1,737 were reported in 1915. *The Hawaiian Islands*

Work begun on the Isthmus of Panama during the Gold Rush, when it was one of the routes to California, had been transferred to the Church of England, but after the acquisition of the Canal Zone it was returned to the Episcopal Church, and expanded. In 1919, a missionary district was created to include the Zone and the republics of Panama and Colombia. It ministered to American personnel, a large percentage of whom had expressed a preference for the Episcopal church, and to large colonies of negroes *The Canal Zone* originally brought in from the British West Indies for work on the canal.

Work Among
the Negroes The work of the Church among the Indians and negroes was carried on in a more systematic manner during this period than it had been during the preceding one. The Freedman's Commission, whose organization was mentioned at the beginning of the present chapter, spent $90,000 during the first three years of its existence, supporting twenty-six teachers during its first year (1866), sixty-two during its second, and sixty-five during its third. The number of pupils in its schools increased from 1,600 to 5,000 during the same period. Most of the instruction, at first, was necessarily elementary, but in 1868 it started a high school at Charleston. In 1870 the Commission was made permanent, and given the name of Commission on Home Missions to Colored People. The Board of Missions had recommended the raising of $50,000 for the work, but by 1871 the Commission had succeeded in raising only $21,308. Its failure was partly due to its unwillingness to employ a salaried agent, as there was a prejudice in the Church against those unromantic but necessary officers. Nevertheless, the Commission had succeeded in supporting, or helping to support, seventeen schools. By 1875 the number of schools assisted had increased to thirty-one. By 1890 the commission had expanded its efforts to include specifically religious as well as educational work. In that year it was supporting sixty-two white and forty-four negro clergy, one hundred and seventeen Sunday schools, sixty-five parochial schools and twelve industrial schools. It is estimated that the contributions received from colored people, of which it had only an imperfect record, were about equal to those received from white people for negro work.

In 1906 the American Church Institute for Negroes was organized to obtain support for the larger negro schools of the Episcopal Church, including St. Augustine's School, Raleigh, the Bishop Payne Divinity School, St. Paul's Industrial School, St. Athanasius' School, Vicksburg Industrial School, and St. Mark's School. It also set a standard of instruction for the schools associated with it. Its organization had been approved by the Board of Missions, though not specifically authorized by General Convention. As was mentioned in the preceding chapter, the work among negroes at this time led to a demand for a negro episcopate which was finally satisfied in part by the canon on suffragans.

It will be remembered that at the beginning of the Civil War the only important Indian work being carried on by the Church was among the Oneidas in Wisconsin and among the Chippeways in Minnesota, where Breck had started his mission. Bishop Whipple, who, in addition to building up the Church among the white people of Minnesota, carried on and extended Breck's Indian work, was one of the first to urge upon the Church as a whole a proper realization of its duty to the red man. In 1868 he submitted to the Board of Missions a vigorous report in which he denounced the general mistreatment of the Indian by the white man, and urged the Church to take some action in his behalf. In 1871, partly as a result of this appeal and partly, it would seem, in response to a suggestion from President Grant, the General Convention directed the Board of Missions to set up a Commission on Indian Affairs, and the House of Deputies appointed a committee of its own to coöperate with this Commission in defending the rights of the Indian. At the same time, a special missionary jurisdiction, called Niobrara, was set up to include the Indian reservations in what is now South Dakota, and in western Nebraska. The Indians

The new jurisdiction was placed temporarily under the supervision of Bishop Clarkson, of Nebraska and Dakota. In 1871 he reported there were five Indian and three white clergymen at work within this area, and urged the appointment of a bishop. This recommendation was complied with in 1873, when the Right Rev. William Hobart Hare was consecrated Bishop of Niobrara. Bishop Hare was a son of the first Dean of the Philadelphia Divinity School, and had served for several years as Secretary of the Foreign Committee of the Board of Missions. During his long episcopate, he identified himself heart and soul with the Indians and their welfare. In 1875 the Indian Commission reported that it had stations at White Earth and Mendota in Minnesota; at Niobrara, Santee, Yankton, Ponka, Yanktonnais, Mackenzie's Point and Upper Brulé in the Niobrara Jurisdiction, and at Cheyenne, Wyoming. Some of these, moreover, were large reservations where several missionaries were stationed, the greatest Bishop Hare number, eight white and two Indian ministers, being on the Niobrara Reservation.

In 1885 Bishop Walker of North Dakota received a delegation from five hundred Chippeway Indians then located in the Turtle Mountains in the northern part of that state. Forty of them had been converted to Christianity while living near the White Earth mission, and their fidelity had so impressed the rest of the tribe that they applied to Walker for a missionary. As a result, he succeeded in establishing a school among them.

In 1900 Bishop Hare, the title of whose jurisdiction had been changed to South Dakota, besides having charge of the white work in that state, was responsible for Indian missions on ten reservations, grouped together in the Niobrara Deanery. His Indian work included ninety congregations, with fifty-seven church buildings and 3,200 communicants, ministered to by six white and fifteen Indian clergymen, and assisted by about fifteen lay helpers and catechists. There were approximately 10,000 baptized persons associated with the mission out of a total Indian population of 25,000. Regular Sunday services were held at about eighty different points. There were also four industrial boarding schools for Indians in the jurisdiction, supported partly by the Missionary Society, partly by the Woman's Auxiliary, and partly by government aid, which had, however, been recently reduced.

Oklahoma

In 1905 Bishop Brooke of Oklahoma and Indian Territory reported the operation of a number of day schools in the latter part of his jurisdiction. He found these more useful than boarding schools for the Indians in that region, as they encouraged the parents of the children to settle in one place.

China

The seeds sown in the foreign field in the earlier period of our missionary history began to bear fruit after the Civil War, and an increasing number of converts was regularly reported from most of the foreign stations. In 1865, Channing Moore Williams, the first Episcopal missionary to Japan, was elected to succeed Bishop Boone as Bishop of China and Japan. By 1871 the China mission was served by seven presbyters, besides the bishop, two native priests, six foreign female missionaries, and two lay missionaries of the masculine sex. A hospital had been started in 1868. According to Bishop Williams, the number of baptisms in the three years between 1866 and 1871 was only eighteen less and the number of confirmations was twenty-seven more than in the twenty-one years of the mission's previous existence.

In 1874, Bishop Williams was relieved of his responsibility for China, and allowed to concentrate upon the work in Japan as Bishop of Yedo. The Rev. S. I. J. Schereschewsky, the translator of the Bible, was elected Bishop of Shanghai. He immediately set about founding St. John's College (now a University), which has made an important contribution to the cause of Christian education in China, as has its younger sister, Boone University at Wuchang. Bishop Schereschewsky resigned in 1883 and was succeeded by the Right Rev. William Jones Boone, who was in turn succeeded by the Right Rev. Frederick Rogers Graves in 1893. In 1901 the Chinese work was divided into the missionary districts of Shanghai, under Bishop Graves, and Hankow, under the Right Rev. J. Addison Ingle, who was succeeded in 1904 by the Right Rev. Logan H. Roots. In 1910 Hankow was divided by the organization of the Missionary District of Wuhu, later Anking, of which the Right Rev. David Trumbull Huntington became bishop. In 1912 the Church in China was given a semi-independent status by the organization of the work of the Anglican communion in that country into the *Chung Hua Sheng Kung Hui,* or Chinese Holy Catholic Church. In 1890 China reported 460 communicants. By 1915 the number had increased to 3,479.

Japan, in 1865, was just beginning her rapid acquisition of European customs. Christian converts were still being persecuted. In 1874 the edicts against Christianity were relaxed, and in the same year Bishop Williams, as already mentioned, was relieved of his Chinese jurisdiction and made Bishop of Yedo (later Tokyo). Thereafter the growth of the Church in Japan was rapid. The first baptism reported from that country was in 1866 and there had been no more until 1872. In 1874, twenty-one persons were baptized. In 1887, the Japanese missions of the Church of England and the Episcopal Church were organized into the *Nippon Sei Ko Kwai,* or Holy Catholic Church in Japan. In 1890 Japan reported more communicants (865) than any other foreign field. By 1915 their number had increased to 3,181. The work in Japan, as in China, was strengthened by the founding of educational and medical institutions, the two most important being St. Luke's Hospital and St. Paul's University in Tokyo. In 1898 the country was divided into the missionary districts of Tokyo and Kyoto. Tokyo was continued under the Right Rev. John McKim, who had been elected in 1893, and Kyoto was placed under the Right Rev. S. C. Partridge, who was succeeded by the Right Rev. Henry St. George Tucker in 1912.

Liberia

The mission to Liberia, which was under Bishop Payne, was reported as being in a flourishing condition in 1865, and it so continued under Bishop Payne and his successors, Bishop Penick and Bishop Ferguson. In the first ten years of Bishop Ferguson's episcopate (1883-93), there were more baptisms than in the fifty previous years of the mission's existence. In 1890, Liberia reported 576 communicants and by 1915 the number had grown to 2,501.

Latin America

Work which had been started in various Latin American countries by the Evangelical American Church Missionary Society was taken over by the Board of Missions in the years following the Civil War. The mission to Haiti, when it came under the control of the Board in 1865, had three ministers and a catechist. In 1874 the General Convention recognized the independence of the Protestant Episcopal Church of Haiti, but with the understanding that it would continue to receive aid from the Board of Missions. The Right Rev. James Theodore Holly was consecrated its first bishop. This action set an important precedent which was to be followed by the creation of national churches in Mexico, China, and Japan. Haiti, however, lost its independent status after the death of Bishop Holly in 1911, and was administered by neighboring bishops until 1923, when the Right Rev. Harry Roberts Carson became its bishop. An independent Church was organized in Mexico, under the Right Rev. Henry Chauncey Riley, Bishop of Mexico Valley, but the experiment was not successful. In 1883, as a result of disagreements within his Church and between himself and the Board of Missions, Bishop Riley was asked to resign. Thereafter the Mexican work was without a bishop until the Right Rev. Henry D. Aves was consecrated in 1904. Work begun by the American Church Missionary Society in Cuba and Brazil was not taken over by the Board of Missions until 1905, but bishops had been sent to these countries before that year. The Right Rev. Lucien Lee Kinsolving had become Bishop of Southern Brazil in 1899, and the Right Rev. Albion W. Knight had been consecrated for Cuba in 1904. Bishop Knight was succeeded by the

Right Rev. Hiram R. Hulse in 1915. In 1915 Haiti reported 843 communicants; Mexico, 1,906; Brazil, 1,304, and Cuba, 1,677.

A number of changes in the constitution of the Domestic and Foreign Missionary Society were made during this period, but none of them was of a fundamental nature. For a time, the General Convention constituted itself the Board of Missions, and the working organization was called the Board of Managers. In 1877, when party strife had begun to subside, the American Church Missionary Society became a recognized auxiliary of the general Society and by 1915 it had ceased to function except to administer its endowments. The most important development of the period, so far as the support of missionary work was concerned, was the organization of the Woman's Auxiliary to the Board of Missions in 1868, to coördinate the work formerly done by a large number of unrelated women's missionary societies. Its organization was largely the work of Miss Mary A. and Miss Julia C. Emery, and the latter continued for many years to be its active leader. Its first title was the Ladies Domestic Missionary Relief Association, but it assumed the more familiar designation when it was four years old. It originally functioned chiefly in supplying boxes of clothing and other goods to supplement the salaries of the missionaries, and to provide them with materials for relieving others, but after the institution of the United Thank Offering of prayer and material gifts in 1890, it became an important source of financial support as well. Miss Emery also organized a Junior Auxiliary to enlist the support of young girls in the work. By 1910 the Woman's Auxiliary had a branch in every diocese and missionary district of the Church. *The Spirit of Missions* continued its useful work in the field of publicity throughout the period, and for a time the Domestic Committee operated a missionary paper for children, known variously as *The Young Christian Soldier, The Christian Soldier and Children's Guest,* and *The Young Christian Soldier and the Carrier Dove.*

The Woman's Auxiliary

CHAPTER XVII

Between Two Wars

THE American people had never before fought a war in which they were so united as in the First World War, nor one with which they became so quickly disillusioned afterwards. As a result, there were few important social institutions or leaders who could look back upon their wartime utterances and actions with entirely unmixed feelings. A strong pacifist movement had developed in this country in the years before the War, and the administration in power was composed mainly of pacifists. When, therefore, the leader of that administration finally pronounced in favor of war, it was natural to assume that every possible means of keeping peace had been exhausted. As soon as war was declared, if not before, the administration began making systematic use of the varied means of propaganda presented by the modern press and other mediums of publicity, employing these with a skill learned of modern psychology. This activity, moreover, merely continued an effective propaganda previously carried on in the United States by the Allied Powers, and in a short time laws were passed to silence any contrary testimony. It is not surprising, therefore, that most Americans were convinced that in entering the War we were merely repelling German aggression, and that we were fighting to preserve democracy and secure a permanent peace. In the years that followed, it became evident that the War did not, in fact, attain these ends, and many people saw reason to believe that, in the original issues of the struggle, the right was not so exclusively on one side as they had supposed. In the reaction that followed, many, especially of the post-war generation, were probably more severe than was necessary in their judgment of those leaders of public opinion who rallied to the support of our suddenly militant government after the declaration of war in the spring of 1917.

The record of the Episcopal Church during the War was about
the same as that of other American denominations. Most of the
clergy supported the War more or less vigorously, some of them
becoming army chaplains or participating in the struggle in other
ways, and a certain amount of war work was carried on in most
parishes. Those ministers who felt obliged to take a pacific attitude
were subjected to a good deal of popular abuse and, sometimes, to
the disapproval of their ecclesiastical superiors. The most serious
case of this sort was that of the Right Rev. Paul Jones, Missionary
Bishop of Utah. Bishop Spalding, Bishop Jones' predecessor, had
established a tradition of liberal social thought for the See which
the latter carried on after his own election in 1914. After the
United States entered the War, Bishop Jones' utterances and his
connection with various radical organizations caused suspicions to
arise as to his loyalty. When the House of Bishops held a special
meeting in October, 1917, to fill some vacancies in the missionary
episcopate, his Council of Advice called the attention of the House
to the situation. After experimenting with various resolutions, the
Bishops directed the Presiding Bishop to appoint a committee of
investigation and granted the accused Bishop a "leave of absence"
while the investigation was pending. At the request of this committee, Bishop Jones submitted his resignation to the House when
it reconvened in April, 1918, but the Bishops declined to
accept it because they were unwilling to admit the propriety of
a member of their order resigning "in deference to an excited
state of public opinion," as Jones had indicated that he was doing.
He, therefore, tendered a resignation which gave no reasons of
any sort, and this was accepted "in view of Bishop Jones' impaired
usefulness," but "with full recognition of the right of every member of this House to freedom of speech in political and social
matters, subject to the law of the land." Before adjourning, the
House sent a telegram of congratulation to General Pershing upon
his confirmation in the Church.

A certain amount of pacifist sentiment also manifested itself at
Berkeley Divinity School, in Connecticut, during the War, and the
school was subjected to a good deal of abuse from its neighbors in
Middletown as a result. It was not exposed to any formal ecclesiastical censure, however.

When the General Convention met in 1919 the war spirit was

War Spirit in the General Convention of 1919

still strong, and a number of resolutions were passed which would seem to have been influenced by it. The Churchwomen's League for Patriotic Service was given official approval, and the Board of Missions was urged to establish a bureau of Christian Americanization. Gratitude was expressed for "that host of noble American youth who, for the sake of God's cause, were careless of their lives even unto death," and approval was expressed of the establishment of the American Field of Honor in France. A resolution was also passed in favor of setting up the Church of the Holy Trinity in Paris as "America's War Memorial Church in Europe for her Hero Dead." On the other hand, a resolution was passed urging the entrance of the United States in the League of Nations and the Bishops passed one in favor of pardoning wartime prisoners. In the latter resolution, however, the Deputies did not concur.

Post-war Reaction

In 1920 a president was elected who was pledged to "Bring the country back to normalcy," and while one may be permitted to doubt that that is the word which exactly describes the resulting condition, it is certain that things were very different from what they had been during the War or before it. Post-war decades are likely to be periods of reaction and lethargy, as a result, it may be presumed, of emotional and economic fatigue. In the present case the reaction was intensified by the rapid disillusionment with the wartime ideals, and the consequent discrediting of the Progressive leaders who had sponsored them. The old Progressive movement, in fact, had completely disintegrated within a few years after the War, and a new type of Liberalism had to be developed, which did not begin to achieve cohesiveness until after a crisis had been developed by the secondary post-war depression at the end of the decade. With the collapse of Progressivism, there came a general cynicism with respect to all professions of lofty ideals, and a vigorous "revolt of youth," and of many who were not young, against all traditional restraints upon the pursuit of pleasure. This is also a common post-war phenomenon, but in the present case it was more vocal than usual, and it apparently involved a general rejection of Victorian sexual standards, which had been receiving a severe pounding from liberals ever since the closing decade of the nineteenth century. It was also intensified by the general rebellion of people of all ages against the unfortunate experiment of prohibition. In the resulting confusion quite a few people sought hysterically for ideals which were new enough not to have been discredited, and others turned for refuge to a somewhat neurotic hedonism.

On the subject of prohibition, the most conspicuous, though not the most important, issue of the twenties, the Church took no official stand, but many of its members were in the opposition, believing that the measure involved a denial of moral freedom and individual responsibility. The Church Temperance Society, which, since its organization in 1881, had emphasized voluntary measures of reform, became converted to prohibition during the First World War. After six years' experience with the experiment, it changed its position again, and advocated modification of the Volstead Act, as the law which provided for the enforcement of the eighteenth, or prohibition, amendment was called. In 1927, it conducted a poll of the clergy of the Church which showed that 72.2 per cent of them found prohibition a failure in their own localities, and 67.4 per cent favored modification of the enforcement act, though only 49.2 per cent advocated repeal of the amendment.

Such an age was naturally a difficult one for the Church, as it was for any institution that was committed to ideals of long standing, and, though the total number of its members increased, there was a slight decrease in the ratio of its baptized membership to the total population. Nevertheless, though much was said about the problems confronting the Church, its internal history was not much affected by the spirit of the age. Some new agencies were developed in the effort to regain the younger generation, the most important being the employment of special student pastors at the larger universities of the country, and the organization of the Young People's Fellowship, an institution which differed from the earlier Church organizations for young men and women in being open to both sexes. A society of lay evangelists, known as the Church Army, which had been organized in England, was transplanted to this country and has done some work here. In 1931 it was given official approval by General Convention.

The only thoroughly new movement which developed during the period was that which was known variously as "Buchmanism," "The First Century Christian Fellowship," and "The Oxford Group Movement." It represented an experiential type of religion, Buchmanism and resembled early Methodism in its emphasis upon conversion and public testimony. Unlike Methodism, however, it was not distinctly a preaching movement, and it showed itself most successful in personal evangelism among the upper classes. Eventually, under the name of Moral Rearmament, it lost its religious emphasis, becoming a crusade for economic and political conservatism.

Catholicism
and
Liberalism

In general, the internal development of the Episcopal Church between wars seems to have followed the same tendencies of Catholicization and Liberalization which were apparent in the earlier period. It might be expected that the growth of these two apparently contrary tendencies would lead to a steadily sharpening conflict, but on the whole the tendency was towards coalescence, producing, on the one hand, a somewhat liberalized Catholicism and, on the other, engendering a greater appreciation of the Catholic tradition among many Liberals. Such a tendency may be regarded either as a sign of growing maturity and open-mindedness in the Church, or as a symptom of decay, or both, according to one's point of view. In the history of most institutions, liberalism performs the same function as the ripening process in fruits. Up to a certain point the process is necessary to bring complete maturity and the full usefulness which that implies, but beyond that point the same process leads to decay, and, unless it is interrupted, as it often is, by the introduction of some new vitalizing force, to death. It is, however, practically impossible to locate the exact point at which the change takes place even when we are able to review the whole process after it has been completed, and to attempt to locate that point while the process is still going on would be rash indeed.

Modernist
Controversy

There was a brief conflict between Liberalism and Orthodoxy at the beginning of the period when the expression by some of the leading "Modernists" in the Church of doubts as to the historicity of the Virgin Birth and the Bodily Resurrection of Christ led the House of Bishops at a special session in 1923 to issue a Pastoral Letter insisting upon these beliefs as taught by the Church, and asserting that their historical accuracy was supported by "the best scholarship of the day." The implication conveyed in the Pastoral that those who rejected these doctrines could not honestly remain in the Church, and a threat that had been made to try a less conspicuous Modernist in another diocese, called forth a vigorous protest from Dr. Leighton Parks, one of the outstanding leaders of the movement, in a sermon which he preached in St. Bartholomew's Church, New York, on December 16, 1923. His assertion in that sermon that, if the position of the Pastoral were correct, he himself, Bishop Lawrence of Massachusetts, Dr. Worcester of Boston, and other leading Modernists ought to be brought to trial, naturally provoked a certain amount of excitement, but the dispute subsided in a surprisingly short time. After that there was, apparently, a tacit agreement on both sides not to force the issue.

About the same time that this discussion was going on, Bishop William Montgomery Brown of Arkansas was deposed for teachings contrary to those of the Episcopal Church, having denied, among other things, the existence of a personal God, and expressed doubts as to the historical existence of Christ. The event did not, however, have any great effect upon the Church, as Bishop Brown's views were too radical to have developed much of a party. Another bishop, Frederick Joseph Kinsman, of Delaware, had been lost to the Episcopal Church at the beginning of the decade through his conversion to Roman Catholicism.

The growing approximation of Catholicism and Liberalism found expression in a movement consciously describing itself as Liberal Catholicism, which expressed its views in the publication of a collection of *Essays Catholic and Critical*, by a number of English clergymen in 1926, and of another series called *Liberal Catholicism in the Modern World*, by a group of Americans in 1934. The movement represented an effort to retain the chief features of the Catholic Tradition while, at the same time, accepting whole-heartedly the results of Biblical criticism and of scientific research in all fields of knowledge. Remaining substantially orthodox in its teaching, it tended to favor a wider latitude of belief than did the older Anglo-Catholicism and to show a greater readiness to re-express traditional beliefs in new thought forms. It showed also an interest in social problems. Liberal Catholicism

A Liberal Evangelical movement likewise developed, seeking to stress the positive contributions of the Reformation and of Evangelical Protestantism while retaining the non-controversial spirit which is essential to Liberalism. While recognizing the value of the Catholic witness to the corporate life of the Church, the adherents of the movement believed that "The spirit of Evangeli- The Liberal Evangelicals calism is the essential guardian of the Church against the reversions to a lower level of religious life that constantly threaten it, externalism, ritualism, intellectualism." To guard this spirit they organized themselves into local groups for prayer and study. As Liberals, they desired "freedom in the Church for historical study, for theological interpretation, and for reverent experimentation in worship . . . to set the Spirit free to reveal the truth of God to our own time." In its subsequent development, this party showed an increasing tendency to stress the traditional values of Evangelicalism more than those of Liberalism, possibly under the influence of the "neo-orthodox" movement, which won the allegiance of many former Protestant Liberals in the thirties and early forties.

A number of important institutional changes marked the interwar period. One of these, the organization of the Church Pension Fund, took place before the War, but so shortly before that its operation was a characteristic of the later period. In our treatment of the colonial Church, we had occasion to mention the organization of a number of insurance schemes for the relief of widows and orphans of clergymen. Some of these survived the Revolution, but they met the needs of only a small portion of the clergy. During the early nineteenth century, no provision was made for those who were not reached by these older funds, possibly because the simplicity of the economic system and the frequency of remarriage made it comparatively unnecessary. In 1853 the General Convention instituted a fund for the relief of clergymen's widows which was discontinued in 1868 for want of support but revived later under the title of the General Clergy Relief Fund. Unlike the colonial funds, it was a charitable enterprise, not a system of insurance, and it was never adequate to meet the demands upon it.

The Church Pension Fund

As the economic strain upon the middle class grew increasingly severe with the passing years, and the economic position of women and children grew steadily worse, a demand for a more adequate pension system to provide both for widows and orphans and for aged clergymen developed within the Church as well as elsewhere. That it was effectively answered was due mainly to the self-sacrificing exertions of the Right Rev. William Lawrence, Bishop of Massachusetts, supported by the expert assistance of

Mr. Monell Sayre. Bishop Lawrence's attention was first drawn to the problem when he discovered that many aged bishops and other clergymen were obliged to remain in harness long after their efficiency had been impaired because they lacked the money upon which to retire. After his election as a trustee of the General Clergy Relief Fund, he had an opportunity to observe the inefficiency of the charity system at first hand.

In 1910 Bishop Lawrence introduced into General Convention a resolution for the appointment of a joint Commission to consider the whole question of clerical support, though apparently with the expectation that it would deal chiefly with the pension problem. Most of the work of the Commission fell, of course, upon his shoulders. With the aid of Mr. Sayre, who had been recommended to him as probably knowing more about pensions than anyone else in the country, he set to work to invent a system which, while being voluntary in character, would, nevertheless, have in it the strongest possible elements of moral compulsion. The result was a system based upon sound insurance principles, with the assessments, which were in proportion to the salary, being paid, not by the clergyman, but by his parish or other employing institution.

This system was finally approved by the General Convention of 1916, but the problem still remained of raising an initial fund of five million and fifty thousand dollars which was considered necessary to put it into successful operation. This was, at the time, an almost unprecedented sum to raise by voluntary subscription. Bishop Lawrence resigned his diocese to devote himself to the task, and succeeded in getting the fund over-subscribed by the spring of 1917. In doing so, he developed methods of campaigning which were put to use again in many of the wartime "drives."

The next important institutional development of the period was the coördination of the missionary and other activities of the general Church under the leadership of the Presiding Bishop, assisted by a National Council, which thus replaced the old Board of Missions. The first step towards this change was made by providing that the office of Presiding Bishop should be elective, instead of being filled by seniority as it had been before. Amendments for this purpose were introduced at several General Conventions, but the change was not finally approved until 1919. It was not to take effect until the death of the then incumbent, Bishop Tuttle, but the

The Presiding Bishop and Council

organization of the National Council was carried out at once through a revision of the constitution of the Missionary Society. Under the Council were to be departments of Missions and Church Extension, Religious Education, Christian Social Service, Finance, Publicity, and the Nationwide Campaign. Most of these, except the missionary department and the one last named, represented Commissions of General Convention which had previously been uncoördinated. The first Presiding Bishop to be elected to the office was the Right Rev. John Gardner Murray, Bishop of Maryland, who was chosen in 1926. The term of office was six years, but Bishop Murray died in 1929, and was succeeded by the Right Rev. Charles Palmerston Anderson of Chicago, who only lived until the following year. His successor was the Right Rev. James DeWolf Perry of Rhode Island. In 1934 he was relieved of administrative work, so that he might devote his time to spiritual leadership.

The executive functions formerly performed by the Presiding Bishop were entrusted to the President of the National Council, to which office the Right Rev. Philip Cook was chosen. The work of the Council was organized in two divisions. The first included the departments of Domestic Missions, Foreign Missions (which also administered the work in our extracontinental territories), Religious Education, and Christian Social Service. The second division included the departments of Finance and Publicity, and the Field Department. Full-time leadership of the National Council was restored to the Presiding Bishop in 1937, and his tenure was extended to the age of retirement, which was fixed at sixty-eight years. The Right Rev. Henry St. George Tucker, Bishop of Virginia, and formerly Bishop of Kyoto, Japan, was elected to the post.

The First World War showed the effectiveness which could be achieved by large-scale "drives" for raising money, and after it was over an attempt was made to apply the lesson in the Church by organizing a "Nationwide Campaign" to raise money for its missionary and other activities. The drive was only moderately successful, but it was succeeded by several similar efforts. In some of the later drives an effort was made to call forth a spiritual revival as well, but it is probable that to the mind of the average layman they continued to appear chiefly as expedients for raising money. The Forward Movement, which was set on foot by the General Convention of 1934, concentrated its efforts entirely upon deepening the devotional life of the Church, especially through the distribution of daily Bible readings and meditations. The movement began a new ten-year program in 1941, following plans laid down by the Presiding Bishop.

The period witnessed a second revision of the American Book of Common Prayer, which was begun in 1913 and given final approval by the General Convention of 1928. It resulted in some alteration in the order of the Communion Service, the Lord's Prayer being placed before the Prayer of Humble Access, which was, in turn, moved up, in order to come immediately before the Administration of the Elements. The Baptismal Service was modified to provide a single service that could be used either for infants or adults. Some changes were also made in the Burial Service and the Marriage Service, including the omission from the latter of the promise of obedience. A number of special prayers were added, the translation of the Psalter was revised, and provision was made for a greater flexibility in the use of the Psalms and Scripture lessons. *Prayer Book Revision*

The development of an interest in child psychology and the effort to turn the art of teaching into a science, which were characteristic of the twentieth century, had their effect upon the Sunday schools of the Church, and resulted in the adoption of a more elaborate systematization of the classes and the attempt to secure technically trained teachers. As a result of this tendency, a Commission on Religious Education was created before the War, becoming a department of the National Council afterward. An effort was also made to develop a single course of instruction for the whole Church, so that children transferring from one Sunday school to another would find the same subjects being taught. For this purpose the *Christian Nurture Series* was worked out, and adopted by a great many parishes. *Religious Education*

The Order of Deaconesses did not prove as popular with women Church workers as its sponsors hoped that it would, and only a small portion of such workers joined it. At the General Convention of 1931 an effort was made to increase the appeal of the order to young women by relaxing some of the restrictions upon its members. The requirement that they could not marry while in the order was repealed, and they were freed from the necessity of wearing a habit at all times. In 1934 the privilege of marriage was withdrawn, but the deaconesses were allowed to make addresses if licensed by the bishop.

Efforts for promoting Church unity continued throughout the period. In 1919, as the result of a concordat with the Congregational Church, a canon was passed allowing for the ordination of ministers to serve in congregations outside of the Episcopal Church with the understanding that the congregations were to continue under episcopally-ordained ministers, that the Lord's Supper would be administered in the Words of Institution, and only the baptized admitted to it. A hope was also expressed that the rite of Confirmation would ultimately be adopted by such Churches. The stipulation that the congregations would be expected to remain under episcopally-ordained ministers was not in the original concordat, and its addition by our Church caused the arrangement to become largely inoperative. At the same session, Cardinal Mercier, who, in addition to his heroic work in Belgium during the German occupation, had been associated with efforts at a *rapprochement* between the Roman and Anglican communions which have since been condemned by the Pope, was presented to the Convention.

In 1925 General Convention voted to coöperate with the Federal Council of Churches in the departments of Social Service, Race Relations, International Justice and Good Will, Research and Education, Religious Press, Finance, and Army and Navy Chaplaincies. In 1927 the Episcopal Church participated in the First World Conference on Faith and Order at Lausanne, Switzerland, where representatives of all the leading Christian bodies except the Roman Catholic Church discussed the problems of unity. It took part in a second such conference held in Edinburgh in 1937, and in a conference on Christian Life and Work held in Oxford the same year.

During the thirties the Joint Commission of General Convention on the approaches to Unity held conferences with a number of Protestant bodies, including the Lutheran, Methodist, and Reformed Episcopal churches. The General Convention of 1937 invited the Presbyterian Church to enter into negotiations directed towards the achievement of organic unity. This invitation was accepted by the Presbyterians, and committees of the two bodies drafted a concordat which affirmed the doctrines that they held in common, and proposed inter-communion and exchange of pulpits. No action was taken on this compact by General Convention, either in 1940 or 1943, but negotiations were continued.

Numerous conversations were also held with representatives of the Eastern Orthodox Church, and there was some practical coöperation in this country, but no official act of communion took place. In 1934 inter-communion with the Old Catholics, as worked out by the Lambeth Conference, was approved by General Convention, and a canon on alien rites was adopted which made it possible to receive into communion with this Church individual congregations professing the Catholic Creed but not using our forms of worship. An effort to give practical application to the canon by the election of the Right Rev. John Torok, a bishop in Eastern Orthodox orders, as Suffragan Bishop of Eau Claire was, however, defeated by the House of Bishops.

The Church continued to show an active interest in social questions. The Commission on Christian Social Service became a department of the National Council, and carried on the work of issuing publications, holding conferences, and giving advice to the charitable institutions of the Church. General Convention, while not issuing any clear pronouncement upon fundamental economic or political issues, apparently felt that all sorts of minor social problems came within its competence, and resolutions were passed against mob violence, religious and racial intolerance, opium, and the marriage of the unfit, and in favor of the Boy Scouts, kindness to animals, and the Near East Relief, as well as upon many other subjects of a similar character. Approval was expressed of the various disarmament conferences and the arbitration of international disputes, and aggressive war was declared a crime. Labor and Capital were invited to adopt the principle of "partnership as an expression of Christian brotherhood in business." In 1934 adherence to the World Court was advocated, and resolutions were adopted opposing the Church's blessing of war in any way, appointing a commission to coöperate with other denominations in opposing war, endorsing a world conference on war and peace, and calling upon the Federal Government to recognize the rights of conscientious objectors. Through a parliamentary

Interests in Social Questions

blunder on the part of the Liberals, no resolutions on economic
questions were adopted, but the Bishops in their Pastoral Letter
described the present economic order as one of "lamentable
inadequacy." A resolution was adopted advocating the legalization
of instruction in birth control under proper regulations.

During the General Convention of 1937 the Church League for
Industrial Democracy held noon meetings, which were attended
by capacity crowds. That convention appointed a joint commission
to study the causes of lynching, and adopted some resolutions on
social questions. The adoption of the federal Social Security Act
in 1935 led to a demand by some leaders of the Church for the
inclusion of lay employees of religious bodies in its benefits, but
this suggestion was opposed by representatives of the Pension
Fund.

Marriage and
Divorce

In 1931 the General Convention adopted a canon regarding marriage and divorce which involved some modification of the traditional position of the Episcopal Church upon that subject. It
provided for instruction and a delay before marriage, and continued the prohibition of the marriage by Church ministers of
divorced persons, except the innocent party to a divorce for adultery, but it also provided for the annulment of a marriage in certain cases. When this took place, remarriage was to be permitted.
Moreover, when a minister thought that persons desirous of receiving Confirmation or Communion had been married contrary
to the Word of God and the discipline of the Church, he was to
refer the matter to the bishop, who should give his judgment in
writing "after due enquiry . . . and taking into consideration the
godly discipline both of justice and mercy," an expression which
would seem to imply that he might admit them even if they had
been so married. Persons who had been married by civil authority
and had any doubt as to the validity of their union might also
submit their cases to the bishop for judgment, a rule which was
presumably also intended to cover cases of remarriage. Further
revision of this canon was proposed by the Joint Commission on
Marriage and Divorce in 1937, but its recommendations were not
approved by General Convention.

Missionary
Work

The missionary work of the Church went on as usual in most
places during the war, but there was a certain amount of interruption in some jurisdictions. Bishop Brent engaged extensively in

war work, and it would seem that his doing so distracted his attention from the affairs of the Philippines, for when his successor, the Right Rev. Gouverneur Frank Mosher, went out in 1920, he found some phases of the work in an unsatisfactory condition. The cathedral at Manila had been nearly destroyed by white ants, the cathedral dormitory was temporarily closed, the settlement work had been given up, and so had the cathedral school for American girls. It should be observed, however, that two years had elapsed between Bishop Brent's resignation and the election of his successor, which might account for the decline. Bishop Ferguson of Liberia had died in 1916, and his successor, the Right Rev. Walter Henry Overs, was not consecrated until 1919. When he arrived he found many of the mission structures badly broken down, and had to assume the difficult task of rebuilding. He resigned in 1925 and was succeeded by the Right Rev. Robert Erskine Campbell of the Order of the Holy Cross, which had long been carrying on an important work in that field.

The economic depression which prevailed throughout the United States during the thirties seriously curtailed missionary receipts and necessitated frequent reductions in the budget of the National Council. In 1936, an additional drastic cut led to widespread protest and an emergency fund was raised to meet the deficiency, but lowered budgets continued to be the rule through 1940, when the council adopted the smallest one in twenty years. In spite of these difficulties, the General Convention of 1937 was sufficiently adventurous in its missionary spirit to direct the beginning of work in India, a field that formerly had been left to the Church of England. The Japanese invasion of China brought disaster to many of the Church's missions there even before the rest of the world was engulfed in war. The 1937 General Convention authorized an appeal for $300,000 to aid Episcopalians in the Chinese war zone. *The Foreign Field*

This convention also passed two canons of some importance affecting the ministry. One required a physical and mental examination of all candidates for ordination. The other, an amendment to the canon providing for a court of review in trials for heresy, opened the path of appeal to presbyters and deacons as well as bishops.

A few other events of this period require mention. The formation of a negro episcopate, transcending diocesan lines, was advocated by the Province of Sewanee, but opposed by the southern bishops. The Anglo-Catholic Congress, in 1936, became the American Church Union. It was the third organization to adopt this name. The first flourished in the sixties and seventies of the nineteenth century. The second, formed in 1908, became the Churchman's Alliance, which subsequently expired. Early in 1938, a committee of English Churchmen issued a comprehensive report on doctrine, designed to harmonize the traditional teachings of the Anglican Communion with modern thought. Though it had no official significance for the American Episcopal Church, it excited a good deal of interest and discussion.

CHAPTER XVIII

Toward the Future

THE advent of a second and more terrible World War brought
confusion and distress to the mind of the Church, as it did to the
rest of the country. This confusion was increased by the fact that
the most influential peace movement in the United States was
linked to the theory known as "Isolationism," which held that
the countries of North and South America could avoid involve-
ment in a "foreign war" by remaining aloof from the affairs of
the rest of the world. Such a point of view the Episcopal Church,
with its world missionary outlook and its close relationship to
the other branches of the Anglican Communion, could hardly
be expected to share.

When the beginnings of the new conflict became apparent, in
1936, the House of Bishops urged the calling of a conference of
all nations signatory to the Kellogg anti-aggression pact, to see if
active hostilities could be averted. When the European phase of
the war broke out officially, in the fall of 1939, some leaders of
the Church immediately took the position that the United States
could not and should not remain aloof from the struggle against
Fascism, but a majority of Episcopalians probably shared the
(then) hope of most of their countrymen that this nation could
remain neutral. The Episcopal Pacifist Fellowship was organized
on Armistice Day, 1939, to serve as a rallying center for those
who were prepared to pledge themselves not to give moral support
to any war.

After the fall of France, in 1940, the President of the United
States, a communicant of the Church, called upon Congress for
the passage of a national conscription law, and advocated giving
Great Britain all possible aid short of actual military participation,
thus placing the country half in the war and half out of it. The
draft act, the first to be adopted when the United States was

legally at peace, was supported by some Episcopalians and opposed by others, as was the passage of the lend-lease bill, by which the program of aid to Britain was implemented. On Armistice Day, 1941, just a month before the Japanese attack on Pearl Harbor brought about full American participation in the war, prayers for world peace were offered in Episcopal churches throughout the country, at the request of the Presiding Bishop. When Allied troops landed in Normandy, in June, 1944, most churches were opened to join in the nation's prayers for their success.

Chaplains

As soon as the first draft act went into effect, in October, 1940, the National Council made an appropriation for the support of the Army and Navy Commission to oversee and aid the work of Episcopalian chaplains in the armed forces. Under the chairmanship of Bishop Henry Knox Sherrill, this body acted as a clearing agency for the Government in the appointment of chaplains, received monthly reports from them, and preserved a record of baptisms, marriages, and burials performed by them. It paid their pension premiums and furnished them with a small discretionary fund and supplied them with literature. It presented special "war crosses" to all Episcopalians in military service. After the beginning of demobilization, it aided in the replacement of chaplains in parochial work. The General Convention of 1943 recommended its absorption by the National Council as soon as the emergency character of its work was ended, and this recommendation was carried out in the spring of 1946. Other agencies of the Church, including diocesan Army and Navy commissions and the Church Periodical Club, also aided the work of the chaplains.

The Episcopal Church was one of the first American denominations to exceed its quota of chaplains, and it had a waiting-list during most of the war. According to the final report of the Commission, a total of 557 clergymen of the Church served with the Army and Navy. Eleven of these died in service, nine being killed in action. An Episcopalian chaplain, the Rev. Frederick B. Howden, one of those killed in action, was left with the heroic defenders of Corregidor, the last American stronghold to resist the Japanese invasion of the Philippines. Another chaplain, the Rev. Ernest Sinfield, was with the first troops to break the German Siegfried Line. The Church also participated in the work of the

Service Men's Christian League, an interdenominational organization devoted to promoting the religious life of the armed forces.

The General Convention of 1934 had appointed a Joint Commission on Non-Combatant Service to seek for conscientious objectors belonging to the Episcopal Church the same exemption from active military service that had been granted in previous wars to Friends and members of other unqualifiedly pacifist denominations. This commission was unable to obtain any special legislation before the outbreak of the Second World War, but when the conscription act of 1940 was passed it provided for the assignment to non-military work camps of all persons, regardless of denominational affiliation, who could persuade their draft boards or boards of review that their scruples against fighting were of religious origin. Earlier in the same year, the National Council, carrying out the orders of General Convention, had invited conscientious objectors belonging to the Church to register with the commission.

Conscientious Objectors

The objectors, except some who engaged in special work, did not receive any salary, nor were their families given any dependency allowance. Their needs, over and above the minimum maintenance provided by the government, were met by the "peace churches"—the Friends, Mennonites, and United Brethren. When the Joint Commission on Non-Combatant Service made its report in the spring of 1946, $46,000 had been advanced by these bodies for the care of Episcopalian objectors, and it was believed that another $10,000 would be needed before they were all returned to civilian life. Of the sum already expended, $44,096 had been repaid, $10,096 from funds raised by the commission, under the chairmanship of Bishop William Appleton Lawrence, and $34,000 from funds raised by the Episcopal Pacifist Fellowship. Bishop William Proctor Remington, a member of the commission, represented the Church on the National Service Board for Conscientious Objectors. Mrs. Henry Hill Pierce represented the Episcopal Pacifist Fellowship on the same body.

The rapid development and decentralization of war industries brought boom conditions to many small and some larger communities, creating special problems for the churches in or near them. No national plan was adopted to meet this situation. Possibly none could have been, in view of its diverse and often unpredictable aspects. Some dioceses adopted special programs to meet the needs of the new industrial centers. In others, the task was left to individual parishes.

Peace
Resolution

General Convention in 1943 adopted a resolution in favor of establishing "an International Authority based on law, and provided with power to enforce that law." This hope found at least partial realization in 1945, with the formation of the United Nations, and the approval by the Senate of American participation therein. The charter of this new world organization reflected in some degree the influence of the Federal Council of Churches' Commission on a Just and Durable Peace, in whose work the Episcopal Church had shared.

Missions
and the War

The war in the Asiatic theater had a disastrous effect on the many missionary projects that lay in its wide path. Converts were killed or scattered, missionaries driven out, and buildings destroyed. American workers had to be withdrawn entirely from Japan, leaving the Church there to the care of the Japanese clergy, but the policy of building up a national Church, with a native episcopate, probably made this withdrawal less catastrophic than it would have been at an earlier time.

At home, the war-born prosperity relieved to some extent the financial difficulties of the National Council. In the spring of 1941, the council was able, for the first time since 1932, to adopt a budget without any cuts, and without appealing to the Church to raise a deficiency fund. The budget for 1942 was $12,348 higher than that proposed for 1941, though less than the amount actually raised in that year. Later, this budget was increased by the inclusion of a sum for the aid of British missions stricken by the war. This assistance had been directed by the General Convention of 1940, but the money was raised as a separate fund in 1941.

After the cessation of hostilities, the National Council undertook the raising of a Reconstruction and Advance Fund of $8,800,-000, of which ten per cent was assigned for general relief in war-torn countries. A total of $7,057,919 was finally raised by a committee headed by Bishop Henry Wise Hobson.

Events
at Home

Within the United States, the work of the Church continued with only minor modifications during the war. A new revision of the hymnal was approved by General Convention in 1940, though wartime printing difficulties delayed its publication. An amendment to the constitution, requiring bishops to submit their resignations on reaching the age of seventy-two, was proposed in 1940 and ratified in 1943. Questions as to the exact legal effect of this amendment were settled by rules adopted by the House of Bishops in 1946. Suffragan bishops were granted a vote in the House of Bishops in 1943. A canon was adopted requiring the Presiding Bishop to resign his diocesan jurisdiction. General Convention voted in favor of full participation in the Federal Council of Churches in 1940, and, in 1942, the Presiding Bishop was honored by election as president of the council.

The Church Historical Society became an official agency of the Church, in 1940, with an appropriation from General Convention for the preservation of Church records. The same convention directed the Presiding Bishop to designate one Sunday each year as Theological Education Sunday, for the purpose of taking up collections for Church seminaries, a practice that had been adopted earlier by the alumni of General Seminary. The Graduate School of Religion, founded in Cincinnati by Dr. William S. Keller in 1923, was merged with the Episcopal Theological School at Cambridge, its dean, the Rev. Joseph Fletcher, joining the Cambridge faculty.

Some success was experienced in using new modes of communication and transportation in conveying the Christian message. New Methods The Episcopal Church of the Air, founded in 1931 as a unit of the Columbia Broadcasting System's Church of the Air, gave its hundredth broadcast in 1944, with a sermon by the Archbishop of York, who was then visiting the United States. The Episcopalian part of this program was conducted by the Rev. G. Warfield Hobbs, until his retirement in 1944. During 1947, the National Council sponsored a program over a group of southern stations, and, in 1948, it began one over a national network. On February 29, 1948, a sermon by the Presiding Bishop was heard simultaneously in churches throughout the country, having been broadcast by nearly six hundred stations, from coast to coast. Moving pictures were used by the Department of Promotion of the National Council and other agencies as a means of education and fund raising. Truck and trailer chapels were used for rural work in a number of dioceses, and the Diocese of Southern Ohio purchased and equipped a trailer cathedral for the use of Bishop Hobson.

The General Convention of 1946 set two historic precedents in electing the first layman, former Supreme Court Justice Owen J. Roberts, as president of the House of Deputies, and in seating the first woman deputy, Mrs. Randolph H. Dyer. It rejected, however, a proposal to amend the first article of the constitution by substituting "lay persons" for "laymen" in the clause defining eligibility for membership in the house. It approved a budget of $10,856,887 for the next triennium, in addition to a special fund of $3,000,000 for relief in war-torn areas. Bishop Henry Knox Sherrill, of Massachusetts, was chosen to succeed Bishop Tucker as Presiding Bishop.

The question of union with the Presbyterian Church was referred back to the Joint Commission on Approaches to Unity, with instructions to draft a declaration of the Episcopalian position in harmony with the Quadrilateral, and to request a declaration of the Presbyterian position. The Lambeth Conference was asked to study the whole question of unity. The convention adopted a new marriage canon which listed a number of circumstances held to be such as to prevent a true Christian marriage. A divorced communicant desiring to remarry, or a communicant desiring to marry a divorced person, could apply to his bishop, who might refer the matter to his council of advice, or to a diocesan court, if there was one. If it was found that any of the specified circumstances had existed at the time of the original marriage, remarriage might be permitted.

Joint resolutions were adopted urging the strengthening of the United Nations, or the formation of a new, democratic world-federation, and advocating an amnesty for persons arrested for conscientious resistance to the draft law. The House of Bishops adopted a resolution condemning the thought of war with Russia, but the deputies failed to concur. The first National Youth Conference of the Episcopal Church met at the same time as the General Convention. It also passed a resolution against war with Russia.

On April 7, 1948, the Most Reverend Isabelo de los Reyes and two other bishops of the Philippine Independent Church were consecrated by Bishop Norman S. Binsted, assisted by Bishops Harry S. Kennedy and Robert F. Wilner. This body, organized in 1902, as the result of a secession from the Roman Catholic Church, had early sought the cooperation of the Episcopal Church, but discouraged by misunderstandings between its principal founder, Father Gregorio Aglipay, and Bishop Brent, it had, for a time, fallen under Unitarian influence. Through the leadership of Bishop de los Reyes, in cooperation with Bishop Binsted, it adopted an unequivocally Trinitarian statement of doctrine, and met other conditions regarded as prerequisite to the granting of the episcopate. The consecration was authorized by the House of Bishops in November, 1947.

The first Lambeth Conference since 1930 met in 1948 and adopted resolutions on a number of topics of current interest. Representatives of the Episcopal Church and other Anglican bodies participated in a meeting of the World Council of Churches at Amsterdam in the same year.

During the first three decades of the twentieth century, when immigration reached its peak, though the Episcopal Church continued to make substantial gains in the number of its communicants, the ratio of its communicant membership to the total population showed only a slight increase. Restrictive legislation, passed in the twenties, drastically reduced the influx of newcomers, greatly slowing up the rate of population increase. During the decade of 1930-1940, the first in which this change was reflected in the census, the ratio of communicant membership increased 5.7 points, as compared with 4.99 points for the entire thirty years preceding. Of fifty-one dioceses which had a higher increase in ratio points than the Church as a whole (ranging from 5.86 to 143.94), twenty-five were located east of the Mississippi, twenty-one in the region between the Mississippi and the Pacific states, and five in the Pacific states, but all of the six dioceses highest on the list were in the Middle West. Sixteen dioceses suffered a loss in ratio standing. Of these, ten were in the East, three in the Middle West, and three in the West Coast states.

According to the federal religious census for 1936, the Episcopal Church had suffered an actual loss in baptized membership of 123,721, or six per cent since the preceding census of 1926. This meant that the Church's gain of communicants by conversion was not, up to that time, sufficient to offset its low rate of natural increase. There was no religious census in 1946, but statistics given in the *Living Church Annual* showed that the downward trend

Growth

had been reversed, with a gain of 292,138 baptized persons in the continental United States between 1937 and 1948.

Of twenty-eight dioceses having a higher ratio of communicants to population than the Church as a whole in 1940 (regardless of increase), twenty-three were in the East and five in the Middle West, indicating that the Episcopal Church was still predominantly an eastern denomination. This was also shown by the statistics for 1948. In that year, the Church had 1,575,485 communicants in continental United States, sixty per cent in the region east of the Mississippi and north of the Mason-Dixon line; nineteen per cent in the area south of that line and east of the Mississippi; fourteen per cent in the country between the Mississippi and the Pacific states, and seven per cent in the Pacific area. These percentages did show a slight westward trend as compared with those for 1935, when the division was: sixty-four and one-half per cent in the Northeast, nineteen per cent in the Southeast, eleven and one-half per cent in the Middle West, and five per cent in the Pacific states.

Among the American territories, Honolulu reported 5,589 communicants in 1948, an increase of 2,001 since 1935. Alaska had 2,028 communicants, an increase of 398. The Canal Zone reported 5,620, a growth of 4,195 since the first bishop was consecrated for that jurisdiction in 1920. Puerto Rico had 4,127 communicants, which, with 3,474 in the Virgin Islands, previously included with Puerto Rico, made a total of 7,601, an increase of 1,455 since 1935. The Philippine Islands became an independent republic on July 4, 1946. In 1948, the Episcopal Church there had 7,999 communicants, an increase of 1,276 since 1935.

In spite of war and civil confusion, China, the largest foreign field, had 2,247 more communicants in 1948 than in 1935, making a total of 11,279 for the American-supported dioceses of *Chung Hua Sheng Kung Hui*: Anking (1,420); Hankow (2,440); and Shanghai (7,419). Japan was no longer reported in 1948 because the three dioceses of *Nippon Sei Ko Kwai* formerly aided by the Episcopal Church are no longer under the jurisdiction of the American church. In Liberia the number of communicants had declined from 5,539 in 1935 to 3,945 in 1948.

In Latin America the picture was more favorable. Haiti reported 12,465 communicants in 1948, an increase of 7,030 since

1935. The Church in Cuba had increased its communicant membership from 3,141 to 6,685. Southern Brazil had gained 3,339 communicants to make a 1948 total of 7,397. Mexico, which had suffered a slight loss between 1915 and 1935, because of revolutionary conditions, was gaining once more, its communicants having increased from 1,867 in 1935 to 2,262 in 1948. The Dominican Republic had 1,933 communicants, an increase of 867 since 1935.

The Church at the opening of 1949 faced the exciting future with its spiritual and material resources elaborately organized, perhaps too elaborately for maximum efficiency. Supreme authority was vested in the General Convention, composed of the House of Bishops and the House of Clerical and Lay Deputies. Members of the House of Deputies were elected by the diocesan conventions, which also had general governing powers within their respective dioceses, but a good deal of independence was still left to the self-supporting parishes, governed by rectors, wardens, and vestries. Between the diocesan and General conventions were eight provincial synods with limited powers.

Organization of the Church

Most of the general missionary and other work of the Church was under the National Council, elected by General Convention, the provinces, and the Woman's Auxiliary, with the Presiding Bishop, elected by the House of Bishops, at its head. Its work was divided among six departments: the Home Department, with divisions for domestic missions, college work, the Army and Navy, and town and country; the Overseas Department, in charge of foreign and territorial missions; the Department of Christian Education; the Department of Christian Social Relations; the Department of Finance; and the Department of Promotion. Aiding the work of the National Council, but having an independent existence, were: the Woman's Auxiliary, the American Church Institute for Negroes, the Church Society for College Work, the Church Army, and the Episcopal Social Work Conference.

The Order of Deaconesses, the Laymen's League, the Church Historical Society, and the Church Pension Fund, with its subsidiaries, the Church Life Insurance Corporation and the Church Fire Insurance Corporation, though authorized by General Convention, were not under the National Council. General Convention also appointed a number of joint commissions. Most of these were to study special problems and report to later conventions, but some of them had the oversight of important work, independent of the National Council. The Forward Movement was directly under the Presiding Bishop, who also had advisory commissions on laymen's work, and college work.

The Theological seminaries of the Church were: General Theological Seminary, New York City; Berkeley Divinity School, New Haven; Bexley Hall, Gambier, Ohio; Bishop Payne Divinity School, Petersburg, Virginia; Church Divinity School of the Pacific, Berkeley, California; Episcopal Theological School, Cambridge; Nashotah House, Nashotah, Wisconsin; Philadelphia Divinity School; School of Theology of the University of the South, Sewanee, Tennessee; Seabury-Western Theological Seminary, Evanston, Illinois; and Virginia Theological Seminary, Alexandria. In addition to the graduate courses offered by most of the seminaries, special opportunities for supplementary study were provided for the clergy by the College of Preachers of Washington Cathedral; the Graduate School of Applied Religion, affiliated with the Episcopal Theological School; Windham House, maintained by the Woman's Auxiliary as a study center for missionaries on furlough; and Calvary Clergy School, operated by Calvary Church, New York, for "supervised internship in pastoral training." There were also a number of diocesan and provincial summer schools and conferences for both ministers and lay workers. Two institutions provided training for deaconesses: the Department of Women of the Philadelphia Divinity School and St. Margaret's House, Berkeley, California.

Not many colleges were affiliated with the Church. The University of the South was owned and controlled by twenty-two southern dioceses. St. Augustine's College, Raleigh, North Carolina, was associated with the American Church Institute for Negroes. Other church-related colleges were Bard College, Annandale, New York; Hobart and William Smith Colleges, Geneva, New York; Kenyon College, Gambier, Ohio; Trinity College, Hartford, Connecticut; and Canterbury College, Danville, Indiana. In the field of secondary education, the Church was much more strongly represented, 137 schools of that level being connected with it.

Organizations concerned with education, in addition to those already mentioned, were: the Association for Promoting the

Theological Seminaries

Other Educational Work

Interests of Church Schools, Colleges, and Seminaries; the Bishop Page Foundation; the Episcopal Educational Association; the National Center for Devotion and Conference; the National Association of Directors of Christian Education; and St. Philip's Society for Teaching Missions. The Society for the Increase of the Ministry, the Evangelical Education Society, and the Protestant Episcopal Education Society of Virginia aided candidates for Orders. The Society for the Promotion of Religion and Learning in the State of New York helped Church colleges and seminaries.

The United Movement of the Church's Youth, with the National Youth Commission as its executive committee, was devoted to promoting a program of education and worship for the young. Organizations for young people were: the Junior Department of the Brotherhood of St. Andrew; the Association of Canterbury Clubs; the Junior Division of the Daughters of the King; the Order of the Fleur de Lis; the Girls' Friendly Society; the Junior Order of Layreaders; the Order of St. Vincent for Acolytes; Pi Alpha Fraternity; the Servants of Christ the King (devotional); the Order of Sir Galahad; and Tau Delta Alpha Sorority. A National Youth Convention met triennially.

There were a number of religious communities for men: the Order of the Holy Cross; the Society of St. John the Evangelist; the Order of St. Benedict; the Order of St. Francis; the Society of the Catholic Commonwealth; the Community of the Holy Spirit; the Congregation of the Companions of the Holy Saviour; the Society of the Good Shepherd; the Oratory of the Good Shepherd; St. Barnabas Brotherhood; the Order of St. Augustine; the Brothers of St. Joseph; and the Brothers of St. Paul. For women there were: All Saints Sisters of the Poor; the Deaconesses of St. Clare's House; the Order of Deaconesses of the Diocese of Alabama; the Sisterhood of the Holy Child Jesus; the Sisterhood of the Holy Nativity; the Poor Clares of Reparation and Adoration; the Order of St. Anne; the Order of St. Helena; the Community of St. John the Baptist; the Sisterhood of St. John the Evangelist; the Society of St. Margaret; the Community of St. Mary; the Community of St. Saviour; the Teachers of the Children of God; the Community of the Transfiguration; and the Community of the Way of the Cross.

Religious Communities

Devotional organizations not requiring a community life were:

the Brotherhood of the Way of the Cross; the Company of the Love of Jesus; the Confraternity of the Blessed Sacrament; the Guild of All Souls; the Guild of the Ascension; the Guild of the Holy Cross; the Guild of the Holy Ghost the Comforter; The Company of the Holy Grail; the Living Rosary of Our Lady and St. Dominic; the Order of the Good Samaritan; The Order of the Thousandfold; and the Society of the Companions of the Holy Cross.

General societies for fellowship and work in the Church were: the National Federation of Church Clubs; the Anglican Society; the Brotherhood of St. Andrew; the Daughters of the King; and the Laymen's League.

Social Work
The Episcopal Church had city mission societies in twenty-two communities; seventy-one hospitals and convalescent homes; eleven guest and rest houses; sixty-five institutions for child care; sixty-two homes for the aged; twenty-one settlement houses; and four maternity centers. The Episcopal Service for Youth was devoted to assisting young people in solving personal problems. The Episcopal League for Social Action, formerly the Church League for Industrial Democracy, worked for a general improvement in social and economic conditions.

Special Organizations
The Fellowship of St. Luke, and the Life Abundant Movement sought to further spiritual healing. Work among the deaf was promoted by the Church Mission to Deaf Mutes and the Conference of Church Workers among the Deaf; rural work by the National Episcopal Conference on Rural Work, the National Town-Country Church Institute, and the Rural Workers' Fellowship. The Confraternity of Unity was dedicated to bringing about a reunion with the Papacy. Editors of diocesan papers were organized in the National Diocesan Press. The spiritual needs of special professions were served by the Episcopal Actors' Guild, the Guild of St. Barnabas for Nurses, and the Seamen's Church Institute. There were two general Church libraries: the National Council Library and the Church Periodical Club, besides the more specialized library of the Church Historical Society.

Other organizations for doing special work or promoting special interests within the Church were: the Ember Guild; the National Committee of Diocesan Altar Guilds; the American Church Building Fund Commission; the American Church Union, Inc.;

the American Friends of Pusey House; the Church Congress; the Church Literature Foundation, Inc.; the Church Missions Publishing Company; the Clerical Union for the Maintenance and Defence of Catholic Principles; Ekklesia Nicene Crusaders; the Episcopal Pacifist Fellowship; the Episcopal Evangelical Fellowship; the Federation of Catholic Priests; the National Guild of Churchmen; the New York Bible and Common Prayer Book Society; the Bishop White Prayer Book Society; the Orthodox and Anglican Fellowship; the Protestant Episcopal Society for the Promotion of Evangelical Knowledge; the Protestant Episcopal Evangelists; the Seabury Society for the Preservation of Glebe House; Shrine Mont; and the Retiring Fund for Deaconesses.

The official missionary publication of the Church was *Forth*, formerly the *Spirit of Missions. The Living Church Annual* served Periodicals the Church as a year book of statistical and other information. Periodicals concerned with general Church matters were: *The Church Militant; The Churchman; Episcopal Church Times; The Living Church; Southern Churchman;* and *The Witness. Anglican Theological Review* and *Historical Magazine of the Protestant Episcopal Church* were scholarly quarterlies. Magazines with special interests were: *The Cathedral Age; Churchways* (parish methods); *Colored Churchman; Messager Evangelique; Sharing* (personal religion and healing); and *The Deaf Churchman.* A number of Church organizations published magazines of their own. These were: *The A.C.U. News* (American Church Union); *The Church Review* (Church Society for College Work); *Co-Partners* (Church Army); *Cowley* (Society of St. John the Evangelist); *Highlights* (Girls' Friendly Society); *Holy Cross Magazine* (Order of the Holy Cross); *The Hinterland* (Holy Cross Liberian Mission); *The Royal Cross* (Daughters of the King); *The Little Chronicle* (Order of St. Francis); *The Rural Messenger* (Rural Workers' Fellowship); and *St. Andrew's Cross* (Brotherhood of St. Andrew).

BIBLIOGRAPHY

I. OFFICIAL AND SEMI-OFFICIAL DOCUMENTS

A. *Colonial*

Chamberlayne, C. G., ed., *The Vestry Book and Register of Bristol Parish, Virginia, 1720-1789,* Richmond, 1898.

Chamberlayne, C. G., ed., *The Vestry Book of Christ Church Parish, Middlesex County, Virginia, 1663-1767,* Old Dominion Press, Richmond, 1927.

Chamberlayne, C. G., ed., *The Vestry Book of Kingston Parish, Mathews County, Virginia,* Old Dominion Press, Richmond, 1929.

Chamberlayne, C. G., ed., *The Vestry Book of Petsworth Parish, Gloucester County, Virginia, 1677-1793,* Library Board, Richmond, 1933.

Chamberlayne, C. G., ed., *The Vestry Book of Blisland Parish, New Kent and James City Counties, Virginia, 1721-1786,* Library Board, Richmond, 1935.

Chamberlayne, C. G., ed., *The Vestry Book and Register of St. Peter's Parish, New Kent and James City Counties, Virginia, 1684-1786,* Library Board, Richmond, 1937.

Hawks Transcripts. Ms. copies of letters, reports, etc., bearing on the colonial Church, from files of S. P. G. and Bishop of London, in New York Historical Society Library, New York City. Published in part in:

Hawks, F. L., and Perry, W. S., eds., *Documentary History of the Episcopal Church in Connecticut,* New York, 1863, 2 vols.

Perry, W. S., ed., *Historical Collections Relating to the American Colonial Church,* Hartford, 1870 ff., 4 vols.

Society for the Propagation of the Gospel, *Abstracts of Proceedings,* London, 1704-83

B. *Post-Revolutionary*

Diocese of Illinois, *Memorial to the Standing Committees,* Chicago, 1875.

Diocese of Massachusetts, *Correspondence between the Bishop and the Rectors of the Parish of the Advent,* Boston, 1856.

Diocese of North Carolina, *Statement of the Difficulties between the Diocese and Dr. Ives, Lately Bishop of Said Diocese,* Fayetteville, 1853.

Diocesan Journals of important dioceses.

Domestic and Foreign Missionary Society, *Proceedings, 1823-1920.*

General Convention, *Journals.*

General Theological Seminary, *Proceedings of the Board of Trustees,* 1821—

House of Bishops, *Pastoral Letters.*

Judd, S. C., *The Legality of the Election of Dr. DeKoven,* Chicago, 1875.

Parish records and histories, published or ms.

Presiding Bishop and Council, *Annual Report, 1920—*

Protestant Episcopal Church, *The Decision of the Bishops Who United in the Consecration of the Rev. Henry U. Onderdonk, D.D.,* Philadelphia, 1827.

Protestant Episcopal Church, *Proceedings of the Court Convened for the Trial of the Right Rev. Benjamin T. Onderdonk, D.D.,* New York, 1845.

Protestant Episcopal Church, *Proceedings of the Court Assembled for the Trial of the Rt. Rev. George Washington Doane, D.D., LL.D.,* New York, 1853.

Protestant Episcopal Church, In the *Court of Review*: "In the Matter of the Presentment of Bishop William Montgomery Brown"; "On Appeal from Trial Court," Cleveland, 1925.

II. UNOFFICIAL MANUSCRIPTS

Hobart, J. H., mss., 1800-30. In the New York Historical Society Library.

Jarvis, Abraham, mss. Owned by Rev. H. C. Robbins.

Johnson, S. R., mss. In General Theological Seminary Library.

Kemper, Jackson, mss. In Wisconsin Historical Society Library.

Smith, William, mss. In the New York Historical Society Library.

White, William, mss. In the New York Historical Society Library.

III. PERIODICALS

Church Journal, New York.

Church Review, New York.

The Churchman, Hartford and New York, 1804—.

Historical Magazine of the Protestant Episcopal Church, Philadelphia.

The Living Church, Chicago, Milwaukee, and New York, 1878—.

The Living Church Annual, Milwaukee and New York, 1890—. Published, 1890-99, as *Living Church Quarterly.*

Southern Churchman, Richmond, 1835—.

The Spirit of Missions (now, *Forth*), New York, 1836—.

Swords' *Pocket Almanac,* New York, 1816-60.

Whittaker's *Churchman's Almanac,* New York, 1874-1908.

The Witness, Chicago and New York.

IV. PAMPHLETS

A. *Colonial*

Apthorp, East, *Considerations on the Character and Conduct of the Society for the Propagation of the Gospel,* Boston, 1763.

Blackburne, Francis, *A Critical Commentary on Archbishop Secker's Letter to the Right Honorable Horatio Walpole,* London, 1770.

Bray, Thomas, *The Acts of Dr. Bray's Visitation Held at Annapolis in Maryland,* London, 1700.

Bray, Thomas, *A General View of the English Colonies in America with Respect to Religion,* London, 1698.

Bray, Thomas, *A letter from Dr. Bray to Such as Have Contributed Towards the Propagating of Christian Knowledge in the Plantations,* London, 1700.

Bray, Thomas, *A Memorial Representing the Present Case of the Church in Maryland,* London, 1700.

Bray, Thomas, *A Memorial Representing the Present*

State of Religion on the Continent of North America, London, 1700.

Bray, Thomas, *Proposals for the Encouragement and Promoting of Religion and Learning in the Foreign Plantations,* London, 1701.

Bray, Thomas, *Several Circular Letters to the Clergy of Maryland,* London, 1701. This and the preceding Bray pamphlets have been reprinted by the Thomas Bray Club.

Caner, Henry, *A Candid Examination of Dr. Mayhew's Observations,* Boston, 1763.

Chandler, T. B., *An Appeal to the Public in Behalf of the Church of England in America,* New York, 1767.

Chandler, T. B., *The Appeal Defended,* New York, 1769.

Chandler, T. B., *The Appeal Farther Defended,* New York, 1771.

Chandler, T. B., *A Free Examination of the Critical Commentary on Archbishop Secker's Letter,* New York, 1774.

Cooper, Miles, and others, *An Address from the Clergy of New York and New Jersey to the Episcopalians of Virginia,* New York, 1771.

Gwatkin, Thomas, *A Letter to the Clergy of New York and New Jersey,* Williamsburg, 1772.

Hobart, Noah, *A Serious Address to the Members of the Episcopal Separation in New England,* Boston, 1748.

Inglis, Charles, *A Vindication of the Bishop of Landlaff's Sermon,* New York, 1768.

Inglis, Charles, *State of the Anglo-American Colonies in 1776,* n.d.

Mayhew, Jonathan, *Observations on the Charter and Conduct of the Society for the Propagation of the Gospel,* London, 1763.

Miller, John, *A Description of the Province and City of New York, 1695,* London, 1843.

Smith, John, *Advertisements for the Unexperienced Planters of New England or Any Where,* London, 1631. Repr., *Collections,* Massachusetts Historical Society, 1833, ser. 3, vol. III.

Wetmore, James, *Vindication of the Professors of the Church of England in Connecticut,* 1747.

Wolley, Charles, *A Two Year's Journal in New York,* London, 1701. Repr., Cleveland, 1902.

B. *Post-Revolutionary*

Allen, Benjamin, *A Letter to the Right Reverend John Henry Hobart, D.D.,* Philadelphia, 1827.

Allen, Benjamin, *Second Letter to the Right Reverend John Henry Hobart, D.D.,* Philadelphia, 1827.

Binney, Horace, *The Case of the Right Rev. Henry U. Onderdonk, D.D.,* Philadelphia, 1853.

Freeman, G. W., *The Rights and Duties of Slaveholders,* Charleston, 1837.

Griswold, A. V., *Convention Addresses,* Boston, 1818 and 1825, and Middlebury, 1827.

Hobart, J. H., *An Address to Episcopalians on the Subject of the American Bible Society,* New York, 1816.

Hobart, J. H., *A Charge to the Clergy of the Protestant Episcopal Church in the State of New York,* New York, 1815.

Hobart, J. H., *The Churchman,* New York, 1819.

Hobart, J. H., *The Corruptions of the Church of Rome Contrasted with Certain Protestant Errors,* New York, 1818.

Hobart, J. H., *The High Churchman Vindicated,* New York, 1826.

Hobart, J. H., *Letter to the Vestry of Trinity Church in Answer to a Pamphlet Entitled, "A Solemn Appeal to the Church,"* New York, 1811.

Hobart, J. H., *A Pastoral Letter on the Subject of the Protestant Episcopal Clerical Association,* New York, 1829.

Hobart, J. H., *A Pastoral Letter Relative to Measures for the Theological Education of Candidates for Orders,* New York, 1820.

Hobart, J. H., *A Statement to the Episcopalians in the State of New York,* New York, 1812.

Hopkins, J. H., *The Law of Ritualism,* New York, 1867.

Ives, L. S., *The Priestly Office: A Pastoral Letter to the Clergy of North Carolina*, New York, 1849.

Ives, L. S., *A Pastoral Letter to the Clergy and Laity of His Diocese*, New York, 1849.

Jay, William, *Caste and Slavery in the American Church*, New York, 1843.

Jay, William, *A Letter to the Right Reverend Bishop Hobart Occasioned by the Strictures on Bible Societies in His Late Charge to the Convention of New York*, New York, 1823.

Johnson, E. M., *The Communion of Saints*, Brooklyn, 1848.

Jones, Cave, *Dr. Hobart's System of Intolerance Exemplified in His Late Proceedings against His Colleague, the Author*, New York, n.d.

Jones, Cave, *A Solemn Appeal to the Church*, New York, 1811.

Meade, William, *Pastoral Letter on the Duty of Affording Religious Instruction to Those in Bondage*, Richmond, 1853.

Meade, William, *Statement in Reply to Some Parts of Bishop Onderdonk's Statement*, New York, 1845.

Muhlenberg, W. A., *An Exposition of the Memorial of Sundry Presbyters*, New York, 1854.

Muhlenberg, W. A., *Memorial of Sundry Presbyters of the Protestant Episcopal Church*, 1853.

Muhlenberg, W. A., *What the Memorialists Want*, New York, 1856.

Onderdonk, B. T., *A Statement of the Facts and Circumstances Connected with the Recent Trial of the Bishop of New York*, New York, 1845.

Onderdonk, B. T., and others, *A Full and True Statement of the Examination and Ordination of Mr. Arthur Carey*, New York, 1843.

Parks, Leighton, *Intellectual Integrity*, New York, 1923.

Potter, H. C., *The Citizen in His Relation to the Industrial Situation*, New York, 1902.

Seymour, G. F., *An Open Letter to the Right Rev. William*

C. Doane in Reference to the Consecration of the Right Rev. Dr. Brooks, Springfield, Illinois, 1892.

Smith, B. B., *The Church Temperance Society,* New York, 1881.

Smith, Hugh, and Anthon, Henry, *A Statement of Facts in Relation to the Recent Ordination in St. Stephen's Church,* New York, 1843.

White, William, *The Case of the Episcopal Churches in the United States Considered,* Philadelphia, 1783.

White, William, *The Integrity of Christian Doctrine and the Sanctity of Christian Practice United in Christian Preaching,* New York, 1811.

White, William, *The Past and Future, a Charge on Events Connected with the Organization of the Protestant Episcopal Church,* Philadelphia, 1834.

Anonymous:

The Liberal Evangelicals: Purpose, Program and Organization, 1933.

Resolutions Adopted at a Meeting of Episcopalians at Mechanics Hall; also Two Letters from the Hon. John Jay, New York, 1812.

A Statement of the Facts and Reasonings in Support of the Remonstrance against the Consecration of the Rev. Henry U. Onderdonk, D.D., Philadelphia, 1827.

V. Miscellaneous Sources

A. *Colonial*

Bradford, William, *History of Plymouth Plantation,* Scribner, New York, 1908.

Johnson, Samuel, *Works,* ed. by H. W. Schneider, Columbia University Press, 1929, 4 vols.

Randolph, Edward, *Letters and Official Papers,* Boston, 1899, 4 vols.

Slafter, E. F., *John Checkley, or the Evolution of Religious Tolerance in Massachusetts Bay,* Boston, 1897, 2 vols.

Smith, William, *Works,* Philadelphia, 1803, 2 vols.

Tyler, L. G., ed., *Narratives of Early Virginia, 1606-1625,* Scribner, New York, 1907.

Winthrop, John, *Journal,* Scribner, New York, 1908, 2 vols.

Collections of the Protestant Episcopal Historical Society, New York, 1851. Only year published.

B. *Post-Revolutionary*

Caswall, Henry, *America and the American Church,* London, 1839.

Gavin, F. S. B., ed., *Liberal Catholicism and the Modern World,* Morehouse-Gorham Co., New York, 1934.

Grammer, C. E., ed., *Abiding Values of Evangelicalism,* Evangelical Education Society, Philadelphia, 1938.

Griswold, A. V., *Discourses on the Most Important Doctrines and Duties of the Christian Religion,* Philadelphia, 1830.

Hobart, J. H., *An Apology for Apostolic Order and Its Advocates,* New York, 1807.

Hobart, J. H., and others, A *Collection of the Essays on the Subject of Episcopacy,* New York, 1806.

Hobart, J. H., *A Companion for the Altar,* New York, 1803.

Hobart, J. H., *A Companion for the Book of Common Prayer,* New York, 1805.

Hobart, J. H., *A Companion for the Festivals and Fasts,* New York, 1804.

Hopkins, J. H., *A Scriptural, Ecclesiastical and Historical View of Slavery,* New York, 1864.

Huntington, W. R., *The Church Idea,* Boston, 1870.

Ives, L. S., *The Trials of a Mind in Its Progress to Catholicism,* Boston, 1854.

Kemper, Jackson, *Journal of an Episcopalian Missionary's Tour to Green Bay, 1834, and Documents Relating to the Episcopal Church and Mission in Green Bay, 1825-41,* Madison, 1898. Repr. from *Collections* of the Wisconsin State Historical Society, vol. XIV.

Lowndes, Arthur, ed., *Archives of General Convention,* New York, 1911, 6 vols. Hobart Correspondence, 1798-1806.

Mason, J. M., *Essays on Episcopacy and the Apology for*

Apostolic Order and Its Advocates Reviewed, New York, 1844.

McIlvaine, C. P., *Oxford Divinity Compared with That of the Romish and Anglican Churches,* London, 1841.

Muhlenberg, W. A., *Evangelical Catholic Papers,* New York 1875, 2 vols.

Newman, J. H., and others, *Tracts for the Times,* New York, 1839, 3 vols.

Newton, R. H., *The Morals of Trade,* New York, 1876.

Newton, R. H., *Social Studies,* New York, 1887.

Perry, W. S., ed., *Historical Notes Illustrating the Organization of the Protestant Episcopal Church,* Claremont, New Hampshire, 1874.

Potter, Alonzo, ed., *Memorial Papers,* Philadelphia, 1857.

Rylance, J. H., *Lectures on Social Questions,* New York, 1880.

Selwyn, E. G., ed., *Essays Catholic and Critical,* Macmillan, New York, 1930.

Sprague, P. W., *Christian Socialism. What and Why,* New York, 1891.

Temple, William, ed., *Essays and Reviews,* Boston, 1862.

Vail, T. H., *The Comprehensive Church,* Hartford, 1841.

Walworth, C. A., *The Oxford Movement in America,* New York, 1895.

Waylen, Edward, *Ecclesiastical Reminiscences of the United States,* New York, 1846.

White, William, *Commentaries Suited to Occasions of Ordination,* New York, 1833.

White, William, *Comparative Views of the Controversy between the Calvinists and the Arminians,* Philadelphia, 1817, 2 vols.

White, William, *Counter-Apology against Robert Barclay, Quaker Apologist,* Unpublished ms. in archives of Christ Church, Philadelphia.

White, William, *Lectures on the Catechism of the Protestant Episcopal Church,* Philadelphia, 1813.

White, William, *Memoirs of the Protestant Episcopal Church,* New York, 1880.

Prohibition As We See It, Church Temperance Society, New York, 1928.

VI. Biographies and Autobiographies

Allen, A. V. G., *Phillips Brooks, 1835-93,* Dutton, New York, 1907.

Allen, T. G., *Memoir of the Rev. Benjamin Allen,* Philadelphia, 1832.

Ayres, Anne, *The Life and Work of William Augustus Muhlenberg,* New York, 1894.

Barry, J. G. H., *Impressions and Opinions,* Morehouse-Gorham Co., New York, 1931.

Beardsley, E. E., *Life and Correspondence of the Right Reverend Samuel Seabury, D.D.,* Boston, 1881.

Boucher, Jonathan, *Reminiscences of an American Loyalist, 1738-1789,* Houghton Mifflin, Boston, 1925.

Brand, W. F., *Life of William Rollinson Whittingham,* New York, 1886, 2 vols.

Breck, Charles, *Life of the Reverend James Lloyd Breck, D.D.,* New York, 1886.

Brown, W. M., *My Heresy,* John Day Co., New York, 1931.

Carus, William, *Memorials of the Right Reverend Charles Pettit McIlvaine, D.D., D.C.L.,* New York, 1882.

Chase, Philander, *Reminiscences,* Boston, 1848, 2 vols.

Clark T. M., *Reminiscences,* New York, 1895.

Crapsey, A. S., *The Last of the Heretics,* Knopf, New York, 1924.

Croswell, Harry, *A Memoir of the Late Rev. William Croswell, D.D.,* New York, 1853.

Cummins, A. M., *Memoir of George David Cummins,* New York, 1878.

Doane, W. C., *A Memoir of the Life of George Washington Doane, Bishop of New Jersey,* New York, 1860.

Dyer, Heman, *Records of an Active Life,* New York, 1886.

Gadsden, C. E., *An Essay on the Life of the Right Reverend Theodore Dehon, D.D.,* Charleston, 1833.

Gailor, T. F., *Some Memories,* Southern Publishers, Kingsport, Tennessee, 1937.

Grafton, C. C., *A Journey Godward*, Milwaukee, 1910.

Green, W. M., *Memoir of the Rt. Rev. James Hervey Otey, D.D.*, New York, 1885.

Greene, Howard, *The Reverend Richard Fish Cadle*, Waukesha, 1936.

Harris, R. V., *Charles Inglis*, General Board of Religious Education, Toronto, 1937.

Henshaw, J. P. K., *Memoir of the Life of the Right Rev. Richard Channing Moore*, Philadelphia, 1842.

Hodges, George, *Henry Codman Potter, Seventh Bishop of New York*, New York, 1915.

Hopkins, J. H., Jr., *Life of the Late Right Reverend John Henry Hopkins, First Bishop of Vermont and Seventh Presiding Bishop*, New York, 1873.

Howe, M. A. DeW., *Memoirs of the Life and Services of the Rt. Rev. Alonzo Potter*, Philadelphia, 1871.

Howe, M. A. DeW., *The Life and Labors of Bishop Hare*, New York, 1911.

Jarratt, Devereux, *Life*, Baltimore, 1806.

Jenkins, Thomas, *The Man of Alaska, Peter Trimble Rowe*, Morehouse-Gorham Co., New York, 1943.

Johns, John, *A Memoir of the Life of the Right Rev. William Meade, D. D.*, Baltimore, 1867.

Kip, W. I., *The Early Days of My Episcopate*, New York, 1892.

Lawrence, William, *Memories of a Happy Life*, Houghton Mifflin Co., Boston, 1926.

Lyddekker, J. W., *The Life and Letters of Charles Inglis*, S. P. C. K., London, 1936.

McNamara, John, *Three Years on the Kansas Border*, New York, 1856.

McVickar, John, *The Early and Professional Years of Bishop Hobart*, Oxford, 1838.

O'Grady, John, *Levi Silliman Ives, Pioneer Leader in Catholic Charities*, P. J. Kennedy & Sons, New York, 1933.

Pennington, E. L., *Apostle of New Jersey, John Talbot, 1645-1727*, Church Historical Society, Philadelphia, 1938.

Polk, W. M., *Leonidas Polk, Bishop and General*, New York, 1915, 2 vols.

Rainsford, W. S., *A Preacher's Story of His Work*, New York, 1904.

Scudder, V. D., *Father Huntington*, Dutton, New York, 1940.

Slattery, C. L., *David Hummell Greer*, New York, 1921.

Smith H. W., *Life and Correspondence of the Rev. William Smith, D.D.*, Philadelphia, 1880, 2 vols.

Sprague, W. B., ed., *Annals of the American Episcopal Pulpit*, New York, 1859.

Stone, J. S., *Memoir of the Life of the Rt. Rev. Alexander Viets Griswold, D.D.*, Philadelphia, 1844.

Stone, J. S., *Memoir of the Life of James Milnor, D.D., Late Rector of St. George's Church, New York*, New York, 1848.

Stowe, W. H., and others, *The Life and Correspondence of Bishop William White*, Morehouse-Gorham Co., New York, 1937.

Suter, J. W., *The Life and Letters of William Reed Huntington*, Appleton-Century, New York, 1925.

Talbot, Ethelbert, *My People of the Plains*, New York, 1906.

Turner, S. H., *Autobiography*, New York, 1863.

Tuttle, D. S., *Reminiscences of a Missionary Bishop*, New York, 1906.

Utley, G. B., *The Life and Times of Thomas John Claggett*, Chicago, 1913.

Ver Mehr, J. L., *Checkered Life*, San Francisco, 1877.

Walker, Cornelius, *The Life and Correspondence of Rev. William Sparrow, D.D.*, Philadelphia, 1876.

Whipple, H. B., *The Lights and Shadows of a Long Episcopate*, New York, 1899.

White, Greenough, *An Apostle of the Western Church*, New York, 1900.

White, Greenough, *A Saint of the Southern Church*, New York, 1897.

Wilson, Bird, *Memoir of the Life of the Right Reverend William White*, Philadelphia, 1839.

Zabriskie, A. C., *Arthur Selden Lloyd*, Morehouse-Gorham Co., New York, 1942.

VII. GENERAL HISTORIES AND MONOGRAPHS

Brewer, C. H., *Early Episcopal Sunday Schools,* Morehouse-Gorham Co., New York, 1933.

Brydon, G. M., "The Clergy of the Established Church in Virginia," *Virginia Magazine of History and Biography.*

Brydon, G. M., *The Episcopal Church among the Negroes of Virginia,* Virginia Diocesan Library, Richmond, 1937.

Brydon, G. M., *The Established Church in Virginia and the Revolution,* Virginia Diocesan Library, Richmond, 1930.

Chorley, E. C., *Men and Movements in the American Episcopal Church,* Scribner, New York, 1946.

Cross, A. L., *Anglican Episcopate and the American Colonies,* Harvard University Press, Cambridge, 1902.

Curtis, W. R., *The Lambeth Conferences,* Columbia University Press, New York, 1942.

De Mille, G. E., *The Catholic Movement in the American Episcopal Church,* Church Historical Society, Philadelphia, 1941.

De Mille, G. E., *A History of the Diocese of Albany, 1704-1923,* Church Historical Society, Philadelphia, 1946.

Dix, Morgan, *A History of the Parish of Trinity Church in the City of New York,* New York, 1898 ff., 6 vols.

Eckenrode, H. J., *The Revolution in Virginia,* Houghton Mifflin, Boston, 1916.

Foote, H. W., *Annals of King's Chapel,* Boston, 1882-96, 2 vols.

Goodwin, E. L., *Colonial History of the Church in Virginia,* Morehouse-Gorham, New York.

Greene, M. L., *The Development of Religious Liberty in Connecticut,* Boston, 1905.

Hawks, F. L., *Contributions to the Ecclesiastical History of the United States of America,* New York, 1836-39, 2 vols.

Keith, C. P., *Chronicles of Pennsylvania,* Philadelphia, 1917, 2 vols.

Klingberg, F. J., *Anglican Humanitarianism in Colonial New York,* Church Historical Society, Philadelphia, 1940.

Lauer, P. E., *Church and State in New England,* Baltimore, 1892.

Lingley, C. R., *The Transition in Virginia from Colony to Commonwealth*, New York, 1910.

Manross, W. W., *The Episcopal Church in the United States, 1800-1840*, Columbia University Press, New York, 1938.

Meade, William, *Old Churches, Ministers and Families of Virginia*, Philadelphia, 1857, 2 vols.

Michael, O. S., *The Sunday School in the Development of the American Church*, Milwaukee, 1904.

Miller, Spencer, and Fletcher, J. F., *The Church and Industry*, Longmans, Green & Co., New York, 1930.

Muller, J. A., *The Episcopal Theological School, 1867-1943*, E. T. S., Cambridge, 1943.

Pascoe, C. F., *Two Hundred Years of the S. P. G.*, London, 1901.

Pennington, E. L., "The Work of the Bray Associates in Pennsylvania," *Pennsylvania Magazine of History*.

Perry, W. S., *The Alleged "Toryism" of the Clergy of the United States*, 1896(?).

Perry, W. S., *The History of the American Episcopal Church*, Boston, 1885, 2 vols.

Reed, S. M., *State and Church in Massachusetts, 1691-1740*, University of Illinois Press, Urbana, 1914.

Stowe, W. H., *Immigration and the Growth of the Episcopal Church*, Joint Commission on Strategy and Policy, Richmond, 1942.

Stowe, W. H., *A Missionary Frontier of the Future: The Foreign White Stock in America*, 1939.

Stowe, W. H., *1930-1940, An Encouraging Decade for the Episcopal Church*, Church Historical Society, Philadelphia, 1946.

Stowe, W. H., *A Short History of the Church in New Jersey*, n.d.

Temple, S. A., *The Theological Writings of Bishop White*, Kings Crown Press, New York, 1946.

Tucker, H. St. G., *The History of the Episcopal Church in Japan*, Scribner, New York, 1938.

Weeks, S. B., *The Religious Development in the Province of North Carolina*, Baltimore, 1892.

Zabriskie, A. C., and others, *Anglican Evangelicalism*, Church Historical Society, Philadelphia. 1944.

INDEX

Abolition (*see* Slavery)

Adams, John, 196

Adams, Rev. William, 259-260

Address from the Clergy of New York and New Jersey to the Episcopalians in Virginia, 167

Aglipay, Gregorio, 365

Alabama, Diocese of, 257, 260

Alaska, 335, 336, 366

Albany, New York, 122, 123, 148

Alexandria, Virginia, 242

Alien rights, canon on, 354

All Saints' Church, New York City, 276

All Saints' Sisters of the Poor, 369

All Souls' Church, New York City, 311

Allen, Rev. A. V. G., 304

Allen, Rev. Benjamin, 251, 253

Allerton, Isaac, 23

Allison, Rev. Francis, 170

Amadas, Philip, 3, 4

America and the American Church, 248

American Church Building Fund Commission, 370

American Church Institute for Negroes, 338, 367, 368

American Church Missionary Society—organized, 262; becomes auxiliary of Domestic and Foreign Missionary Society, 262, 343; receipts of, 325; begins work in Latin America, 342

American Church Union, 358, 370-71

American Colonization Society, 218

American Friends of Pusey House, 371

'American Whig," 170

Amherst, Lord Jeffrey, 122, 145

'Anatomist" (William Smith), 170

Anderson, C. P., presiding bishop, 352

Andover, Massachusetts, 93

Andrews, Rev. John—in Revolution, 181; accuses William Smith, 198; opposes Purcell, 204; interview of, with Coke and Asbury, 205

Andrews, Rev. William, 144

Andros, Sir Edmund—governor of New England, 30, 31; aids Church in Boston, 32; imprisoned, 33; deposes Nicolaus Van Rens-

selaer, 35; governor of Virginia, 66-68; dispute of, with Blair, 67

Anglican Society, 370

Anglican Theological Review, 371

Anglo-Catholic Congress, 315, 358

Anglo-Catholicism—in Church of the Advent, 264; origin of, in Oxford Movement, 266-273; liberalization of, 273, 348, 349; in General Seminary, 274-278; growth of, 314, 315; Liberal Catholic Movement within, 349

Anglo-Catholics—theology of, 268-273; attitude of, towards Roman Catholicism, 271, and towards medieval thought and practice, 271, 272; theory of, regarding sacraments, 273; missionary work of, 273; social interests of some, 273; charged with "Romanizing," 274, 275, 314; favor free churches, 304; support Brooks, 310, 311; attitude of, towards Higher Criticism, 312, 313

Anking, Missionary District of, 341, 366

Anne, Queen, 44, 120, 160

Anthon, Rev. Henry, 276, 277

Anvik, Alaska, mission to, 335, 336

Apocrypha, Carey's view of, 276

Apology for Apostolic Order and Its Advocates, An, 221

Apostles' Creed, 189, 196

Appeal Answered, 169

Appeal Defended, 169

Appeal Further Defended, 169

Appeal to the Public on Behalf of the Church of England in America, 169

Apthorp, Rev. East, 100, 145, 169

Archdeacon, suggested for colonies, 164

Argall, Gov., of Virginia, 10

Arkansas, Missionary Jurisdiction of, 260, 331, 332

Army and Navy Commission, 360

Arnold, Rev. Jonathan, 104

Arrowsmith, I., 126

Asbury, Bishop Francis, 205, 206

"Associates of the late Dr. Bray, the" 148, 149, 153

Association for Promoting the Interests of Church Schools, Colleges, and Seminaries, 369

162-164; intermittent appeals for, 164, 165; campaign for, reopened in sixties, 164, 165; appointment of, rumored among dissenters, 164; effect of colonial politics on campaign for, 166, 167, 170; pamphlet controversy on, 168-170; newspaper controversy over, 170

Bishops, English—carry out Stuart policies, 158; temporal power of, 155, 156

Blackburne, Archdeacon Francis, 169

Blackwell, Rev. Robert, 181

Blair, Commissary James—career of, 44, 46, 47; founds College of William and Mary, 65, 66; controversies of, 67-68; protests against lack of induction in Virginia, 70; death of, 71

Blair, Rev. John, in North Carolina, 88, 89

Blaxton, William, "old planter," 27

Bliss, Rev. W. P. D., 318

Board of Missions (see Domestic and Foreign Missionary Society)

Bondet, Rev. Daniel—in Westchester, 117, 118; among Indians, 143

"Book Annexed," 321

Book of Common Prayer—first use of, in North America, 2; services of, read in Maine, 5; use of, in Virginia under Commonwealth, 14, 15; use of, at Merrymount, 22; use of, in Salem, 24; efforts to introduce, into New England, 29; use of, in South Carolina, 81; prayers for King required by, 174; Athanasian Creed omitted from, 189; revisions of, 195, 200, 320, 321, 353; attitude of Evangelicals towards, 215; in Confederate States, 290; attitude of Ritualists towards, 295; said to contain law of Church on ritual, 297

Boone, Bishop W. J. (I)—missionary to China, 263; Bishop of China, 263

Boone, Bishop W. J. (II), in Shanghai, 341

Boone University, Wuchang, 341

Bosomworth, Rev. Thomas, 91, 141

Boston—settled by Puritans, 25; choice of ministers at, 26; "old planters," 26, 27; beginnings of the Church in, 30-33; opposition to witchcraft panic in, 93; French Church in, 97; work among Negroes in, 152; laity in, favorable to Independence, 175, 176; Church in, 1811, 230; early indifference to missions in, 230; St. Paul's Church, 240; Church of the Advent, 264, 283, 284

Boucher, Rev. Jonathan, 149

Bowen, Rev. Nathaniel—in Charleston, 234; rector of Grace Church, New York City, 234;

Bishop of South Carolina, 235; agent for General Seminary, 240

Boyle, Robert, 47, 68, 138

Braddock's defeat, 141

Bradford, Gov. William, 21, 22

Bray, Commissary Thomas—in Maryland, 46, 76; founds religious societies, 47-49; urges sending a bishop to the colonies, 159; receives letter from Urmiston, 170

Brazil (see Southern Brazil)

Breck, Rev. J. L.—founder of Nashotah, 259; goes to Minnesota, 260, 261; work of, among Indians, 261, 265, 339; goes to California, 261; examined by Bishop Onderdonk, 275; listed, 327

Brent, Bishop C. H., 337, 357, 365

Brewer, Bishop L. R., in Montana, 334

Bridge, Rev. Christopher, at King's Chapel, 50, 95; in Newport, 95, 107; in Westchester, 118

Bridges, John, 98

Bridgewater, Massachusetts, Church in, 230

Briggs, Rev. C. A., 312

Bright, Rev. Francis, 27, 28

Bristol, Rhode Island—Congregationalists in, 107; Church in, 108, 229-231

Broad Churchmanship, 307

Brooke, Bishop F. K., 340

Brooke, Rev. John, 133, 134, 135

Brooklyn, New York—first Church services in, 179; St. Ann's Church, 223

Brooks, Bishop Phillips—at first Church Congress, 309; career of, 310; theological views of, 310; objection to consecration of, 310, 311; proposes greeting to Congregationalists, 317

Brotherhood of St. Andrew, 322, 369-371

Brotherhood of the Way of the Cross, 370

Brotherhoods, religious, 314, 315

Brothers of St. Joseph, 369

Brothers of St. Paul, 369

Brown, Rev. Daniel, "Yale Convert," 103

Brown, Stewart, 326

Brown, Bishop W. M., tried for heresy, 349

Browne, Rev. Arthur—in Providence, 108; in Portsmouth, 109; opposes Dickinson, 111; answers Mayhew, 168

Browne, Rev. Isaac, in Suffolk County, 121

Browne, Rev. Marmaduke—sent to Newport, 108, 109; in New Hampshire, 109; work of, among Negroes, 153

Browne brothers, opposition of, in Salem, 24

Texas, Diocese of, 261, 292, 333
Thirty-nine Articles—and Tract Ninety, 269,
270; early respect for, 269, 270; adopted by
American Church, 270; Carey's view of, 276
Thomas, Rev. John, 121, 127
Thomas, Rev. Samuel, 82, 139
Thomson, J. M., ̇̇o3
Thomson, Rev. William, 132
Tibbs, Rev. William, 60
Tillotson, Archbishop John, 66
"Timothy Tickle," 170
Tobacco Acts, 71, 73, 74, 78, 79
Tohoku, Missionary District of, 366
Tokyo, Missionary District of. 342
Toleration, Religious (see Religious toleration)
Toleration Act, in colonies, 72, 105
Torok, Rev. John, 355
Tory clergy, 174-179, 181, 182
Tract Ninety, 269, 270
Tract Thirty-eight, 269
Tractarianism (see Oxford Movement)
Tractarians—stand of on Rituals, 272, 294; ac-
cused of "Romanizing," 274, 275
Transubstantiation, 273, 276, 284
Trapnell, Rev. Joseph, 283
Trinity Church, Boston—organized, 95, 99;
Phillips Brooks, rector, 310
Trinity Church, New York City—rector of,
asked to visit Stratford, 101; organized, 113,
114, 116; Vesey rector of, 114-116; obtains
"Queen's Farm," 116; gift of, to King's Col-
lege, 124; work among Negroes in, 148; in
Revolution, 178, 179; Hobart and Griswold
consecrated in, 222; Cave Jones consecrated
in, 223; aids missions, 225, 226; Hobart
rector of, 227; Berrian rector of, 276; Carey
ordained in, 277
Trinity College, Hartford—founded, 244, 245;
at present, 368
Tryon, Governor and General—secures Establishment in North Carolina, 89; receives petition from Mansfield, 176; burns Norwalk
and Fairfield, 177
Tucker, Bishop H. St. G.—in Japan, 342; Presiding Bishop, 352, 363, 364
Turner, Rev. S. H.—professor in General Seminary, scholarship of, 246; patron of Missionary Society, 253; suspected of Rationalism,
278
Tuttle, Bishop D. S.—in Montana and Idaho,
329, 330, 334; Presiding Bishop, 351
Tyng, Rev. S. H., Sr., 296
Tyng, S. H., Jr., trial of, 296

Union Theological Seminary, 312
Unitarians and Phillips Brooks, 310
United Movement of the Church's South, 369
United Nations, 362, 364
United Thank Offering, 343
University of Maryland, 235
University of the South, 304, 368
Unlawfulness of the Common Prayer Worship,
33
Upfold, Bishop George, in Indiana, 260
Urmiston, Rev. John—in North Carolina, 89;
in Philadelphia, 129; drunkenness of, 89,
129, 170; charges of. against Talbot, 129,
170
Urquhart, Rev. William, in Jamaica, 119
Usher, Bishop James, 191
Usher, Rev. John, in Rhode Island, 108
Utah, conditions in, 330, 331

Valle Crucis, religious community at, 284
Van Buren, Bishop J. H., in Puerto Rico, 337
Van Ingen, Dr., assist Breck, 261
Van Rensselaer, Nicolaus, 35
Van Rensselaers, the, won to Church, 123
Varnod, Rev. Francis, interest of, in Indians, 140
Vaughan, Rev. Edward, 134, 135
VerMehr, Rev. J. L. H., in California, 261, 327
Vermont, Diocese of—obtains lands, 55; and
Peters case, 204; in Eastern Diocese, 228; in
1811, 230; withdraws from Eastern Diocese,
231; Hopkins, Bishop of, 242; elects Bishop
Hall, 311
Vesey, Rev. William—called to Trinity Church,
New York, 113, 114; ordained, 115; death
of, 116; aids Church in Westchester, 117;
opposes Neau, 148
Vestries, beginnings of, 9, 15, 16; in Maryland,
75
Vicary, Rev. John, in Philadelphia, 128
Vicksburg Industrial School, 338
Viets, Rev. Roger, tutor of Griswold, 228
Vinton, Bishop A. H.—at first Church Con-
gress, 309; and Phillips Brooks, 310
Vinton, Rev. Francis, 290, 291
Virgin Birth—denied by MacQueary and Crapsey,
314; controversy over, 348, 349
Virgin Islands, 335
Virginia, colonial—named for Queen Elizabeth,
3; settlement of, 6, 7, 8; "Dale's Laws" in,
8, 9; Church discipline in, 8, 9, 11, 17, 47,
68; Herico Parish in, 9; first assembly in, 10;
college projected in, 10, 11; religious laws
in, 11-13, 15, 16; dissent in, 13, 14, 72, 73;